McGraw-Hill
Mathematics

Gary G. Bitter

Carole E. Greenes

Shirley A. Hill

Evan M. Maletsky

Linda Schulman

Gwen Shufelt

Max A. Sobel

Linda L. Thompson

Consulting Editor
Max A. Sobel

Webster Division,
McGraw-Hill
Book Company

New York   St. Louis   San Francisco

Authors

Gary G. Bitter
Professor of Computer and Mathematics Education
Arizona State University

Carole E. Greenes
Associate Professor of Education
Boston University

Shirley A. Hill
Professor of Mathematics and Education
University of Missouri at Kansas City

Evan M. Maletsky
Professor of Mathematics & Computer Science
Montclair State College

Linda Schulman
Associate Professor of Mathematics
Lesley College

Gwen Shufelt
Director Educational Microcomputing Unit
University of Missouri at Kansas City

Max A. Sobel
Professor of Mathematics & Computer Science
Montclair State College

Linda L. Thompson
Consultant
Arizona State Department of Education

Editorial Development

Joanne E. Kane, Dominic Costa, Don Richert, Linda Nicholson, Pat Hunter-Hicklin

Editing and Styling: Linda Richmond, Maureen Meehan

Art and Design: Rosemary O'Connell, Clint Anglin, Valerie Greco, Terry Harmon, Kay Wanous

Photo Editing: Suzanne V. Skloot, Nancy Dyer, Safra Nimrod, Nancy Grimes, Ilene Cherna

Production Manager: Angela Biola

Special Assistant: Vivian Alessi

Series Design: Donald R. Long Design

Cover Design: Group 4, Inc.

This book was set in 12 point Helvetica Light by York Graphic Services. The color separation was done by York Graphic Services.

ISBN 0–07–012626–7

    3   4   5   6   7   8   9   10   DOWDOW   95   94   93   92   91   90   89   88   87

CONTENTS

1 Numeration, Addition, and Subtraction

2 Multiplication

3 Division

4 Decimals: Addition and Subtraction

5 Decimals: Multiplication and Division

6 Measurement

7 Number Relationships

Fractions: Addition and Subtraction

Fractions: Multiplication and Division

Ratio and Percent

Geometry

12 Perimeter, Area, and Volume

13 Statistics and Probability

14 Integers

1

NUMERATION, ADDITION, AND SUBTRACTION

Thousands

■ Our numeration system is based on 10.
The value of each place is 10 times the
value of the place to its right.

$$10 \text{ ones} = 1 \text{ ten}$$
$$10 \text{ tens} = 1 \text{ hundred}$$
$$10 \text{ hundreds} = 1 \text{ thousand}$$
$$10 \text{ thousands} = 1 \text{ ten-thousand}$$
$$10 \text{ ten-thousands} = 1 \text{ hundred-thousand}$$

■ In naming large numbers, the digits are
grouped into periods. Each period is a
group of three digits. Commas separate
the periods.

In 1790, this was the population of Virginia.

THOUSANDS PERIOD			ONES PERIOD		
hundred-thousands	ten-thousands	one-thousands	hundreds	tens	ones
6	9	1	7	3	7

The digit 6 means 6 hundred-thousands, or 600,000.
The digit 9 means 9 ten-thousands, or 90,000.
The digit 1 means 1 thousand, or 1,000.
What does the digit 3 mean?

Write: 691,737
Read: six hundred ninety-one thousand, seven hundred thirty-seven

Another way to read large numbers
is to think about the periods: 691 thousand 737

■ In **expanded form:**

$$691,737 = 600,000 + 90,000 + 1,000 + 700 + 30 + 7$$

Try These

What does the digit 4 mean in each number?

1. 5,435
2. 48,620
3. 234,567
4. 408,215

Write each number.

5. 62 thousand 903
6. 745 thousand 12
7. 312 thousand 900

Write each number in expanded form.

8. 8,651
9. 416,618
10. 51,806
11. 549,016

Exercises

What does the digit 2 mean in each number?

1. 625
2. 47,332
3. 2,136
4. 625,047
5. 216,158
6. 459,625
7. 26,481
8. 267,903

Use 258,731. Write the digit that is in each place.

9. ten-thousands place
10. hundreds place
11. hundred-thousands place
12. ones place
13. tens place
14. thousands place

Write each number.

15. 7 thousand 216
16. 9 thousand 37
17. 24 thousand 800
18. 50 thousand 925
19. 206 thousand 14
20. 300 thousand 752
21. four hundred nine thousand, two hundred fifty
22. five hundred thousand, nineteen

Write each number in expanded form.

23. 6,257
24. 18,510
25. 75,063
26. 427,598

Write the number for the underlined words.

27. In 1790, the population of Lexington, Kentucky, was <u>eight hundred thirty-four</u>.

28. In 1980, the population of Lexington was <u>one hundred ninety thousand, six hundred eighty-six</u>.

Comparing and Ordering

You can compare numbers by starting at the left and comparing the digits in each place.

- Compare 45,589 and 45,642.

    Line up the digits.

    Compare the ten-thousands.

    $\boxed{4}$5 , 5 8 9
    $\boxed{4}$5 , 6 4 2
    same

    Compare the thousands.

    4$\boxed{5}$, 5 8 9
    4$\boxed{5}$, 6 4 2
    same

    Compare the hundreds.

    4 5 , $\boxed{5}$8 9
    4 5 , $\boxed{6}$4 2
    5 **is less than** 6
    5 < 6
    so
    45,589 < 45,642

- Compare 192,346 and 96,385.

    Line up the digits.

    Compare the hundred-thousands.

    $\boxed{1}$9 2 , 3 4 6
    $\boxed{}$9 6 , 3 8 5
    1 hundred-thousand **is greater than**
    0 hundred-thousands
    so
    192,346 > 96,385

- Order from least to greatest:
    48,213   9,924   46,831

    $\boxed{4}$8 , 2 1 3
    $\boxed{}$9 , 9 2 4   9,924 is the least.
    $\boxed{4}$6 , 8 3 1

    Compare 48,213 and 46,831.

    4$\boxed{8}$, 2 1 3
    4$\boxed{6}$, 8 3 1   46,831 < 48,213

    The order from least to greatest is
    9,924; 46,831; 48,213.

Try These

Write >, <, or =.

1. 4,342 ▓ 4,326   **2.** 37,056 ▓ 37,052   **3.** 275,300 ▓ 274,200

4. 82,156 ▓ 82,156   **5.** 364,500 ▓ 364,550   **6.** 35,960 ▓ 135,475

Write in order from least to greatest.

7. 45,682   44,997   45,882   45,880

8. 678,431   678,531   75,894   678,441

Exercises

Write >, <, or =.

1. 275 ▓ 527   **2.** 8,080 ▓ 8,080   **3.** 5,448 ▓ 548

4. 9,077 ▓ 9,770   **5.** 16,257 ▓ 16,527   **6.** 98,124 ▓ 98,124

7. 84,500 ▓ 8,500   **8.** 673,080 ▓ 678,370   **9.** 176,040 ▓ 76,400

10. 75,000 ▓ 574,900   **11.** 451,275 ▓ 415,275   **12.** 723,599 ▓ 24,600

Write in order from least to greatest.

13. 3,875   3,762   3,964   3,698

14. 26,864   26,798   26,654   27,183

15. 426,589   462,589   426,985   426,859

16. 768,530   786,530   86,350   768,305   768,350

Find the greatest digit that will make each sentence true.

★ **17.** 49,▓35 < 49,735   ★ **18.** 662 > 6▓2   ★ **19.** 9,▓56 < 9,856

This table shows the number of trucks and buses produced in several countries in 1 year.

Solve each problem.

20. Which country produced the fewest trucks and buses in this year?

21. Which countries produced fewer trucks and buses than Italy?

22. Write the number of trucks and buses in order from least to greatest.

TRUCK AND BUS PRODUCTION	
Country	Number
Australia	53,488
Brazil	68,186
France	290,610
Italy	115,315
Mexico	51,653

Rounding Numbers

■ Sometimes an exact number is important, and sometimes a rounded number is all that is needed.

There were 46,742 tickets purchased for Friday's game.

About 50,000 people attended the game on Friday.

■ A number line can help you to round numbers.
Round 6,324 to the nearest ten.

6,324 is between 6,320 and 6,330.
It is nearer to 6,320 than to 6,330.
6,324 rounds down to 6,320.

■ You can use this rule for rounding numbers.

> *Look at the digit to the right of the place you are rounding to. If the digit is less than 5, round down. If the digit is 5 or greater, round up.*

Round 26,842 to the nearest thousand.
Look at the digit in the hundreds place.   2 6 , ⑧4 2
Compare this digit with 5.   8 > 5
Round up.
26,842 rounded to the nearest thousand is 27,000.

■ To round money to the nearest dollar, look at the cents. If the cents amount is $.50 or more, round up to the next dollar.

Round the cost of each item to the nearest dollar.

Since the cents amount is $.50, round up to $33. The tennis racket costs about $33.

Since the cents amount is less than $.50, round down to $2. The tennis balls cost about $2.

Try These

Round to the nearest ten.

1. 54   **2.** 3,163   **3.** 718   **4.** 42,367   **5.** 210,175

Round to the nearest thousand.

6. 3,764   **7.** 14,650   **8.** 145,100   **9.** 43,500   **10.** 712,252

Round to the nearest dollar.

11. $2.95   **12.** $7.15   **13.** $35.05   **14.** $9.50   **15.** $1.49

Exercises

Round to the nearest hundred.

1. 312   **2.** 910   **3.** 2,617   **4.** 13,257   **5.** 4,875
6. 1,150   **7.** 127,560   **8.** 36,245   **9.** 87   ★ **10.** 13,998

Round to the nearest ten-thousand.

11. 74,300   **12.** 55,000   **13.** 18,015   **14.** 42,897   **15.** 75,281
16. 325,125   **17.** 934,600   **18.** 691,874   ★ **19.** 99,000   ★ **20.** 8,392

Round to the nearest dollar.

21. $36.15   **22.** $98.75   **23.** $125.10   **24.** $72.50   **25.** $1.50
26. $.98   **27.** $9.17   **28.** $99.85   **29.** $.63   **30.** $215.10

Round 68,459 to each place indicated.

31. the nearest ten   **32.** the nearest hundred   **33.** the nearest thousand

Solve each problem.

34. I am a 3-digit number. I round to 360 to the nearest ten. What is the greatest number I can be?

35. I am a 4-digit number. I round to 5,800 to the nearest hundred. What is the least number I can be?

★ **36.** I am a 3-digit number. I round to 650 to the nearest ten. If you added 1 to me, I would round to 660 to the nearest ten. What number am I?

★ **37.** I am a 3-digit number. I round to 420 to the nearest ten. The sum of my digits is 7. What number am I?

Millions

■ From 1971 to 1979, this many immigrants came to the United States.

MILLIONS PERIOD			THOUSANDS PERIOD			ONES PERIOD		
hundred-millions	ten-millions	one-millions	hundred-thousands	ten-thousands	one-thousands	hundreds	tens	ones
		3	9	6	2	6	7	5

The digit 3 means 3 millions, or 3,000,000.

Write: 3,962,675
Read: 3 million 962 thousand 675

■ From 1961 to 1970, 3,321,777 immigrants came to the United States.

Compare 3,962,675 and 3,321,777.

3 ,⑨6 2 , 6 7 5   9 > 3, so
3 ,③2 1 , 7 7 7   3,962,675 > 3,321,777

■ From 1951 to 1960, 2,515,479 immigrants came to the United States.
      2,515,479 to the nearest million
      is 3,000,000.

Try These

What does the digit 5 mean in each number?

1. 45,372,281   **2.** 506,463,000   **3.** 697,583,202   **4.** 350,116,000

Write each number.

5. 86 million 372 thousand   **6.** 935 million   **7.** 640 million 275
8. four hundred sixty-two million, five hundred thousand, seven

Write >, <, or =.

9. 64,615,233 ■ 64,415,233   **10.** 586,410,233 ■ 58,642,233

Exercises

What does the digit 8 mean in each number?

1. 785,612,355   **2.** 91,180,500   **3.** 864,233,179   **4.** 38,242,105

5. 43,278,022   **6.** 5,654,382   **7.** 815,200,000   **8.** 4,816,021

Use 765,283,149. Write the digit that is in each place.

9. ten-thousands place   **10.** hundred-millions place   **11.** ones place

Write each number.

12. 16 million 372 thousand 478   **13.** 27 million 9 thousand 538

14. 87 million 500 thousand 15   **15.** 400 million 750

16. one hundred fifty-three million, seven hundred thousand

17. five hundred million, seventy-four thousand, two

Write >, <, or =.

18. 4,276,300 ▨ 4,267,300   **19.** 72,876,100 ▨ 72,878,100

20. 309,090,009 ▨ 309,090,009   **21.** 196,894,650 ▨ 196,896,450

Round to the nearest million.

22. 5,276,415   **23.** 16,524,210   **24.** 84,097,295

25. 742,769,518   **26.** 998,765,000   **27.** 809,500,500

This table shows the number of immigrants who entered the United States between 1821 and 1900.

Solve each problem.

28. During which 10-year period did the greatest number of immigrants arrive?

29. During which 10-year periods did more than 3 million immigrants arrive?

★ **30.** During which 10-year periods did fewer than 2,500,000 immigrants arrive?

★ **31.** During which 10-year periods did more than 2 million but fewer than 3 million immigrants arrive?

IMMIGRANTS ADMITTED FROM ALL COUNTRIES	
Year	Number
1821–1830	143,439
1831–1840	599,125
1841–1850	1,713,251
1851–1860	2,598,214
1861–1870	2,314,824
1871–1880	2,812,191
1881–1890	5,246,613
1891–1900	3,687,564

Billions

■ In 1 year, about this many kilograms of wheat were produced in the world.

BILLIONS PERIOD			MILLIONS PERIOD			THOUSANDS PERIOD			ONES PERIOD		
hundred-billions	ten-billions	one-billions	hundred-millions	ten-millions	one-millions	hundred-thousands	ten-thousands	one-thousands	hundreds	tens	ones
4	8	0	3	0	0	0	0	0	0	0	0

The digit 4 means 4 hundred-billions, or 400,000,000,000.
The digit 8 means 8 ten-billions, or 80,000,000,000.

Write: 480,300,000,000
Read: 480 billion 300 million

■ Compare billions the same way you did millions.
Compare 19,368,207,455 and 19,342,708,561.

1 9 , 3 6 8 , 2 0 7 , 4 5 5   6 > 4, so
1 9 , 3 4 2 , 7 0 8 , 5 6 1   19,368,207,455 > 19,342,708,561

■ You also round billions the same way you did millions.

907,318,264,532 to the nearest billion is 907,000,000,000.

Try These

What does the digit 4 mean in each number?

1. 514,123,007,311   **2.** 460,126,173,615   **3.** 14,635,722

Write each number.

4. 4 billion 700 million 175   **5.** 78 billion 532 million 218 thousand
6. thirty-six billion, five hundred million, three hundred six

Write >, <, or =.

7. 431,514,262,011 ■ 431,513,892,911   **8.** 6,204,019,245 ■ 6,204,020,135

Exercises

What does the digit 3 mean in each number?

1. 43,022,516,112
2. 2,643,547,789
3. 325,109,248,662
4. 734,214,711,896
5. 517,322
6. 315,216,482,495

Use 321,687,900,455. Write the digit that is in each place.

7. ten-billions place
8. hundred-millions place
9. billions place
10. hundred-billions place
11. hundred-thousands place
12. hundreds place

Write each number.

13. 47 billion 395 thousand 168
14. 2 billion 26 million 124 thousand 735
15. 39 billion 400 million 60 thousand 247
16. seventy-eight billion, two hundred thirty-five million, four hundred thousand
17. seven billion, two hundred forty-one million, fourteen thousand
18. five hundred sixty-two billion, thirty-four million, eight hundred fifty

Write >, <, or =.

19. 7,642,500,789 ▦ 7,624,500,789
20. 23,149,872,015 ▦ 23,159,872,015
21. 78,926,014,681 ▦ 78,296,014,681
22. 4,151,263,910 ▦ 14,151,263,904
23. 510,160,702,000 ▦ 510,160,702,000
24. 193,004,781,242 ▦ 193,004,691,242
25. 602,500,847,197 ▦ 602,500,874,197
26. 11,248,322,454 ▦ 11,248,322,454

Round to the nearest billion.

27. 4,519,236,340
28. 37,101,962,700
29. 389,871,504,216

Solve each problem.

30. Which product was produced in the greatest quantity? The least quantity?

31. Which products round to 400,000,000,000 when rounded to the nearest hundred-billion?

32. List the products in order of the number of kilograms produced. Begin with the greatest number.

WORLD AGRICULTURAL PRODUCTION (1980)	
Product	Kilograms Produced
corn for grain	405,000,000,000
rice	396,000,000,000
soybeans	80,600,000,000
wheat	439,000,000,000

Problem Solving: Strategies

FINDING INFORMATION

A **schedule** contains information about buses, trains, or airplanes. A schedule can help you solve problems.

This is a schedule of nonstop flights from Houston to Los Angeles. These are some codes used in the schedule:

"LV" means the time the plane leaves Houston.
"ARR" means the time the plane arrives in Los Angeles.
"AL" means the name of the airline.
"FLT" means the flight number.

What time does ABC flight number 963 leave Houston and arrive in Los Angeles?

ABC flight number 963 leaves Houston at 7:15 A.M. and arrives in Los Angeles at 8:29 A.M.

FLIGHTS FROM HOUSTON TO LOS ANGELES			
LV	ARR	AL	FLT
7:15 A.M.	8:29 A.M.	ABC	963
8:45 A.M.	10:00 A.M.	TRANS	265
10:00 A.M.	11:15 A.M.	Aero	485
11:58 A.M.	1:13 P.M.	ABC	851
12:45 P.M.	2:00 P.M.	Aero	423
2:00 P.M.	3:15 P.M.	ABC	743

Using the Strategy

Use the schedule to answer each question.

1. What time does Aero flight number 485 leave Houston?

2. What time does TRANS flight number 265 arrive in Los Angeles?

3. Which airline has a flight that leaves Houston at 2:00 P.M.?

4. Which airline has the most flights to Los Angeles?

5. Which flight leaves earlier, Aero 423 or ABC 851?

6. Which flight arrives in Los Angeles at 2:00 P.M.?

7. Which flight would you take to get to Los Angeles before 9 A.M.?

8. Which flight arrives in Los Angeles after 3 P.M.?

9. Which flight gets to Los Angeles earlier, Aero 485 or ABC 851?

10. Which flights leave Houston after noon?

11. Mr. Johnston is flying from Houston to Los Angeles. He has a 1 P.M. meeting at the Los Angeles airport the same day. What is the latest flight he could take?

12. Mr. Klein needs to be in a meeting at 2 P.M. in Los Angeles. He estimates that it takes an hour to drive from the airport to the meeting place. Should he take flight ABC 851 the same day?

ACTIVITY

USING A SCHEDULE

1. Go to a train or bus station. Get a schedule that gives information about trains or buses leaving your community.

2. Use the schedule to complete a table like this one.

3. Plan a 1-day or overnight trip using the schedule. Decide where you will go, what time you will leave your home, and which bus or train you will take. What will you do in the place you are visiting? What bus or train will you take home?

Time	Communities You Can Reach
1 hour or less	
2 hours or less	
3 hours or less	

Properties of Addition and Subtraction

■ Here are two ways you can write addition and subtraction facts.

$$7 \atop +8 \atop \overline{15}$$ ← addends / ← sum

$$7 + 8 = 15$$
addends sum

$$9 \atop -4 \atop \overline{5}$$ ← difference

$$9 - 4 = 5$$

■ Addition has some special properties that can help you add mentally.

ORDER
You can change the order of the addends.
The sum is the same.
You can use the order property to check addition.

$$8 + 5 = 13$$
$$5 + 8 = 13$$

ZERO
When one addend is 0,
the sum is the other addend.

$$0 + 5 = 5$$
$$3 + 0 = 3$$

GROUPING
You can change the grouping of
the addends.
The sum is the same.
The parentheses mean *do this first*.
If there are no parentheses, you can add in any order.

$$(6 + 5) + 8$$
$$11 \quad + 8 = 19$$

$$6 + (5 + 8)$$
$$6 + \quad 13 \quad = 19$$

■ These patterns in subtraction can help you find differences mentally.

When you subtract a number from
itself, the difference is 0.

$$2 - 2 = 0$$
$$6 - 6 = 0$$

When you subtract 0 from a number,
the difference is that number.

$$8 - 0 = 8$$
$$4 - 0 = 4$$

■ Subtraction does not have the grouping property.

$$(9 - 4) - 3$$
$$5 \quad - 3 = 2$$

$$9 - (4 - 3)$$
$$9 - \quad 1 \quad = 8$$

The answers are not the same.

■ Addition and subtraction are related.

$$3 + 9 = 12 \qquad 12 - 9 = 3$$
$$9 + 3 = 12 \qquad 12 - 3 = 9$$

You can check subtraction by adding.

Try These

Add or subtract.

1. $2 + 9$ **2.** $4 + 8$ **3.** $10 - 5$ **4.** $5 + 8$ **5.** $18 - 9$ **6.** $6 + 4$ **7.** $13 - 8$

8. $14 - 7$ **9.** $9 + 6$ **10.** $14 - 9$ **11.** $3 + 6 + 2$
12. $7 + 0$ **13.** $9 - 0$ **14.** $5 + 4 + 7$ **15.** $15 - 7$

Exercises

Add or subtract.

1. $15 - 6$ **2.** $9 + 5$ **3.** $17 - 9$ **4.** $5 + 6$ **5.** $9 + 0$ **6.** $7 \; 2 + 8$ **7.** $5 \; 4 + 6$

8. $10 - 7$ **9.** $13 - 9$ **10.** $11 - 4$ **11.** $2 + 8 + 4$
12. $6 + 8$ **13.** $8 + 6$ **14.** $3 + 5 + 8$ **15.** $4 - 4$

Write two addition sentences and two subtraction sentences using the three numbers.

16. 3, 5, 8 **17.** 6, 3, 9 **18.** 8, 4, 12 **19.** 5, 8, 13

Compute. Do as many as you can mentally.

20. $(4 + 6) - 7$ **21.** $(8 - 2) + 5$ **22.** $(3 + 6) - (4 + 1)$
23. $14 - (13 - 7)$ **24.** $(9 + 8) - (3 + 5)$ **25.** $(15 - 6) + 7$
26. $(3 + 5) + 4$ **27.** $3 + (5 + 4)$ **28.** $13 - (8 + 5)$

THINK AND TRY

USING LOGICAL REASONING

Six people were in a room. Each person shook hands once with every other person in the room. How many handshakes were there?

Adding 2-Digit and 3-Digit Numbers

■ Mr. Nagin is the superintendent for Redwood Condominium. He ordered 38 screen doors for Section A and 54 screen doors for Section B. How many screen doors did Mr. Nagin order in all?

Add 38 and 54 to find how many in all.

Sometimes you have to regroup to add.

Add the ones. Regroup.	Add the tens.	Check.
1 38 +54 2	1 38 +54 92	54 +38 92 ✔

12 ones is 1 ten 2 ones.

Mr. Nagin ordered 92 screen doors.

■ Sometimes you need to regroup more than once.

Add: 205 + 198

Add the ones. Regroup.	Add the tens. Regroup.	Add the hundreds.	Check.
1 205 +198 3	11 205 +198 03	11 205 +198 403	198 +205 403 ✔

■ You add money the same way you add **whole numbers**. Whole numbers are the numbers 0, 1, 2, 3, 4, and so on.

Add: $6.75 + $.97 + $8.60

$$\begin{array}{r} 2\,1 \\ 675 \\ 97 \\ +860 \\ \hline 1{,}632 \end{array} \qquad \begin{array}{r} 2\ 1 \\ \$\ 6.75 \\ .97 \\ +\ \ 8.60 \\ \hline \$16.32 \end{array}$$

Remember: Write the $ and the . in the answer.

Try These

Add. Check each answer.

1. 32
+47

2. 39
+57

3. 216
+324

4. $2.53
+ 6.79

5. 475
+ 7

6. 36 + 45 + 72

7. 148 + 374 + 215

8. $7.96 + $8.48

Exercises

Add.

1. 92
+65

2. 67
+26

3. $.08
+ .75

4. 62
+486

5. 765
+123

6. $6.23
+ .95

7. $7.96
8.48
+ 2.03

8. 48
72
+72

9. 315
184
+ 67

10. 209
54
+618

11. 435 + 86

12. $7.40 + $1.68

13. 461 + 39

14. 139 + 24 + 63

15. 516 + 278 + 134

16. 212 + 47 + 536

 Ed, Carol, and Milagros drove from _A_ to _I_. Find the path of each person.

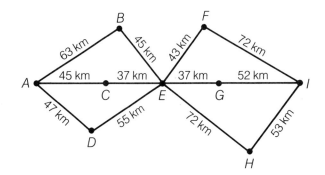

17. Ed drove 207 kilometers.

18. Carol drove 233 kilometers.

19. Milagros drove 217 kilometers.

Solve each problem. You may choose paper and pencil or a calculator.

20. Mr. Nagin bought 24 combination locks and 79 key locks. How many locks did he buy in all?

21. Mr. Nagin spent $9.25 on paint and $4.49 on a brush. How much money did he spend in all?

22. Mr. Nagin calls a plumber. The plumber is paid $15 per hour. He works for 3 hours. How much is the plumber paid?

★ **23.** The gardener orders sod. Section A needs 124 pieces. Section B needs twice that many pieces. How many pieces are needed altogether?

Adding Greater Numbers

■ The Irving Motor Corporation shipped 7,519 cars and 3,684 trucks to dealers in New Jersey. How many vehicles did they ship altogether?

To find how many altogether, add 7,519 and 3,684.

Add the ones. Regroup.	Add the tens. Regroup.	Add the hundreds. Regroup.	Add the thousands. Regroup.
$\overset{1}{7{,}519}$	$\overset{11}{7{,}519}$	$\overset{1\ 11}{7{,}519}$	$\overset{1\ 11}{7{,}519}$
$+3{,}684$	$+3{,}684$	$+3{,}684$	$+3{,}684$
3	03	203	11,203

The Irving Motor Corporation shipped 11,203 vehicles.

■ You can **estimate** mentally to check whether or not an answer is reasonable.

Add: 169,275 + 53,884

$$\begin{array}{r} \overset{111\ 1}{169{,}275} \\ +\ \ 53{,}884 \\ \hline 223{,}159 \end{array}$$

Estimate to check.

Circle the first digit in each addend. Round each addend to the circled place. Add.

$$\begin{array}{r} ①69{,}275 \longrightarrow 200{,}000 \\ +\ ⑤3{,}884 \longrightarrow +\ 50{,}000 \\ \hline 250{,}000 \end{array}$$

The sum seems reasonable since 223,159 is close to 250,000.

Try These

Add. Estimate to check.

1. 4,096
   +1,983

2. 9,125
   + 876

3. $383.81
   +   48.16

4. 127,308
   + 85,265

5. $3,780 + $927

6. 8,456 + 9,375 + 3,420

Exercises

Add. Estimate to check.

1.	1,746 +8,201	**2.**	63,821 + 2,765	**3.**	$27.80 + 11.52	**4.**	8,217 + 891	**5.**	26,508 + 9,384

6.	194,872 + 23,514	**7.**	$826.18 + 97.24	**8.**	526,190 +487,546	**9.**	229,764 +196,134	**10.**	$4,861.25 + 875.98

11.	635,204 +387,519	**12.**	205 86 +897	**13.**	$15.75 9.95 76.43 + 24.18	**14.**	75,624 316 1,746 + 214	**15.**	$ 129 2,574 3,716 542 + 117

16. 6,372 + 7,124 + 82,456

17. 24 + 106 + 2,648

18. $36.12 + $7.95 + $54.68

19. 15,812 + 198,017 + 64,943

20. 85,624 + 92,101 + 6,864

21. 526 + 4,257 + 89,515 + 9,334

 Add. Use a calculator to check.

22. 3,124 + 58,709 + 611 + 2,005

23. 46,123 + 70,531 + 2,954 + 6,101

Estimate. Then use a calculator to find an exact answer.

24. 6,492 + 3,155

25. 462 + 7,920

26. 21,405 + 39,216 + 18,000

27. 3,405 + 67,948

28. 2,639 + 8,347

29. 1,694 + 54,273 + 9,065

Solve each problem. You may choose paper and pencil or a calculator.

30. The base price of a car is $7,280. Find the total cost with air conditioning, power steering, and disc brakes.

31. The base price of a car is $6,975. Find the total cost with air conditioning, tinted glass, stereo, and defogger.

★ **32.** Ms. Connolly chooses a car with a base price of $7,950. She orders the three most expensive items of optional equipment. Find the total cost.

OPTIONAL EQUIPMENT	
Equipment	Cost
air conditioning	$625
bucket seats	$278
power steering	$265
tinted glass	$ 96
stereo AM/FM	$468
defogger	$ 77
disc brakes	$317

Subtracting 2-Digit and 3-Digit Numbers

■ Lisa owns the Book Nook. She sold 75 paperbacks and 47 hardcover books this week. How many more paperbacks than hardcover books did she sell?

Subtract 47 from 75 to find how many more.

Sometimes you need to regroup tens to get more ones.

Regroup.
Subtract the ones.

$$\begin{array}{r} \overset{6}{\cancel{7}}\ \overset{15}{\cancel{5}} \\ -4\ 7 \\ \hline 8 \end{array}$$

Subtract the tens.

$$\begin{array}{r} \overset{6}{\cancel{7}}\ \overset{15}{\cancel{5}} \\ -4\ 7 \\ \hline 2\ 8 \end{array}$$

Check.

$$\begin{array}{r} 28 \\ +47 \\ \hline 75 \end{array} ✔$$

Lisa sold 28 more paperbacks than hardcover books.

■ Sometimes you need to regroup more than once.

Subtract: 724 − 595

Regroup.
Subtract the ones.

$$\begin{array}{r} \overset{1}{7}\ 2\ \overset{14}{\cancel{4}} \\ -5\ 9\ 5 \\ \hline 9 \end{array}$$

Regroup.
Subtract the tens.

$$\begin{array}{r} 6\ \overset{11}{\cancel{1}}\ 14 \\ 7\ \cancel{2}\ \cancel{4} \\ -5\ 9\ 5 \\ \hline 2\ 9 \end{array}$$

Subtract the hundreds.

$$\begin{array}{r} 6\ \overset{11}{\cancel{1}}\ 14 \\ 7\ \cancel{2}\ \cancel{4} \\ -5\ 9\ 5 \\ \hline 1\ 2\ 9 \end{array}$$

Check.

$$\begin{array}{r} 129 \\ +595 \\ \hline 724 \end{array} ✔$$

■ You subtract money the same way you subtract whole numbers.

Subtract: $6.35 − $2.98

$$\begin{array}{r} 5\ \overset{12}{\cancel{2}}\ 15 \\ \cancel{6}\ \cancel{3}\ \cancel{5} \\ -2\ 9\ 8 \\ \hline 3\ 3\ 7 \end{array}$$

$$\begin{array}{r} 5\ \overset{12}{\cancel{2}}\ 15 \\ \$\cancel{6}.\cancel{3}\ \cancel{5} \\ -\ 2.9\ 8 \\ \hline \$3.3\ 7 \end{array}$$

> *Remember: Write the $ and the . in the answer.*

Try These

Subtract. Check each answer.

1. 84
  − 36

2. 58
  − 29

3. $4.80
  − .67

4. 625
  − 169

5. 709
  − 64

6. 93 − 67

7. $862 − $490

8. 112 − 47

9. 894 − 36

Exercises

Subtract.

1. 78
  − 32

2. 81
  − 64

3. $3.75
  − 1.24

4. 430
  − 53

5. 246
  − 128

6. 384 − 123

7. $576 − $54

8. 313 − 184

9. $3.64 − $.97

Add or subtract.

10. 42
  − 33

11. 57
  + 29

12. 109
  + 654

13. 428
  − 75

14. $5.17
  − 1.09

15. 561 + 84

16. $4.27 − $1.38

17. $7.26 + $5.05

18. 630 − 297

Compute.

19. (462 − 90) + 235

20. 462 − (90 + 235)

21. $9.24 − ($3.75 − $1.12)

22. (870 + 185) + 313

23. ($1.87 − $.49) + $2.85

24. 673 − (141 + 282)

Solve each problem.

25. Lisa orders 126 novels and 88 biographies. How many more novels than biographies does Lisa order?

26. A customer buys a cookbook for $6.19. She gives the clerk $6.25. How much change should she receive?

27. There are 127 books. 47 of the books are mysteries. How many books are not mysteries?

28. Lisa orders 213 books. She receives a shipment of 125 books. How many more books must be sent?

★ 29. A carton contains 75 books. A clerk unpacks 32 books. Then he unpacks another 19 books. How many books are left in the carton?

★ 30. There was $750 in the library fund. The librarians spent $439 on books and $95 on magazines. How much money was left in the fund?

Problem Solving: Applications

CHOOSING THE OPERATION

Westwood Elementary School is a small school with only one class at each grade level.

The bar graph shows the number of students in each class on October 1, 1985. How many more students were in the first grade than in the kindergarten?

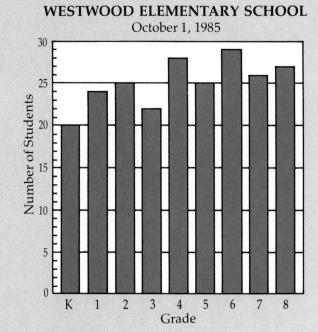

WESTWOOD ELEMENTARY SCHOOL
October 1, 1985

READ   There were 24 students in the first grade. There were 20 students in the kindergarten.

PLAN   Subtract 20 from 24 to find how many more were in the first grade.

DO
$$\begin{array}{r} 24 \\ -20 \\ \hline 4 \end{array}$$
There were 4 more students in the first grade than in the kindergarten.

CHECK   Did you read the graph correctly?
Did you do the subtraction correctly?
Add to check your subtraction: $20 + 4 = 24$

Try These

Solve each problem. Use the graph on page 22.

1. Which grade had the greatest number of students?

2. Which grade had the least number of students?

3. How many more students were there in the 4th grade than in the 3rd grade?

4. How many students were in kindergarten and 1st grade altogether?

5. What was the total number of students in grades 6, 7, and 8?

6. Estimate the number of students at Westwood. Check your estimate by finding the total.

Exercises

This graph shows the number of students in each class on February 1, 1986.

Solve each problem.

1. How many months had passed when this graph was made?

2. Which grades had fewer students on February 1 than on October 1?

3. How many fewer students were in the 6th grade on February 1 than on October 1?

4. Which grades had more students on February 1 than on October 1?

5. How many more students were in the 5th grade on February 1 than on October 1?

WESTWOOD ELEMENTARY SCHOOL
February 1, 1986

6. What was the total number of students in grades 6, 7, and 8?

7. What was the total number of students in Westwood at the beginning of February?

8. Had the total number of students increased or decreased from October to February? By how many?

★ 9. What was the average number of students in the 7th grade during this 4-month period?

★ 10. About half of the 6th graders ate lunch in school. About how many 6th graders ate lunch in school each day in February?

Zeros in Subtraction

■ Sometimes you have to regroup across one or more 0s.

The Abacus Theater box office sold 804 tickets in 1 week. 156 of the tickets were for the Friday night performance of *Cinderella*. How many tickets were sold for other performances?

Subtract 156 from 804 to find the answer.

There are no tens. Regroup hundreds first.	Regroup tens.	Subtract.	Check.
$\begin{array}{r} \overset{7\ 10}{8\rlap{/}0\ 4} \\ -1\ 5\ 6 \\ \hline \end{array}$	$\begin{array}{r} \overset{9}{}\ \ \\ \overset{7\ \rlap{/}{10}\ 14}{8\ \rlap{/}0\ \rlap{/}4} \\ -1\ 5\ 6 \\ \hline \end{array}$	$\begin{array}{r} \overset{9}{}\ \ \\ \overset{7\ \rlap{/}{10}\ 14}{8\ \rlap{/}0\ \rlap{/}4} \\ -1\ 5\ 6 \\ \hline 6\ 4\ 8 \end{array}$	$\begin{array}{r} 648 \\ +156 \\ \hline 804 \ \checkmark \end{array}$

648 tickets were sold for other performances.

■ Souvenir programs are available at the theater. 400 programs were printed. 75 programs were sold during one performance. How many programs are left?

To find how many are left, subtract 75 from 400.

Regroup hundreds first.	Regroup tens.	Subtract.	Check.
$\begin{array}{r} \overset{3\ 10}{4\rlap{/}0\ 0} \\ -\ \ 7\ 5 \\ \hline \end{array}$	$\begin{array}{r} \overset{9}{}\ \ \\ \overset{3\ \rlap{/}{10}\ 10}{4\ \rlap{/}0\ \rlap{/}0} \\ -\ \ 7\ 5 \\ \hline \end{array}$	$\begin{array}{r} \overset{9}{}\ \ \\ \overset{3\ \rlap{/}{10}\ 10}{4\ \rlap{/}0\ \rlap{/}0} \\ -\ \ 7\ 5 \\ \hline 3\ 2\ 5 \end{array}$	$\begin{array}{r} 325 \\ +\ 75 \\ \hline 400 \ \checkmark \end{array}$

325 programs are left.

Try These

Subtract. Check each answer.

1. $\begin{array}{r} 306 \\ -\ 58 \\ \hline \end{array}$
2. $\begin{array}{r} 500 \\ -175 \\ \hline \end{array}$
3. $\begin{array}{r} \$60 \\ -\ 27 \\ \hline \end{array}$
4. $\begin{array}{r} 604 \\ -386 \\ \hline \end{array}$
5. $\begin{array}{r} 205 \\ -148 \\ \hline \end{array}$

6. $\$7.00 - \$3.92$
7. $800 - 534$
8. $401 - 97$
9. $\$43.06 - \$19.19$

Exercises

Subtract.

1. 900 −156	**2.** 302 − 79	**3.** 701 −697	**4.** $6.00 − .85	**5.** $498 − 268
6. 522 −135	**7.** $900 − 497	**8.** 104 − 99	**9.** $7.03 − 5.69	**10.** 560 −291

11. 800 − 86 **12.** $5.00 − $2.15 **13.** 632 − 48 **14.** $700 − $368

Add or subtract.

15. 200 − 142 **16.** 508 + 364 **17.** $8.20 − $5.95 **18.** 279 + 321
19. 923 + 88 **20.** $4.91 − $1.86 **21.** 790 − 584 **22.** $6.17 + $.35

Compute.

23. 900 − (114 + 231) **24.** 380 + (79 + 25) **25.** ($6.00 − $3.45) + $6.79
26. ($403 + $797) − $355 **27.** (745 − 182) − 49 **28.** 745 − (182 − 49)

Copy and complete.

★ **29.** 500 − ■ = 426 ★ **30.** $6.35 − ■ = $1.49
★ **31.** ■ − $1.35 = $5.65 ★ **32.** ■ − 296 = 106

Solve each problem.

33. The Abacus Theater seats 600 people. On Friday evening, 124 seats were empty. How many seats were occupied?

34. 1 adult ticket costs $3.75. Mrs. Wong buys a ticket and a program that costs $.95. How much does Mrs. Wong spend in all?

★ **35.** There were two performances of *Cinderella*. 418 people saw the first performance. 75 fewer people saw the second performance. How many people saw *Cinderella* altogether?

★ **36.** Mr. Bruce buys 1 adult ticket for $3.75. He also buys 2 children's tickets for $1.85 each. How much does he pay in all? How much change does he receive from $10?

Subtracting Greater Numbers

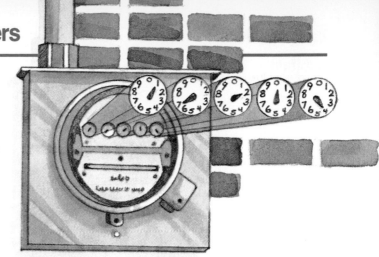

- The present reading on the electric meter at the Wainwright Building is 17,204 kilowatt-hours. The reading before this was 9,658 kilowatt-hours. How many kilowatt-hours of electricity were used?

Subtract 9,658 from 17,204 to find how many.

Regroup. Subtract the ones.	**Subtract the tens.**	**Regroup. Subtract the hundreds.**	**Regroup. Subtract the thousands.**
9 1 10 14 1 7,2 0 4 − 9,6 5 8 ——— 6	9 1 10 14 1 7,2 0 4 − 9,6 5 8 ——— 4 6	11 9 6 1 10 14 1 7,2 0 4 − 9,6 5 8 ——— 5 4 6	16 11 9 0 6 1 10 14 1 7,2 0 4 − 9,6 5 8 ——— 7,5 4 6

7,546 kilowatt-hours of electricity were used.

- You can estimate mentally to check whether or not an answer is reasonable.

Subtract: 609,214 − 78,536

11 10
5 10 8 1 0 14
6 0 9,2 1 4
− 7 8,5 3 6
——————
5 3 0,6 7 8

Circle the first digit in each number. Round each number to the circled place. Subtract.

Estimate to check.

⑥0 9 , 2 1 4 → 600,000
− ⑦8 , 5 3 6 → − 80,000
——————————
520,000

The difference seems reasonable since 530,678 is close to 520,000.

Try These

Subtract. Estimate to check.

1. 8,015
  −2,567

2. 24,162
  − 9,575

3. $825.00
  − 637.45

4. 521,164
  − 89,565

5. 294,018
  −123,529

6. 43,272 − 4,956

7. 502,300 − 175,800

8. $3,812.04 − $197.51

Exercises

Subtract. Estimate to check.

1. 3,601 −1,287	**2.** 4,700 −1,265	**3.** 5,002 −1,756	**4.** $65.00 − 24.15	**5.** 7,026 − 458
6. 28,962 −13,784	**7.** 319,250 − 47,627	**8.** 475,245 −265,780	**9.** $70,000 − 6,500	**10.** 361,007 − 57,235

11. 2,648 − 1,436

12. 5,642 − 3,475

13. $3,000 − $2,995

Add or subtract.

14. 5,000 − 2,681

15. $34.58 + $19.75

16. 18,126 + 9,799

17. 47,220 − 8,465

18. $825.19 − $178.50

19. $419.00 + $586.42

This table shows some readings on the electric meter at the Wainright Building.

Solve each problem.

20. Copy and complete the table.

21. What was the total number of kilowatt-hours used?

★ **22.** In November, the electric bill was $3,850.97. In December, the bill was $4,214.35. How much more than $7,000 was spent these 2 months?

NUMBER OF KILOWATT-HOURS		
Present Reading	Previous Reading	Amount Used
9,241	7,856	▦
10,314	9,241	▦
11,880	10,314	▦
15,444	11,880	▦

 KEEPING IN SHAPE

Write >, <, or =.

1. 375 ▦ 357

2. 4,163 ▦ 4,165

3. 528,920 ▦ 75,164

4. 14,605 ▦ 1,465

5. 981,742 ▦ 981,742

6. 26,053 ▦ 26,503

7. 8,749 ▦ 12,035

8. 724,036 ▦ 742,063

9. 67,802 ▦ 67,082

Problem Solving: Applications

ESTIMATING SUMS AND DIFFERENCES

■ Sometimes you do not need an exact answer. An estimate may be good enough.

The St. Lawrence Seaway is 3,771 kilometers long. The St. Lawrence River is 1,224 kilometers long. About how much longer is the seaway than the river?

To find the answer, estimate the difference.

Round each number and subtract.

$$
\begin{array}{r}
③,7\,7\,1 \longrightarrow 4{,}000 \\
-①,2\,2\,4 \longrightarrow -1{,}000 \\
\hline
3{,}000
\end{array}
$$

The seaway is about 3,000 kilometers longer than the river.

■ Mary Jackson works in a tollbooth. The amount of money she collects each hour is recorded. Mary's record for 3 hours is shown below. Estimate the amount of money she collected.

   $64.50 $92.65 $57.20

To find the answer, estimate the sum.

$$
\begin{array}{r}
\$ ⑥4\,.\,5\,0 \longrightarrow \$\ 60 \\
⑨2\,.\,6\,5 \longrightarrow 90 \\
+\ ⑤7\,.\,2\,0 \longrightarrow +\ 60 \\
\hline
\$210
\end{array}
$$

About $210 was collected.

Try These

Estimate to solve each problem.

1. The Tacoma Narrows Bridge is 853 meters long. The Ambassador International Bridge is 564 meters long. About how much longer is the Tacoma Narrows Bridge?

2. Ms. Goldstein went on a 2-day business trip. She spent $83.42 on Monday and $68.29 on Tuesday. Estimate the amount she spent altogether.

Exercises

Choose estimation, paper and pencil, or a calculator to solve.

1. The Green family drove 455 kilometers to a hotel. The next day they drove 148 kilometers to an amusement park. About how many kilometers did they drive in all?

2. The Amazon River is 6,437 kilometers long. The Volga River is 3,690 kilometers long. How much longer is the Amazon River?

3. Mr. Lee went on a business trip. He spent $124.80 on gasoline, $31.20 on tolls, and $179.00 on hotels. Estimate the amount he spent altogether.

4. A salesman drove 175 kilometers to see a customer. Then he drove 83 kilometers to pick up an order. How many kilometers did the salesman drive in all?

5. The Nile River is 6,650 kilometers long. The Rio Grande is 3,610 kilometers shorter. About how long is the Rio Grande?

6. The Walt Whitman Bridge is 610 meters long. The Severn Bridge is 378 meters longer. Estimate the length of the Severn Bridge.

7. On Sunday, 2,512 cars passed through the city tollbooths. On Monday, 5,380 cars passed through the tollbooths. How many more cars passed through the tollbooths on Monday?

8. The Erie Canal is 544 kilometers long. Three other canals in New York State are a total of 284 kilometers long. About how many kilometers of canals are in New York State altogether?

9. The Lake Pontchartrain Causeway is 38,352 meters long. The Chesapeake Bay Bridge-Tunnel is 9,947 meters shorter. Estimate the length of the Chesapeake Bay Bridge-Tunnel.

★ 10. Ms. García was given $100 per day for expenses for a 3-day business trip. She spent $73.20 the first day, $78.08 the second, and $89.23 the third. About how much did she have left?

Problem Solving: Applications

TOO MUCH INFORMATION

Sometimes there is too much information in a problem. You must decide what information you do need to solve the problem.

Tati flew from New York to Berlin, Germany, for a 2-week vacation. The distance from New York to Berlin is about 6,400 kilometers. She traveled about 900 kilometers the first week she was in Germany and about 600 kilometers the second week. About how many kilometers did she travel while in Germany?

Find the information you need. Tati traveled about 900 kilometers the first week and about 600 kilometers the second week.

Add 900 and 600 to find about how many kilometers she traveled while in Germany.

$$\begin{array}{r} 900 \\ +600 \\ \hline 1,500 \end{array}$$

Tati traveled about 1,500 kilometers while in Germany.

Try These

Solve each problem.

1. George works for a travel agency. In January, his travel sales were $94,642. In February, his travel sales were $112,486. His goal for March is $120,000. What was the total of his travel sales for January and February?

2. Ms. Yakamura went to Spain and to France. Her suitcase weighed 23 kilograms. She traveled 3,172 kilometers in Spain and 2,269 kilometers in France. About how many more kilometers did she travel in Spain than in France?

Exercises

Solve each problem.

1. Fred made two business trips last month. The first one cost his company $1,425.72. The second one cost his company $928.48. His sales for the month were $216,428.45. How much did his two business trips cost his company?

2. Lucy spent $1,300 on her trip to Hawaii. She flew 4,115 kilometers from New York City to San Francisco. The flight from San Francisco to Honolulu was 3,832 kilometers. About how many kilometers did Lucy fly from New York City to Honolulu?

3. Get-Away Travel Agency has two agents, Ms. Chan and Mr. Katz. In February, Ms. Chan's sales were $4,615, and Mr. Katz's sales were $3,845. Ms. Chan's commission was $184.60, and Mr. Katz's commission was $153.80. What were the total sales for the agency in February?

4. Mr. Kern is a salesman for a computer-chip company. He flew 57,200 kilometers last year. He flew 42,300 kilometers on business trips. Mr. Kern sold $850,000 worth of computer chips on those trips. About how far did he fly last year for reasons other than business?

5. Ms. Ortega rented a car and drove it 890 kilometers. She paid $108.00 for the rental fee, $133.50 for the mileage charge, and $31.25 for gasoline. How much did Ms. Ortega pay in all?

6. Justin took a trip by bus. His fare was $128.95. He spent $19.50 on food. If he had gone by train, his fare would have been $134.25. How much more is the train fare than the bus fare?

7. The catering truck delivered 215 chicken dinners and 175 beef dinners to the plane. The flight attendants served all the beef dinners and 180 chicken dinners. The flight took 4 hours. How many dinners did the flight attendants serve?

★ 8. Mr. and Mrs. May are planning a vacation. It would cost them $215 each to fly during the day. If they flew at night, the cost would be $158 each. If they took the train, the cost would be $140 each. How much money would they save altogether by flying at night instead of during the day?

CHAPTER CHECKPOINT

What does the digit 7 mean in each number? (pp. 2–11)

1. 472
2. 78,014
3. 763,124
4. 47,210,000
5. 710,563,000
6. 79,000,831,123

Write each number. (pp. 2–11)

7. 18 thousand 206
8. 355 thousand 74
9. 2 million 700 thousand 11
10. 93 million 160
11. six hundred eight thousand, one hundred seventy
12. twenty million, five hundred three thousand, twelve
13. two billion, one hundred fifty-four million, six thousand

Write >, <, or =. (pp. 4–11)

14. 4,751 ▓ 4,752
15. 126,380 ▓ 96,130
16. 23,146,887 ▓ 23,148,887
17. 6,047,115 ▓ 16,004,121
18. 175,424,313 ▓ 175,424,313
19. 30,180,045,772 ▓ 30,180,025,991

Round each number to the given place. (pp. 6–11)

20. 745 to the nearest hundred
21. 18,743 to the nearest thousand
22. 683,192 to the nearest ten-thousand
23. $12.55 to the nearest dollar
24. 49,822,103 to the nearest million
25. 33,772,151,918 to the nearest ten-billion

Add. (pp. 14–19)

26. $\begin{array}{r} 75 \\ +18 \\ \hline \end{array}$
27. $\begin{array}{r} 246 \\ +537 \\ \hline \end{array}$
28. $\begin{array}{r} \$1.25 \\ +\ 6.49 \\ \hline \end{array}$
29. $\begin{array}{r} 4,803 \\ +\ 721 \\ \hline \end{array}$
30. $\begin{array}{r} 32,441 \\ +19,756 \\ \hline \end{array}$

31. 417 + 26
32. $57.20 + $21.55
33. 833 + 64 + 297

Subtract. (pp. 20–27)

34. $\begin{array}{r} 72 \\ -35 \\ \hline \end{array}$
35. $\begin{array}{r} 614 \\ -289 \\ \hline \end{array}$
36. $\begin{array}{r} \$5.21 \\ -\ .83 \\ \hline \end{array}$
37. $\begin{array}{r} 400 \\ -127 \\ \hline \end{array}$
38. $\begin{array}{r} 703 \\ -685 \\ \hline \end{array}$

39. 700 − 62
40. $3.41 − $.58
41. 41,026 − 2,945

Add or subtract. Estimate to check. (pp. 14–27)

42. $173.24
   + 96.82

43. 3,124
   − 1,560

44. 27,011
   − 9,428

45. 239,143
   + 786,059

46. $718.00
   − 247.63

47. 406
   178
   + 52

48. $18.05
   7.95
   + 4.63

49. 520,075
   − 83,194

50. 28,749
   603
   + 1,551

51. 703,801
   − 576,233

52. $82.00 − $4.76

53. 6,092 + 7,181

54. 50,072 − 28,193

55. 100,304 − 88,566

56. 193,454 + 67,439

57. 15,234 + 1,987 + 663

Choose estimation or paper and pencil to solve. (pp. 2–31)

58. Lisa bought a paperback book rack for $268. She bought a rack for travel guides that cost $405. How much more did the rack for travel guides cost?

59. During July, 86 people moved into a condominium. During August, 124 people moved in. During September, 249 people moved in. How many people moved in altogether?

60. Ms. Herrera is an airline pilot. She flew 4,642 kilometers in April and 7,263 kilometers in May. About how many kilometers did Ms. Herrera fly in those 2 months?

61. The tour center sold 243 county maps at $1.50 each. It sold 158 state maps at $2.75 each. How many more county maps did the tour center sell?

This schedule shows the trains leaving Center City for Woodsville, Glentown, and Harris.

62. Ms. Louis checks the train schedule. She wants to take the train that arrives in Woodsville at 4:57. What time does that train leave Center City?

LEAVE	ARRIVE		
Center City	Woodsville	Glentown	Harris
3:40 P.M.	3:59 P.M.	4:31 P.M.	4:41 P.M.
4:36 P.M.	4:57 P.M.	5:30 P.M.	5:40 P.M.
5:01 P.M.	5:28 P.M.	6:00 P.M.	6:13 P.M.

63. Mrs. Stern takes the 3:40 train from Center City. What time will she arrive in Glentown?

64. Mr. Lee takes the 5:01 train from Center City. What time will he arrive in Harris?

COMPUTERS AND PROBLEM SOLVING

How many BASIC statements and commands do you remember?

1. What is a variable?

2. What command erases everything from the computer's temporary memory?

3. What symbol tells the computer to multiply? To divide?

4. What statement temporarily stops the program so the user can add a piece of information?

5. What does GOTO tell the computer to do?

6. What instruction tells the computer to do something only when certain things are true?

7. What is a string variable?

8. What will the computer do when it receives this statement: LET NA$ = "ALAN"?
What does the $ mean?

9. Explain the meaning of this message.
   ?SYNTAX ERROR IN 50

10. What is the purpose of a FOR. . .NEXT loop?

This BASIC program asks you to input two numbers, and then to choose a symbol to show how the numbers are related.

```
NEW
10   PRINT "WHAT IS YOUR FIRST NUMBER?"
20   INPUT N1
30   PRINT "WHAT IS YOUR SECOND NUMBER?"
40   INPUT N2
50   PRINT "IS "; N1; " >, <, OR = "; N2; "?"
60   INPUT ANSWER$
70   IF N1 < N2 AND ANSWER$ = "<" THEN GOTO 110
80   IF N1 > N2 AND ANSWER$ = ">" THEN GOTO 110
90   IF N1 = N2 AND ANSWER$ = "=" THEN GOTO 110
100   PRINT "THAT'S NOT THE ANSWER I GET.": GOTO 120
110   PRINT "RIGHT!!"
120   END
```

Each of the IF. . .THEN statements in the program checks two conditions. Line 70 checks:

1. Is it true that N1 is less than N2?

2. Is it true that the user input <?

If both of these conditions are true, the computer will jump to line 110. Otherwise, the computer will go on to line 100.

Solve each problem.

1. How does the computer respond when the user doesn't type the right answer?

2. Change line 100 to let the user respond until there is a right answer.

3. In this program, how many conditions are checked for true/false?

★ 4. Modify the program to ask whether the user wants to input a new set of numbers.

ENRICHMENT

ROMAN NUMERALS

■ Centuries ago, the Romans used a system for naming numbers that is different from the system we use.

Roman Numeral	I	V	X	L	C	D	M
Our Number	1	5	10	50	100	500	1,000

■ They used these rules:

1. Add when a letter is repeated.

   XXX means 10 + 10 + 10, or 30.
   CC means 100 + 100, or 200.

2. Add when a letter for a number follows a letter for a greater number.

   MC means 1,000 + 100, or 1,100.
   LXX means 50 + 10 + 10, or 70.

3. Subtract when a letter for a number comes before a letter for a greater number.

   IX means 10 − 1, or 9.   XL means 50 − 10, or 40.

Write our number.

1. VIII	**2.** XV	**3.** DC	**4.** IV	**5.** DCCII
6. DXC	**7.** CXX	**8.** CCLXX	**9.** CMIII	**10.** XIV
11. MIV	**12.** XCIV	**13.** MDXLVI	**14.** CDVI	**15.** CCXIX
16. XLVII	**17.** CCCXXVII	**18.** CXCII	**19.** CDXLIV	**20.** CMXLI

Write the Roman numeral.

21. 16	**22.** 25	**23.** 42	**24.** 63	**25.** 250
26. 1,522	**27.** 2,612	**28.** 89	**29.** 615	**30.** 23
31. 55	**32.** 971	**33.** 942	**34.** 864	**35.** 655
36. 1,021	**37.** 1,253	**38.** 3,941	**39.** 662	**40.** 2,494

Write the Roman numeral that comes next.

41. XV   **42.** XXIX   **43.** MCXLI   **44.** DLIII   **45.** CXCIX   **46.** XLIV

What does the digit 6 mean in each number?

1. 3,650

2. 126,802

3. 1,640,937

4. 26,142,009

5. 634,110,258

6. 6,247,358,901

Write each number.

7. 106 thousand 45

8. 3 million 211 thousand 57

9. 28 million 543

10. 1 billion 479 million

11. one hundred four million, fifty thousand, twenty-six

12. twelve billion, nine million, three hundred thousand, one

Write >, <, or =.

13. 37,258 ▓ 37,208

14. 681,433 ▓ 91,344

15. 80,144,215 ▓ 80,144,220

16. 3,278,994,121 ▓ 3,278,994,121

Round each number to the given place.

17. 26,529 to the nearest thousand

18. $479.35 to the nearest dollar

19. 97,143,608 to the nearest ten-million

20. 28,460,300,115 to the nearest billion

Add or subtract.

21.
$$378 + 426$$

22.
$$205 - 97$$

23.
$$\$51.34 - 18.65$$

24.
$$42,568 + 59,134$$

25.
$$16,400 - 5,873$$

26. 254 + 1,096 + 777

27. 80,412 − 5,635

28. 4,744 + 951 + 16,088

Solve each problem.

29. San Diego Stadium has 52,568 seats. There were 49,759 seats occupied for the game. How many seats were empty?

30. The attendance for the game on Saturday was 51,279. There were 52,186 people at the Sunday game. What was the total attendance?

31. Bob paid $7.50 to get into the game and $.75 for a program. How much did he spend altogether?

32. Doreen buys a hat for $5.50. She pays with a $10 bill. How much change should she receive?

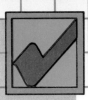

SKILLS CHECK

Choose the correct answer.

1. In 1,036,427,589, which digit is in the ten-millions place?

a. 2
b. 3
c. 4
d. 6

2. What is the number for two billion, six million, five hundred nine?

a. 2,006,509
b. 2,006,000,509
c. 2,006,509,000
d. NG

3. Which number is greater than 473,185?

a. 470,524
b. 473,085
c. 473,180
d. 474,185

4. What is 1,352,897 rounded to the nearest hundred-thousand?

a. 1,300,000
b. 1,352,900
c. 1,400,000
d. NG

5. $(8 + 6) - (5 + 4)$

a. 5
b. 13
c. 14
d. 23

6.   184
  + 79

a. 63
b. 153
c. 253
d. NG

7.   36,521
  +68,477

a. 94,998
b. 104,998
c. 914,998
d. 1,049,980

8   2,005
  −1,839

a. 166
b. 274
c. 1,834
d. NG

9.   354,102
  − 63,215

a. 90,887
b. 290,887
c. 290,997
d. 311,113

10. Lee had $12.34. He bought a hat for $9.75. How much money does he have left?

a. $2.59
b. $2.69
c. $3.41
d. $22.09

11. There are 2,879 cans of soup. A shipment of 1,950 cans arrives. About how many cans of soup is that in all?

a. 3,000 cans
b. 4,000 cans
c. 5,000 cans
d. NG

12. In 3 days, Sue spent $8.46, $9.53, and $12.31. How much did she spend in all?

a. $5.68
b. $17.99
c. $29.20
d. $30.30

MULTIPLICATION

2

Properties of Multiplication

■ You bought 4 bags of oranges. There are 6 oranges in each bag. How many oranges did you buy in all?

There are 4 sets of 6.

Multiply to find how many in all.

$4 \times 6 = 24$

You bought 24 oranges in all.

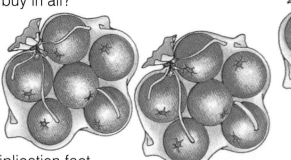

■ Here are two ways to write a multiplication fact.

$$\begin{array}{r} 7 \\ \times 5 \\ \hline 35 \end{array}$$ factors

35 ← product

$5 \times 7 = 35$ ← product

factors

■ A product is a **multiple** of each of its factors.

35 is a multiple of 5.
35 is a multiple of 7.

Here are some of the multiples of 6:

0, 6, 12, 18, 24, 36, 42

> 0 is a multiple of every number.

■ Multiplication has some special properties that can help you multiply mentally.

ORDER
You can change the order of the factors.
The product is the same.

$3 \times 4 = 12$
$4 \times 3 = 12$

GROUPING
You can change the grouping of the factors.
The product is the same.
The parentheses mean *do this first*.
If there are no parentheses, you can multiply in any order.

$(3 \times 2) \times 4 \qquad 3 \times (2 \times 4)$
$\downarrow \qquad\qquad\qquad \downarrow$
$6 \ \times 4 = 24 \quad 3 \times \ 8 \ = 24$

ONE
When one factor is 1,
the product is the other factor.

$9 \times 1 = 9$
$1 \times 9 = 9$

ZERO
When one factor is 0,
the product is 0.

$6 \times 0 = 0$
$0 \times 6 = 0$

Try These

Multiply.

1. $\begin{array}{r} 9 \\ \times 8 \\ \hline \end{array}$
2. $\begin{array}{r} 8 \\ \times 9 \\ \hline \end{array}$
3. $\begin{array}{r} 6 \\ \times 1 \\ \hline \end{array}$
4. $\begin{array}{r} 0 \\ \times 7 \\ \hline \end{array}$
5. $\begin{array}{r} 6 \\ \times 6 \\ \hline \end{array}$
6. $\begin{array}{r} 8 \\ \times 8 \\ \hline \end{array}$
7. $\begin{array}{r} 8 \\ \times 7 \\ \hline \end{array}$

8. 3×9
9. $6 \times (1 \times 7)$
10. $(6 \times 1) \times 7$
11. $0 \times 4 \times 3$

Solve.

12. Name five multiples of 7.
13. Name five multiples of 4.

Exercises

Multiply.

1. $\begin{array}{r} 2 \\ \times 9 \\ \hline \end{array}$
2. $\begin{array}{r} 9 \\ \times 2 \\ \hline \end{array}$
3. $\begin{array}{r} 4 \\ \times 7 \\ \hline \end{array}$
4. $\begin{array}{r} 5 \\ \times 9 \\ \hline \end{array}$
5. $\begin{array}{r} 0 \\ \times 4 \\ \hline \end{array}$
6. $\begin{array}{r} 8 \\ \times 4 \\ \hline \end{array}$
7. $\begin{array}{r} 6 \\ \times 9 \\ \hline \end{array}$

8. $\begin{array}{r} 1 \\ \times 9 \\ \hline \end{array}$
9. $\begin{array}{r} 7 \\ \times 7 \\ \hline \end{array}$
10. $\begin{array}{r} 5 \\ \times 8 \\ \hline \end{array}$
11. $\begin{array}{r} 7 \\ \times 8 \\ \hline \end{array}$
12. $\begin{array}{r} 3 \\ \times 6 \\ \hline \end{array}$
13. $\begin{array}{r} 6 \\ \times 8 \\ \hline \end{array}$
14. $\begin{array}{r} 9 \\ \times 0 \\ \hline \end{array}$

15. 4×5
16. $(2 \times 3) \times 3$
17. $2 \times (3 \times 3)$
18. $8 \times 0 \times 1$

Compute. Do as many as you can mentally.

19. $70 - (9 \times 6)$
20. $(4 \times 4) + 23$
21. $(3 + 5) \times 9$
22. $17 - (13 + 4)$
23. $4 \times (2 + 6)$
24. $1 \times 8 \times 7$
25. $(14 - 9) \times 7$
26. $(5 \times 6) + 13$

Solve.

27. Name six multiples of 3.
28. Name six multiples of 8.

Solve each problem.

29. Dave buys 3 packages of peaches. There are 8 peaches in each package. How many peaches is that?

30. Mrs. King buys 7 boxes of apples. There are 9 apples in each box. How many apples are there in all?

31. Craig works part-time in the fruit store. He worked 4 hours on Monday, 3 hours on Tuesday, and 5 hours on Thursday. How many hours did he work in all?

★ 32. There are 6 packages of tomatoes with 7 tomatoes in each. There are 5 boxes of plums with 9 plums in each. Are there more tomatoes or plums? How many more?

Multiplying by 1-Digit Numbers

■ A pool is 23 meters long. Sue swam its length 8 times. How far did she swim?

Multiply 23 by 8 to find out how far she swam.

Multiply the ones by 8. Regroup.

$$
\begin{array}{r}
^{2} \\
23 \\
\times\ 8 \\
\hline
4
\end{array}
$$

24 ones is 2 tens 4 ones.

Multiply the tens by 8. Add the regrouped tens.

$$
\begin{array}{r}
^{2} \\
23 \\
\times\ 8 \\
\hline
184
\end{array}
$$

Sue swam 184 meters.

■ Multiply: 469 × 7

$$
\begin{array}{r}
7 \\
\times 469 \\
\hline
\end{array}
$$

> Use the order property to rewrite this example.

$$
\begin{array}{r}
^{4\,6} \\
469 \\
\times\ \ 7 \\
\hline
3{,}283
\end{array}
$$

■ You can estimate mentally to check whether or not an answer is reasonable.

Multiply: 6 × 2,809

Estimate to check.

$$
\begin{array}{r}
^{4\ \ \ 5} \\
2{,}809 \\
\times\ \ \ \ \ 6 \\
\hline
16{,}854
\end{array}
$$

Circle the first digit.
Round to the circled
place. Multiply.

$$
\begin{array}{r}
②{,}809 \longrightarrow\ \ \ 3{,}000 \\
\times\ \ \ \ \ \ 6 \longrightarrow \times\ \ \ \ \ 6 \\
\hline
18{,}000
\end{array}
$$

The product seems reasonable since 16,854 is close to 18,000.

■ You multiply money the same way you multiply whole numbers.

Multiply: 3 × $107.85

$$
\begin{array}{r}
^{2\ 21} \\
10{,}785 \\
\times\ \ \ \ \ \ 3 \\
\hline
32{,}355
\end{array}
$$

$$
\begin{array}{r}
^{2\,2\ 1} \\
\$107.85 \\
\times\ \ \ \ \ \ 3 \\
\hline
\$323.55
\end{array}
$$

> Remember: Write the $ and the . in the answer.

Try These

Multiply. Estimate to check.

1. $\begin{array}{r} 78 \\ \times\ 4 \\ \hline \end{array}$

2. $\begin{array}{r} 8 \\ \times 127 \\ \hline \end{array}$

3. $\begin{array}{r} \$9.36 \\ \times\quad 4 \\ \hline \end{array}$

4. $\begin{array}{r} 2,625 \\ \times\quad 7 \\ \hline \end{array}$

5. $\begin{array}{r} 68,442 \\ \times\qquad 6 \\ \hline \end{array}$

6. 26 × 9

7. 8 × 309,264

8. 3 × $4.69

9. 3,987 × 7

Exercises

Multiply. Estimate to check.

1. $\begin{array}{r} 92 \\ \times\ 7 \\ \hline \end{array}$

2. $\begin{array}{r} 216 \\ \times\ 6 \\ \hline \end{array}$

3. $\begin{array}{r} \$6.45 \\ \times\quad 9 \\ \hline \end{array}$

4. $\begin{array}{r} 3,850 \\ \times\quad 8 \\ \hline \end{array}$

5. $\begin{array}{r} 9 \\ \times 397 \\ \hline \end{array}$

6. $\begin{array}{r} \$82.17 \\ \times\qquad 6 \\ \hline \end{array}$

7. $\begin{array}{r} 57,008 \\ \times\qquad 7 \\ \hline \end{array}$

8. $\begin{array}{r} 675,470 \\ \times\qquad 4 \\ \hline \end{array}$

9. $\begin{array}{r} 5 \\ \times 5,427 \\ \hline \end{array}$

10. $\begin{array}{r} 193,674 \\ \times\qquad 8 \\ \hline \end{array}$

11. 4 × 81

12. 3 × $.75

13. 1,857 × 9

14. 49,683 × 6

15. 5 × 274

16. 93 × 8

17. 7 × 2,016

18. 3 × 4,659

Compute.

19. 9 × (4,062 − 143)

20. 425,654 − (5 × 37,056)

21. (324 + 57) × 7

22. (37,289 × 8) − 279,653

23. (419 + 283) × 9

24. 6 × (15,601 − 743)

Solve each problem.

25. The track at Clinton Park is 800 meters long. Carmen ran around it 4 times. How far did she run?

26. Jan buys a sweat suit for $28.13. She gives the clerk $30.20. How much change should she receive?

 KEEPING IN SHAPE

1. 73,280 − 4,162
2. 6,004 − 2,327
3. 7,824 + 9,368
4. $6.98 + $25.51

5. 386 + 2,154
6. 7,302 − 854
7. $19.25 − $3.86
8. 43,079 + 6,511

9. 1,825 + 6,087
10. 2,251 − 1,647
11. 5,701 − 655
12. 15,604 + 3,513

Problem Solving: Applications

TWO-STEP PROBLEMS

Sometimes a problem requires more than one step.

Joe bought 3 records that cost $6.95 each. The tax was $1.25. What was the total bill?

Step 1   To find the total price without tax, multiply $6.95 by 3.

$$\begin{array}{r} \overset{2\ 1}{} \$\ 6.95 \\ \times \quad\quad 3 \\ \hline \$20.85 \end{array}$$

The total price without tax is $20.85.

Step 2   Then add the tax to $20.85.

$$\begin{array}{r} \overset{1\ 1}{} \$20.85 \\ + \quad 1.25 \\ \hline \$22.10 \end{array}$$

The total bill was $22.10.

Try These

Solve each problem.

1. Carey bought 4 classical music tapes. The tapes cost $3.99 each. The tax was $.88. What was the total bill?

2. There are 8 display racks with 37 records each. Of these, 65 are classical music records. How many are not classical music records?

3. Mr. Fernandez ordered 4 video-tapes. The tapes cost $11.75 each. There was no tax. He sent a check for $45 instead of the correct amount. How much more does he owe?

4. Mr. Klein orders 455 records. He receives 5 boxes with 75 records in each box. How many fewer records than he ordered did Mr. Klein receive?

Exercises

Solve each problem. Explain the way you solved each problem.

1. Lisa bought a transistor radio for $13.95. The tax was $.84. She gave the clerk $20.00. How much change did Lisa receive?

2. Songbooks cost $3.95 each. 1 piece of sheet music costs $1.50. How much would 8 songbooks cost?

3. Mr. Clark places 12 copies of a new record in a window display. There are 4 racks in the store with 15 copies each of the new record. How many copies of the record are there altogether?

4. In the folk music section, there are 175 records in 6 racks. There are 46 records in one rack and 58 in another rack. How many folk records are in the rest of the racks?

5. There are 1,857 tapes in the stockroom. A shipment of 745 tapes arrives. About how many tapes are in the stockroom now?

6. Tina works in the record store. She earns $5.25 an hour. Tina works 6 hours per day, 5 days per week. How much money does she earn in a week?

Menu	
salad	$3.25
yogurt	$1.95
soup: cup	$ .85
bowl	$1.35
milk	$ .50
juice	$ .75

7. Tina ordered lunch for some of the people who work at the record store. She ordered 3 salads and a bowl of soup. What was the total cost of the food?

★ 8. The next day Tina ordered 2 salads, 3 yogurts, a cup of soup, and 3 juices. What was the total cost of the food?

Multiplying by Multiples of 10

■ Notice the pattern when you multiply by 10.

$$\begin{array}{r} 6 \\ \times 10 \\ \hline 60 \end{array} \qquad \begin{array}{r} 27 \\ \times 10 \\ \hline 270 \end{array} \qquad \begin{array}{r} 543 \\ \times\ 10 \\ \hline 5{,}430 \end{array} \qquad \begin{array}{r} 1{,}981 \\ \times\ \ \ \ 10 \\ \hline 19{,}810 \end{array}$$

■ You can use this pattern to multiply by 10 mentally.

Multiply: 10 × 639

$$\begin{array}{r} 639 \\ \times\ \ 10 \\ \hline 6{,}390 \end{array}$$

> *To multiply by 10, write a 0 in the ones place. Then multiply by 1.*

■ You can use this rule to multiply by multiples of 10.

Multiply: 20 × 341

Write the 0 in the ones place.

$$\begin{array}{r} 341 \\ \times\ 20 \\ \hline 0 \end{array}$$

← 2 × 10

0 ← shows multiplying by 10

Multiply by 2.

$$\begin{array}{r} 341 \\ \times\ 20 \\ \hline 6{,}820 \end{array}$$

2 × 341

> *To multiply by a number ending in 0, write a 0 in the ones place. Then multiply by the rest of the number.*

Try These

Multiply. Do as many as you can mentally.

1. $\begin{array}{r} 9 \\ \times 10 \\ \hline \end{array}$	**2.** $\begin{array}{r} 36 \\ \times 30 \\ \hline \end{array}$	**3.** $\begin{array}{r} 60 \\ \times 85 \\ \hline \end{array}$	**4.** $\begin{array}{r} \$1.36 \\ \times\ \ \ \ 40 \\ \hline \end{array}$	**5.** $\begin{array}{r} 4{,}167 \\ \times\ \ \ \ \ 10 \\ \hline \end{array}$

6. 50 × 8

7. 603 × 10

8. 50 × 284

9. 90 × $325.62

Exercises

Multiply. Do as many as you can mentally.

1. 87 $\times 50$	**2.** 321 $\times 10$	**3.** 4,178 $\times 7$	**4.** 50 $\times 4,006$	**5.** $2.37 $\times 20$
6. 60 $\times 728$	**7.** $52.18 $\times 90$	**8.** $16.79 $\times 8$	**9.** 37,104 $\times 10$	**10.** 97,231 $\times 40$

11. 50×89 **12.** 10×385 **13.** 764×9 **14.** $10 \times \$4.89$

15. $674 \times 60 \times 10$ **16.** $8 \times 7,286 \times 30$ **17.** $10 \times 3,280 \times 40$

Compute.

18. $(30 \times 1,285) - 2,092$ **19.** $80 \times (16,475 + 23,362)$ **20.** $13,486 + (20 \times 34,692)$

21. $(2,605 \times 10) - 3,789$ **22.** $43,126 - (875 \times 9)$ **23.** $40 \times (1,392 + 8,741)$

Write >, <, or =.

24. $80 \times 60 \blacksquare 8 \times 600$ **25.** $40 \times 90 \blacksquare 4 \times 9,000$

26. $5 \times 80 \blacksquare 50 \times 80$ **27.** $30 \times 50 \blacksquare 5 \times 300$

★ **28.** $(70 \times 20) + 600 \blacksquare (7 \times 300) - 100$ ★ **29.** $(8 \times 400) + 800 \blacksquare (20 \times 80) + 400$

★ **30.** $(70 \times 90) - 800 \blacksquare (70 \times 80) - 100$ ★ **31.** $(30 \times 50) + 100 \blacksquare (3 \times 500) - 100$

Solve each problem mentally or with paper and pencil.

32. There are 10 students from each class in the school band. There are 14 classes. How many students are in the band?

33. There are 1,250 seats in the school auditorium. At the concert, 160 seats were empty. How many seats were occupied?

34. There are 30 students in Mrs. Pearl's class. Each student sold 15 tickets to the school concert. How many tickets did the class sell altogether?

35. Mr. Sands took 50 glee club members to a music festival. The student tickets cost $2.25 each. The bus cost $250.00. What was the total cost of the trip?

36. The school band includes wind instruments. There are 12 flutes, 10 clarinets, 25 horns, 4 tubas, 14 trumpets, 10 saxophones, and 6 trombones. How many wind instruments are there in all?

★ **37.** The music director ordered 8 music stands at $29.50 each. He also ordered 10 band uniforms at $85.45 each and 20 pieces of sheet music at $1.50 each. What was the total cost of the order?

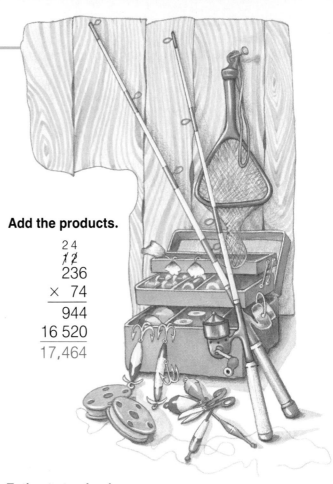

Dan orders merchandise for a chain of sporting-equipment stores. He orders 236 fishing reels for each of 74 stores. How many fishing reels does he order?

Multiply 236 by 74 to find the answer.

Think: 74 = 70 + 4

Multiply by 4.

```
  12
 236
×  74
─────
 944  ← 4 × 236
```

Multiply by 70.

```
    24     ┌Cross out
    12  ← │before you
   236     └multiply.
  ×  74
  ─────
   944
 16 520  ← 70 × 236
```

Add the products.

```
   24
   12
  236
×  74
─────
  944
16 520
──────
17,464
```

Dan orders 17,464 fishing reels.

Multiply: 46 × 6,017

```
    2
    14
  6,017
 ×   46
 ──────
 36 102
240 680
───────
276,782
```

Estimate to check.

Circle the first digit of each factor.
Round each factor to the circled place.
Multiply.

```
⑥, 0 1 7  →    6,000
×    ④6  →  ×    50
              ───────
              300,000
```

The product seems reasonable since 276,782 is close to 300,000.

Multiply: 37 × $295.18

```
 $295.18
 ×    37
 ───────
 2 066 26
 8 855 40
 ────────
$10,921 66
```

Remember: Write the $ and . in the answer.

Estimate to check.

```
$②9 5.1 8  →   $   300
×      ③7  →  ×     40
               ────────
               $12,000
```

Multiply. Estimate to check.

1. 78 ×24	**2.** 754 × 43	**3.** $4.55 × 25	**4.** 12 ×3,754	**5.** 9,707 × 89

6. 57 × 38 **7.** 304 × 89 **8.** 70 × 6,485 **9.** 16 × $28.40

Multiply. Estimate to check.

1. 64 ×51	**2.** $3.25 × 63	**3.** 72 ×419	**4.** 2,609 × 79	**5.** $70.07 × 80
6. 647 × 58	**7.** 1,372 × 6	**8.** 2,315 × 42	**9.** 19,987 × 70	**10.** 36 ×68,007
11. 87 ×66	**12.** $69.00 × 48	**13.** 8,757 × 92	**14.** 12,978 × 8	**15.** 10,899 × 65

16. 82 × 35 **17.** 60 × 23,547 **18.** 9,086 × 7 ★ **19.** 46 × 23,090 × 38

 Compute. Use a calculator to check.

20. (67 × 404) + 3,571   **21.** 51 × (7,659 − 1,488)   **22.** (24 + 427) × 65
23. (40 × 623) − 8,451   **24.** (723 + 568) × 37   **25.** (5,002 − 863) × 88

THINK AND TRY

MISSING DIGITS

Copy and complete.

1.	**2.**	**3.**	**4.**
3 6 7 × 2 ■ ――― 1 4 6 8 7 3 ■ 0 ――― ■,8 0 ■	2 ■ 7 × 3 ■ ――― 1 8 9 6 7 ■ 1 0 ――― 9,0 0 6	1 ■ 9 × 4 ■ ――― 6 1 9 5 ■ ■ 6 0 ――― ■,■ 5 5	2 6 ■ ■ × ■ 9 ――― 2 3 7 3 3 ■ ■ ■ ■ 8 0 ――― ■ ■ ■,■ 1 3

Problem Solving: Strategies

GENERALIZING

To solve a problem, it sometimes helps to make up a similar problem that is simpler. Then solve it first.

A rocket is moving toward Saturn at a speed of 12,432 miles per hour. At this rate, how many miles would it travel in a day? (There are 24 hours in a day.)

Make up a similar problem that is simpler.

A blimp is traveling at a speed of 8 miles per hour. At this rate, how many miles would it travel in 3 hours?

The blimp travels 8 miles each hour. In 3 hours, it would travel 3 times as far. Multiply 8 by 3 to find how many miles the blimp would travel in 3 hours.

$$3 \times 8 = 24$$

The blimp would travel 24 miles in 3 hours.

Use the same idea to solve the original problem. Multiply 12,432 by 24 to find how many miles the rocket would travel.

```
   12,432
 ×     24
   49 728
  248 640
  298,368
```

The rocket would travel 298,368 miles in a day.

Using the Strategy

For each problem, solve the simpler problem first. Then solve the original problem.

Original Problem

1. a. A man ran at a rate of 375 feet per minute for 6 minutes. How many feet did he run?

2. a. Suppose a computer can perform 12,400 calculations per second. How many calculations can it perform in a minute? (There are 60 seconds in a minute.)

Simpler Problem

b. A man walked at a rate of 75 feet per minute for 6 minutes. How many feet did he walk?

b. Suppose a machine can perform 4 calculations per second. How many calculations can it perform in 5 seconds?

Solve each problem. Make up a similar problem that is simpler, and solve it first if necessary.

3. A test car traveled at a speed of 66 feet per second for 7 seconds before hitting a barrier. How many feet did it travel in that time?

4. A bus is driven at 45 miles per hour. There are 31 passengers. At that rate, how many miles would it travel in 4 hours?

5. A computer printer can print 1,230 lines per minute. How many lines can the computer print in 10 minutes?

6. A man is paid $2.30 for each computer part he puts together. How much would he be paid for putting together 58 parts?

ACTIVITY

FINDING A PATTERN

In each exercise, draw the points so that you cannot connect more than two of them with one line segment.

1. Draw four points on your paper. How many different line segments can you draw that connect pairs of these points?

2. Now draw five points. How many different line segments can you draw that connect pairs of these points?

3. Now draw 6 points. How many different line segments can you draw that connect pairs of these points?

Multiplying by Multiples of 100 and 1,000

■ These patterns can help you multiply by 100 and by 1,000 mentally.

$$\begin{array}{r} 7 \\ \times 100 \\ \hline 700 \end{array} \qquad \begin{array}{r} 68 \\ \times 100 \\ \hline 6,800 \end{array} \qquad \begin{array}{r} 3,549 \\ \times \quad 100 \\ \hline 354,900 \end{array}$$

> To multiply by 100, write a 0 in the ones place and in the tens place. Then multiply by 1.

$$\begin{array}{r} 7 \\ \times 1,000 \\ \hline 7,000 \end{array} \qquad \begin{array}{r} 68 \\ \times 1,000 \\ \hline 68,000 \end{array} \qquad \begin{array}{r} 3,549 \\ \times 1,000 \\ \hline 3,549,000 \end{array}$$

> To multiply by 1,000, write a 0 in the ones place, in the tens place, and in the hundreds place. Then multiply by 1.

■ You can use these rules to multiply by multiples of 100 and 1,000.

Multiply: 300×857 Multiply: $7,000 \times 42,013$

$$\begin{array}{r} 857 \\ \times 300 \\ \hline 257,100 \end{array} \qquad \begin{array}{r} 42,013 \\ \times \quad 7,000 \\ \hline 294,091,000 \end{array}$$

3×857 $7 \times 42,013$

> To multiply by a number ending in 0s, write the 0s. Then multiply by the rest of the number.

Try These

Multiply. Do as many as you can mentally.

1. $\begin{array}{r} 49 \\ \times 100 \end{array}$
2. $\begin{array}{r} 607 \\ \times 1,000 \end{array}$
3. $\begin{array}{r} 2,536 \\ \times 4,000 \end{array}$
4. $\begin{array}{r} \$42.95 \\ \times \quad 600 \end{array}$
5. $\begin{array}{r} 74,018 \\ \times \quad 300 \end{array}$

6. $1,000 \times 4,893$
7. $700 \times 3,298$
8. $8,000 \times 22,146$

Exercises

Multiply. Do as many as you can mentally.

1. 13
$\times$ 200

2. 845
$\times$ 60

3. 4,050
$\times$ 9,000

4. $.85
$\times$ 300

5. 98,725
$\times$ 1,000

6. 7,193
$\times$ 10

7. 456
$\times$ 84

8. $7.75
$\times$ 100

9. 8,942
$\times$ 600

10. 85,003
$\times$ 7,000

11. 100 $\times$ 92

12. 75 $\times$ 32,168

13. 8,000 $\times$ 9,016

Compute. Do as much as you can mentally.

14. 100 $\times$ (4,179 + 386)

15. (8,041 − 279) $\times$ 1,000

16. 24,065 − (30 $\times$ 470)

17. 500 $\times$ (5,133 − 639)

18. 21,469 + (900 $\times$ 56,447)

19. (126,895 + 41) $\times$ 800

 Find each product on the left. Then guess each product on the right. Check each guess.

20. 56 $\times$ 630 $\longrightarrow$ 560 $\times$ 63

21. 326 $\times$ 750 $\longrightarrow$ 3,260 $\times$ 75

22. 124 $\times$ 7,600 $\longrightarrow$ 1,240 $\times$ 760

23. 67 $\times$ 4,200 $\longrightarrow$ 670 $\times$ 420

24. 42 $\times$ 8,600 $\longrightarrow$ 4,200 $\times$ 86

25. 980 $\times$ 240 $\longrightarrow$ 9,800 $\times$ 24

Solve each problem. You may choose paper and pencil or a calculator.

26. Gary invests in the stock market. He buys 300 shares of utility stock. Each share costs $14. How much money does he spend?

27. Mrs. Tribit owns 4,000 shares of PAK stock. She sells it for $25.50 a share. How much money does she receive?

28. Mr. Ramirez buys 2,000 shares of a computer stock for $18.75 a share. Later he sells the stock for $21.25 a share. How much profit does Mr. Ramirez make?

29. 1 share of EVET sold for $86.40. Ira bought 500 shares. He sold all of it a month later for $75 a share. How much did Ira lose?

Multiplying by Greater Numbers

■ Anne Sheldon owns Flowermart Distributors. She needs to know when the stock is low. Roses are packed 144 to a case. There are 162 cases in stock. How many roses is that?

Multiply 144 by 162 to find how many.

Think: 162 = 100 + 60 + 2

Multiply by 2.	**Multiply by 60.**	**Multiply by 100.**	**Add the products.**
144	144	144	144
×162	×162	×162	×162
288 ⟵ 2 × 144	288	288	288
	8 640 ⟵ 60 × 144	8 640	8 640
		14 400 ⟵ 100 × 144	14 400
			23,328

There are 23,328 roses in stock.

■ Multiply: 203 × 5,867

Think: 203 = 200 + 3

Multiply by 3.	**There are no tens to multiply by. Multiply by 200.**	**Add the products.**
5,867	5,867	5,867
× 203	× 203	× 203
17 601 ⟵ 3 × 5,867	17 601	17 601
	1 173 400 ⟵ 200 × 5,867	1 173 400
		1,191,001

■ Multiply: 4,391 × 8,259

Think: 4,391 = 4,000 + 300 + 90 + 1

Estimate to check.

```
      8,259        ⑧, 2 5 9 ⟶        8,000
    × 4,391       ×④, 3 9 1 ⟶      × 4,000
      8 259                       32,000,000
    743 310
  2 477 700
 33 036 000
 36,265,269
```

The product seems reasonable since 36,265,269 is close to 32,000,000.

Try These

Multiply. Estimate to check.

1. 316
  × 275

2. 219
  × 503

3. 483
  × 211

4. 123
  × 3,456

5. 6,613
  × 2,587

6. 427 × 109

7. 1,387 × 514

8. 3,752 × 84,651

Exercises

Multiply. Estimate to check.

1. 321
  × 431

2. 2,764
  ×   207

3. $65.27
  ×   345

4. 5,107
  × 6,000

5. 6,008
  × 1,472

6. 804
  × 300

7.   73
  × 42,654

8. 20,742
  ×   608

9. $60.45
  ×   339

10. 40,015
  × 2,163

11. 78 × 221

12. 845 × $31.59

13. 583 × 702

14. 3,030 × 5,672

15. 16,752 × 4,019

16. 881 × 19,257 × 382

Compute. Use a calculator to check.

17. (304 × 216) − 64,819

18. 275 × (3,104 + 957)

19. 155 + (3,108 × 2,647)

20. 517,418 + (62,120 × 712)

21. 17,214 − (231 × 47)

22. 6,345 × (73 + 45)

Solve each problem. You may choose paper and pencil or a calculator.

23. Neil takes an order for 250 lilies. Each lily costs $1.85. What is the total cost of this order?

24. Anne had 5,800 tulips in stock. A customer picked up 1,925 tulips. About how many tulips are left?

25. Lilac bushes cost $4.95 each. Each rosebush costs $7.45. Mr. Mogil orders 175 lilac bushes. What is the total cost of his order?

26. There are 15 cartons with 40 flowerpots in each. There are 25 more flowerpots on the shelf. How many flowerpots are there in all?

27. Neil ordered 3,000 carnations. He received 18 cases with 150 carnations in each case. How many more carnations should he receive?

★ **28.** Baskets cost $.78 each. 10 mums cost $3.25. Mr. Schwartz buys 180 baskets and 600 mums. How much money does he spend?

Problem Solving: Applications

ESTIMATING PRODUCTS

■ There are 221 bookshelves in the library. Each shelf holds 39 books. About how many books are there?

Estimate the product of 221 and 39. Round each factor and multiply.

$$
\begin{array}{r}
②21 \longrightarrow 200 \\
\times\ ③9 \longrightarrow \times\ 40 \\
\hline
8{,}000
\end{array}
$$

There are about 8,000 books.

■ The principal ordered 300 new math books. Each book cost $7.16. Estimate the total cost of the order.

Estimate the product of 300 and $7.16.

$$
\begin{array}{r}
\$⑦.16 \longrightarrow \$7 \\
\times\ ③00 \longrightarrow \times 300 \\
\hline
\$2{,}100
\end{array}
$$

The books cost about $2,100 altogether.

Try These

Solve each problem.

1. There are 12 boxes in the storage closet. Each box contains 34 books. Estimate the total number of books.

2. Mrs. Carson ordered 175 computer books. Each book cost $5.95. About how much did the books cost altogether?

3. Kim is a librarian. She earns $375 each week. About how much does Kim earn in 1 year (52 weeks)?

Exercises

Choose estimation, paper and pencil, or a calculator to solve.

1. The children's library has 17 bookcases. Each bookcase holds 125 books. About how many books are there in all?

2. There are 32 drawers in the card catalog. Each drawer contains 325 cards. Estimate the number of cards in the card catalog.

3. The February issue of *Computer Fun* magazine had 53 pages in it. About 70,000 copies of that issue were printed. About how many pages were printed for the issue?

4. The library subscribes to 9 magazines that are published 52 times a year. How many of those magazines does the library receive altogether in a year?

5. In the fiction section, there are 86 shelves holding about 30 books each. Estimate the number of fiction books.

6. The library contains 8,619 books. A computer report shows that 2,215 books are checked out. About how many books are in the library?

7. The librarian orders 5 reference books for $29.95 each. How much is the total cost of the order?

8. Each piece of microfilm contains 22 editions of the daily newspaper. There are 183 pieces of microfilm. How many editions of the newspaper is that altogether?

9. There was $7,854.96 in the library bank account. A deposit of $4,132.00 was made with money the library received as donations. About how much money is in the account now?

10. There are 7 encyclopedias in the library. Each encyclopedia has 24 volumes. Estimate how many volumes there are altogether.

★ 11. The library charges $.08 per day for overdue books. One day there were 52 books turned in that were 1 day overdue. About how much money was collected for those overdue books?

Exponents

■ There is a short way to write $2 \times 2 \times 2 \times 2 \times 2$.
Use an **exponent**. An exponent tells how many $\qquad 2 \times 2 \times 2 \times 2 \times 2 = 2^5$
times a number is used as a factor.

Read: 2 to the 5th power

The exponent 5 tells you that 2 is used as a factor five times.
Since $2 \times 2 \times 2 \times 2 \times 2 = 32$, $2^5 = 32$.

■ Here are some more examples:

$$3^2 = 3 \times 3 = 9 \qquad 4^3 = 4 \times 4 \times 4 = 64$$

3^2 is usually read "three squared" and
4^3 is usually read "four cubed."

■ Exponents make it easy to show powers of 10.

POWERS OF 10		
Number	10 as a Factor	Exponent Form
10	10	10^1
100	10×10	10^2
1,000	$10 \times 10 \times 10$	10^3
10,000	$10 \times 10 \times 10 \times 10$	10^4
100,000	$10 \times 10 \times 10 \times 10 \times 10$	10^5
1,000,000	$10 \times 10 \times 10 \times 10 \times 10 \times 10$	10^6

■ Exponents can be used to write some
numbers as a whole number times a
power of 10.

$$5,000,000 = 5 \times 1,000,000$$
$$5,000,000 = 5 \times 10^6$$

Read: 5 times 10 to the 6th power

$$6,000,000,000 = 6 \times 10^9$$

Read: 6 times 10 to the 9th power

Try These

Copy and complete.

1. $8 \times 8 = 8^{\blacksquare}$

2. $6 \times 6 \times 6 \times 6 = 6^{\blacksquare}$

3. $4 \times 4 \times 4 = 4^{\blacksquare}$

Multiply to find each product.

4. 2^4　　**5.** 7^2　　**6.** 3^3　　**7.** 10^5　　**8.** 5^2　　**9.** 4^6

Exercises

Show each product using an exponent.

1. $3 \times 3 \times 3$

2. $8 \times 8 \times 8 \times 8$

3. $10 \times 10 \times 10$

Multiply to find each product.

4. 3^4　　**5.** 2^5　　**6.** 4^3　　**7.** 9^4　　**8.** 6^6　　**9.** 10^4
10. 5^3　　**11.** 7^4　　**12.** 2^8　　**13.** 17^2　　**14.** 58^2　　**15.** 12^4

Write each number.

16. $3 \times 1{,}000$

17. $10 \times 10 \times 10 \times 10 \times 10$

18. $3 \times 1{,}000{,}000$

19. $23 \times 10{,}000$

20. 8×10^7

21. 40×10^6

Write each using an exponent.

22. $2 \times 10 \times 10 \times 10 \times 10$

23. $6 \times 1{,}000$

24. $3 \times 10{,}000$

25. $8 \times 100{,}000$

26. $5{,}000{,}000$

27. $17{,}000{,}000{,}000$

 THINK AND TRY

USING EXPONENTS

Scientists often use exponents to name large numbers.

Solve each problem.

1. There are about 3×10^{25} molecules in a kilogram of water. A gallon of water weighs about 4 kilograms. About how many molecules are there in a gallon of water?

2. In 1 year, light travels about 9×10^{12} kilometers. Light from the star Proxima Centauri takes about 4 years to reach Earth. About how many kilometers is Proxima Centauri from us?

Problem Solving: Applications

MORE THAN ONE WAY TO SOLVE

Joe has two part-time jobs. He earns
$8 each morning working in a pet
store. He earns $5 each afternoon
delivering groceries. How much does
Joe earn in 25 days?

There are two ways to solve this problem.

One way: Add to find how
much Joe earns in 1 day.

$$\begin{array}{r} \$\ 8 \text{ morning job} \\ +\quad 5 \text{ afternoon job} \\ \hline \$13 \end{array}$$

Joe earns $13 each day.

Multiply to find how
much Joe earns in 25 days.

$$\begin{array}{r} \$\ 13 \\ \times\quad 25 \\ \hline 65 \\ 260 \\ \hline \$325 \end{array}$$

Joe earns $325 in 25 days.

Another way: Multiply to find how much Joe earns
at each job in 25 days.

$$\begin{array}{r} 25 \\ \times \$8 \\ \hline \$200 \text{ morning job} \end{array} \qquad \begin{array}{r} 25 \\ \times \$5 \\ \hline \$125 \text{ afternoon job} \end{array}$$

Add to find how much Joe earns
from both jobs.

$$\begin{array}{r} \$200 \\ +\ 125 \\ \hline \$325 \end{array}$$

Joe earns $325 in 25 days.

Try These

Solve each problem.
To check, solve the problem a different way.

1. Nancy works in a garden supply store. She packs 3 climbing rose plants and 4 tea rose plants in a package. How many plants are there in 65 packages?

2. There are 5 sixth-grade classes. Each class made 10 mobiles and 10 dioramas for the school art sale. How many items at the sale were made by sixth graders?

Exercises

Solve each problem. Explain the way you solved each problem.

1. Each day, Jan works at 2 different stores. She earns $4 at one and $7 at the other. How much does she earn in 22 days?

2. Each week Steve has 2 baby-sitting jobs. He earns $6 on Friday and $8 on Saturday. How much does he earn in 52 weeks?

3. Peter sells copies of a game he invented. The game has 12 red pieces and 12 white pieces. For 50 games, how many pieces must he make altogether?

4. Patrick has 2 paper routes. He delivers 138 papers each morning and 157 papers each afternoon. About how many papers does he deliver in 1 month (30 days)?

5. Sarah strings beads to make jewelry. For each necklace, she uses 350 small beads and 150 large beads. For each bracelet, Sarah uses 200 small beads. How many beads are in 100 necklaces?

6. Danny has 2 summer jobs. He earns $6 a week plant-sitting for a neighbor. He also earns $15 a week caring for another neighbor's dog. How much does Danny earn in 12 weeks?

7. Roberta makes wall hangings. She cuts 8 shapes from each piece of fabric. She has 50 pieces of fabric. How many shapes can Roberta cut from 3 red pieces, 4 blue pieces, and 5 yellow pieces?

8. Esther has a gift certificate worth $25. She buys a tennis racket for $52.89 and a sweatshirt for $8.75. Esther gives the clerk the gift certificate and a $50 bill. How much change should she receive?

CHAPTER CHECKPOINT

Multiply. (pp. 40–43)

1. 8 $\times 7$	**2.** 36 $\times\ 9$	**3.** $4.17 $\times\ \ 6$	**4.** 5 $\times 254$	**5.** 32,086 $\times\ \ \ 7$

6. $52.49 $\times\ \ \ \ 3$	**7.** 6 $\times 4,904$	**8.** 73,128 $\times\ \ \ \ 9$	**9.** 140,328 $\times\ \ \ \ \ 5$	**10.** 579,116 $\times\ \ \ \ \ \ 4$

11. $(4 \times 7) \times 6$ **12.** $4 \times (7 \times 6)$ **13.** $9 \times 0 \times 3$
14. $5 \times \$.84$ **15.** $12{,}483 \times 9$ **16.** $8 \times 6{,}747$

Multiply. (pp. 46–49)

17. 4 $\times 10$	**18.** 37 $\times 50$	**19.** 264 $\times\ 38$	**20.** $9.95 $\times\ \ \ 40$	**21.** 3,402 $\times\ \ \ 26$

22. 8,332 $\times\ \ \ 70$	**23.** $14.61 $\times\ \ \ \ 45$	**24.** 92,083 $\times\ \ \ \ \ 10$	**25.** 17,522 $\times\ \ \ \ \ 38$	**26.** 48,006 $\times\ \ \ \ \ 39$

27. 36×84 **28.** $60 \times 1{,}297$ **29.** $54 \times \$32.78$

Multiply. (pp. 52–55)

30. 48 $\times 300$	**31.** 516 $\times 207$	**32.** 1,293 $\times\ \ 465$	**33.** $26.81 $\times\ \ \ \ 182$	**34.** 54,377 $\times\ \ \ \ 900$

35. 3,149 $\times 1,000$	**36.** 21,308 $\times\ \ \ 650$	**37.** $75.20 $\times\ \ \ \ 394$	**38.** 6,821 $\times 3,049$	**39.** 19,556 $\times\ \ 4,000$

40. 100×751 **41.** $204 \times \$8.65$ **42.** $3{,}127 \times 940$

Estimate each product. (pp. 42–43, 48–49, 54–55)

43. 82 $\times 51$	**44.** 7,016 $\times\ \ \ 49$	**45.** 67,091 $\times\ \ \ \ \ 8$	**46.** 135 $\times 6,048$	**47.** $8.71 $\times\ \ \ 213$

48. 175×225 **49.** $\$420.22 \times 32$ **50.** $1{,}000 \times 843$
51. $\$625 \times 831$ **52.** $73 \times 21{,}844$ **53.** $40{,}523 \times 37{,}144$

Multiply to find each product. (pp. 58–59)

54. 2^3 **55.** 8^2 **56.** 3^4 **57.** 4^3 **58.** 10^5 **59.** 9^2

Write each using an exponent. (pp. 58–59)

60. $4 \times 10 \times 10 \times 10$ **61.** $3 \times 10,000$ **62.** $7 \times 100,000$

63. 8,000,000   **64.** 90,000,000   **65.** 12,000,000,000

Choose estimation or paper and pencil to solve each problem. (pp. 40–61)

66. The Good Eats Restaurant orders 7 cases of tomato sauce. Each case contains 25 cans of tomato sauce. How many cans are ordered?

67. David grows fruit for the restaurant. He planted 165 rows of seedlings. There were 28 seedlings in each row. How many seedlings did he plant?

68. The cash register total for a day was $1,268. At this rate, about how much money would the restaurant make in a month (30 days)?

69. Mr. Charles ordered 175 drinking glasses. Each glass cost $1.15. About how much do the glasses cost altogether?

70. The restaurant had 145 paper tablecloths in stock. A shipment of 375 tablecloths arrives. 38 tablecloths are used during the day. How many tablecloths are now in stock?

71. 12 tables in the restaurant are set for 4 people. Each table is set with 4 dinner plates and 4 salad plates. How many plates is that altogether?

72. Mr. Charles buys 4 boxes of silverware. Each box contains 12 forks and 18 spoons. How many pieces of silverware is that in all?

73. The chef uses 6 ounces of cheese in each chef's salad. She makes 125 chef's salads. How many ounces of cheese does she use?

74. Mr. and Mrs. Derek ordered 2 chef's salads and 2 juices. What was the total cost of their order?

75. Carol orders lunch for 3 people in her office. She orders 3 tuna sandwiches and 1 cottage cheese platter. What is the total cost of her order?

Menu	
tuna sandwich	$1.95
cottage cheese platter	$2.45
chef's salad	$4.95
juice	$ .75
milk	$ .50

COMPUTERS AND PROBLEM SOLVING

■ This program uses a FOR. . .NEXT loop to display the powers of 10 from 1 to 6.

```
NEW
10   FOR N = 1 TO 6
20   PRINT "10 RAISED TO THE POWER OF  "; N; "  IS  ";
30   PRINT 10 ^ N
40   NEXT N
50   END
```

The symbol ^ tells the computer to raise 10 to the power of the exponent, N. An exponent must always follow the symbol ^.

Solve each problem.

1. How many times will the program go through the FOR. . .NEXT loop?

2. What is the largest number that line 30 will display?

■ You could rewrite this program and insert lines to show how many times 10 is used as a factor.
But it would be easier to add a subroutine.

A subroutine is a set of program lines that does a specific job. Place a subroutine after the END statement, and use the GOSUB statement to send the computer to the subroutine from one or many points in your main program.

For every GOSUB, the computer notes a return address, which is the number of the next program line. After it stores the return address in its memory the computer jumps to the subroutine.

Start the subroutine at line number 1000.

```
1000   PRINT "TENS NEEDED TO FACTOR  "; 10 ^ N;":"
1010   FOR T = 1 TO N
1020   PRINT "10  ";
1030   NEXT T
1040   PRINT " "
1050   RETURN
```

To get this subroutine to work, you must add the GOSUB command to the main program. Place the GOSUB inside the FOR. . .NEXT loop so the computer performs the subroutine each time a power of 10 is displayed.

```
35   GOSUB 1000
```

Solve each problem.

1. What is the computer's return address for the GOSUB?

2. What is the purpose of PRINT " " in line 1040?

3. What would happen if you typed GOSUB 1020 on line 35? Why?

★ **4.** Modify the program to accept any number and print the first six powers of the number.

ENRICHMENT

MULTIPLICATION OF EVEN GREATER NUMBERS

■ Most calculators cannot show more than 8 digits. But there is a way to use a calculator to help you multiply when the answer has more than 8 digits.

Multiply: $74 \times 12{,}436{,}000$

Since $12{,}436{,}000 = 12{,}436 \times 1{,}000$,
$74 \times 12{,}436{,}000 = (74 \times 12{,}436) \times 1{,}000$.

Use a calculator.	Multiply by 1,000 on paper.
12,436	920,264
$\times$ 74	$\times$ 1,000
920,264	920,264,000

So $74 \times 12{,}436{,}000 = 920{,}264{,}000$.

■ Multiply: $12{,}436{,}543 \times 74$

Here is a way to use a calculator to help you do this.

$$12{,}436{,}543 \times 74 = (12{,}436{,}000 + 543) \times 74$$
$$= (12{,}436{,}000 \times 74) + (543 \times 74)$$

You found the first of these two products in the first example. All you have to do is find 543×74 and add.

$$
\begin{array}{rcr}
12{,}436{,}000 \times 74 & \longrightarrow & 920{,}264{,}000 \\
+ \qquad 543 \times 74 & \longrightarrow & +\qquad 40{,}182 \\
\hline
12{,}436{,}543 \times 74 & \longrightarrow & 920{,}304{,}182
\end{array}
$$

Multiply using this method.

1. 4,236,542
    $\times$ 931

2. 321,284,483
    $\times$ 65

3. 8,519,342
    $\times$ 4,185

4. $516{,}329 \times 6{,}235$

5. $92 \times 6{,}215{,}832$

6. $423 \times 384 \times 1{,}792$

7. $39 \times 4{,}062 \times 421$

PLANNING A CANNED FOOD DRIVE

Your class is planning a canned food drive for your area. You are in charge of the project. How will you organize it?

Some Questions to Explore
- To whom will the food be sent?
- How will the food get to its final destination?
- Where will you get cans of food?
- How will you sort the cans?

Some Strategies to Explore
Consider the first two questions. You can use the strategies of finding information and organizing information to help answer the questions.

- Contact local hospitals, nursing homes, and so on.
- Find information about who may need your services.
- Organize the information in a list.
- Make a map to determine the most efficient way to deliver the food.

Decide what strategies you will use to answer the other questions above. List other questions and strategies you need to explore. Then solve the problem.

SKILLS CHECK

Choose the correct answer.

1. In 32,461,057,890, which number is in the ten-billions place?

a. 2
b. 3
c. 6
d. NG

2. What is 674,281 rounded to the nearest hundred-thousand?

a. 600,000
b. 670,000
c. 674,000
d. 700,000

3. $27.45 − $8.99

a. $18.46
b. $21.54
c. $28.46
d. $36.44

4. 71,623 + 82,497

a. 53,120
b. 153,010
c. 154,120
d. 164,120

5. 620,104
    − 58,967

a. 61,137
b. 561,137
c. 638,863
d. 679,071

6. 478,266
    + 35,109

a. 403,365
b. 443,157
c. 513,475
d. NG

7. 56 × 483

a. 26,048
b. 26,648
c. 26,938
d. 27,048

8. 2,147
    × 608

a. 145,996
b. 1,281,026
c. 1,305,376
d. NG

9. Compute: 2^5

a. 10
b. 16
c. 25
d. 32

10. 1 slice of cheese contains 109 calories. How many calories are there in 6 slices?

a. 614 calories
b. 654 calories
c. 1,104 calories
d. NG

11. Lee spent $4.38 on a sandwich, soup, and an apple. He paid with $10.00. How much change did Lee receive?

a. $5.62
b. $6.22
c. $6.72
d. $14.38

12. There are 6,000 seats in the auditorium. 4,812 seats are occupied. How many seats are empty?

a. 1,188 seats
b. 2,298 seats
c. 10,812 seats
d. NG

DIVISION

3

Division

■ 28 students are touring the United Nations. They are in groups of 7 students each. How many groups are there?

Divide 28 by 7 to find how many groups.

$$28 \div 7 = 4$$

There are 4 groups.

■ Here are two ways to write a division fact.

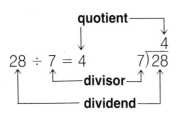

■ These patterns in division can help you find quotients mentally.

When you divide by 1, the quotient is the same as the dividend. $9 \div 1 = 9$

When you divide a number other than 0 by itself, the quotient is 1. $6 \div 6 = 1$

When you divide 0 by a number other than 0, the quotient is 0. $0 \div 7 = 0$
You never divide by 0.

■ Multiplication and division are related.

$$4 \times 7 = 28 \qquad 28 \div 7 = 4$$
$$7 \times 4 = 28 \qquad 28 \div 4 = 7$$

You can check that $28 \div 7 = 4$ is correct by multiplying: $4 \times 7 = 28$

■ Sometimes when you divide there may be a **remainder**.

Divide: $8\overline{)77}$

Find the quotient.

$$
\begin{array}{r}
9 \\
8\overline{)77} \\
72 \\
\hline
5
\end{array}
$$
← Multiply: 9×8
← Subtract: $77 - 72$

Show the remainder.

$$
\begin{array}{r}
9 \text{ R}5 \\
8\overline{)77} \\
72 \\
\hline
5
\end{array}
$$

Check.

$$
\begin{array}{r}
9 \\
\times 8 \\
\hline
72 \\
+ \ 5 \\
\hline
77
\end{array}
$$
← quotient
← divisor

← remainder
← dividend

Try These

Divide. Check each answer.

1. $8\overline{)40}$ **2.** $4\overline{)38}$ **3.** $8\overline{)0}$ **4.** $6\overline{)48}$ **5.** $3\overline{)19}$ **6.** $7\overline{)3}$ **7.** $2\overline{)15}$

8. $7 \div 1$ **9.** $64 \div 8$ **10.** $9 \div 9$ **11.** $51 \div 9$

Exercises

Divide.

1. $6\overline{)54}$ **2.** $9\overline{)74}$ **3.** $8\overline{)47}$ **4.** $5\overline{)45}$ **5.** $9\overline{)7}$ **6.** $6\overline{)35}$ **7.** $8\overline{)72}$

8. $5\overline{)39}$ **9.** $8\overline{)8}$ **10.** $7\overline{)45}$ **11.** $9\overline{)30}$ **12.** $6\overline{)50}$ **13.** $1\overline{)19}$ **14.** $9\overline{)45}$

15. $8\overline{)70}$ **16.** $6\overline{)38}$ **17.** $5\overline{)30}$ **18.** $5\overline{)0}$ **19.** $5\overline{)49}$ **20.** $8\overline{)48}$ **21.** $7\overline{)21}$

22. $7\overline{)49}$ **23.** $6\overline{)4}$ **24.** $6\overline{)58}$ **25.** $7\overline{)42}$ **26.** $4\overline{)19}$ **27.** $3\overline{)23}$ **28.** $3\overline{)27}$

29. $7 \div 7$ **30.** $20 \div 3$ **31.** $35 \div 4$ **32.** $17 \div 2$

33. $55 \div 6$ **34.** $81 \div 9$ **35.** $32 \div 5$ **36.** $56 \div 8$

37. $60 \div 8$ **38.** $11 \div 2$ **39.** $0 \div 4$ **40.** $22 \div 5$

Compute. Do as much as you can mentally.

41. $(16 \div 4) \div 2$ **42.** $3 + (18 \div 3)$ **43.** $(21 + 8) \div 9$

44. $(50 - 8) \div 6$ **45.** $7 \times (30 \div 5)$ **46.** $58 \div (2 + 5)$

Solve each problem.

47. A United Nations guide is talking to 40 students. They are in 5 study groups. Each group has the same number of students. How many are in each group?

48. Mrs. Brewster works 40 hours per week. She earns $8 per hour. This week she worked 8 hours less than usual. How many hours did she work this week?

49. Jim bought 6 rings in the gift shop. The total cost was $48. Each ring cost the same amount. How much did each ring cost?

50. There are 36 ambassadors at a meeting. Each ambassador has 4 staff people present. How many staff people are at the meeting?

51. There were 35 people in Cathy's morning tour. 42 people took her afternoon tour. How many people took Cathy's tours that day?

★ **52.** 62 people are waiting for a guided tour. Each guide takes a group of 8 people. How many guides are needed?

Dividing by 1-Digit Numbers

■ Containers of milk are put in cases. Each case holds 6 containers. How many cases are needed for 87 containers?

Divide 87 by 6 to find the number of cases.

Think: Are there enough tens to divide? Yes, because 6 < 8.
         The quotient has two digits.

Find the tens.	**Find the ones.**	**Show the remainder.**	**Check.**
Think: 6)8̄	Think: 6)2̄7̄		

$$\begin{array}{r} 1\ \_ \\ 6)\overline{8\ 7} \\ 6 \\ \hline 2\ 7 \end{array}$$

← Multiply: 1×6

← Subtract: $8 - 6$
Bring down the 7.

$$\begin{array}{r} 1\ 4 \\ 6)\overline{8\ 7} \\ 6 \\ \hline 2\ 7 \\ 2\ 4 \\ \hline 3 \end{array}$$

$$\begin{array}{r} 1\ 4\ R3 \\ 6)\overline{8\ 7} \\ 6 \\ \hline 2\ 7 \\ 2\ 4 \\ \hline 3 \end{array}$$

$$\begin{array}{r} 14 \\ \times\ 6 \\ \hline 84 \\ +\ 3 \\ \hline 87 \end{array} \checkmark$$

This means that there will be 14 full cases and 3 containers left. So 15 cases will be needed altogether.

■ Divide: 7)2,891

Think: Are there enough thousands to divide? No, because 7 > 2.
         Are there enough hundreds to divide? Yes, because 7 < 28.
         The quotient has three digits.

Find the hundreds.	**Find the tens.**	**Find the ones.**	**Check.**
Think: 7)2̄8̄	Think: 7)9̄	Think: 7)2̄1̄	

$$\begin{array}{r} 4\ \_\ \_ \\ 7)\overline{2,8\ 9\ 1} \\ 2\ 8 \\ \hline 9 \end{array}$$

$$\begin{array}{r} 4\ 1\ \_ \\ 7)\overline{2,8\ 9\ 1} \\ 2\ 8 \\ \hline 9 \\ 7 \\ \hline 2\ 1 \end{array}$$

$$\begin{array}{r} 4\ 1\ 3 \\ 7)\overline{2,8\ 9\ 1} \\ 2\ 8 \\ \hline 9 \\ 7 \\ \hline 2\ 1 \\ 2\ 1 \\ \hline 0 \end{array}$$

$$\begin{array}{r} 413 \\ \times\ \ 7 \\ \hline 2,891 \end{array} \checkmark$$

Try These

Divide. Check each answer.

1. 3)94   **2.** 4)137   **3.** 6)69   **4.** 7)463   **5.** 5)342   **6.** 7)157

7. $75 \div 5$ **8.** $489 \div 8$ **9.** $233 \div 3$ **10.** $520 \div 6$

Exercises

Divide.

1. $9\overline{)99}$ **2.** $7\overline{)156}$ **3.** $8\overline{)248}$ **4.** $9\overline{)199}$ **5.** $6\overline{)884}$ **6.** $7\overline{)84}$

7. $2\overline{)87}$ **8.** $6\overline{)76}$ **9.** $5\overline{)68}$ **10.** $4\overline{)463}$ **11.** $4\overline{)97}$ **12.** $3\overline{)162}$

13. $3\overline{)87}$ **14.** $5\overline{)682}$ **15.** $3\overline{)75}$ **16.** $6\overline{)51}$ **17.** $3\overline{)216}$ **18.** $6\overline{)366}$

19. $2\overline{)184}$ **20.** $8\overline{)96}$ **21.** $4\overline{)136}$ **22.** $7\overline{)799}$ **23.** $3\overline{)225}$ **24.** $5\overline{)170}$

25. $91 \div 8$ **26.** $173 \div 2$ **27.** $234 \div 4$ **28.** $369 \div 3$

29. $83 \div 9$ **30.** $645 \div 4$ **31.** $596 \div 7$ **32.** $256 \div 8$

Compute.

33. $(42 \times 9) \div 6$ **34.** $(42 \div 6) \times 9$ **35.** $(728 \div 8) \div 7$

36. $126 \div (6 + 3)$ **37.** $(136 + 248) \div 8$ **38.** $(136 \div 8) + (248 \div 8)$

Solve each problem.

39. Laura drove the milk-delivery truck 162 miles. She used 9 gallons of gas. How many miles did she drive on each gallon?

40. 63 students are taking a trip to the Anderson Dairy. No more than 5 students can travel in a car. How many cars are needed?

41. There are 42 pints of milk in each case. Carol delivers 7 cases of milk to Archie's Market. How many pints of milk does Archie's Market receive?

★ **42.** The Anderson Dairy sells 288 containers of yogurt to 3 markets. All 3 markets receive the same number of containers. 6 containers are sold as a unit. How many units does each market receive?

THINK AND TRY

USING LOGICAL REASONING

A frog falls into a well that is 12 yards deep.
Each day the frog climbs up 3 yards.
At night, it slips back 2 yards.
How many days will it take the frog to get out?

Think about it!
The answer is not 12 days.
Hint: Make a diagram.

More on Dividing

■ Sometimes the quotient has a 0 in it.

Divide: 5)3,512

Think: Are there enough thousands to divide? No, because 5 > 3.
Are there enough hundreds to divide? Yes, because 5 < 35.
The quotient has three digits.

Find the hundreds.	**Find the tens.**	**Find the ones.**	**Check.**
Think: 5)35	Think: 5)1	Think: 5)12	

```
   7 _ _            7 0 _            7 0 2 R2
5)3,5 1 2        5)3,5 1 2        5)3,5 1 2              702
  3 5              3 5              3 5                ×    5
 ───              ───              ───                3,510
    1                1                1             +      2
                     0                0                3,512 ✔
                    ──               ──
                    1 2              1 2
                                     1 0
                                    ──
                                      2
```

■ Sometimes the quotient has more than one 0.

Divide: 3)18,241

```
   6,0 8 0 R1          Check.
3)1 8,2 4 1              6,080
  1 8                 ×       3
 ──                   ────────
    2                   18,240
    0                 +       1
   ──                 ────────
    2 4                 18,241 ✔
    2 4
   ──
      1
      0
     ──
      1
```

■ You divide money the same way you divide whole numbers.

```
  1 605              $16.05
6)9,630            6)$96.30
```

> Remember: Write the $ and the . in the answer.

Divide. Check each answer.

1. $8\overline{)818}$ 2. $5\overline{)544}$ 3. $6\overline{)1,476}$ 4. $3\overline{)12,194}$ 5. $4\overline{)\$44.00}$ 6. $7\overline{)\$17.50}$

7. $4,818 \div 8$ 8. $\$7.49 \div 7$ 9. $8,694 \div 2$ 10. $10,020 \div 5$

Divide.

1. $2\overline{)618}$ 2. $7\overline{)917}$ 3. $3\overline{)7,936}$ 4. $5\overline{)5,546}$ 5. $3\overline{)847}$ 6. $2\overline{)7,527}$

7. $5\overline{)\$284.65}$ 8. $9\overline{)1,982}$ 9. $8\overline{)\$40.32}$ 10. $4\overline{)835}$ 11. $3\overline{)13,550}$ 12. $4\overline{)\$69.00}$

13. $5\overline{)10,103}$ 14. $5\overline{)27,354}$ 15. $7\overline{)30,000}$ 16. $8\overline{)\$30.40}$ 17. $8\overline{)89,209}$ 18. $6\overline{)19,364}$

19. $906 \div 3$ 20. $413 \div 4$ 21. $\$65.43 \div 9$ 22. $1,473 \div 7$

23. $76,000 \div 8$ 24. $\$70.63 \div 7$ 25. $47,897 \div 6$ 26. $\$723.60 \div 9$

Compute.

27. $(641 \times 8) \div 8$ 28. $641 \times (8 \div 8)$ 29. $462 - (1,784 \div 8)$

30. $(7,473 - 4,622) \div 6$ 31. $(864 \div 8) + (6,381 \div 9)$ 32. $407 \times (623 \div 7)$

Solve each problem.

33. Cobb's Furniture Store received a shipment of 9 lamps, each the same price. The total cost of the shipment was $451.26. How much did each lamp cost?

34. Mr. Nussbaum works in a furniture factory. He has 253 chairs to pack. He can pack 8 chairs in a crate. How many crates does he need altogether?

35. Mrs. Baxter buys a living room set. She buys 2 end tables. Each end table costs $229. She also buys a coffee table for $309. How much does Mrs. Baxter spend for her living room set?

36. Nancy has saved $1,000. She buys a bed for $159 and a mattress for $290. She also buys a dresser for $215, a mirror for $119, and a night table for $89. How much money does Nancy have left?

37. A furniture manufacturer delivers to 5 stores. Each store receives 48 dining room chairs and 36 living room chairs. How many chairs are delivered in all?

★ 38. Nils buys a sofa for $828.30. He makes a down payment of $75.30. He will pay the balance in 6 equal payments. How much will each payment be?

Averages

Carmela Rivera keeps a record of how much she spends for gas. The last five times she stopped for gas she spent $15.75, $21.40, $17.00, $23.50, and $19.25. What was the average amount Carmela spent each time she stopped for gas?

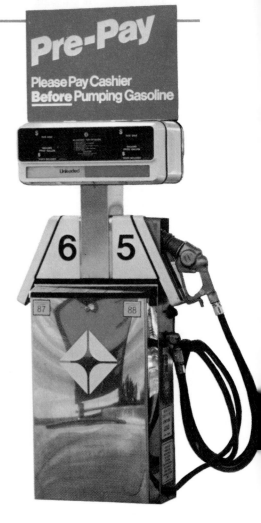

To find an average:

1. Add the numbers.
2. Divide the sum by the number of items.

Add the amount Carmela spent in five stops.	**Then divide the sum by 5, the number of stops.**
$15.75	
21.40	
17.00	
23.50	
+19.25	
$96.90	

$$\begin{array}{r} \$19.38 \\ 5\overline{)\$96.90} \\ \underline{5} \\ 46 \\ \underline{45} \\ 1\,9 \\ \underline{1\,5} \\ 40 \\ \underline{40} \\ 0 \end{array}$$

Carmela spent an average of $19.38 each time she stopped for gas.

Sometimes the sum is given.

Carmela drove her car 360 miles in 8 hours. What was her average speed in miles per hour?

Divide 360 by 8 to find her average speed.

$$\begin{array}{r} 45 \\ 8\overline{)360} \\ \underline{32} \\ 40 \\ \underline{40} \\ 0 \end{array}$$

Carmela's average speed was 45 miles per hour.

Try These

Find each average.

1. 25, 21, 28, 20, 26   **2.** $125, $183, $154

3. 6, 8, 10, 9, 12, 7, 11   **4.** $.44, $.38, $.40, $.42, $.36

5. 364, 285, 350, 297   **6.** 75, 125, 107, 93, 100

Exercises

Find each average.

1. 21, 34, 44   **2.** $4, $3, $5, $4

3. 81, 82, 91, 78   **4.** 91, 68, 75, 84, 52

5. $9.00, $10.50, $9.50, $11.00   **6.** 57, 61, 57, 57, 58

7. 68, 53, 39, 94, 65, 24, 42   **8.** 62, 65, 66, 70, 74, 75, 82, 85, 96

 Find each average.

9. 3,725; 4,152; 8,124; 9,762; 5,112; 6,925

10. 46,316; 52,875; 43,904; 51,867; 45,883

11. 318,275; 299,608; 314,678; 309,243; 286,302; 312,418; 297,843

Solve each problem. You may choose paper and pencil or a calculator.

12. Francis spent $15.21 for 9 gallons of gasoline. What was the average cost of each gallon?

13. On 7 tests, Sally made scores of 80, 85, 90, 95, 82, 88, and 75. What was her average score?

14. Harriet Davis drives a truck for a furniture company. In 6 months, she drove 34,692 miles. What was the average number of miles she drove each month?

15. In 8 football plays, Anthony gained 3 yards, 0 yards, 4 yards, 25 yards, 2 yards, 11 yards, 6 yards, and 37 yards. What was his average gain per play?

16. Paul is a salesman for a sweater company. He sells the sweaters to store owners. In 4 weeks, he traveled 312 miles, 294 miles, 325 miles, and 289 miles. What is Paul's average weekly mileage?

★ **17.** Kevin took a science test each week in November. He made scores of 82, 90, and 76 on the first three tests. What must his test score be the fourth week to have an average score of 83?

Dividing by Multiples of 10

■ Jim drove 780 miles on 30 gallons of gas. How many miles per gallon was that?

Divide 780 by 30 to find the number of miles per gallon.

Think: Are there enough hundreds to divide? No, because 30 > 7.

Are there enough tens to divide? Yes, because 30 < 78.
The quotient has two digits.

Find the tens.

Think: 30)78

$$
\begin{array}{r}
2 \\
30\overline{)7\ 8\ 0} \\
6\ 0 \\
\hline
1\ 8\ 0
\end{array}
$$

Find the ones.

Think: 30)180

$$
\begin{array}{r}
2\ 6 \\
30\overline{)7\ 8\ 0} \\
6\ 0 \\
\hline
1\ 8\ 0 \\
1\ 8\ 0 \\
\hline
0
\end{array}
$$

Jim got 26 miles per gallon.

■ Divide: 30)15,247

Think: There are enough hundreds to divide, because 30 < 152.

$$
\begin{array}{r}
5\ 0\ 8\ \text{R7} \\
30\overline{)1\ 5,2\ 4\ 7} \\
1\ 5\ 0 \\
\hline
2\ 4 \\
0 \\
\hline
2\ 4\ 7 \\
2\ 4\ 0 \\
\hline
7
\end{array}
$$

Check.

$$
\begin{array}{r}
508 \\
\times\ \ 30 \\
\hline
15,240 \\
+\ \ \ \ \ 7 \\
\hline
1\ 5,2\ 4\ 7\ \checkmark
\end{array}
$$

Try These

Divide. Check each answer.

1. 40)242
2. 80)325
3. 60)2,400
4. 50)6,570
5. 496 ÷ 60
6. 2,600 ÷ 30
7. $80.40 ÷ 40

Exercises

Divide.

1. $70\overline{)501}$ **2.** $30\overline{)1,642}$ **3.** $50\overline{)2,645}$ **4.** $20\overline{)12,880}$

5. $60\overline{)2,600}$ **6.** $30\overline{)2,700}$ **7.** $90\overline{)998}$ **8.** $50\overline{)\$119.00}$

9. $30\overline{)7,642}$ **10.** $9\overline{)3,415}$ **11.** $50\overline{)\$25.00}$ **12.** $80\overline{)64,000}$

13. $90\overline{)4,871}$ **14.** $40\overline{)4,150}$ **15.** $40\overline{)\$126.00}$ **16.** $90\overline{)800}$

17. $867 \div 30$ **18.** $630 \div 7$ **19.** $\$113.40 \div 60$

20. $284 \div 90$ **21.** $\$3,500 \div 50$ **22.** $70,568 \div 70$

Compute.

23. $(890 + 310) \div 40$ **24.** $1,467 - (240 \div 60)$ **25.** $694 \times (6,300 \div 70)$

26. $(280 \div 20) + (990 \div 30)$ **27.** $(16,400 \div 40) - 410$ **28.** $(20,356 - 9,214) \div 20$

Solve each problem.

Alice bought a new car. It had a sticker on it like the one at the right that showed the estimated miles per gallon.

ESTIMATED MILES PER GALLON
CITY   24
HIGHWAY   32

29. On the first 20 gallons of gas, Alice drove 420 miles. What was the average number of miles per gallon?

30. Did Alice get the mileage advertised on the sticker?

31. The base price of Alice's car was $9,797. She ordered an automatic transmission for $465 and tinted glass for $90. What was the total price of the car?

32. Richard paid $12,487 for his new car. That price includes $936 for insurance, $45 to register the car, and $860 in tax. What was the price of the car alone?

33. Richard drives 14 miles each way to work. How many miles does Richard drive round trip each week (5 working days)?

★ **34.** Richard's car averages 20 miles per gallon of gas. If gas costs $1.35 per gallon, how much will it cost Richard to drive his car 2,400 miles?

Dividing by 2-Digit Numbers

■ Ed Bailey is a poultry farmer. He has 915 chickens. 39 chickens fit in each chicken coop. How many coops can he fill?

Divide 915 by 39 to find how many he can fill.

Think: There are enough tens to divide, because $39 < 91$.

Find the tens.

39 rounds to 40.
Think: $40\overline{)91}$

$$
\begin{array}{r}
2 \\
39\overline{)9\,1\,5} \\
7\,8 \\
\hline
1\,3\,5
\end{array}
$$

Find the ones.

Think: $40\overline{)135}$

$$
\begin{array}{r}
2\,3\ \text{R18} \\
39\overline{)9\,1\,5} \\
7\,8 \\
\hline
1\,3\,5 \\
1\,1\,7 \\
\hline
1\,8
\end{array}
$$

He can fill 23 chicken coops.

■ Divide: $53\overline{)21{,}539}$

Think: There are enough hundreds to divide, because $53 < 215$.

Find the hundreds.

53 rounds to 50.
Think: $50\overline{)215}$

$$
\begin{array}{r}
4 \\
53\overline{)2\,1{,}5\,3\,9} \\
2\,1\,2 \\
\hline
3\,3
\end{array}
$$

Find the tens.

Think: $50\overline{)33}$

$$
\begin{array}{r}
4\,0 \\
53\overline{)2\,1{,}5\,3\,9} \\
2\,1\,2 \\
\hline
3\,3 \\
0 \\
\hline
3\,3\,9
\end{array}
$$

Find the ones.

Think: $50\overline{)339}$

$$
\begin{array}{r}
4\,0\,6\ \text{R21} \\
53\overline{)2\,1{,}5\,3\,9} \\
2\,1\,2 \\
\hline
3\,3 \\
0 \\
\hline
3\,3\,9 \\
3\,1\,8 \\
\hline
2\,1
\end{array}
$$

Check.

$$
\begin{array}{r}
406 \\
\times\ 53 \\
\hline
1\ 218 \\
20\ 30 \\
\hline
21{,}518 \\
+\quad 21 \\
\hline
21{,}539\ \checkmark
\end{array}
$$

Try These

Divide. Check each answer.

1. $24\overline{)156}$ **2.** $42\overline{)800}$ **3.** $54\overline{)2,160}$ **4.** $37\overline{)\$90.65}$

5. $121 \div 31$ **6.** $2,478 \div 41$ **7.** $8,378 \div 38$

Exercises

Divide.

1. $47\overline{)289}$ **2.** $62\overline{)12,200}$ **3.** $54\overline{)5,955}$ **4.** $38\overline{)3,050}$

5. $19\overline{)1,995}$ **6.** $42\overline{)9,250}$ **7.** $23\overline{)\$69.00}$ **8.** $57\overline{)5,985}$

9. $93\overline{)36,200}$ **10.** $86\overline{)\$79.12}$ **11.** $64\overline{)65,024}$ **12.** $54\overline{)2,116}$

13. $35\overline{)42,360}$ **14.** $66\overline{)\$535.26}$ **15.** $49\overline{)49,056}$ **16.** $20\overline{)8,428}$

17. $640 \div 32$ **18.** $\$90.00 \div 45$ **19.** $1,476 \div 36$
20. $1,295 \div 30$ **21.** $\$185.00 \div 37$ **22.** $26,362 \div 85$

Find each missing divisor.

★ **23.** $\blacksquare\overline{)754}$ (30 R4)   ★ **24.** $\blacksquare\overline{)3,750}$ (76 R26)   ★ **25.** $\blacksquare\overline{)4,032}$ (67 R12)

★ **26.** $\blacksquare\overline{)2,699}$ (71 R1)   ★ **27.** $\blacksquare\overline{)1,679}$ (27 R5)   ★ **28.** $\blacksquare\overline{)8,190}$ (190 R20)

Solve each problem. You may use a calculator to check.

29. Eggs are being packed into cartons. Each carton holds 1 dozen (12) eggs. How many cartons are needed for 600 eggs?

30. Ed delivers 15 cases of eggs to the market. There are 30 dozen eggs in each case. How many eggs does the market receive?

31. Yuri works 40 hours each week. He earns $170.00. How much does he earn each hour?

32. The chickens laid 386 eggs one hour and 534 eggs the next hour. How many eggs were laid in all?

★ **33.** Each of the 915 chickens eats 8 ounces of feed a day. How many ounces of feed does Ed need each day? How many pounds does he need? (Hint: 16 ounces = 1 pound)

★ **34.** A case of 30 cartons of Ed's extra-large eggs costs $15.90. A case of 24 cartons of his jumbo eggs costs $14.64. How much more does each carton of jumbo eggs cost?

Correcting Estimates

■ Sometimes when you are dividing, your first estimate may be too large.

Divide: 22)419

Find the tens.

22 rounds to 20.
Think: 20)41

$$\begin{array}{r} 2 \\ 22\overline{)4\ 1\ 9} \\ 4\ 4 \end{array}$$ ⎡ 44 > 41
⎢ 2 is too
⎣ large.

Try 1.

$$\begin{array}{r} 1 \\ 22\overline{)4\ 1\ 9} \\ 2\ 2 \\ \hline 1\ 9\ 9 \end{array}$$

Find the ones.

Think: 20)199

$$\begin{array}{r} 1\ 9\ \text{R1} \\ 22\overline{)4\ 1\ 9} \\ 2\ 2 \\ \hline 1\ 9\ 9 \\ 1\ 9\ 8 \\ \hline 1 \end{array}$$

■ Sometimes your first estimate may be too small.

Divide: 26)1,076

Find the tens.

26 rounds to 30.
Think: 30)107

$$\begin{array}{r} 3 \\ 26\overline{)1,0\ 7\ 6} \\ 7\ 8 \\ \hline 2\ 9 \end{array}$$ ← 29 > 26
3 is too small.

Try 4.

$$\begin{array}{r} 4 \\ 26\overline{)1,0\ 7\ 6} \\ 1\ 0\ 4 \\ \hline 3\ 6 \end{array}$$

Find the ones.

Think: 30)36

$$\begin{array}{r} 4\ 1\ \text{R10} \\ 26\overline{)1,0\ 7\ 6} \\ 1\ 0\ 4 \\ \hline 3\ 6 \\ 2\ 6 \\ \hline 1\ 0 \end{array}$$

■ Divide: 68)3,878

Find the tens.

68 rounds to 70.
Think: 70)387

$$\begin{array}{r} 5 \\ 68\overline{)3,8\ 7\ 8} \\ 3\ 4\ 0 \\ \hline 4\ 7\ 8 \end{array}$$

Find the ones.

Think: 70)478

$$\begin{array}{r} 5\ 6 \\ 68\overline{)3,8\ 7\ 8} \\ 3\ 4\ 0 \\ \hline 4\ 7\ 8 \\ 4\ 0\ 8 \\ \hline 7\ 0 \end{array}$$ ← 70 > 68
6 is too small.

Try 7.

$$\begin{array}{r} 5\ 7\ \text{R2} \\ 68\overline{)3,8\ 7\ 8} \\ 3\ 4\ 0 \\ \hline 4\ 7\ 8 \\ 4\ 7\ 6 \\ \hline 2 \end{array}$$

Check.

$$\begin{array}{r} 57 \\ \times 68 \\ \hline 456 \\ 3,420 \\ \hline 3,876 \\ +\quad 2 \\ \hline 3,878 \end{array}$$ ✔

Divide. Check each answer.

1. $24\overline{)156}$ 2. $31\overline{)121}$ 3. $36\overline{)\$150.48}$ 4. $27\overline{)1,647}$

5. $371 \div 47$ 6. $4,639 \div 66$ 7. $\$1,764 \div 36$

Exercises

Divide.

1. $47\overline{)289}$ 2. $42\overline{)800}$ 3. $38\overline{)2,698}$ 4. $32\overline{)1,997}$

5. $57\overline{)3,500}$ 6. $54\overline{)2,116}$ 7. $63\overline{)5,514}$ 8. $34\overline{)\$191.42}$

9. $86\overline{)7,912}$ 10. $24\overline{)610}$ 11. $78\overline{)\$65.52}$ 12. $66\overline{)53,526}$

13. $27\overline{)\$118.26}$ 14. $62\overline{)12,200}$ 15. $56\overline{)35,916}$ 16. $93\overline{)36,200}$

17. $526 \div 59$ 18. $1,295 \div 34$ 19. $2,753 \div 42$

20. $8,774 \div 93$ 21. $11,352 \div 28$ 22. $\$934.66 \div 34$

Compute.

23. $(4,032 + 4,127) \div 41$ 24. $(5,666 - 975) \div 56$ 25. $(6,293 \div 31) \times 58$

26. $(2,680 \div 20) + 752$ 27. $908 \times (6,400 \div 80)$ 28. $(796 + 421) - (786 \div 6)$

29. $445 \times (6,370 \div 98)$ 30. $(2,306 - 917) \div 48$ 31. $(346 + 759) \div (80 - 21)$

Solve each problem.

32. A new Indian exhibit is coming to the museum. For the opening ceremony, 288 chairs are needed. There are 48 seats in each row. How many rows of seats are there?

33. The gift shop has 4,290 postcard-sized prints of the exhibit pieces. There are 55 prints of each exhibit piece. How many exhibit pieces were photographed?

34. Floor plans were printed so visitors could locate the pieces in the new exhibit. The printers delivered 14 boxes. There were 250 floor plans in each box. How many floor plans were printed?

★ 35. Tickets to the opening cost $5.75 if you preregister. If you buy a ticket when you arrive, you pay $1.25 more. 200 people preregister. 65 people buy tickets when they arrive. How much money is collected by the museum?

Problem Solving: Strategies

FINDING INFORMATION

■ Sometimes you can use a table to help you solve a problem.

In this table, highway distances between cities are given in miles.

	Seattle	Bismarck	San Francisco	Los Angeles	Salt Lake City	Denver	Dallas
Seattle		1,195	808	1,131	836	1,307	2,078
Bismarck	1,195		1,604	1,617	916	671	1,141
San Francisco	808	1,604		379	752	1,235	1,753
Los Angeles	1,131	1,617	379		715	1,059	1,387
Salt Lake City	836	916	752	715		504	1,242
Denver	1,307	671	1,235	1,059	504		781
Dallas	2,078	1,141	1,753	1,387	1,242	781	

What is the distance from Salt Lake City to San Francisco?

Find the row for Salt Lake City. Move across that row until you find the column for San Francisco. Read the number in that box. It is 752.

The distance from Salt Lake City to San Francisco is 752 miles. The distance from San Francisco to Salt Lake City is also 752 miles.

Find the distance from Denver to Los Angeles. You will find the same distance from Los Angeles to Denver.

■ If you want to drive from Denver to Los Angeles by way of Salt Lake City, how many miles will you drive?

Denver to Salt Lake City   504 miles
Salt Lake City to Los Angeles   +715 miles
                                    1,219 miles

You will drive 1,219 miles.

Why are there no numbers in some of the boxes?

Using the Strategy

Solve each problem.

1. If you want to drive from Dallas to Salt Lake City in 3 days, how many miles per day must you average?

2. If you want to drive from San Francisco to Salt Lake City in 2 days, how many miles per day must you average?

3. If you drive an average of 50 miles per hour, about how long will it take to drive from San Francisco to Los Angeles?

4. Only part of the table below is completed. Use the given information to complete the table.

Highway Distances (in miles)					
	Charleston, S.C.	Charlotte, N.C.	Columbia, S.C.	Nashville, Tenn.	Norfolk, Va.
Charleston, S.C.		210		539	440
Charlotte, N.C.				421	310
Columbia, S.C.	113	94			
Nashville, Tenn.			437		672
Norfolk, Va.			389		

 ACTIVITY

USING ESTIMATION

A country music band is going on a tour in a van. They start in San Francisco. They go to Seattle, Denver, and Dallas. Then they return to San Francisco.

1. Find the total number of miles they will drive. Round your answer to the nearest 10 miles.

2. Assume the van gets 15 miles per gallon. Estimate the number of gallons of gas it will use by dividing the answer to exercise 1 by 15.

Dividing by Multiples of 100

■ 46,800 newspapers are printed each day by the *Daily Bugle*. The papers are piled in groups of 900 and placed on the loading dock. How many piles are there?

Divide 46,800 by 900 to find the number of piles.

Think: There are enough tens to divide, because 900 < 4,680.

Find the tens.	Find the ones.	Check.
Think: $900)\overline{4,680}$	Think: $900)\overline{1,800}$	

$$
\begin{array}{r}
5\_\ \\
900)\overline{4\,6,8\,0\,0} \\
4\,5\,0\,0 \\
\hline
1\,8\,0\,0
\end{array}
\qquad
\begin{array}{r}
5\,2 \\
900)\overline{4\,6,8\,0\,0} \\
4\,5\,0\,0 \\
\hline
1\,8\,0\,0 \\
1\,8\,0\,0 \\
\hline
0
\end{array}
\qquad
\begin{array}{r}
900 \\
\times\ 52 \\
\hline
1,800 \\
45\,000 \\
\hline
46,800\ \checkmark
\end{array}
$$

There are 52 piles of papers.

■ Divide: $200)\overline{81,643}$

Find the hundreds.	Find the tens.	Find the ones.

$$
\begin{array}{r}
4\_\_ \\
200)\overline{8\,1,6\,4\,3} \\
8\,0\,0 \\
\hline
1\,6\,4
\end{array}
\qquad
\begin{array}{r}
4\,0\_ \\
200)\overline{8\,1,6\,4\,3} \\
8\,0\,0 \\
\hline
1\,6\,4 \\
0 \\
\hline
1\,6\,4\,3
\end{array}
\qquad
\begin{array}{r}
4\,0\,8\ \text{R43} \\
200)\overline{8\,1,6\,4\,3} \\
8\,0\,0 \\
\hline
1\,6\,4 \\
0 \\
\hline
1\,6\,4\,3 \\
1\,6\,0\,0 \\
\hline
4\,3
\end{array}
$$

Try These

Divide. Check each answer.

1. $700)\overline{6,948}$ 2. $500)\overline{45,873}$ 3. $400)\overline{\$3,344.00}$ 4. $200)\overline{64,895}$

5. $52,708 \div 600$ 6. $\$3,200 \div 800$ 7. $265,319 \div 300$

Exercises

Divide.

1. $400\overline{)2{,}519}$ **2.** $600\overline{)28{,}095}$ **3.** $700\overline{)\$3{,}941.00}$ **4.** $300\overline{)29{,}784}$

5. $100\overline{)85{,}386}$ **6.** $500\overline{)4{,}692}$ **7.** $200\overline{)12{,}000}$ **8.** $400\overline{)\$600.00}$

9. $600\overline{)191{,}687}$ **10.** $200\overline{)2{,}975}$ **11.** $900\overline{)\$2{,}700.00}$ ★ **12.** $300\overline{)967{,}425}$

13. $8{,}925 \div 700$ **14.** $160{,}420 \div 500$ **15.** $24{,}650 \div 100$

16. $\$516.00 \div 200$ **17.** $640{,}000 \div 800$ ★ **18.** $848{,}999 \div 600$

Copy and complete.

★ **19.** ■ $\div 300 = 6$ R27   ★ **20.** ■ $\div 86 = 24$ R6

★ **21.** ■ $\div 600 = 309$ R58   ★ **22.** $57{,}623 \div$ ■ $= 64$ R23

★ **23.** $98{,}874 \div$ ■ $= 123$ R474   ★ **24.** $12{,}256 \div$ ■ $= 126$ R34

Solve each problem.

25. Jethro sells 400 newspapers each day. He sells newspapers 7 days a week. The price of each paper is $.35. How much money does Jethro collect each day?

26. The Main Street Newsstand is open 300 days each year. It sold 184,500 papers this year. What was the average number of papers sold each day?

27. Ames Department Store is planning its advertisement campaign for the year. It wants to spend no more than $12,500 for advertisements. How many $400 advertisements can the store buy?

★ **28.** 25 delivery trucks are used on weekends. Each truck picks up 100 bundles of newspapers. There are 18 newspapers in each bundle. How many newspapers are picked up in all?

KEEPING IN SHAPE

1. 8×71 **2.** $6 \times \$1.75$ **3.** 60×86 **4.** $90 \times \$5.45$

5. 42×318 **6.** $85 \times 2{,}473$ **7.** $600 \times 3{,}948$ **8.** $679 \times 4{,}521$

9. $7 \times 2{,}609$ **10.** $4{,}831 \times 56$ **11.** $372 \times \$6.98$ **12.** 704×906

Dividing by 3-Digit Numbers

■ The Centerville Post Office delivered 8,398 pieces of mail in 1 week. They deliver to 221 locations. What was the average number of pieces delivered to each location?

Divide 8,398 by 221 to find the answer.

Find the tens.

221 rounds to 200.
Think: $200\overline{)839}$

$$\begin{array}{r} 4\_\_ \\ 221\overline{)8,398} \\ 884 \end{array}$$ ← 884 > 839
4 is too large.

Try 3.

$$\begin{array}{r} 3\_\_ \\ 221\overline{)8,398} \\ 663 \\ \hline 1768 \end{array}$$

Find the ones.

Think: $200\overline{)1768}$

$$\begin{array}{r} 38 \\ 221\overline{)8,398} \\ 663 \\ \hline 1768 \\ 1768 \\ \hline 0 \end{array}$$

Each location received an average of 38 pieces of mail.

■ Divide: $396\overline{)277,284}$

Find the hundreds.

396 rounds to 400.
Think: $400\overline{)2,772}$

$$\begin{array}{r} 6\_\_ \\ 396\overline{)277,284} \\ 2376 \\ \hline 396 \end{array}$$ ← 396 = 396
6 is too small.

Try 7.

$$\begin{array}{r} 7\_\_ \\ 396\overline{)277,284} \\ 2772 \\ \hline 8 \end{array}$$

Find the tens.
Find the ones.

$$\begin{array}{r} 700\ \text{R84} \\ 396\overline{)277,284} \\ 2772 \\ \hline 8 \\ 0 \\ \hline 84 \\ 0 \\ \hline 84 \end{array}$$

Try These

Divide. Check each answer.

1. $317\overline{)9,000}$ 2. $432\overline{)9,863}$ 3. $273\overline{)\$666.12}$ 4. $652\overline{)198,418}$

5. $92,354 \div 721$ 6. $39,518 \div 407$ 7. $\$4,432.44 \div 516$

Exercises

Divide.

1. $205\overline{)1{,}562}$ **2.** $486\overline{)2{,}673}$ **3.** $845\overline{)70{,}562}$ **4.** $423\overline{)\$359.55}$

5. $539\overline{)16{,}073}$ **6.** $105\overline{)11{,}098}$ **7.** $395\overline{)\$790.00}$ **8.** $237\overline{)9{,}418}$

9. $682\overline{)31{,}487}$ **10.** $246\overline{)\$484.62}$ **11.** $200\overline{)180{,}000}$ **12.** $427\overline{)10{,}084}$

13. $289\overline{)13{,}590}$ **14.** $584\overline{)409{,}086}$ **15.** $879\overline{)\$12{,}306.00}$ ★ **16.** $225\overline{)739{,}182}$

17. $5{,}920 \div 483$ **18.** $22{,}420 \div 295$ **19.** $\$683.76 \div 231$
20. $17{,}783 \div 208$ ★ **21.** $395{,}406 \div 118$ ★ **22.** $902{,}875 \div 714$

Compute.

23. $(200 \times 600) \div 400$ **24.** $521 \times (2{,}464 \div 22)$ **25.** $4{,}967 - (7{,}056 \div 126)$
26. $(900 \div 30) + 627$ **27.** $(32{,}086 - 10) \div 324$ **28.** $718 \times (1{,}935 \div 215)$

Solve each problem. You may choose paper and pencil or a calculator.

29. A grocery store pays $285.00 to mail out 750 fliers. How much does it cost to mail each flier?

30. The post office receives 33,600 catalogs boxed in groups of 200. How many boxes are there?

31. 230,000 new stamps are issued. 175,600 have already been delivered to post offices. How many more stamps need to be delivered?

32. There are 144 post office boxes for rent. Each box is rented for $25 per year. How much does the post office earn from renting the boxes?

33. The postal workers sell about 2,500 first-class stamps each day. They also sell about 350 air-mail stamps and 125 postcards. How many stamps are sold each day?

34. There are 214 packages to deliver. The packages weigh an average of 6 pounds. About how much does the total delivery weigh?

★ **35.** *Gloria's Gift Catalog* is sent out 4 times each year. 4,250 catalogs are mailed each time. Gloria pays $1.19 to mail each issue. How much does Gloria pay for mailing in 1 year?

Estimating Quotients

■ ABC Computer Company makes computers. Each computer it makes contains 6 chips. The company ordered 49,450 chips. About how many computers can it make with that number of chips?

To find about how many, estimate the quotient.

Estimate: $6\overline{)49,450}$

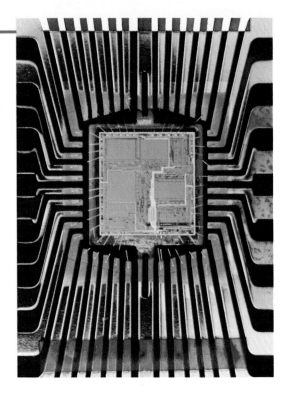

Find the first digit of the quotient.	**Write 0s for the rest of the digits.**
$\dfrac{8}{6\overline{)49,450}}$	$\dfrac{8,000}{6\overline{)49,450}}$

The company could make about 8,000 computers.

■ To estimate when the divisor has more than 1 digit, round the divisor. Then change the dividend to a number that is easy to divide by the rounded divisor.

Estimate: $28\overline{)67,346}$

Round the divisor.	**Change the dividend.**	**Estimate the quotient.**
28 rounds to 30.		
$30\overline{)67,346}$	$30\overline{)60,000}$	$\dfrac{2,000}{30\overline{)60,000}}$

Estimate: $541\overline{)36,279}$

Round the divisor.	**Change the dividend.**	**Estimate the quotient.**
541 rounds to 500.		
$500\overline{)36,279}$	$500\overline{)35,000}$	$\dfrac{70}{500\overline{)35,000}}$

Try These

Estimate each quotient.

1. $4\overline{)3,196}$ **2.** $18\overline{)58,014}$ **3.** $7\overline{)\$62.79}$ **4.** $286\overline{)849,065}$

5. $15,821 \div 37$ **6.** $828 \div 9$ **7.** $236,496 \div 417$

Exercises

Estimate each quotient.

1. $4\overline{)371}$ **2.** $48\overline{)36,172}$ **3.** $6\overline{)2,097}$ **4.** $17\overline{)784,209}$

5. $87\overline{)62,300}$ **6.** $729\overline{)438,192}$ **7.** $58\overline{)\$329.44}$ **8.** $3\overline{)796}$

9. $396\overline{)24,152}$ **10.** $61\overline{)\$2,806.00}$ **11.** $38\overline{)2,761}$ **12.** $41\overline{)358,975}$

13. $56\overline{)47,284}$ **14.** $678\overline{)\$4,922.28}$ **15.** $98\overline{)289,373}$ **16.** $5\overline{)36,409}$

17. $6,595 \div 8$ **18.** $43,197 \div 74$ **19.** $\$1,563.52 \div 224$

20. $55,233 \div 56$ **21.** $\$644.00 \div 28$ **22.** $445,183 \div 893$

23. $51,248 \div 7$ **24.** $74,352 \div 860$ **25.** $43,916 \div 42$

Use estimation to decide whether each answer is reasonable.
Write *yes* if it is reasonable and *no* if it is not reasonable.

26. $4\overline{)276}^{\,169}$ **27.** $32\overline{)\$576.00}^{\,\$18.00}$ **28.** $63\overline{)22,995}^{\,165}$ **29.** $76\overline{)34,352}^{\,152}$

30. $391\overline{)315,146}^{\,806}$ **31.** $9\overline{)8,262}^{\,1,918}$ **32.** $516\overline{)38,184}^{\,24}$ **33.** $48\overline{)172,992}^{\,3,604}$

Decide if you need an estimate or an exact answer. Then solve.

34. An order for 2,404 microcomputers is being packed. 1 carton holds 8 microcomputers. About how many cartons are needed?

35. It costs ABC Computer Company $1,021.25 to mail out 475 progress reports. About how much does it cost to mail 1 progress report?

36. The ABC Computer Company sells 516 screens to the Wainbrite Corporation. All 6 branch offices receive the same number of screens. How many screens does each branch office receive?

37. Kathy worked on developing a new computer program for a total of 82 hours in 4 weeks. Estimate the average number of hours she worked on the program each week.

38. Tony is a salesperson for the ABC Computer Company. In the first 3 weeks of November, he drove a total distance of 1,658 kilometers. Estimate the average number of kilometers he drove each week.

★ **39.** Milano Bakeries bought computers for a total of $7,485.60. They made a down payment of $1,500.00. They will pay the balance in 8 equal payments. How much will each payment be?

Problem Solving: Applications

NOT ENOUGH INFORMATION

The 3 sixth-grade classes at Highpoint Elementary School are going on a field trip to a science museum. There are 24 students in each class. 3 teachers and 6 parents are also going. How many buses will be needed to take all of them to the museum?

Do you have enough information to answer the question? What else do you need to know? You need to know how many people each bus holds.

Suppose each bus holds 30 people.

First, add to find how many people are going.

$$3 \times 24 = 72 \text{ students}$$
$$\begin{array}{r} 3 \text{ teachers} \\ + \ 6 \text{ parents} \\ \hline 81 \text{ people} \end{array}$$

81 people will be going in all.

Then, divide 81 by 30 to find the number of buses needed.

$$\begin{array}{r} 2 \text{ R21} \\ 30\overline{)81} \\ \underline{60} \\ 21 \end{array}$$

3 buses will be needed to hold all 81 people—
2 buses with 30 people and 1 bus with 21 people.

3 buses have 90 seats altogether. Since $81 < 90$, this answer makes sense.

Try These

Write what information is needed to solve each problem.

1. The 72 students were divided into groups to go through the museum. Each group had the same number of students. How many students were in each group?

2. It cost $2.50 for each student to enter the museum. What was the cost for the whole group, including the adults, to enter?

Exercises

If all the necessary information is given, solve the problem.
If information is missing, tell what you need to know.

1. Tim saw a robot that could weld parts for tractors. How many parts could it weld in 8 hours?

2. 32 of the students saw the coal mine exhibit. They had to enter in groups of 6 or fewer. What is the fewest number of groups they could have formed?

3. Kirsten bought 6 postcards at the museum gift shop. The postcards cost $.35 each. The tax was $.17. What was the total cost of the postcards?

4. Rosemary saw a skeleton of a dinosaur. Rosemary weighs 83 pounds. How many students weighing as much as Rosemary would weigh the same as the dinosaur did?

5. Frank learned that to find your weight on the moon, you divide your weight on earth by 6. How much would Frank weigh on the moon?

6. Ruth learned that the moon is about 240,000 miles from the earth. At a rate of 400 miles per hour, about how long would it take to travel to the moon?

7. Paul saw an exhibit about honeybees. He learned that a queen bee may lay 1,800 eggs per day. How many eggs would that be in a week?

8. The sixth graders presented a play to raise money for another trip. They charged $1.50 for adults' tickets and $.75 for children's tickets. How much money did they make?

CHAPTER CHECKPOINT

Divide. (pp. 70–75, 78–83)

1. $6\overline{)36}$ **2.** $9\overline{)0}$ **3.** $8\overline{)77}$ **4.** $1\overline{)25}$

5. $3\overline{)72}$ **6.** $3\overline{)675}$ **7.** $6\overline{)1,947}$ **8.** $4\overline{)489}$

9. $3\overline{)\$19.83}$ **10.** $7\overline{)4,493}$ **11.** $2\overline{)\$20.18}$ **12.** $9\overline{)9,756}$

13. $50\overline{)1,074}$ **14.** $40\overline{)4,600}$ **15.** $60\overline{)\$86.40}$ **16.** $30\overline{)9,690}$

17. $81\overline{)650}$ **18.** $23\overline{)4,945}$ **19.** $68\overline{)21,809}$ **20.** $61\overline{)\$278.16}$

21. $49\overline{)3,994}$ **22.** $56\overline{)4,691}$ **23.** $66\overline{)53,540}$ **24.** $63\overline{)55,146}$

25. $200\overline{)1,800}$ **26.** $900\overline{)57,623}$ **27.** $700\overline{)\$4,900.00}$ **28.** $500\overline{)430,825}$

29. $502\overline{)150,684}$ **30.** $267\overline{)\$630.12}$ **31.** $479\overline{)791,064}$ **32.** $384\overline{)185,270}$

33. $7 \div 7$ **34.** $51 \div 7$ **35.** $280 \div 4$

36. $896 \div 4$ **37.** $\$75.25 \div 5$ **38.** $600 \div 30$

39. $8,568 \div 42$ **40.** $86,177 \div 600$ **41.** $68,927 \div 148$

Estimate each quotient. (pp. 90–91)

42. $6\overline{)2,967}$ **43.** $19\overline{)768}$ **44.** $86\overline{)\$270.90}$ **45.** $218\overline{)152,600}$

46. $8,916 \div 28$ **47.** $198,318 \div 384$ **48.** $17,915 \div 6$ **49.** $\$202.02 \div 37$

Find each average. (pp. 76–77)

50. 26, 34, 48, 36   **51.** $86, $95, $78, $99, $82

52. 198, 247, 176, 283   **53.** 608, 545, 712, 639

54. $846, $923, $957, $814   **55.** 26, 31, 48, 37, 53

56. 275, 318, 297, 309, 321   **57.** 65, 68, 70, 74, 65, 82, 73, 79

**Solve each problem. If information is missing, tell what you
need to know.** (pp. 70–93)

58. Inez has 66 inches of wire. She cuts it into pieces that are 8 inches long. How many 8-inch pieces are there? How many inches of wire are left?

59. A carton containing 8 cookbooks arrives at the bookstore. The carton costs $41.52. How much does each cookbook cost?

60. Fred drove 598 miles on 23 gallons of gas. What was the average number of miles per gallon?

61. Chris has taken 4 math tests. His scores were 92, 86, 78, and 88. What was his average grade?

62. There are 1,086 students in the Eastside School District. A bus can carry 48 students. How many buses are needed to take all the students to a concert?

63. A truckload of 2,250 apple trees arrives at the orchard. The apple trees are being planted in 45 rows. How many trees should be planted in each row?

64. A department store pays $863.10 to mail out 685 catalogs. How much does each catalog cost?

65. Suki wants to buy a calculator. She has $25.68. How much more does she need?

66. Alice and Carl walked 15 kilometers in 3 hours. They walked the same distance each hour. How many kilometers did they walk each hour?

67. Fred drove a total of 1,940 kilometers in 6 days. Estimate the average number of kilometers he drove each day.

68. Kim bakes spinach pies for a restaurant. Each pie is cut into 8 equal pieces. How many people can be served from all the pies?

69. A store sold 575 T-shirts in one month. The store was open 26 days that month. About how many T-shirts were sold each day?

In this table, airline distances between cities are given in miles.

	San Francisco	New Orleans	New York
San Francisco		1,926	2,571
New Orleans	1,926		1,171
New York	2,571	1,171	

70. Felipe flew to San Francisco. If it took 3 hours to fly from New Orleans to San Francisco, what was the average speed?

71. If you flew from San Francisco to New York at an average speed of 483 miles per hour, about how long would it take?

COMPUTERS AND PROBLEM SOLVING

■ Division and subtraction are related. To divide 6 by 2, you can subtract 2 from 6 again and again, counting the number of subtractions.

6 − 2 = 4	1 subtraction
4 − 2 = 2	2 subtractions
2 − 2 = 0	3 subtractions

The quotient is 3, the number of times you subtracted 2. It would take you far too much time to divide large numbers this way. But the computer can perform the subtractions quickly.

Here is a program to divide 456 by 17. The computer subtracts 17 over and over. The variable Q counts the number of subtractions. The variable DV is the dividend.

```
NEW
10   REM THIS PROGRAM DIVIDES BY SUBTRACTING
20   LET DV = 456: REM 456 IS THE DIVIDEND
30   LET Q = 0: REM SET THE COUNTER TO 0
40   LET Q = Q + 1: REM ADD 1 TO THE COUNTER
50   LET DV = DV − 17: REM 17 IS THE DIVISOR
60   IF DV < 17 THEN GOTO 80
70   GOTO 40: REM REPEAT THE SUBTRACT LOOP
80   PRINT "THE QUOTIENT IS "; Q
90   IF DV > 0 THEN PRINT "THE REMAINDER IS "; DV
100   END
```

Solve each problem.

1. In line 60 the computer checks a condition. What happens when DV < 17 is false?

2. How many times will the computer find this condition false?

3. What happens when DV < 17 is true?

4. How many times will the computer find this condition true?

The programmer used the REM statement to add notes to make the program easier to understand. The first line of the program is a REM statement that explains what the program will do. REM statements can be alone on a line, or at the end of a line.

Solve each problem.

1. Why use a GOTO loop between lines 70 and 40 instead of a FOR. . .NEXT loop?

2. What does the IF. . .THEN in line 90 prevent?

3. Add a line before the end of the program to check the result.

4. Modify the program to work with any dividend and any divisor.

ENRICHMENT

ORDER OF OPERATIONS

■ Here are some names for the number 8.   Here are some names for the number 7.

$12 - 4$ $35 \div 5$
$2 \times 2 \times 2$ $(2 \times 2) + 3$
$16 \div (7 - 5)$ $3 + 2 + 2$

All of these are called **expressions**. To simplify an
expression without parentheses, certain operations must be
done in a special order.

1. Multiply and divide from left to right.
2. Then add and subtract from left to right.

┌──────── Subtract.   ┌──────── Multiply.
$12 - 7 + 4 = 5 + 4 = 9$ $8 + 3 \times 4 = 8 + 12 = 20$
└──── Then add.   └──────── Then add.

$7 \times 2 + 4 \div 2 = 14 + 2 = 16$

■ Remember that parentheses mean *do this first*. They can be
used to change the usual order of operations.

┌──────── Add.   ┌──────── Add.
$12 - (7 + 4) = 12 - 11 = 1$ $(8 + 3) \times 4 = 11 \times 4 = 44$
└──────── Then subtract.   └──── Then multiply.

$7 \times (2 + 4) \div 2 = 7 \times 6 \div 2 = 42 \div 2 = 21$

Compare the answers with and without parentheses.

Simplify.

1. $14 - 3 - 2$
2. $14 - (3 - 2)$
3. $14 - 3 + 2$
4. $3 + 4 \times 6$
5. $(3 + 4) \times 6$
6. $3 \times 6 + 4 \times 6$
7. $56 \div 4 \div 2$
8. $56 \div (4 \div 2)$
9. $56 \times 2 \div 4$
10. $24 \div 4 \times 3$
11. $24 \div (4 \times 3)$
12. $24 \times 3 \div 4$
13. $2 + 3 \times 4 + 7 - 3$
14. $(2 + 3) \times 4 + 7 - 3$
15. $36 \div 4 \times 2 + 1 - 7$
16. $36 \div 4 \times (2 + 1) - 7$

What does the digit 8 mean in each number?

1. 684

2. 86,017

3. 867,249

4. 8,906,000

5. 896,375,200

6. 68,000,000,467

Write each number.

7. 46 thousand 514

8. 462 thousand 90

9. nine hundred twelve million, five hundred thousand, sixteen

Write >, <, or =.

10. 6,851 ▧ 6,581

11. 346,207 ▧ 346,207

12. 46,175,926 ▧ 46,157,962

13. 50,270,408,996 ▧ 50,270,480,996

Round each number to the given place.

14. 674 to the nearest ten

15. $18.76 to the nearest dollar

16. 8,571 to the nearest thousand

17. 46,172,814 to the nearest ten-million

Add. Estimate to check.

18.	**19.**	**20.**	**21.**	**22.**
96	$3.68	4,603	88,516	739,201
+24	+ 5.49	+ 978	+19,475	14,688
				+179,195

Subtract. Estimate to check.

23.	**24.**	**25.**	**26.**	**27.**
62	512	$8.00	6,407	$605.95
−49	−186	− 2.79	−1,968	− 437.18

Multiply. Estimate to check.

28.	**29.**	**30.**	**31.**	**32.**
64	$6.85	763	1,274	568
× 9	× 8	× 40	× 38	×432

Divide.

33. 4)‾37‾

34. 3)‾963‾

35. 9)‾1,140‾

36. 7)‾$140.56‾

(Continued)

Divide.

37. $50)\overline{\$268.00}$ **38.** $64)\overline{86,475}$ **39.** $33)\overline{6,303}$ **40.** $428)\overline{18,276}$

Compute.

41. $684 + 96$ **42.** 75×84 **43.** $\$6.00 - \$2.89$

44. $76 \div 4$ **45.** 40×40 **46.** $179 + 86 + 2,164$

47. $86,741 \div 200$ **48.** $\$5.67 \times 600$ **49.** $62,014 - 19,567$

Solve each problem.

50. Mrs. Mazor bought a calculator, a package of file cards, and a tape dispenser. How much money did she spend?

51. A customer buys a package of file cards, a box of envelopes, and a package of paper. Estimate the cost.

52. The Everett Corporation ordered 9 calculators on Tuesday. What is the cost of the order?

Item	Price (no tax added)
typewriter	$375.25
calculator	$ 68.50
file cards (per package)	$ 3.70
envelopes (per box)	$ 6.85
paper (per package)	$ 9.15
stapler	$ 16.89
tape dispenser	$ 7.50

53. Mrs. Byron bought 1 package each of envelopes and file cards. How much change should she have received from $20?

54. A package of typewriter ribbons sells for $32.70. There are 6 ribbons in each package. Estimate the cost of each ribbon.

55. Jim works at the office supply store and the drug store. He earns $15 a day at one job and $9 a day at the other. How much does he earn in 18 days?

56. Ed sold $4,650 worth of supplies in May. In June, he sold $6,207 worth of supplies. His goal for July was $7,500. What was the total of his sales for May and June?

57. Ed sold 86 calculators in January, 98 calculators in February, and 125 calculators in March. What was the average number of calculators Ed sold in those months?

58. A shipment of 5,200 envelopes arrives at the office supply store. There are 400 envelopes in each box. How many boxes are in this shipment?

4

DECIMALS:
ADDITION AND SUBTRACTION

Tenths and Hundredths

- A **fraction** or a **decimal** may be used to tell what part of a region is shaded.

This region is divided into 10 equal parts.

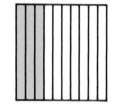

Write: $\frac{3}{10}$ or 0.3 ⌐ This is a **decimal point**.

Read: three tenths or zero point three

This region is divided into 100 equal parts.

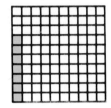

Write: $\frac{7}{100}$ or 0.07

Read: seven hundredths or zero point zero seven

- A **mixed number** or a decimal may be used to tell how much is shaded.

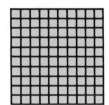

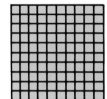

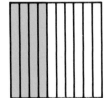

Write: $2\frac{4}{10}$ or 2.4

Read: two and four tenths or two point four

> The decimal point separates the ones and the tenths.

- Decimals can also be shown on a number line. Each tenth is divided into 10 hundredths.

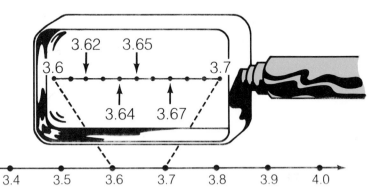

0.3 and 0.30 name the same number. They are **equivalent decimals**.

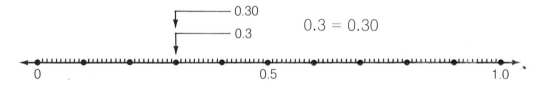

0.30
0.3

$0.3 = 0.30$

Try These

Write a decimal to tell how much is shaded.

1. 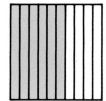 **2.** 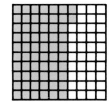 **3.**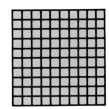

Write as a decimal.

4. 5 tenths

6. seven and two tenths

5. 62 hundredths

7. two and fifteen hundredths

Exercises

Write as a decimal.

1. 54 and 3 tenths

3. 7 and 5 hundredths

5. eighty-five and four tenths

2. 24 and 4 hundredths

4. 20 and 9 tenths

6. one hundred fifty and seventy-five hundredths

Copy and complete.

7. 0.67 = 6 tenths ▩ hundredths

9. 0.08 = ▩ tenths ▩ hundredths

8. 5.4 = 5 and ▩ tenths

10. 0.32 = ▩ tenths ▩ hundredths

Write the decimal shown by each labeled point.

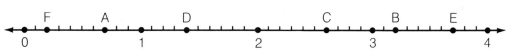

11. *A*   **12.** *B*   **13.** *C*   **14.** *D*   **15.** *E*   **16.** *F*

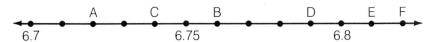

17. *A*   **18.** *B*   **19.** *C*   **20.** *D*   ★ **21.** *E*   ★ **22.** *F*

Write an equivalent decimal.

23. 0.5	**24.** 0.20	**25.** 0.3	**26.** 0.40	**27.** 0.60	**28.** 1.7
29. 0.10	**30.** 8.0	**31.** 0.90	**32.** 11.00	**33.** 0.1	**34.** 1.40
35. 7.6	**36.** 3.70	**37.** 10.4	**38.** 7.90	**39.** 65.3	**40.** 100.80

Decimals: Place Value

To show decimals, a place value chart can be extended to the right of the ones place.

hundred-thousands	ten-thousands	thousands	hundreds	tens	ones	.	tenths	hundredths	thousandths	ten-thousandths	hundred-thousandths
			3	8	4	.	2	5			
					0	.	0	8	9		
					0	.	0	0	6	0	8

To read a decimal, begin with the first non-zero digit.
Then read the place value of the last digit.

Write: 384.25
Read: 384 and 25 hundredths

In 384.25, the 8 means 8 tens, or 80.

Write: 0.089
Read: 89 thousandths

In 0.089, the 8 means 8 hundredths, or 0.08.

Write: 0.00608
Read: 608 hundred-thousandths

In 0.00608, the 8 means 8 hundred-thousandths, or 0.00008.

Try These

What does the digit 6 mean in each number?

1. 256.831   **2.** 98.962   **3.** 615.987   **4.** 8,658,210   **5.** 4,592.0064

6. 31.461   **7.** 16,142.5   **8.** 384.691   **9.** 867.304   **10.** 14.34869

Write each decimal.

11. 97 hundredths   **12.** 8 and 15 thousandths   **13.** 256 and 176 thousandths

Exercises

What does the digit 4 mean in each number?

1. 61.342   **2.** 14,257.8   **3.** 9.25643   **4.** 27.842   **5.** 354.983

6. 942.307   **7.** 9,362.0047   **8.** 764.19   **9.** 6,233.476   **10.** 418.7589

Use 3,901.84627. Write the digit that is in each place.

11. tenths place   **12.** thousands place   **13.** hundredths place

14. thousandths place   **15.** hundreds place   **16.** ten-thousandths place

Write each decimal.

17. 418 thousandths   **18.** 95 and 20 hundredths   **19.** 46 and 159 thousandths

20. 6 and 18 thousandths   **21.** 654 ten-thousandths   **22.** 356 and 6 hundredths

23. seven and four hundred and one thousandth

★ **24.** sixty-three and five hundred nineteen ten-thousandths

★ **25.** five millionths

26. two hundred seventy-three ten-millionths

THINK AND TRY

USING DECIMALS

There are 100 letters in these two facts about America:
    About twenty of every one hundred Americans live in country
    towns or villages. About five out of one hundred live on farms.

Write a decimal to show what part of the set of letters describes each group.

1. the e's   **2.** vowels   **3.** consonants

Comparing and Ordering Decimals

■ You can use a number line to compare decimals.

0	0.1	0.2	0.3	0.4	0.5	0.6	0.7	0.8	0.9	1.0	1.1	1.2	1.3	1.4	1.5

0.7 is to the right of 0.4, so 0.7 > 0.4.   1.2 is to the left of 1.3, so 1.2 < 1.3.

■ You can also compare decimals by starting at the left and comparing the digits in each place.

Compare 213.2 and 36.43.

Line up the decimal points.

Compare the hundreds.

$$2\,1\,3\,.\,2$$
$$3\,6\,.\,4\,3$$

2 hundreds > no hundreds, so 213.2 > 36.43.

■ Compare 6.725 and 6.75.

Line up the decimal points.

Compare the ones.   Compare the tenths.   Compare the hundredths.

6 . 7 2 5   6 . 7 2 5   6 . 7 2 5
6 . 7 5   6 . 7 5   6 . 7 5
same   same   2 < 5
                                                                  so
                                                          6.725 < 6.75

■ Write 3.679, 3.874, and 3.601 in order from least to greatest.

3 . 6 7 9
3 . 8 7 4   3.874 is the greatest.
3 . 6 0 1

Compare 3.679 and 3.601.

3 . 6 7 9   3.601 < 3.679
3 . 6 0 1

The order from least to greatest is 3.601, 3.679, 3.874.

Try These

Write >, <, or =.

1. 0.60 ▨ 0.6

2. 0.2 ▨ 0.21

3. 3.754 ▨ 12.754

4. 0.1 ▨ 0.15

5. 1.142 ▨ 0.984

6. 0.1 ▨ 0.0100

Exercises

Write >, <, or =.

1. 2.43 ▨ 2.45

2. 31.17 ▨ 2.18

3. 7.08 ▨ 6.09

4. 0.09 ▨ 0.009

5. 1.01 ▨ 0.95

6. 78.046 ▨ 78.0046

7. 6.414 ▨ 34.2

8. 1.352 ▨ 1.3520

9. 364.5 ▨ 365.40

10. 9.002 ▨ 9.02

11. 14.2504 ▨ 14.2540

12. 321.052 ▨ 321.321

Write in order from least to greatest.

13. 316.172   316.127   316.107   316.17

14. 74.5   4.054   4.54   4.005

15. 2.094   2.49   2.904   2.94   2.409   2.049

Bob Burke is a mechanic. He uses a feeler gauge to measure gaps in spark plugs in inches.

Solve each problem.

16. What is the smallest gap he can measure with the gauges shown?

17. What is the largest gap he can measure?

18. List the gauge sizes in order from least to greatest.

 THINK AND TRY

USING CLUES

What number am I? Use the clues to find each answer.

1. I am a decimal number with 2 digits to the right of the decimal point. I am less than 0.3 and greater than 0.2. The sum of my digits is 9.

2. I am a decimal number. I am greater than 0.68 and less than 0.69. The sum of my digits is 21. What are some numbers I could be?

Rounding Decimals

■ You can use a number line to round decimals.

Round 6.37 to the nearest tenth.

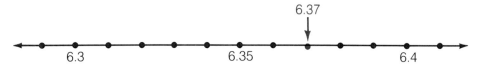

6.37 is between 6.3 and 6.4.
6.37 is closer to 6.4 than to 6.3.
6.37 rounded to the nearest tenth is 6.4.

■ You can use this rule for rounding decimals.

> *Look at the digit to the right of the place you are*
> *rounding to. If the digit is less than 5, round down.*
> *If the digit is 5 or greater, round up.*

Round 27.0964 to the nearest thousandth.

27.096④   Look at the digit in the ten-thousandths place.
4 < 5   Compare this digit with 5.
            Round down.

27.0964 rounded to the nearest thousandth is 27.096.

■ Round 52.938 to the nearest whole number.

52.⑨38   Look at the digit in the tenths place.
9 > 5   Compare this digit with 5.
            Round up.

52.938 rounded to the nearest whole number is 53.

Try These

Round to the nearest tenth.

1. 3.64   **2.** 0.792   **3.** 1.35   **4.** 0.924   **5.** 87.63

Round to the nearest thousandth.

6. 6.05218   **7.** 0.0678   **8.** 12.8121   **9.** 4.6725   **10.** 248.0055

Exercises

Round to the nearest hundredth.

1. 42.176   **2.** 9.614   **3.** 0.315   **4.** 1.015   **5.** 8.292

6. 5.028   **7.** 0.703   **8.** 0.4545   **9.** 4.597   **10.** 39.0648

Round to the nearest whole number.

11. 7.8   **12.** 13.9   **13.** 74.3   **14.** 3.78   **15.** 100.85

16. 47.05   **17.** 3.518   **18.** 0.283   **19.** 32.3997   **20.** 84.0098

Round to the nearest thousandth.

21. 0.64389   **22.** 16.8921   **23.** 34.00075   **24.** 67.206754   **25.** 189.09702

Round to the nearest dollar.

26. $2.75   **27.** $18.18   **28.** $56.95   **29.** $176.50   **30.** $216.49

Round 7.19827 to each given place.

31. the nearest tenth   **32.** the nearest hundredth

33. the nearest thousandth   **34.** the nearest ten-thousandth

Solve each problem. Write whether each number in the newspaper article is *exact* or *rounded*.

35. 2,000

36. $5,189.75

37. $3,468.92

38. $900

DELLWOOD FAIR A SUCCESS

About 2,000 people attended the Dellwood Fair on Saturday. Craft booth sales totaled $5,189.75. Refreshment stand sales totaled $3,468.92. Profits of over $900 are being donated to local charities.

KEEPING IN SHAPE

1. 5)95   **2.** 7)496   **3.** 9)$81.72   **4.** 28)4,675

5. 32 ÷ 4   **6.** $96 ÷ 3   **7.** 244 ÷ 80   **8.** 9,941 ÷ 16

Problem Solving: Strategies

GUESSING AND CHECKING

One way to solve a problem is to guess what the answer might be and then to check your guess. If your guess is not correct, you may be able to see how to make a better guess.

Sandra has $4.20 in quarters and dimes. Altogether she has 21 coins. How many coins of each kind does she have?

Make a guess. Suppose she has 10 quarters. Then she must have 11 dimes, since she has 21 coins altogether. Find how much 10 quarters and 11 dimes are worth.

$$
\begin{array}{rr}
10 \times \$.25 = & \$2.50 \\
11 \times \$.10 = & +\ 1.10 \\
\hline
& \$3.60
\end{array}
$$

$3.60 is too small an amount. Make another guess. Try more quarters. Suppose she has 16 quarters. Then she must have 5 dimes.

$$
\begin{array}{rr}
16 \times \$.25 = & \$4.00 \\
5 \times \$.10 = & +\ \ .50 \\
\hline
& \$4.50
\end{array}
$$

$4.50 is too large an amount. Make another guess. Try fewer quarters. Suppose she has 14 quarters. Then she must have 7 dimes.

$$
\begin{array}{rr}
14 \times \$.25 = & \$3.50 \\
7 \times \$.10 = & +\ \ .70 \\
\hline
& \$4.20 \ \checkmark
\end{array}
$$

That checks. Sandra has 14 quarters and 7 dimes.

Using the Strategy

Solve each problem.

1. Keith has $.70 in nickels and dimes. He has 10 coins altogether. How many coins of each kind does he have?

2. Amy has $1.90 in quarters and nickels. She has 18 coins altogether. How many coins of each kind does she have?

3. Shu has $3.25 in quarters and dimes. He has 16 coins altogether. How many coins of each kind does he have?

4. Erin has $2.55 in quarters, dimes, and nickels. She has 18 coins altogether. How many coins of each kind does she have?

5. The product of two numbers is 48. Their sum is 16. What are the numbers?

6. The sum of two numbers is 115. Their difference is 29. What are the numbers?

7. Joel bought 30 stamps for $4.53. Some of them were $.22 stamps, and some of them were $.13 stamps. How many of each type did he buy?

8. Eve bought 34 stamps for $5.02. Some of them were $.17 stamps, and some of them were $.13 stamps. How many of each type did she buy?

 ACTIVITY

MAKING A LIST

You have a penny, a nickel, a dime, a quarter, and a half-dollar in your pocket. You are going to take out two coins. Make a list of all the different possibilities. You can use P to stand for the penny, N to stand for the nickel, and so on.

One possibility is PN, the penny and the nickel. NP is not considered a different possibility, since NP also means the penny and the nickel. Altogether, there are 10 different possibilities.

Adding Decimals

■ Add decimals as you would whole numbers.

Linda made a food mixture for wild birds. She used 62.78 kilograms of sunflower seed and 33.24 kilograms of cracked corn. How many kilograms of food mix did she make?

Add 62.78 and 33.24 to find how many kilograms.

Line up the decimal points. Add the hundredths. Regroup.

$$\begin{array}{r} 1 \\ 62.78 \\ +33.24 \\ \hline 2 \end{array}$$

Add the tenths. Regroup.

$$\begin{array}{r} 1\ 1 \\ 62.78 \\ +33.24 \\ \hline 02 \end{array}$$

Add the whole numbers. Write the decimal point in the sum.

$$\begin{array}{r} 1\ 1 \\ 62.78 \\ +33.24 \\ \hline 96.02 \end{array}$$

Linda made 96.02 kilograms of food mix for wild birds.

■ Sometimes you add decimals with different numbers of decimal places.

Add: 26 + 0.17 + 9.2 + 3.405

Write equivalent decimals for 26, 0.17, and 9.2.

$$\begin{array}{r} 26.000 \\ 0.170 \\ 9.200 \\ +3.405 \\ \hline \end{array}$$

Add. Write the decimal point in the sum.

$$\begin{array}{r} 1 \\ 26.000 \\ 0.170 \\ 9.200 \\ 3.405 \\ \hline 38.775 \end{array}$$

Try These

Add.

1. $\begin{array}{r} 3.1 \\ +24.6 \\ \hline \end{array}$

2. $\begin{array}{r} \$16.09 \\ +\ \ 7.05 \\ \hline \end{array}$

3. $\begin{array}{r} 35.375 \\ +\ 9.50 \\ \hline \end{array}$

4. $\begin{array}{r} 20.05 \\ +16.955 \\ \hline \end{array}$

5. $\begin{array}{r} 140.15 \\ +386.25 \\ \hline \end{array}$

6. $8.06 + $21.75

7. 3.8 + 42 + 7.56

8. 0.346 + 9.27 + 3.4

Exercises

Add.

1. 2.4
      +1.3

2. $4.78
      + 3.56

3. 11.07
      + 9.8

4. 0.376
      +0.84

5. $32.00
      + 19.68

6. $3.46
      + 2.32

7. 4.6648
      +2.827

8. 26.743
      +39.845

9. $17.31
      + 86.26

10. 312.059
       + 42.1824

11. 3.45
       0.783
       +1.2

12. 24.984
       2.82
       + 0.1259

13. 136.4
       65.96
       + 20.0

14. $4.03
       3.75
       + 1.22

15. 35.7
       1.98
       + 0.1

16. 2.3 + 8.9

17. 8.9 + 2.3

18. $3.86 + $47.00

★ **19.** 20.821 + 1.78 + 20 + 15.64571

★ **20.** 0.86312 + 8.41 + 106

★ **21.** 72.8 + 19.00672 + 127.937 + 58

 Use a calculator.

22. Press ⊞ ⊡ ⑤ ⚌ ⚌ ⚌ ⚌ and continue pressing ⚌ .
Guess which of these numbers will appear on your display.
Then check.

   2.15   5.5   5   10   5.2   2.5   5.55

23. Press ⊞ ⊡ ③ ⚌ ⚌ ⚌ ⚌ and continue pressing ⚌ .
Guess which of these numbers will appear on your display
if you go far enough. Then check them on your calculator.

   5.4   0.54   2.6   1.2   1.33   1.11   3   2

Solve each problem. You may choose paper and pencil or a calculator.

24. During December, Linda used 51.8 kilograms of bird food. During January, she used 71.45 kilograms. How many kilograms of bird food did she use in the 2 months?

25. Norman buys cracked corn for $8.89. He also buys sunflower seed for $11.96 and safflower seed for $3.00. How much money does he spend altogether?

26. Beth buys an 8-kilogram bag of bird food. The bird food costs $12.00. What is the cost per kilogram?

27. During February, Walter used 15.25 kilograms of thistle seed and 12.5 kilograms of safflower seed. Which is the greater amount?

Subtracting Decimals

■ Subtract decimals as you would whole numbers.

Albert works for the Water Department in Brookby County. He has a 0.754-liter sample of water from Jack's River. He uses 0.362 liter of that water to run a bacteria test. How much water is left?

Subtract 0.362 from 0.754 to find the answer.

Line up the decimal points. Subtract the thousandths.	**Regroup. Subtract the hundredths.**	**Subtract the tenths. Write the decimal point in the difference.**
$$\begin{array}{r} 0.754 \\ -0.362 \\ \hline 2 \end{array}$$	$$\begin{array}{r} {}^{6}\,{}^{15} \\ 0.7\,\cancel{5}\,4 \\ -0.3\,6\,2 \\ \hline 9\,2 \end{array}$$	$$\begin{array}{r} {}^{6}\,{}^{15} \\ 0.7\,\cancel{5}\,4 \\ -0.3\,6\,2 \\ \hline 0.3\,9\,2 \end{array}$$

0.392 liter of water is left.

■ Sometimes you subtract decimals with different numbers of decimal places.

Subtract: 7.2 − 0.35

Write an equivalent decimal for 7.2.	**Subtract.**	**Check.**
$$\begin{array}{r} 7.20 \\ -0.35 \end{array}$$	$$\begin{array}{r} {}^{11} \\ {}^{6}\,\cancel{7}\,{}^{10} \\ 7.\cancel{2}\,\cancel{0} \\ -0.3\,5 \\ \hline 6.8\,5 \end{array}$$	$$\begin{array}{r} 6.85 \\ +0.35 \\ \hline 7.20 \end{array}\ \checkmark$$

Try These

Subtract. Check each answer.

1. $\begin{array}{r} 300.3 \\ -182.4 \end{array}$ 2. $\begin{array}{r} 3.065 \\ -1.548 \end{array}$ 3. $\begin{array}{r} \$82.65 \\ -\ \ 13.77 \end{array}$ 4. $\begin{array}{r} 7.86 \\ -2.903 \end{array}$ 5. $\begin{array}{r} 3.1 \\ -0.008 \end{array}$

6. 5.9 − 1.6   7. 6.75 − 0.467   8. 12.064 − 9.38

Exercises

Subtract.

1. 12.7
－ 1.8

2. 3.76
－2.812

3. 0.645
－0.643

4. 8.962
－8

5. $26.47
－ 13.98

6. 30.4
－29.61

7. 4
－3.1

8. 94.03
－37.8

9. $72.19
－ 19.71

10. 300.0942
－256.879

11. 0.75
－0.3684

12. 30.4
－ 0.569

13. $10.01
－ 9.26

14. 136.5
－ 28.74

15. 16.9973
－ 1.0709

16. 7.8 － 2.93

17. $35.00 － $17.45

18. 8.45 － 5.186

19. $4.78 － $1.25

20. 407.4 － 9.3216

21. 60.133 － 45.0655

Copy and complete.

★ **22.** 32.54 － ▦ = 30.94

★ **23.** 3.4 － ▦ = 0.554

★ **24.** 18.3 － ▦ = 12.01

**Add or subtract.
Use a calculator to check.**

25. $95.71
＋ 75.95

26. 2.025
－0.621

27. 405.6
＋299.2

28. 3.20
－1.759

29. 9.8
－0.375

30. 0.842 － 0.59

31. $46.90 － $18.00

32. 41.46 － 12.2864

Solve each problem. You may choose paper and pencil or a calculator.

33. This is a map of an area in Brookby County. How many kilometers long is the shorter trail from Trail Head to Jack's River? How many kilometers farther is the longer trail?

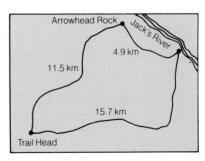

34. Albert keeps a record of the rainfall in Brookby County. In January, it rained 4.8 centimeters. The normal rainfall for January is 7.2 centimeters. How many centimeters below normal was the rainfall?

★ **35.** Albert makes a mixture of 0.5 liter of water and 0.275 liter of a chemical. He uses 0.395 liter of the mixture for Test A. How much will be left if he uses another 0.185 liter for Test B?

Decimals: Addition and Subtraction   115

Estimating Sums and Differences

■ Mr. Esposito works in a lumberyard. Yesterday he put 41.3 gallons of gas in the company truck. Today he put in 27.4 gallons. Estimate the number of gallons he put in altogether.

To find the answer, estimate the sum of 41.3 and 27.4.

Circle the first digit of each addend.
Round each number to the circled place.
Then add to estimate the sum.

$$
\begin{array}{r}
④1.3 \longrightarrow 40 \\
+②7.4 \longrightarrow +30 \\
\hline
70
\end{array}
$$

He put in about 70 gallons altogether.

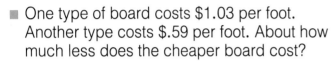

■ One type of board costs $1.03 per foot. Another type costs $.59 per foot. About how much less does the cheaper board cost?

To find about how much less, estimate the difference between $1.03 and $.59.

Circle the first digit in each number.
Round each number to the circled place.
Then subtract to estimate the difference.

$$
\begin{array}{r}
\$①.03 \longrightarrow \$1.00 \\
- \quad ⑤9 \longrightarrow - \quad .60 \\
\hline
\$ \ .40
\end{array}
$$

The cheaper board costs about $.40 less per foot.

■ You can also use estimation to check addition and subtraction.

$$
\begin{array}{r}
⑤23.735 \longrightarrow 500 \\
+③71.62 \longrightarrow +400 \\
\hline
895.355 \qquad 900
\end{array}
$$

The sum seems reasonable since 895.355 is close to 900.

$$
\begin{array}{r}
⑧2.61 \longrightarrow 80 \\
-③1.8 \longrightarrow -30 \\
\hline
50.81 \qquad 50
\end{array}
$$

The difference seems reasonable since 50.81 is close to 50.

Try These

Estimate each answer.

| **1.** 7.8 $+1.2$ | **2.** 68.01 -31.92 | **3.** 18.96 $+\ 8.04$ | **4.** $\$.75$ $+\ .24$ | **5.** 672.1 -121.8 |

6. $\$4.16 - \$2.89$ **7.** $46.472 + 22.9$ **8.** $5.89 - 2.1$

Exercises

Estimate each answer.

| **1.** 7.98 -4.29 | **2.** 3.51 $+9.68$ | **3.** 15.14 $-\ 8.96$ | **4.** $\$6.73$ $-\ 1.89$ | **5.** 365.2 $+123.6$ |

| **6.** 7.24 -4.345 | **7.** $\$3.45$ $-\ 1.85$ | **8.** 5.836 -0.98 | **9.** 69.34 $+18.365$ | **10.** 28.05 $+\ 5.79$ |

11. $3.46 + 7.83$ **12.** $2.38 - 0.967$ **13.** $\$315.08 - \$126.75$
14. $32.19 - 18.95$ **15.** $\$42.50 + \$62.95$ **16.** $85.05 - 49.64$
17. $64.38 + 7.2$ **18.** $5.91 + 0.8$ **19.** $82.04 - 5.763$

Use estimation to decide whether each answer is reasonable.
Write *yes* if it is reasonable and *no* if it is not reasonable.

| **20.** 44.1 $+19.18$ $\overline{63.28}$ | **21.** $\$38.59$ $-\ 17.11$ $\overline{\$29.48}$ | **22.** 9.2 $+3.15$ $\overline{18.35}$ | **23.** 11.8 $-\ 6.7$ $\overline{8.1}$ | **24.** 104.96 $+\ 86.5$ $\overline{291.46}$ |

Decide if you need an estimate or an exact answer. Then solve.

25. Mr. Kwan is redecorating the living room. He bought a piece of paneling for $19.55 including tax. He paid with a $50 bill. About how much change should he receive?

26. Kim rode her bicycle 1.6 miles to a friend's house. Then she rode 3.1 miles to the lumberyard and 1.8 miles home. How far did she ride altogether?

★ **27.** Daniel runs the forklift at the lumberyard. He works from 7:00 A.M. to 2:00 P.M. He works 6 days each week and earns $6.85 per hour. How much does Daniel earn in 4 weeks?

★ **28.** It takes Eileen about 30 minutes to assemble 1 shelving unit. She is going to assemble 32 shelving units. If she works on this project 4 hours per day, about how many days will it take her?

Problem Solving: Applications

CHECKBOOK RECORD

■ Jennifer Mason wrote a check to pay for some new shoes.

This check tells the First National Bank that Ms. Mason wants the bank to take $37.84 from her checking account and pay it to the Johnson Shoe Company.

Jennifer Mason 512
200 W. 16th Street
San Jose, California   *April 7* 19 *86*
Pay to the Order of *Johnson Shoe Co.* $ *37.84*
Thirty-Seven and *84/100* ———— Dollars
First National Bank
⑈3ᬂ00ᬂ39⑈:035·ᬂ6ᬂ2095⑈ᬂ0513   *Jennifer Mason*

The entry at the top of the balance column shows that there was $826.37 in Ms. Mason's account before she wrote the check. She then recorded the information in her checkbook record.

She wrote the date, the check number, and the name of the company. Then she wrote the amount of the check in the withdrawal column and in the balance column. She subtracted the amount of the check from her balance and wrote the difference on the next line of the balance column.

Date	Check Number	Description	Withdrawal		Deposit		Balance	
							826	37
4-7	512	Johnson Shoe	37	84			37	84
							788	53
4-9		Deposit			373	12	373	12
							1,161	65

■ On April 9, Ms. Mason made a deposit of $373.12. She wrote the date in the first column and the word "Deposit" in the third column. Then she wrote the amount of the deposit in the deposit column and in the balance column. She added the amount of the deposit to her new balance and wrote the sum on the next line of the balance column.

Try These

Copy Ms. Mason's checkbook record. Enter each check and deposit in the record, and find each balance.

1. On April 10, she deposited $200.

2. On April 12, she wrote this check to Haas Auto.

Jennifer Mason	513
200 W. 16th Street	
San Jose, California	*April 12* 19*86*

Pay to the Order of *Haas Auto* $ *40.25*

Forty and ²⁵/₁₀₀ ———————— Dollars

First National Bank

⑆3400139⑈035·1612095⑈0513   *Jennifer Mason*

Exercises

Copy Mr. Stover's checkbook record below. Enter each check and deposit in the record, and find each balance.

1. On February 27, Mr. Stover wrote check #658 to Green Bros. for $27.00.

2. On March 1, he deposited $672.29.

3. On March 3, he wrote check #659 to PG&E for $75.32.

4. On March 3, he also wrote check #660 to Pacific Bell for $51.13.

5. On March 4, he made a deposit of $65.10.

6. On March 7, he wrote check #661 to Steven Goldstone for $50.00.

7. On March 8, he wrote check #662 to Yellowstone Hardware for $76.65.

8. On March 11, he deposited $314.00.

Date	Check Number	Description	Withdrawal	Deposit	Balance	
					403	50

CHAPTER CHECKPOINT

Write a decimal to tell how much is shaded. (pp. 102–103)

1. 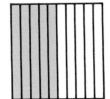   2. 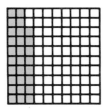   3.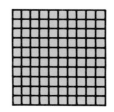

Write an equivalent decimal. (pp. 102–103)

4. 0.80   **5.** 0.4   **6.** 4.30   **7.** 26.50   **8.** 3.6   **9.** 82.90

Write as a decimal. (pp. 102–105)

10. 9 and 5 tenths   **11.** 625 thousandths

12. 214 and 56 thousandths   **13.** 42 and 96 hundredths

14. thirty-five thousandths   **15.** twelve and fifty-two hundredths

What does the digit 2 mean in each number? (pp. 104–105)

16. 25.146   **17.** 4.752   **18.** 33.026   **19.** 43.2689   **20.** 19.00126

Write >, <, or =. (pp. 106–107)

21. 0.9 ▧ 0.90   **22.** 2.06 ▧ 2.05   **23.** 37.187 ▧ 36.796

24. 1.6 ▧ 1.600   **25.** 0.19 ▧ 0.9   **26.** 45.687 ▧ 45.678

Write in order from least to greatest. (pp. 106–107)

27. 7.086   7.860   7.680   7.186

28. 34.357   33.457   34.753   37.453

Round to the nearest tenth. (pp. 108–109)

29. 8.24   **30.** 9.75   **31.** 25.086   **32.** 83.316   **33.** 95.895

Round to the nearest hundredth. (pp. 108–109)

34. 7.084   **35.** 16.248   **36.** 39.007   **37.** 126.0943   **38.** 62.5762

Add or subtract. (pp. 112–115)

39. 6.8
      +1.3

40. 3.46
      −2.817

41. 26.961
      − 8

42. $64.00
      + 18.62

43. 24.68
       5.967
      + 0.2

44. 14.8
      − 9.9

45. $3.27
      + 1.86

46. $20.00
      − 9.75

47. 0.487
      +0.933

48. 200.8641
      − 97.367

49. 3.45 + 8.26 + 9.76   **50.** 30.06 − 9.2   **51.** 0.015 + 0.75 + 3

Estimate each answer. (pp. 116–117)

52. 6.79
      −3.16

53. $4.59
      + 2.13

54. 16.418
      − 8.8692

55. 37.4
      + 1.893

56. $312.08
      − 187.94

Decide if you need an estimate or an exact answer. Then solve. (pp. 102–117)

57. During June, Mrs. Avery sold 52.8 kilograms of beans. During July, she sold 61.9 kilograms of beans. How many kilograms of beans did she sell in the 2 months?

58. Amelia drove 28.6 kilometers in the morning. Then she drove 52.4 kilometers in the afternoon. About how far did she drive in all?

59. Jim bought a shirt for $9.62 including tax. He paid with a $20 bill. Estimate his change.

60. Fred had 13.4 meters of wire. He cut off 1.6 meters to use to hang a picture. How much wire was left?

Copy Ms. Bloom's checkbook record. Enter each check and deposit in the record, and find each balance. (pp. 118–119)

61. On December 6, Ms. Bloom wrote check #253 for $31.76 to E-Z Hardware.

62. On December 8, she deposited $300.00.

63. On December 9, she wrote check #254 for $80.00 to Pat Durr.

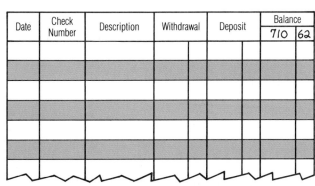

Date	Check Number	Description	Withdrawal	Deposit	Balance
					710 62

COMPUTERS AND
PROBLEM SOLVING

■ If one number is not divisible by another, the quotient will contain a decimal.

<table>
<tr><td>Type:</td><td>]PRINT 10 / 3</td></tr>
<tr><td>The computer displays:</td><td>3.33333333

]▤</td></tr>
</table>

Suppose you want to know how many groups of 3 are in 10. Use the INT function to separate the integer, or whole number, from the decimal.

<table>
<tr><td>Type:</td><td>]PRINT INT (10 / 3)</td></tr>
<tr><td>The computer displays:</td><td>3

]▤</td></tr>
</table>

■ INT is a function. A function tells the computer how to treat a number, or what part of a number to use. Always use a statement like LET, PRINT, or one of the arithmetic operators, with a function.

INT finds and removes the decimal part of a number.

```
]PRINT INT (88)
88

]▤
```

```
]LET A = INT
   (1.99999999)
]PRINT A
1

]▤
```

The program below uses the INT function to help you understand how rounding works.

```
NEW
10   PRINT "TYPE A NUMBER FOR ME TO ROUND."
20   PRINT "GIVE IT ONE DECIMAL PLACE."
30   INPUT NUMBER
40   LET TNUMBER = NUMBER − INT (NUMBER)
50   IF TNUMBER < .5 THEN GOTO 70
60   LET RNUMBER = INT (NUMBER) + 1: GOTO 80
70   LET RNUMBER = INT (NUMBER)
80   PRINT "THE NUMBER ROUNDS TO ";
90   PRINT RNUMBER; "."
100  END
```

Solve each problem.

1. What happens in line 40 of the program?

2. What place does this program round to?

3. When you round, you look at the digit to the right to decide whether to round down or up. How is rounding done in this program?

★ 4. Change line 20 to PRINT "GIVE IT TWO DECIMAL PLACES." Add two lines to make it possible to round to tenths using this program. [Hint: you will have to move the decimal point so the program looks at hundredths instead of tenths.]

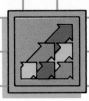

ENRICHMENT

AN UNSOLVED PROBLEM

There are some problems in mathematics for which no one knows the answer yet. They are called **unsolved problems**.

Imagine a machine that works like this:

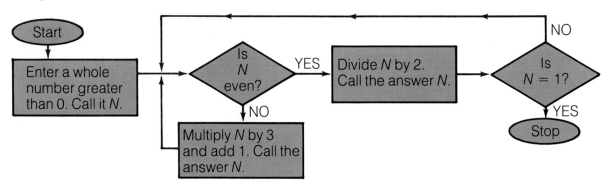

What does the machine do if you enter the number 10?
Follow these steps in the flow chart.

10   First, it lets N equal 10.
↓   Since N is even, it divides N by 2.

5   The answer, 5, becomes the new N.
↓   Since N is not 1, the machine again asks "Is N even?"
↓   Since N is now odd, it multiplies N by 3 and adds 1.

16   The answer, 16, becomes the new N.
↓   Since N is now even, it divides N by 2.

8   The answer, 8, becomes the new N.

The machine keeps dividing by 2 until the answer is 1.
Then it stops.

The complete sequence can be written like this:

$$10 \longrightarrow 5 \longrightarrow 16 \longrightarrow 8 \longrightarrow 4 \longrightarrow 2 \longrightarrow 1$$

The unsolved problem is this: For every whole number greater than 0, will the machine finally get to 1 and stop? The problem is called "unsolved" because no one knows the answer for sure.

Show that the machine finally gets to 1 for each of the following numbers. Write each complete sequence.

1. 4   **2.** 21   **3.** 16   **4.** 6

5. 13   **6.** 7   **7.** 17   **8.** 25

Write each number.

1. 86 thousand 216

2. 37 hundredths

3. eight hundred thousand and forty-nine thousandths

4. thirty-one billion, nine hundred thousand, one hundred one

Write >, <, or =.

5. 670 ▓ 607

6. 48.71 ▓ 48.17

7. 357,290 ▓ 357,209

8. 81.7 ▓ 8.71

9. 3.226 ▓ 3.2260

10. 16,346,124 ▓ 16,364,124

Compute.

11. 75
    +26

12. 25
    × 8

13. 3,000
    − 1,624

14. $8.15
    ×   46

15. 756
      89
    +275

16. 50
    × 6

17. 9.7
    −4.8

18. 265
    × 20

19. $15.89
    + 64.95

20. 821
    ×357

Divide.

21. 6)38

22. 30)975

23. 46)5,483

24. 75)64,389

Estimate each answer.

25. 387 + 196

26. $51.19 − $18.67

27. 61 × 22

28. 7,196 ÷ 80

29. 467.6 + 310.4

30. 875 × 47

Solve each problem.

31. Mr. Moyer bought a bicycle for $146.15. He gave the cashier $150.00. How much change should Mr. Moyer receive?

32. A factory has 30,480 cans of tomatoes to pack. 60 cans are packed in each case. How many cases can be filled?

33. The shop ordered 18 bicycles. Each bicycle cost $87.50. What was the total cost?

34. Harry walked 3.7 miles. Betty walked 4.5 miles. How much farther did Betty walk?

SKILLS CHECK

Choose the correct answer.

1. Round 641 to the nearest ten.

    a. 600
    b. 640
    c. 650
    d. 700

2.
$$\begin{array}{r} \$12.59 \\ + \quad 3.87 \\ \hline \end{array}$$

    a. $15.36
    b. $16.27
    c. $16.45
    d. $16.46

3.
$$\begin{array}{r} 500 \\ - 186 \\ \hline \end{array}$$

    a. 314
    b. 324
    c. 386
    d. 686

4. Compute: 8^3

    a. 24
    b. 512
    c. 6,561
    d. NG

5.
$$\begin{array}{r} 316 \\ \times 194 \\ \hline \end{array}$$

    a. 4,624
    b. 48,404
    c. 61,304
    d. NG

6. $6\overline{)35}$

    a. 5 R2
    b. 5 R5
    c. 6 R1
    d. 7

7. $26,413 \div 3$

    a. 765 R2
    b. 5,201 R1
    c. 8,131 R2
    d. 8,804 R1

8. Which sentence is correct?

    a. $9.05 > 9.050$
    b. $9.05 < 9.050$
    c. $9.05 = 9.050$

9.
$$\begin{array}{r} 30.086 \\ - \quad 9.29 \\ \hline \end{array}$$

    a. 20.796
    b. 20.984
    c. 21.37
    d. 39.376

10. Jacob ordered 420 books for his bookstore. 188 of the books arrived. How many books were not delivered?

    a. 242 books
    b. 588 books
    c. 608 books
    d. NG

11. A track is 350 meters long. Beth ran around the track 5 times. How many meters did she run?

    a. 70 meters
    b. 950 meters
    c. 1,750 meters
    d. 1,875 meters

12. Mary has 8.6 kilograms of soil. She buys a bag of soil that weighs 12.75 kilograms. How much soil does Mary have?

    a. 4.15 kilograms
    b. 13.61 kilograms
    c. 21.35 kilograms
    d. NG

5

DECIMALS:
MULTIPLICATION AND DIVISION

Multiplying Decimals

■ The space shuttle moves at a speed of 7.8 kilometers per second in space. How far does it travel in 3 seconds?

Multiply 7.8 by 3 to find how far.

Multiply decimals as you would whole numbers.

$$
\begin{array}{r}
7.8 \\
\times\ 3 \\
\hline
234
\end{array}
$$

Estimate to help place the decimal point.

$$
\begin{array}{r}
7.8 \longrightarrow\ 8 \\
\times\ 3 \longrightarrow \times 3 \\
\hline
24
\end{array}
$$
←— So, the decimal product is about 24.

Place the decimal point in the product.

$$
\begin{array}{r}
7.8 \\
\times\ 3 \\
\hline
23.4
\end{array}
$$

The space shuttle travels 23.4 kilometers in 3 seconds.

■ You can add the number of decimal places in the factors to place the decimal point in the product.

Multiply: 2.7 × 6.39

$$
\begin{array}{r}
6.39 \\
\times\ 2.7 \\
\hline
4\ 4\ 7\ 3 \\
1\ 2\ 7\ 8\ 0 \\
\hline
1\ 7.2\ 5\ 3
\end{array}
$$

6.39 ←— 2 decimal places
× 2.7 ←— 1 decimal place
17.253 ←— 3 decimal places

Count off as many decimal places in the product as there are in the two factors.

$2 + 1 = 3$

Then check by estimating.
6.39 × 2.7 is about 6 × 3, or 18.
17.253 seems reasonable.

■ Multiply: 0.9 × 6.2

6.2 ←— 1 decimal place
× 0.9 ←— 1 decimal place
5.5 8 ←— 2 decimal places

Multiply: 4 × 3.1

3.1 ←— 1 decimal place
× 4 ←— 0 decimal places
12.4 ←— 1 decimal place

Try These

Multiply.

1. 2.8 ×6.4	**2.** 3.7 ×0.5	**3.** 29.1 × 8	**4.** $42.83 × 5.6	**5.** 73.04 × 0.92

6. 1.8 × 74

7. 0.45 × 20.6

8. 3.07 × 1.264

Exercises

Multiply.

1. 7.3 ×2.5	**2.** 19.4 × 0.6	**3.** 82.4 × 13	**4.** 76 ×4.2	**5.** $38.05 × 9.7
6. 45.8 ×0.32	**7.** $6.61 × 5.8	**8.** 19.07 × 40	**9.** 6.321 × 5.5	**10.** 0.457 × 6.82

11. 67 × $41.83

12. 0.215 × 7.36

13. 0.03 × 27.4

14. 4.09 × 1,367

15. 82.4 × 0.35

16. 60.1 × 3.478

Here is how to find the distance between you and a flash of lightning. Sound travels at about 0.34 kilometer per second. When you see the flash, count the number of seconds until you hear the thunder. Then multiply the number of seconds by 0.34 kilometer.

These were times between seeing the flash and hearing the thunder. For each time, find how far away the lightning was.

17. 5 seconds

18. 13 seconds

19. 9.5 seconds

Solve each problem.

20. One type of astronaut's lunch weighs 357.2 grams. Each lunch contains 50 grams of whole wheat bread. How much would 12 of these lunches weigh?

21. Ms. Parker has 3.5 hours to get to the space shuttle site in time for the launch. The site is 260 kilometers away. If she drives an average of 80 kilometers per hour, will she make it?

22. A satellite is traveling at a speed of 3.27 kilometers per second. How far does it travel in 9.2 seconds?

★ **23.** A rocket is moving at 40.908 kilometers per second. How far will it travel in 1.5 minutes?

More Multiplying Decimals

- Sometimes you need to write one or more 0s in the product in order to place the decimal point.

Multiply: 0.3×0.26

$$
\begin{array}{r}
0.26 \longleftarrow \text{2 decimal places} \\
\times\ 0.3 \longleftarrow \text{1 decimal place} \\
\hline
0.0\,7\,8 \longleftarrow \text{3 decimal places}
\end{array}
$$

Multiply: 0.3×0.026

$$
\begin{array}{r}
0.026 \longleftarrow \text{3 decimal places} \\
\times\ \ 0.3 \longleftarrow \text{1 decimal place} \\
\hline
0.0\,0\,7\,8 \longleftarrow \text{4 decimal places}
\end{array}
$$

- Dolores Ruiz bought 0.43 pound of potatoes. The potatoes cost $.19 per pound. What was the total cost?

Multiply $.19 by 0.43 to find the total cost.

$$
\begin{array}{r}
\$.19 \\
\times 0.43 \\
\hline
5\,7 \\
7\,6\,0 \\
\hline
\$.0\,8\,1\,7
\end{array}
$$

$.0817 rounded to the nearest cent is $.08.
The cost of the potatoes was $.08.

Try These

Multiply.

1. $\begin{array}{r} 1.2 \\ \times 0.03 \\ \hline \end{array}$

2. $\begin{array}{r} 0.045 \\ \times\ \ 0.6 \\ \hline \end{array}$

3. $\begin{array}{r} .13 \\ \times 0.47 \\ \hline \end{array}$

4. $\begin{array}{r} 2.81 \\ \times 0.07 \\ \hline \end{array}$

5. $\begin{array}{r} 0.023 \\ \times\ \ 0.05 \\ \hline \end{array}$

6. 9×0.008

7. 3.4×81.6

8. 0.04×0.127

Multiply. Then round each product to the nearest cent.

9. $0.8 \times \$.11$

10. $2.7 \times \$3.59$

11. $0.46 \times \$.15$

Exercises

Multiply.

1. 3.4×0.02
2. 0.051×0.7
3. 2.1×0.6
4. 0.006×5
5. 0.43×0.22

6. 3.42×0.08
7. 0.09×0.07
8. 21×0.004
9. 0.012×0.05
10. 0.014×0.7

11. 0.06×1.34
12. 0.13×0.097
13. 1.8×3.142
14. $\$3.25 \times 0.03$
15. 25×0.008
16. 0.16×0.022

Multiply. Then round each product to the nearest cent.

17. $0.6 \times \$.12$
18. $0.9 \times \$.43$
19. $4.62 \times \$3.07$

Compute.

20. $(18.4 + 12) \times 6.4$
21. $(5 \times 0.006) \times 4.8$
22. $2.07 \times (15 - 3.89)$
23. $(0.7 \times 36) - 9.51$
24. $42.07 + (81.4 - 34)$
25. $(7.1 + 2.06) \times 0.005$

 Find this product on a calculator: 823 × 464. Find each of the following products without using the calculator. Then use the calculator to check each answer.

26. 82.3×4.64
27. 8.23×46.4
28. 823×0.464
29. 82.3×0.464
30. 8.23×4.64
31. 0.823×4.64
32. 0.823×46.4
33. 0.823×464
34. 0.823×0.464

Solve each problem. You may choose paper and pencil or a calculator.

35. Mr. Ruiz is planning to make roast beef for 8 people. Then he learns that 4 more people are coming. He estimates that each person will eat 0.6 pound of meat. How much meat should Mr. Ruiz buy?

36. Mrs. Ruiz bought 0.32 pound of onions. The onions cost $.30 per pound. How much did Mrs. Ruiz pay for the onions? Round the answer to the nearest cent.

37. Another time, Mr. Ruiz bought a 7.5-pound rib roast. Use the chart to find how long he should roast it if he wants it to be rare.

Roasting Time	
rare	24 minutes per pound
medium	28 minutes per pound
well-done	34 minutes per pound

Problem Solving: Strategies

GENERALIZING

Sometimes you can solve a problem by **finding a pattern**.

There was a multimillionaire who had $100,000,000. He decided to give some of his fortune to his five grandchildren. He gave 0.1 of his fortune to his first grandchild. To the second, he gave 0.1 of the amount he had given the first. He gave each remaining grandchild 0.1 of the amount he had given the one before.

Here is the pattern he used to find the amount each grandchild would receive.

first: $0.1 \times \$100,000,000 = \$10,000,000$

second: $0.1 \times \$10,000,000 = \$1,000,000$

third: $0.1 \times \$1,000,000 = \$100,000$

Use the pattern to predict what the fourth and fifth grandchildren received.

Complete the pattern to check your prediction.

first: $0.1 \times \$100,000,000 = \$10,000,000$

second: $0.1 \times \$10,000,000 = \$1,000,000$

third: $0.1 \times \$1,000,000 = \$100,000$

fourth: $0.1 \times \$100,000 = \$10,000$

fifth: $0.1 \times \$10,000 = \$1,000$

Using the Strategy

Solve each problem.

1. Altogether, how much money did the multimillionaire give to his grandchildren?

2. How much of his $100,000,000 was left?

Since the multimillionaire still had more than $80,000,000 left, he decided to give the fifth grandchild 0.1 of $80,000,000. He gave the fourth grandchild 0.1 of the additional amount he had just given the fifth. He gave the third grandchild 0.1 of the additional amount he had just given the fourth, and so on.

Here is the pattern.

$$\begin{aligned}
\text{fifth:} \quad & 0.1 \times \$80,000,000 = \$8,000,000 \\
\text{fourth:} \quad & 0.1 \times \$8,000,000 = \$800,000 \\
\text{third:} \quad & 0.1 \times \$800,000 = \\
\text{second:} \quad & \\
\text{first:} \quad &
\end{aligned}$$

3. Use the pattern to predict the additional amounts the third, second, and first grandchildren received.

4. Copy and complete the pattern to check your prediction.

5. How much did each grandchild receive in all?

6. Which grandchild received the most money?

 ACTIVITY

FINDING PATTERNS

Compute.

1. 11×11 **2.** 111×111 **3.** $1,111 \times 1,111$

Use the pattern in exercises 1–3 to predict each answer.
Then compute.

4. $11,111 \times 11,111$ **5.** $111,111 \times 111,111$

Compute.

6. $9 \times 2,222$ **7.** $9 \times 3,333$ **8.** $9 \times 4,444$

Use the pattern in exercises 6–8 to predict each answer.
Then compute.

9. $9 \times 5,555$ **10.** $9 \times 6,666$

Dividing a Decimal by a Whole Number

■ John has a pedometer. It measures how far he walks. It shows that he walked 9.75 kilometers while mowing 3 lawns. What was the average number of kilometers he walked mowing each lawn?

Divide 9.75 by 3 to find the average.

Divide decimals as you would whole numbers.

$$
\begin{array}{r}
3\ 25 \\
3\overline{)9.75} \\
9 \\
\hline
7 \\
6 \\
\hline
15 \\
15 \\
\hline
0
\end{array}
$$

Estimate to place the decimal point.

$$3\overline{)9.75} \longrightarrow 3\overline{)10} \quad \begin{array}{l} 3 \end{array}$$

← So the decimal quotient is about 3.

Place the decimal point in the quotient.

$$
\begin{array}{r}
3.25 \\
3\overline{)9.75} \\
9 \\
\hline
7 \\
6 \\
\hline
15 \\
15 \\
\hline
0
\end{array}
$$

John walked an average of 3.25 kilometers mowing each lawn.

■ When dividing a decimal by a whole number, place the decimal point in the answer above the decimal point in the dividend.

Divide: $12\overline{)0.6024}$

Place the decimal point.

$$12\overline{)0.6024}$$

Divide.

$$
\begin{array}{r}
0.0502 \\
12\overline{)0.6024} \\
60 \\
\hline
2 \\
0 \\
\hline
24 \\
24 \\
\hline
0
\end{array}
$$

Check.

$$
\begin{array}{r}
0.0502 \\
\times\ \ \ \ 12 \\
\hline
1004 \\
5020 \\
\hline
0.6024 \ \checkmark
\end{array}
$$

Try These

Divide. Check each answer.

1. $8\overline{)9.76}$ **2.** $4\overline{)\$13.36}$ **3.** $16\overline{)1.232}$ **4.** $7\overline{)4.2}$

5. $\$29.16 \div 27$ **6.** $0.609 \div 3$ **7.** $98.4 \div 2$

Exercises

Divide.

1. $7\overline{)2.1}$ **2.** $9\overline{)12.6}$ **3.** $25\overline{)\$27.25}$ **4.** $3\overline{)0.072}$

5. $18\overline{)54.72}$ **6.** $9\overline{)0.1404}$ **7.** $6\overline{)6.054}$ **8.** $3\overline{)\$6.72}$

9. $25\overline{)0.0825}$ **10.** $4\overline{)\$8.04}$ **11.** $12\overline{)250.8}$ **12.** $14\overline{)42.056}$

13. $5.325 \div 5$ **14.** $64.64 \div 4$ **15.** $0.1095 \div 5$
16. $\$3.84 \div 8$ **17.** $9.018 \div 9$ **18.** $12.096 \div 24$

Compute.

19. $(17.48 + 6.7) \div 6$ **20.** $5.2 \times (19 - 3.54)$ **21.** $(16.08 \div 4) \times 0.05$
22. $(280.35 \div 45) + 7.8$ **23.** $29.8 - (34.051 \div 17)$ **24.** $2.35 \times (4.6 + 9.21)$

Solve each problem.

25. John spends $19.25 at the garden center for 5 kilograms of grass seed. What is the price of each kilogram of seed?

26. Ms. Satz paid John $15.00 to prepare the ground for a vegetable garden. John worked for 4 hours. How much did John earn each hour?

27. John used scrap lumber to repair Mrs. Durst's fence. The pieces he used measured 3.1 meters, 4.3 meters, and 2.8 meters. How many 2-meter sections can John cut from this wood?

★ **28.** John buys fertilizer in 30-kilogram bags. He pays $25.20 for 2 bags of garden fertilizer and $87.30 for 3 bags of lawn fertilizer. How much more does the lawn fertilizer cost per kilogram than the garden fertilizer?

 KEEPING IN SHAPE

Estimate each answer.

1. $6.27 + 4.93$ **2.** $32.45 - 18.6$ **3.** $10.2 - 6.35$ **4.** $8,987 - 4,169$ **5.** $46.57 + 3.382$

6. $8.07 - 1.639$ **7.** $52.6 - 19.74$ **8.** $38.412 + 106.59$
9. $72.4 + 9.63$ **10.** $9,148 + 560$ **11.** $64.5 - 17.25$

Rounding a Quotient

Cheryl does research for a spice manufacturing company. She has 1.32 kilograms of paprika. She wants to divide it into 5 equal parts. About how much should each part weigh? Round the answer to the nearest hundredth of a kilogram.

To find the answer, divide 1.32 by 5 and round the quotient to the nearest hundredth.

To round to the nearest hundredth, you need to know the thousandths place in the quotient.

Place the decimal point.	**Divide.**	**Write a 0 in the dividend. Continue dividing.**

$$
\begin{array}{r}
. \\
5\overline{)1.32}
\end{array}
\qquad
\begin{array}{r}
0.26 \\
5\overline{)1.32} \\
\underline{1\ 0} \\
32 \\
\underline{30} \\
2
\end{array}
\qquad
\begin{array}{r}
0.264 \\
5\overline{)1.320} \\
\underline{1\ 0} \\
32 \\
\underline{30} \\
20 \\
\underline{20} \\
0
\end{array}
$$

1.32 is equivalent to 1.320.

To the nearest hundredth, 0.264 rounds to 0.26.
Each part should weigh about 0.26 kilogram.

Divide 4.7 by 3.
Round to the nearest tenth.

$$
\begin{array}{r}
1.56 \longrightarrow 1.6 \\
3\overline{)4.70} \\
\underline{3} \\
1\ 7 \\
\underline{1\ 5} \\
20 \\
\underline{18} \\
2
\end{array}
$$

Divide 11 by 4.
Round to the nearest hundredth.

$$
\begin{array}{r}
2.75 \longrightarrow 2.75 \\
4\overline{)11.00} \\
\underline{8} \\
3\ 0 \\
\underline{2\ 8} \\
20 \\
\underline{20} \\
0
\end{array}
$$

Try These

Divide. Round each quotient to the nearest tenth.

1. $5\overline{)13.7}$ **2.** $3\overline{)1.76}$ **3.** $4\overline{)4.94}$ **4.** $15\overline{)7}$

Divide. Round each quotient to the nearest hundredth.

5. $2\overline{)4.47}$ **6.** $7\overline{)25}$ **7.** $6\overline{)1.41}$ **8.** $45\overline{)1.107}$

Exercises

Divide. Round each quotient to the nearest tenth.

1. $5\overline{)11.8}$ **2.** $8\overline{)1.85}$ **3.** $9\overline{)13}$ **4.** $7\overline{)0.63}$

5. $14.8 \div 3$ **6.** $4 \div 24$ **7.** $2.66 \div 6$

Divide. Round each quotient to the nearest hundredth.

8. $4\overline{)12.86}$ **9.** $8\overline{)0.344}$ **10.** $9\overline{)2.35}$ **11.** $5\overline{)11.2}$

12. $0.59 \div 5$ **13.** $28 \div 12$ **14.** $7.217 \div 7$

Divide. Round each quotient to the nearest cent.

15. $\$18.76 \div 8$ **16.** $\$42.50 \div 6$ **17.** $\$93.51 \div 15$

Solve each problem. You may use a calculator to check.

18. Cheryl has 17.23 grams of ginger. She wants to divide it into 6 equal parts. About how much will each part weigh? Round the answer to the nearest hundredth.

19. Cheryl spends a total of 34.5 hours working on an experiment over a period of 4 days. That is an average of how many hours per day? Round the answer to the nearest tenth.

20. Each test packet of curry costs $1.90. There are 50 grams in each test packet. What is the price per gram? Round the answer to the nearest cent.

21. Cheryl makes a seasoning mix. She uses 10 grams of pepper, 15 grams of salt, 8.5 grams of ginger, and 7.75 grams of nutmeg. How many grams does she use altogether?

22. Cheryl uses 3.5 grams of cloves in a seasoning mix. She makes 6 batches of the mix. How many grams of cloves does Cheryl use altogether?

★ **23.** 50 grams of cinnamon cost $1.10. What is the price of 20 kilograms of cinnamon?

Problem Solving: Applications

UNIT PRICING

You are buying bran flakes. You see these two boxes. Which is the better buy?

To find the **unit price** for each box, find the price per ounce for each. Divide $1.68 by 15 and $2.89 by 24, and round each quotient to the nearest cent. Then compare the unit prices to find the better buy.

```
    $  .112 ——→ $.11          $  .120 ——→ $.12
 15)$1.680                 24)$2.890
    1 5                        2 4
    ___                        ___
    18                         49
    15                         48
    ___                        ___
    30                         10
    30                          0
    ___                        ___
     0                         10
```

The unit price is about $.11 per ounce.

The unit price is about $.12 per ounce.

15 ounces for $1.68 costs about $.11 per ounce.
24 ounces for $2.89 costs about $.12 per ounce.
So 15 ounces for $1.68 is the better buy.

Try These

Which is the better buy?

1. 10 pounds of potatoes for $2.60 or 25 pounds of potatoes for $5.25

2. 12 ounces of tomato juice for $.89 or 16 ounces of tomato juice for $1.25

3. 6 lemons for $.79 or 8 lemons for $1.10

4. 2 quarts of fruit juice for $1.65 or 5 quarts of fruit juice for $4.00

Exercises

Solve each problem.

1. An 8-ounce bag of peanuts costs $.80. A 12-ounce can of the same kind of peanuts costs $1.08. Which costs less per ounce?

2. A 12-ounce box of Crispy Wheat Crackers costs $.96. A 16-ounce box of D and B Wheat Crisps costs $1.15. Which is the better buy?

3. In one store, oranges are 3 for $.50. In another store, the same kind of oranges are 5 for $.75. Which is the better buy?

4. A box of 6 bran muffins costs $1.38. A box of 12 of the same muffins costs $2.88. Is it better to buy 1 box of 12 or 2 boxes of 6?

5. Brand X apple juice costs $1.14 for a 2-quart bottle. Brand Y apple juice comes in a 1-quart bottle for $.59. Mr. Juno wants 4 quarts of apple juice. Is it better to buy 2 bottles of Brand X or 4 bottles of Brand Y?

6. In Lee's Market, a 5-pound bag of potatoes costs $.79. In Daily's, a 5-pound bag of potatoes costs $.88. Compare the unit prices. How much less does each pound of potatoes cost in Lee's Market?

7. A 4-ounce tube of toothpaste costs $1.25. A 7-ounce tube of the same toothpaste costs $2.15. Which is the better buy?

8. A 15-pound turkey costs $9.75 at C&L Market. A 20-pound turkey costs $12.75 at Kelly Stores. Which store has the better buy?

9. Mrs. Kelly buys 8 ounces of sunflower seeds for $1.84. If the price per ounce is the same, how much would 12 ounces of sunflower seeds cost?

★ 10. A 6-ounce box of raisins costs $.69. A 15-ounce box costs $1.69. A 24-ounce box costs $2.49. You need 30 ounces of raisins. Which boxes should you buy?

Multiplying and Dividing by 10, by 100, and by 1,000

■ Multiply decimals by 10, by 100, and by 1,000. Look for a pattern.

$$\begin{array}{r} 6\,3.4\,2 \\ \times\quad 1\,0 \\ \hline 6\,3\,4.2\,0 \end{array} \qquad \begin{array}{r} 6\,3.4\,2 \\ \times\quad 1\,0\,0 \\ \hline 6,3\,4\,2.0\,0 \end{array} \qquad \begin{array}{r} 6\,3.4\,2 \\ \times\,1,0\,0\,0 \\ \hline 6\,3,4\,2\,0.0\,0 \end{array}$$

There is one 0 in 10. To multiply a decimal by 10, move its decimal point one place to the right.

$10 \times 63.42 = 63.\underset{\curvearrowright}{4}2 = 634.2$

There are two 0s in 100. To multiply a decimal by 100, move its decimal point two places to the right.

$100 \times 63.42 = 63.\underset{\curvearrowright}{4}2 = 6{,}342$

There are three 0s in 1,000. To multiply a decimal by 1,000, move its decimal point three places to the right.

$1{,}000 \times 63.42 = 63.\underset{\curvearrowright}{42}0 = 63{,}420$

■ Divide numbers by 10, by 100, and by 1,000. Look for a pattern.

$$\begin{array}{r} 29.3 \\ 10\overline{)293.0} \end{array} \qquad \begin{array}{r} 2.93 \\ 100\overline{)293.00} \end{array} \qquad \begin{array}{r} 0.293 \\ 1{,}000\overline{)293.000} \end{array}$$

To divide a decimal by 10, move its decimal point one place to the left.

$293 \div 10 = 29\underset{\curvearrowleft}{3.} = 29.3$

To divide a decimal by 100, move its decimal point two places to the left.

$293 \div 100 = 2\underset{\curvearrowleft}{93.} = 2.93$

To divide a decimal by 1,000, move its decimal point three places to the left.

$293 \div 1{,}000 = \underset{\curvearrowleft}{293.} = 0.293$

Try These

Multiply or divide. Do as many as you can mentally.

1. 10×3.645
2. 100×3.645
3. $1{,}000 \times 3.645$
4. 41.28×10
5. 41.28×100
6. $41.28 \times 1{,}000$
7. $7{,}642 \div 10$
8. $7{,}642 \div 100$
9. $7{,}642 \div 1{,}000$
10. $31.2 \div 10$
11. $31.2 \div 100$
12. $31.2 \div 1{,}000$

Exercises

Multiply or divide. Do as many as you can mentally.

1. 10 × 0.3

2. 64 ÷ 10

3. 51.2 × 1,000

4. 18.7 ÷ 100

5. 236 ÷ 1,000

6. 100 × 0.038

7. 9.06 × 1,000

8. 42.1 ÷ 10

9. 375 ÷ 100

10. 520 × 10

11. 1,000 × 0.004

12. 67.2 ÷ 1,000

13. 100 × 37.4

14. 9,431 ÷ 1,000

15. 0.01 ÷ 10

16. 2.66 ÷ 100

17. 42 × 1,000

18. 0.075 × 100

Solve each problem mentally or with paper and pencil.

19. Jim has $13.45 in pennies. He has $4.20 in dimes. How many pennies does he have?

20. Mr. Robertson has 12,432 pennies. How much is that in dollars and cents?

21. A roll of pennies contains 50 pennies. Gina has 10 rolls of pennies. How many dollars is that?

22. Ashani has 472 dimes. How many dimes are there in a dollar? How much does Ashani have in dollars and cents?

THINK AND TRY

FORMING A RULE

How do the answers to a and b compare?

1. a. 365 ÷ 10   **b.** 0.1 × 365   **2. a.** 45.2 ÷ 10   **b.** 0.1 × 45.2

3. a. 245 ÷ 100   **b.** 0.01 × 245   **4. a.** 27 ÷ 100   **b.** 0.01 × 27

5. a. 127 ÷ 1,000 **b.** 0.001 × 127   **6. a.** 52 ÷ 1,000   **b.** 0.001 × 52

7. Make a rule that compares multiplying by 0.1, by 0.01, or by 0.001 to dividing by 10, by 100, or by 1,000.

Use your rule to find each product.

8. 0.1 × 72

9. 0.01 × 454

10. 0.001 × 386

11. 0.01 × 19.6

12. 0.1 × 0.8

13. 0.001 × 17.4

Decimals: Multiplication and Division   141

Dividing by Decimals

■ How are these division problems alike?

$$3\overline{)6}^{\,2} \qquad 30\overline{)60}^{\,2} \qquad 300\overline{)600}^{\,2}$$

Multiply the 3 and the 6 by 10. Multiply the 3 and the 6 by 100.

They all have the same quotient.

If you multiply both the divisor and the dividend by the same number, the quotient remains the same. This is true for any division problem.

In this way, you can change a division problem with a decimal divisor to a division problem with a whole number divisor. The quotients will be the same.

■ Sherry is making yarn dolls. She has 6.72 meters of yarn. She is going to cut it into pieces 0.32 meter long. How many pieces can she cut?

Divide 6.72 by 0.32 to find the number of pieces.

Multiply the divisor and the dividend by 100.

$$0.32\overline{)6.72}$$

Divide.

```
          21.
0.32 )6.72
       6 4
         32
         32
          0
```

Check.

```
    21      ← quotient
  ×0.32     ← original divisor
    42
  6 30
  6.72 ✔   ← original dividend
```

Sherry can cut 21 pieces of yarn.

■ Divide: $0.6\overline{)0.72}$

Multiply the divisor and the dividend by 10.

$$0.6\overline{)0.72}$$

Divide.

```
         1.2
0.6 )0.7 2
      6
      1 2
      1 2
        0
```

Check.

```
    1.2
  ×0.6
   0.72 ✔
```

Try These

Divide. Check each answer.

1. $0.2\overline{)0.24}$ **2.** $0.08\overline{)6.72}$ **3.** $0.3\overline{)0.48}$ **4.** $0.22\overline{)90.64}$

5. $6.82 \div 3.1$ **6.** $0.1908 \div 0.09$ **7.** $0.815 \div 0.163$

Exercises

Divide.

1. $0.5\overline{)7.5}$ **2.** $0.05\overline{)0.75}$ **3.** $0.07\overline{)0.084}$ **4.** $1.6\overline{)3.408}$

5. $6.2\overline{)130.2}$ **6.** $12\overline{)45.6}$ **7.** $0.24\overline{)3.84}$ **8.** $0.157\overline{)1.256}$

9. $37\overline{)888}$ **10.** $0.31\overline{)68.82}$ **11.** $0.04\overline{)9.476}$ **12.** $42\overline{)55.44}$

13. $0.072 \div 0.36$ **14.** $3.18 \div 5.3$ **15.** $2.56 \div 0.32$

16. $2.232 \div 1.8$ **17.** $1.302 \div 0.031$ **18.** $0.2665 \div 0.205$

 Divide. Use a calculator to check.

19. $44.38 \div 0.7$ **20.** $3.432 \div 0.12$ **21.** $0.0084 \div 0.06$

22. $2.784 \div 2.4$ **23.** $8.216 \div 1.04$ **24.** $2.025 \div 0.225$

25. $6.591 \div 5.07$ **26.** $24.16 \div 60.4$ **27.** $0.621 \div 0.23$

Solve each problem. You may choose paper and pencil or a calculator.

28. A mold holds 0.4 liter of plaster of paris. How many molds can be filled with 10.8 liters of plaster of paris?

29. Each candle mold holds 0.09 liter of hot wax. How many candles can be made from 3.15 liters of hot wax?

30. Mr. Davis buys 12 cans of paint. Each can is marked $11.95. Mr. Davis finds out that the paint is on sale for $10.80 a can. How much does Mr. Davis save on 12 cans of paint?

★ **31.** Jason wants to make 6 banners of the same length. He has a piece of fabric 0.5 meter wide and 15.6 meters long. If he is going to make the banners 0.5 meter wide, how long should he make them?

More Dividing by Decimals

■ Sometimes you need to add 0s to the dividend to place the decimal point.

Divide: $0.32\overline{)96}$

Multiply the divisor and the dividend by 100.	Divide.	Check.

$0.32\overline{)96.00}$

$$\begin{array}{r} 3\,0\,0. \\ 0.3\,2\overline{)9\,6.0\,0} \\ \underline{9\,6} \\ 0\,0 \\ \underline{0} \\ 0\,0 \\ \underline{0} \\ 0 \end{array}$$

$$\begin{array}{r} 0.32 \\ \times 300 \\ \hline 96.00 \ \swarrow \end{array}$$

■ Divide 5 by 0.6 and round the quotient to the nearest hundredth. To round to the nearest hundredth, you need to know the thousandths place in the quotient.

Multiply the divisor and the dividend by 10.	Divide.	Write three 0s in the dividend. Continue dividing.

$0.6\overline{)5.0}$

$$\begin{array}{r} 8. \\ 0.6\overline{)5.0} \\ \underline{4\,8} \\ 2 \end{array}$$

$$\begin{array}{r} 8.3\,3\,3 \longrightarrow 8.33 \\ 0.6\overline{)5.0\,0\,0\,0} \\ \underline{4\,8} \\ 2\,0 \\ \underline{1\,8} \\ 2\,0 \\ \underline{1\,8} \\ 2\,0 \\ \underline{1\,8} \\ 2 \end{array}$$

Try These

Divide.

1. $0.7\overline{)91}$ **2.** $1.6\overline{)128}$ **3.** $0.24\overline{)21.6}$ **4.** $0.27\overline{)4.05}$

Divide. Round each quotient to the nearest tenth.

5. $0.3\overline{)2}$ **6.** $4.3\overline{)7.869}$ **7.** $8\overline{)10}$ **8.** $0.14\overline{)3.7}$

Exercises

Divide.

1. $0.8\overline{)136}$ **2.** $3.2\overline{)192}$ **3.** $0.15\overline{)1.2}$ **4.** $0.041\overline{)4.92}$

5. $0.006\overline{)2.04}$ **6.** $68\overline{)197.2}$ **7.** $4.2\overline{)2.037}$ **8.** $1.43\overline{)5.72}$

9. $132.6 \div 6.5$ **10.** $76 \div 0.19$ **11.** $35.1 \div 0.135$

12. $12.6 \div 1.5$ **13.** $0.0272 \div 0.008$ **14.** $9.177 \div 0.21$

Divide. Round each quotient to the nearest tenth.

15. $0.7\overline{)4.49}$ **16.** $6\overline{)19}$ **17.** $5.4\overline{)68.31}$ **18.** $0.82\overline{)20.1}$

19. $7.8 \div 0.23$ **20.** $0.845 \div 3.6$ **21.** $2.6 \div 0.079$

Divide. Round each quotient to the nearest hundredth.

22. $0.9\overline{)8}$ **23.** $0.23\overline{)1.06}$ **24.** $0.16\overline{)4.7}$ **25.** $7\overline{)9}$

26. $0.1554 \div 3.7$ **27.** $57 \div 12$ **28.** $5.6 \div 0.49$

Solve each problem.

29. 7 pieces of machinery are delivered to a factory. The combined weight of these pieces is 363.20 kilograms. What is the average weight of each piece of machinery? Round the answer to the nearest hundredth.

30. Mrs. Johnson is a machine operator. She earns $7.75 per hour. She works 40 hours per week. How much does Mrs. Johnson earn per week?

31. A machine uses 2.4 liters of fuel for each hour of operation. At this rate, how long will it take to use 12 liters of fuel?

★ **32.** It takes a wheel 0.9 second to make 1 revolution. How many revolutions will the wheel make in 9 hours?

Decimals: Multiplication and Division   145

Estimating Products and Quotients

■ Mr. Moore owns a produce store. He is selling pears for $.69 per pound. Estimate how much he would charge for 3.16 pounds of pears.

To find the answer, estimate the product of 3.16 and $.69.

Circle the first digit of each factor. Round each factor to the circled place. Then multiply to estimate the product.

$$
\begin{array}{r}
\$.\textcircled{6}9 \longrightarrow \$.70 \\
\times\textcircled{3}.16 \longrightarrow \times\quad 3 \\
\hline
\$2.10
\end{array}
$$

The pears would cost about $2.10.

■ Mr. Moore has 77.6 pounds of turnips. About how many bags of turnips can he fill if each bag weighs about 1.8 pounds?

To find the answer, estimate the quotient of 77.6 ÷ 1.8.

Round the divisor. Then change the dividend to a number that is easy to divide by the rounded divisor.

Round the divisor.	**Change the dividend.**	**Estimate the quotient.**
1.8 rounds to 2.		
$2\overline{)77.6}$	$2\overline{)80}$	$\begin{array}{r}40\\2\overline{)80}\end{array}$

Mr. Moore can fill about 40 bags with turnips.

Try These

Estimate each product.

1. 24.7
   × 3.6

2. $6.83
   × 1.9

3. 7.12
   ×0.54

4. 4.815
   ×   23

5. 0.609
   × 3.17

Estimate each quotient.

6. $2.7\overline{)58.4}$

7. $13\overline{)\$42.01}$

8. $4.37\overline{)187.6}$

9. $0.61\overline{)1.38}$

Exercises

Estimate each product.

1. $\begin{array}{r} 18.3 \\ \times\ 2.4 \\ \hline \end{array}$ **2.** $\begin{array}{r} 7.34 \\ \times\ 6.5 \\ \hline \end{array}$ **3.** $\begin{array}{r} 11.4 \\ \times 0.26 \\ \hline \end{array}$ **4.** $\begin{array}{r} \$3.75 \\ \times\ \ \ 49 \\ \hline \end{array}$ **5.** $\begin{array}{r} 0.62 \\ \times\ 1.8 \\ \hline \end{array}$

6. $\begin{array}{r} 1.275 \\ \times\ 4.61 \\ \hline \end{array}$ **7.** $\begin{array}{r} 0.82 \\ \times 2.53 \\ \hline \end{array}$ **8.** $\begin{array}{r} \$.55 \\ \times\ 7.8 \\ \hline \end{array}$ **9.** $\begin{array}{r} 174 \\ \times 0.96 \\ \hline \end{array}$ **10.** $\begin{array}{r} 18.43 \\ \times\ 3.09 \\ \hline \end{array}$

11. 47.8×2.395 **12.** 0.36×121.4 **13.** $6.2 \times \$.87$

Estimate each quotient.

14. $3.4\overline{)28.6}$ **15.** $27\overline{)55.81}$ **16.** $5.2\overline{)36.04}$ **17.** $16\overline{)\$38.51}$

18. $4.19\overline{)122.3}$ **19.** $12.7\overline{)88.4}$ **20.** $0.38\overline{)2.24}$ **21.** $0.62\overline{)41.8}$

22. $374.8 \div 9.7$ **23.** $\$453 \div 5.2$ **24.** $8.73 \div 0.26$

Use estimation to decide whether each answer is reasonable.
Write *yes* if it is reasonable and *no* if it is not reasonable.

25. $\begin{array}{r} 13.6 \\ \times\ 8.2 \\ \hline 80 \end{array}$ **26.** $\begin{array}{r} 9.24 \\ \times\ 3.7 \\ \hline 27 \end{array}$ **27.** $\begin{array}{r} 12.8 \\ \times 0.44 \\ \hline 40 \end{array}$ **28.** $\begin{array}{r} 51.32 \\ \times\ 18.7 \\ \hline 1,000 \end{array}$ **29.** $\begin{array}{r} 6.114 \\ \times\ \ \ 93 \\ \hline 54 \end{array}$

30. $2.9\overline{)52.8}^{\ 2}$ **31.** $16\overline{)74.32}^{\ 4}$ **32.** $43.5\overline{)186.2}^{\ 50}$ **33.** $0.97\overline{)8.245}^{\ 8}$

Decide if you need an estimate or an exact answer. Then solve.

34. Mr. Moore paid $11.35 for a case of 48 heads of lettuce. Estimate the cost per head.

35. Paul bought 3.8 pounds of bananas for $.45 per pound. Estimate the total cost of the bananas.

36. Mr. Moore drove his truck 326.5 miles on 12.4 gallons of gasoline. Find the number of miles per gallon. Round to the nearest whole number.

37. A customer buys 3.4 pounds of apples at $.59 per pound. He gives the clerk $5.00. About how much change does the customer receive?

38. Jenny had $11.63. She bought potatoes for $1.95 and melons for $2.29. How much money did she have left?

39. Kate bought 2.6 pounds of grapes for $3.77, 3.4 pounds of plums for $3.03, and 6 oranges for $1.35. Find the unit price for each type of fruit.

Problem Solving: Applications

SALES TAX

Some states charge a sales tax of $.05 on the dollar. To find the amount of the tax, multiply the cost by 0.05.

■ Find the sales tax on a paint brush that costs $3.59.

$$
\begin{array}{r}
\$3.59 \\
\times\ 0.05 \\
\hline
\$.1795
\end{array}
$$

Round $.1795 to the nearest cent (hundredth).
$.1795 rounds to $.18.

To the nearest cent, the sales tax is $.18.

■ Find the total cost of a screwdriver that costs $.75.

Multiply to find the sales tax on $.75.

$$
\begin{array}{r}
\$.75 \\
\times\ 0.05 \\
\hline
\$.0375
\end{array}
$$

Round $.0375 to the nearest cent.
$.0375 rounds to $.04.

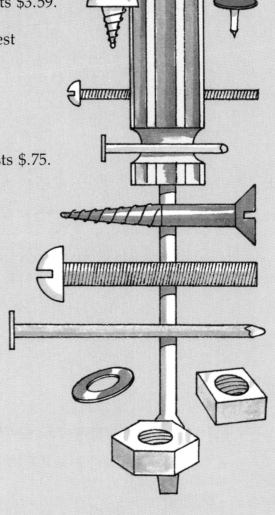

Then add to find the total cost.

$$
\begin{array}{ll}
\text{screwdriver} \longrightarrow & \$.75 \\
\text{tax} \longrightarrow & +\ .04 \\
\hline
\text{total cost} \longrightarrow & \$.79
\end{array}
$$

The total cost of the screwdriver is $.79.

Try These

**Copy and complete each sales ticket.
Use a sales tax of $.05 on the dollar.**

1.

E-Z Hardware Store	
1 hammer	$ 7.95
1 pliers	4.99
1 extension cord	+ 16.29
Subtotal	$ ■
Tax	$ ■
Total	$ ■

2.

E-Z Hardware Store	
3 bolts @ $.49 each	$ ■
5 washers @ $.20 each	■
2 paint brushes @ $3.59 each	■
1 wrench set @ $12.59 each	+ ■
Subtotal	$ ■
Tax	$ ■
Total	$ ■

Exercises

ABC Hardware recently ran this advertisement.

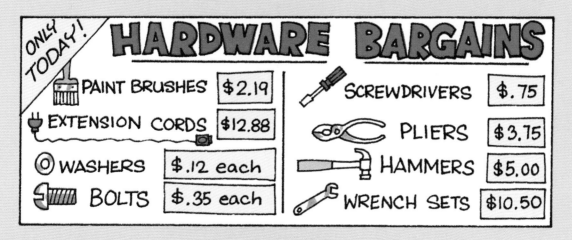

Use the ABC Hardware advertisement and a sales tax of $.06 on the dollar. Copy and complete each sales ticket.

1.

ABC Hardware Store	
5 bolts	$ ■
6 washers	■
1 extension cord	+ ■
Subtotal	$ ■
Tax	$ ■
Total	$ ■

2.

ABC Hardware Store	
3 screwdrivers	$ ■
2 pliers	■
1 wrench set	+ ■
Subtotal	$ ■
Tax	$ ■
Total	$ ■

Solve each problem. Sales tax just went up to $.07 on the dollar. Use the ABC Hardware advertisement and the new sales tax rate.

3. Mr. Jamison buys the hammer that is on sale. Find the sales tax.

4. Fran buys the wrench set that is on sale. Find the sales tax.

5. Mrs. Brooks buys 2 of the paint brushes that are on sale. What is the total cost of her purchase?

6. Jed buys an extension cord, 10 bolts, and the wrench set. What is the total cost of his purchase?

★ **7.** A customer buys pliers, 4 paint brushes, 9 washers, and a hammer. The customer gives the clerk $20.00. How much change should the customer receive?

★ **8.** Ms. Berger buys 2 screwdrivers, 18 bolts, an extension cord, and 3 paint brushes. She gives the clerk $25.00 and a credit slip for $6.59. How much change should the clerk give Ms. Berger?

CHAPTER CHECKPOINT

Multiply. (pp. 128–133, 140–141)

1. 7.2 $\times 0.6$	**2.** 3.16 $\times 0.04$	**3.** 0.032 $\times\ 0.76$	**4.** $2.59 $\times\ 8.4$	**5.** 19.07 $\times\ 36$
6. 0.021 $\times\ 0.34$	**7.** 5.041 $\times\ 2.08$	**8.** $674 $\times\ 1.25$	**9.** 0.014 $\times\ 0.09$	**10.** 0.244 $\times\ 5.18$
11. 3.75 $\times\ 10$	**12.** 18.304 $\times\ 0.25$	**13.** 0.068 $\times\ 100$	**14.** 0.059 $\times\ 0.23$	**15.** 1.4 $\times 1,000$

16. 10×2.3 **17.** 3.4×100 **18.** $1,000 \times 20.65$
19. 0.071×0.06 **20.** $0.039 \times 1,000$ **21.** 2.54×16.09

Divide. (pp. 134–135, 140–145)

22. $4\overline{)16.92}$ **23.** $0.6\overline{)0.42}$ **24.** $0.47\overline{)3.008}$ **25.** $2.3\overline{)50.83}$

26. $8\overline{)16.056}$ **27.** $10\overline{)8.74}$ **28.** $32\overline{)\$153.28}$ **29.** $0.045\overline{)1.71}$

30. $100\overline{)54.23}$ **31.** $0.6\overline{)\$78}$ **32.** $0.125\overline{)0.175}$ **33.** $1,000\overline{)89.3}$

34. $4.6 \div 100$ **35.** $81 \div 10$ **36.** $74.2 \div 1,000$
37. $28.98 \div 0.09$ **38.** $50.7 \div 100$ **39.** $2,159 \div 1,000$

Divide. Round each quotient to the nearest tenth.
(pp. 136–137, 144–145)

40. $5\overline{)3.1}$ **41.** $0.6\overline{)2}$ **42.** $12\overline{)58.56}$ **43.** $3.4\overline{)21.42}$

44. $0.14\overline{)2.947}$ **45.** $16\overline{)23}$ **46.** $48\overline{)7.13}$ **47.** $0.27\overline{)8.97}$

Divide. Round each quotient to the nearest hundredth.
(pp. 136–137, 144–145)

48. $9\overline{)1.404}$ **49.** $0.3\overline{)11}$ **50.** $2.9\overline{)6.15}$ **51.** $18\overline{)54.72}$

52. $0.44\overline{)3.7}$ **53.** $8\overline{)15}$ **54.** $36\overline{)14.472}$ **55.** $0.64\overline{)11.9}$

Estimate each answer. (pp. 146–147)

56. 3.49
 $\times$ 8.6

57. 17.4
 $\times$ 3.3

58. $9.95
 $\times$ 6.2

59. 0.731
 $\times$ 4.18

60. 279
 $\times$0.54

61. $2.7\overline{)14.3}$

62. $11\overline{)518.4}$

63. $32.1\overline{)86.42}$

64. $0.98\overline{)7.15}$

Use the following pattern to find each product:
$22 \times 22 = 484$, $22 \times 222 = 4,884$, $22 \times 2,222 = 48,884$. (pp. 132–133)

65. $22 \times 22,222$

66. $22 \times 222,222$

Decide if you need an estimate or an exact answer. Then solve. (pp. 128–147)

67. Gasoline costs $1.45 per gallon. How much do 8.4 gallons cost?

68. Idaho potatoes are selling for $.59 per pound. Estimate the price of 4.17 pounds.

69. A box of 6 corn muffins costs $1.62. A box of 12 of the same muffins costs $3.12. Is it better to buy 1 box of 12 or 2 boxes of 6?

70. A 16-ounce bottle of shampoo sells for $1.96. A 12-ounce bottle of the same shampoo sells for $1.38. Which is the better buy?

71. Brand A cereal costs $1.73 for a 13-ounce box. Brand B cereal costs $.65 for a 7-ounce box. How much will 3 boxes of Brand B cereal cost?

72. You are going to cut a plastic pipe that is 9.6 meters long into pieces that are 1.2 meters long. How many pieces will you cut?

Copy and complete each sales ticket.
Use a sales tax of $.05 on the dollar. (pp. 148–149)

73.

PJ Department Store	
1 shirt	$10.95
1 sweater	17.99
1 skirt	+ 22.50
Subtotal	$ ▨
Tax	$ ▨
Total	$ ▨

74.

PJ Department Store	
4 bath towels @ $6.39 each	$ ▨
3 hand towels @ 4.55 each	▨
2 face cloths @ 2.99 each	+ ▨
Subtotal	$ ▨
Tax	$ ▨
Total	$ ▨

COMPUTERS AND PROBLEM SOLVING

Suppose you are programming an adventure game. You make up four possible events:

```
10   LET E0$ = "YOU LOSE YOUR COMPASS. FOLLOW THE SUN."
20   LET E1$ = "YOU COME TO A STREAM. SWIM ACROSS."
30   LET E2$ = "YOU DECIDE TO SPEND THE NIGHT ON A MOUNTAIN LEDGE."
40   LET E3$ = "YOU SEE A PLUME OF SMOKE IN THE DISTANCE."
```

Your game would be boring if players always knew exactly which events would occur and when. To make the game more interesting, you can use the BASIC random function RND (1). Let's experiment with the RND function.

Type:
The computer displays:

```
]PRINT RND (1)
.00321787

]▤
```

Type:
The computer displays:

```
]PRINT RND (1)
.99320000

]▤
```

What's the matter with the computer? It gives different results when you give it the same command. It seems unpredictable! That's why RND (1) is so useful for creating adventure games.

■ You are now ready to introduce a random element into your game. Use RND to get random numbers between 0 and 3. Call the random numbers CHANCE. Test CHANCE with IF. . .THEN statements to guide the flow of events. In this program, REM statements mark places where additional events will be added to complete the adventure.

```
50   LET CHANCE = INT (4 * RND (1))
60   IF CHANCE = 0 THEN PRINT E0$
70   IF CHANCE = 1 THEN PRINT E1$
80   IF CHANCE = 2 THEN PRINT E2$
90   IF CHANCE = 3 THEN PRINT E3$
100    REM NEXT, OUR EXPLORER WILL MEET A FRIENDLY TRIBE.
1550   END
2000   REM I WILL WRITE THE SMOKE SUBROUTINE HERE.
3000   RETURN
```

Solve each problem.

1. PRINT RND (1) always gives a result between .00000000 and .99999999. The INT function always removes the decimal part of a number. What will always be the answer to PRINT INT (RND (1))? Why?

2. Explain why PRINT INT (6 * RND (1)) will always give either 0, 1, 2, 3, 4, or 5 as a result. [Hint: what is the highest possible number that 6 * RND (1) can supply?]

ENRICHMENT

SQUARES AND SQUARE ROOTS

■ 5^2 is read "5 squared." It means 5×5, or 25.
25 is called the **square** of 5.
5 is called the **square root** of 25.

■ What is the square of 8.3?

$$(8.3)^2 = 8.3 \times 8.3$$
$$= 68.89$$

The square of 8.3 is 68.89.
The square root of 68.89 is 8.3.

■ What is the square root of 610.09?

You need to find a number whose square is 610.09. You can use a calculator to help you guess and check.

Try 30: $30 \times 30 = 900$. Since $900 > 610.09$, 30 is too great.

Try 20: $20 \times 20 = 400$. Since $400 < 610.09$, 20 is too small. The number is between 20 and 30.

Try 25: $25 \times 25 = 625$. The number is between 20 and 25.

Try 24: $24 \times 24 = 576$. The number is between 24 and 25.

Try 24.3: $24.3 \times 24.3 = 590.49$. The number is between 24.3 and 25.

Try 24.7: $24.7 \times 24.7 = 610.09$. 24.7 works.

The square root of 610.09 is 24.7.

Find the square of each number.

1. 68   **2.** 4.2   **3.** 176   **4.** 3.81   **5.** 27.94

Find the square root of each number.

6. 121   **7.** 1,369   **8.** 56.25   **9.** 372.49   **10.** 1.9881

BUYING A COMPUTER

You have $1,000 in your savings account. You would like to buy a computer with this money. What should you consider before making your purchase?

Some Questions to Explore
- What features are you looking for in a computer?
- Where can you obtain information about prices?
- What software will you buy?
- Do you have enough money to buy all the necessary components?

Some Strategies to Explore
Consider the first question. Use the strategy of organizing information to help answer the question.

- Make a list of planned uses and gather specifications (such as computer memory and number of disk drives).
- Send for brochures.
- Visit stores and watch demonstrations.
- Make a list of the hardware you need.

Decide what strategies you will use to answer the other questions above. List other questions and strategies you need to explore. Then solve the problem.

SKILLS CHECK

Choose the correct answer.

1.
```
   1,293
   6,098
+ 4,775
```
a. 11,096
b. 11,265
c. 12,056
d. 12,166

2. 6,000 − 4,287

a. 1,623
b. 1,713
c. 10,287
d. NG

3.
```
   871
×   59
```
a. 11,294
b. 12,194
c. 47,789
d. 51,389

4. 6,206 ÷ 58

a. 17
b. 47
c. 58 R3
d. 107

5. Round 30.63 to the nearest tenth.

a. 30.6
b. 30.7
c. 31.0
d. NG

6. 29.8 + 4.17

a. 7.15
b. 33.16
c. 33.97
d. 34.05

7.
```
   41.131
−   0.828
```
a. 4.413
b. 40.303
c. 403.03
d. NG

8. 2.8 × 3.4

a. 6.32
b. 8.46
c. 9.52
d. 10.52

9. $100\overline{)9.4}$

a. 0.0094
b. 0.094
c. 0.94
d. 94

10. Bea scores a total of 430 points on 5 tests. What is her average score?

a. 65
b. 78
c. 86
d. NG

11. Tom buys a shirt for $12.79 and a jacket for $18.65. How much money does he spend?

a. $5.86
b. $6.14
c. $30.74
d. $31.44

12. The hiking club orders 25 steaks for a cookout. Each steak weighs 0.45 kilogram. What is the total weight of the order?

a. 9 kilograms
b. 10.5 kilograms
c. 11.25 kilograms
d. 12.5 kilograms

MEASUREMENT

6

Time

■ People have been using clocks to measure time for over 900 years.

Read: one forty-five or
       forty-five minutes past one or
       quarter to two
Write: 1:45

Read: ten twelve or
       twelve minutes past ten
Write: 10:12

■ Use A.M. for the hours from 12 midnight to 12 noon.
Use P.M. for the hours from 12 noon to 12 midnight.

■ Find the time 2 hours 43 minutes after 6:25 A.M.

Think: Start at 6:25 A.M.
       2 hours later is 8:25 A.M.
       43 minutes later is 9:08 A.M.

2 hours 43 minutes after 6:25 A.M.
is 9:08 A.M.

■ Find the time 4 hours 9 minutes before 3:52 P.M.

Think: Start at 3:52 P.M.
       4 hours earlier is 11:52 A.M.
       9 minutes earlier is 11:43 A.M.

4 hours 9 minutes before 3:52 P.M.
is 11:43 A.M.

■ Find the amount of time between 7:38 P.M. and 10:14 P.M.

Think: Start at 7:38 P.M.
       2 hours later is 9:38 P.M.
       36 minutes later is 10:14 P.M.

The amount of time between 7:38 P.M.
and 10:14 P.M. is 2 hours 36 minutes.

Try These

Write each time.

1.

2.

3.

What time is it?

4. 3 hours 36 minutes after 10:15 A.M.

5. 4 hours 9 minutes before 12:25 P.M.

How much time is between these times?

6. 10:12 A.M. and 2:35 P.M.

7. 5:45 P.M. and 11:02 P.M.

Exercises

Write each time.

1.

2.

3.

What time is it?

4. 35 minutes before 2:30 A.M.

6. 4 hours after midnight

8. 3 hours 48 minutes before 1:30 P.M.

5. 1 hour 9 minutes after 6:51 P.M.

7. 2 hours 18 minutes before 11:12 A.M.

9. 6 hours 35 minutes after 10:41 P.M.

How much time is between these times?

10. 4:30 P.M. and 8:26 P.M.

12. 11:15 A.M. and midnight

11. 3:09 A.M. and 9:03 A.M.

13. 9:25 A.M. and 4:42 P.M.

Solve each problem.

14. Celeste traveled from Atlanta, Georgia, to Washington, D.C. She left Atlanta at 10:30 A.M. The trip took 2 hours. What time did she arrive in Washington, D.C.?

★ **15.** Celeste started a walking tour of the city at 9:10 A.M. She stopped for lunch at 11:50 A.M. Then she walked from 12:45 P.M. to 4:30 P.M. For how long did Celeste walk?

Units of Time

- The **second (s)**, the **minute (min)**, the **hour (h)**,
the **day**, the **week**, the **month**, and the **year** are
used to measure time.

1 minute = 60 seconds
1 hour = 60 minutes
1 day = 24 hours

1 week = 7 days
1 year = 365 days
1 year = 12 months

←—— **Leap years
have 366 days.**

- Use the chart to find the number of hours in 2 days 3 hours.

$$2 \text{ days } 3 \text{ hours} = \blacksquare \text{ hours}$$
$$1 \text{ day} = 24 \text{ hours}$$
$$2 \text{ days} = 2 \times 24 \text{ hours}$$
$$2 \text{ days} = 48 \text{ hours}$$
$$2 \text{ days } 3 \text{ hours} = 48 \text{ hours} + 3 \text{ hours}$$
$$2 \text{ days } 3 \text{ hours} = 51 \text{ hours}$$

- Use the chart to find the number of minutes and seconds
in 135 seconds.

$$135 \text{ seconds} = \blacksquare \text{ minutes } \blacksquare \text{ seconds}$$
$$60 \text{ seconds} = 1 \text{ minute}$$
$$135 \text{ seconds} = 2 \text{ minutes } 15 \text{ seconds}$$

$$\begin{array}{r} 2 \text{ R}15 \\ 60\overline{)135} \\ \underline{120} \\ 15 \end{array}$$

- You can add and subtract units of time.

Add: 2 h 30 min + 1 h 43 min

Add the minutes.

$$\begin{array}{r} 2 \text{ h } 30 \text{ min} \\ +1 \text{ h } 43 \text{ min} \\ \hline 73 \text{ min} \end{array}$$

Add the hours.

$$\begin{array}{r} 2 \text{ h } 30 \text{ min} \\ +1 \text{ h } 43 \text{ min} \\ \hline 3 \text{ h } 73 \text{ min} \end{array}$$

Rename the answer.

$$73 \text{ min} = 1 \text{ h } 13 \text{ min}$$
$$3 \text{ h } 73 \text{ min} = 4 \text{ h } 13 \text{ min}$$

Subtract: 5 h 26 min − 3 h 52 min

$$\begin{array}{r} 5 \text{ h } 26 \text{ min} \\ -3 \text{ h } 52 \text{ min} \end{array}$$

26 min < 52 min
Rename 1 h as 60 min.
60 min + 26 min = 86 min

$$\begin{array}{r} \overset{4 \quad\; 86}{\cancel{5} \text{ h } \cancel{26} \text{ min}} \\ -3 \text{ h } 52 \text{ min} \\ \hline 1 \text{ h } 34 \text{ min} \end{array}$$

Try These

Copy and complete.

1. 3 days 6 hours = ■ hours
2. 240 seconds = ■ minutes
3. 6 hours 9 minutes = ■ minutes
4. 56 months = ■ years ■ months
5. 8 weeks 2 days = ■ days
6. 2 years 15 days = ■ days

Compute. Rename when necessary.

7.   3 h 20 min
   + 1 h 45 min

8.   6 h 30 min
   − 2 h 45 min

9.   5 h 24 min
   − 4 h 37 min

10.   4 h 19 min
    +   41 min

Exercises

Copy and complete.

1. 52 hours = ■ days ■ hours
2. 135 minutes = ■ hours ■ minutes
3. 49 months = ■ years ■ month
4. 9 weeks 3 days = ■ days
5. 214 seconds = ■ minutes ■ seconds
6. 2 hours 43 minutes = ■ minutes
7. 5 years 3 months = ■ months
8. 3 days 15 hours = ■ hours
9. 4 minutes 37 seconds = ■ seconds
10. 40 years = ■ months

Compute. Rename when necessary.

11.   4 h 10 min
   + 1 h 45 min

12.   3 h 20 min
   − 1 h 30 min

13.   6 h 51 min
   − 2 h 25 min

14.   5 h 40 min
   + 3 h

15.   9 h 12 min
   − 2 h 48 min

16.   5 h 15 min
   + 3 h 45 min

17.   4 h
   − 3 h 26 min

★ 18.   3 days   5 h
    −   18 h

Solve each problem.

19. Jason had a meeting with the producer at WXYZ at noon. The meeting ended at 3:20 P.M. How long did the meeting last?

20. The tape from a special travel report runs 8 min 20 s. The tape is cut by 5 min 50 s. How long is the travel report now?

21. Jason worked on a special broadcast for 4 h 25 min on Monday. He worked on it 3 h 45 min on Tuesday. How long did Jason work on this broadcast?

★ 22. The camera crew arrived at 1:45 P.M. Equipment failure delayed the taping for 1 h 35 min. The taping ended at 5:09 P.M. How long was the taping session?

Metric Units of Length

- The **meter (m)** is the basic unit of length in the metric system.

  An umbrella is about 1 meter long.
  A door is about 2 meters high.

- The **millimeter (mm)**, the **centimeter (cm)**, the **decimeter (dm)**, and the **kilometer (km)** are also used to measure length in the metric system.

> **1 centimeter = 10 millimeters**
> **1 decimeter = 10 centimeters**
> **1 meter = 100 centimeters**
> **1 kilometer = 1,000 meters**

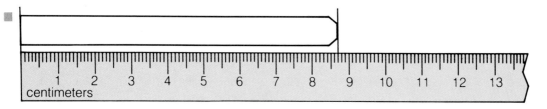

This piece of chalk is between 8 and 9 centimeters long.
It is 9 centimeters long to the nearest centimeter.
It is 87 millimeters long to the nearest millimeter.

Try These

Measure each to the nearest centimeter and to the nearest millimeter.

1.

2.

Write *mm, cm, dm, m,* or *km*.

3. The length of a room may be 5 ▦.
4. The length of a snapshot is about 1 ▦.
5. The thickness of a pencil lead is about 2 ▦.
6. The highway distance from New York to Boston is about 340 ▦.

Exercises

Measure each to the nearest centimeter and to the nearest millimeter.

1.

2. ●————————————————————————●

Write *mm*, *cm*, *dm*, *m*, or *km*.

3. The thickness of a nickel is about 2 ▩.
4. The length of your thumb is about 5 ▩.
5. The highway distance from Denver to Salt Lake City is about 800 ▩.
6. The width of your notebook paper is about 21 ▩.
7. The height of a chair is about 1 ▩.
8. The length of a pencil is about 2 ▩.
9. The width of a calculator may be 7 ▩.

Choose the sensible measurement.

10. A rowboat is about ▩ long.
    a 2 m   **b.** 2 dm   **c.** 2 km
11. A needle is about ▩ long.
    a. 30 cm   **b.** 30 m   **c.** 30 mm
12. The highway distance from Seattle to San Francisco is about ▩.
    a. 1,300 m   **b.** 1,300 km   **c.** 1,300 cm
13. The height of a bicycle is about ▩.
    a. 1 dm   **b.** 1 m   **c.** 1 km
14. The width of a car is about ▩.
    a. 2 dm   **b.** 2 m   **c.** 2 km
15. A fence may be ▩ high.
    a. 150 cm   **b.** 150 mm   **c.** 150 m
16. The Delaware River is about ▩ long.
    a. 630 km   **b.** 630 mm   **c.** 630 cm

This table shows the length of the state coastlines along the Gulf Coast of the United States.

Solve each problem.

17. How long is the gulf coastline of Louisiana?

18. How much longer is the gulf coastline of Florida than that of Texas?

19. How long are the combined gulf coastlines of Alabama and Mississippi?

20. What is the total length of the gulf coastlines?

GULF COASTLINES	
State	Kilometers
Florida	1,232
Alabama	85
Mississippi	70
Louisiana	635
Texas	587

Changing Metric Measurements

■ To name the same measurements in a smaller unit, multiply by 10, by 100, or by 1,000.

To name the same measurements in a larger unit, divide by 10, by 100, or by 1,000.

Most railroad ties are 0.53 m apart. How many centimeters apart are they?

$$0.53 \text{ m} = \blacksquare \text{ cm}$$
$$1 \text{ m} = 100 \text{ cm}$$
$$100 \times 0.53 = 53$$

The railroad ties are 53 cm apart.

A railroad boxcar is about 130 dm long. How many meters long is it?

$$130 \text{ dm} = \blacksquare \text{ m}$$
$$10 \text{ dm} = 1 \text{ m}$$
$$130 \div 10 = 13$$

A railroad boxcar is about 13 m long.

■ Each refrigerator car is 15 m long. A locomotive pulls 100 refrigerator cars. How many kilometers long are the refrigerator cars altogether?

To find the answer in meters, multiply 100 and 15.

$$100 \times 15 \text{ m} = 1,500 \text{ m}$$

To give the answer in kilometers, divide by 1,000.

$$1,500 \text{ m} = \blacksquare \text{ km}$$
$$1,500 \div 1,000 = 1.5 \text{ km}$$

The refrigerator cars are 1.5 km long altogether.

Try These

Copy and complete.

1. 5 cm = ■ mm
2. 3 m = ■ cm
3. 50 cm = ■ dm
4. 860 m = ■ km
5. 0.5 m = ■ cm
6. 186 cm = ■ m
7. 52 cm = ■ m
8. 4,000 m = ■ km
9. 23 mm = ■ m
10. 5.7 km = ■ m
11. 8 dm = ■ cm
12. 200 cm = ■ m

Exercises

Copy and complete.

1. 20 mm = ▓ cm
2. 8 dm = ▓ cm
3. 1.5 cm = ▓ mm
4. 0.4 m = ▓ mm
5. 5 km = ▓ m
6. 4,300 m = ▓ km
7. 0.800 km = ▓ m
8. 924 cm = ▓ m
9. 125 mm = ▓ m
10. 0.475 m = ▓ mm
11. 0.76 m = ▓ cm
12. 7.8 m = ▓ mm
13. 0.5 dm = ▓ mm
14. 9 m = ▓ mm
15. 7,580 mm = ▓ dm

Change to the same units. Write >, <, or =.

16. 1.6 m ▓ 16 cm
17. 500 cm ▓ 0.5 m
18. 400 m ▓ 4 km
19. 1.4 mm ▓ 14 cm
20. 6,000 cm ▓ 60 m
21. 3.6 cm ▓ 360 mm

Solve each problem.

22. A train travels 8.9 km. How many meters is this?

23. A flatcar is 17 m long. A locomotive pulls 85 flatcars. How long are the 85 flatcars altogether in meters? In kilometers?

24. A train was making a 280-km trip. It traveled at an average speed of 55 kph for 4 h. At what average speed must the train travel to reach its destination in 1 more hour?

★ 25. A boxcar is about 13 m long. A locomotive pulls 25 boxcars. About how many kilometers long is this train?

THINK AND TRY

EXPLORING OTHER MEASUREMENTS

The **dekameter (dam)** and the **hectometer (hm)** are also used to measure distances in the metric system. These units are not used very often.

1 dekameter	= 10 meters
1 hectometer	= 10 dekameters
1 kilometer	= 10 hectometers

Copy and complete.

1. 4 dam = ▓ m
2. 18 hm = ▓ dam
3. 59.8 hm = ▓ dam
4. 5 km = ▓ hm
5. 6 m = ▓ dam
6. 0.8 dam = ▓ m
7. 100 hm = ▓ km
8. 75 hm = ▓ km
9. 26 dam = ▓ hm

Metric Units of Capacity and Weight

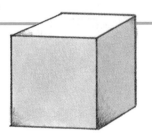

■ The **liter (L)** and the **milliliter (mL)** are used to measure **capacity** in the metric system. Capacity is the amount of a substance that a container can hold.

The large cube holds 1 liter of water. The small cube holds 1 milliliter of water.

1 liter = 1,000 milliliters

An eyedropper holds about 1 milliliter of water. A baby bottle holds about 250 milliliters of liquid. A milk carton holds about 1 liter of milk.

■ **Mass** is the amount of matter contained in an object. Mass can be measured in **milligrams (mg)**, **grams (g)**, and **kilograms (kg)**. These are commonly called units of weight.

1 milliliter of water weighs 1 gram.
1 liter of water weighs 1 kilogram.

1 gram = 1,000 milligrams
1 kilogram = 1,000 grams

A grain of rice weighs about 50 milligrams.
A $1 bill weighs about 1 gram.
A hiking boot weighs about 1 kilogram.

■ You can change measurements from one unit to another.

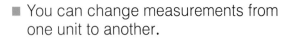

2 L = ▦ mL	4,300 g = ▦ kg
1 L = 1,000 mL	1,000 g = 1 kg
so 2 L = 2,000 mL	so 4,300 g = 4.3 kg

Try These

Write *L* or *mL*.

1. A thimble may hold about 3 ▦.
2. A cooking pot may hold about 4 ▦.
3. A bottle of cough syrup may hold about 300 ▦.
4. A thermos may hold 1 ▦.

Write *mg, g,* or *kg*.

5. A mosquito weighs about 5 ▦.
6. An elephant may weigh 5,000 ▦.
7. A tomato may weigh 20 ▦.
8. A head of cabbage may weigh 1 ▦.

Copy and complete.

9. 500 mL = ▦ L
10. 7,000 g = ▦ kg
11. 0.400 kg = ▦ g
12. 9 L = ▦ mL
13. 1.2 L = ▦ mL
14. 55 g = ▦ kg

Exercises

Choose the sensible measurement.

1. A fishbowl may hold ▦ of water.   **a.** 70 mL   **b.** 7 L   **c.** 700 L
2. A glass may hold ▦ of lemonade.   **a.** 300 mL   **b.** 3 L   **c.** 30 L
3. A football player weighs about ▦.   **a.** 110 g   **b.** 110 kg   **c.** 110 mg
4. An orange weighs about ▦.   **a.** 200 kg   **b.** 200 mg   **c.** 200 g
5. A quarter weighs about ▦.   **a.** 6 g   **b.** 6 mg   **c.** 6 kg
6. A bottle of shampoo holds about ▦.   **a.** 5 mL   **b.** 250 L   **c.** 250 mL
7. An ant weighs about ▦.   **a.** 500 mg   **b.** 500 kg   **c.** 5 kg

Copy and complete.

8. 8 kg = ▦ g
9. 60 mL = ▦ L
10. 4.8 kg = ▦ g
11. 5 L = ▦ mL
12. 8,000 mL = ▦ L
13. 0.5 kg = ▦ g
14. 50 mL = ▦ L
15. 0.9 kg = ▦ g
16. 1.1 L = ▦ mL

Solve each problem.

17. Ernie bought 1.7 kg of green beans. How many grams is that?

18. Ms. Carbone bought a 4-L bottle of juice. How many milliliters is that?

19. Miguel Ramirez bought a roast beef for dinner. It weighed 3.34 kg. How many grams is that?

★ 20. Anna had a liter container of orange juice. She used 200 mL of juice for a recipe. What part of a liter is left?

Problem Solving: Applications

METRIC MEASURES

Julius owns the Aquarium Center. He is building a shelf along one wall of his shop so he can display more tanks. The shelf is 4.6 m long. Each tank is 75 cm long. How many tanks will fit side by side on the shelf?

The shelf is 4.6 m long; the tank is 75 cm long.

Change the measurements to the same unit.

$$4.6 \text{ m} = \blacksquare \text{ cm}$$
$$1 \text{ m} = 100 \text{ cm}$$
$$\text{so} \quad 4.6 \text{ m} = 460 \text{ cm}$$

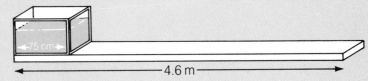

Then divide to find how many tanks will fit.

$$460 \text{ cm} \div 75 \text{ cm} = 6 \text{ R}10$$

$$
\begin{array}{r}
6 \text{ R}10 \\
75\overline{)460} \\
450 \\
\hline
10
\end{array}
$$

6 tanks will fit on the shelf.

Try These

Solve each problem.

1. Julius wants to fill a 15-L tank using a 1,500-mL cup. How many cups of water does he need?

2. A shelf is 2.3 m long. Each tank is 46 cm long. How many tanks will fit on the shelf?

3. Mr. Friedman has 3 L of a pond-cleaning chemical. He uses 750 mL. How much does he have left?

4. Andy bought a piece of plastic tubing. The tubing is 6 m 75 cm long. How many centimeters long is the tubing?

Exercises

Solve each problem.

1. A fish tank can hold 20,000 mL of water. It contains 16 L of water. How many more liters can the tank hold?

2. A bag of fish food weighs 350 g. There are 12 bags in a carton. How many kilograms of fish food are in a carton?

3. A special tank circulates 1 L of water every 4 h. How many milliliters of water are circulated in 1 h?

4. A guppy is 4 cm long. A neon tetra is 38 mm long. A mollie is 3.7 cm long. Which fish is longest?

5. Julius wants to put 1.8 kg of gravel into an aquarium. He has 750 g. How many more kilograms of gravel does he need?

6. The flower of a water lily measures 15 cm across. Another flower measures 95 mm across. What is the difference in their measures?

7. Kate has a 1-kg bag of angel hair for the aquarium filters. She uses 75 g of angel hair for a small filter and 125 g for a large filter. How much angel hair is left in the bag?

8. A customer bought 2.5 kg of pond-cleaning chemical. She used 500 g on the first application. How many more applications of 500 g can she make?

9. A shelf is 2.3 m long. Julius has 2 tanks that are 46 cm long and 1 tank that is 75 cm long on the shelf. Will another tank fit on this shelf? Which size tank will fit?

10. Yvonne buys a 90-g container of fish food for $1.69. She uses 1.5 g of food each day. For how many days can Yvonne feed her fish with this container of food?

11. A female guppy is 3.8 cm long. A male guppy is 19.05 mm long. Which guppy is longer? How much longer? (Give the answer in millimeters.)

12. Paul has 1.5 kg of charcoal for the aquarium filters. He puts 200 g in each of 7 filters. How much charcoal is left?

★ 13. The capacity of a fish tank is 25.6 L. How many kilograms of water will the tank hold?

★ 14. Julius connected pieces of tubing to repair a fountain. The pieces were 2.8 m long, 155 mm long, 6.75 dm long, and 90 cm long. How many meters of tubing did he use?

Problem Solving: Strategies

FINDING INFORMATION

A **double line graph** can provide information that you can use to solve word problems.

The National Weather Service measures and records the depths of major rivers. Large boats can then travel up and down the rivers safely. The map shows the Missouri River and the Kansas River, which flows into the Missouri River at Kansas City. During 8 days in May, the National Weather Service recorded depths for the two rivers. The depths for the Missouri River were recorded at St. Joseph. The depths for the Kansas River were recorded at Kansas City.

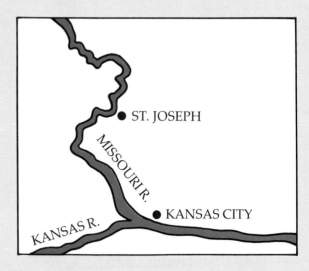

You can use a double line graph to compare the changes in the depths of the two rivers. Dates are shown along the bottom of the graph. The depths of the rivers in feet are shown along the left side of the graph. A dot shows where a date and a depth meet.

The key above the graph shows what the colored lines mean. The red line connects the dots that show the depths of the Missouri River at 6 A.M. on each day. The purple line connects the dots that show the depths of the Kansas River at 6 A.M. on each day.

What was the depth of the Kansas River on May 21?

Find the dot on the purple line above 21. Read across the graph to find the depth. The depth is halfway between 18.2 feet and 18.4 feet.

So the depth of the Kansas River on May 21 was 18.3 feet.

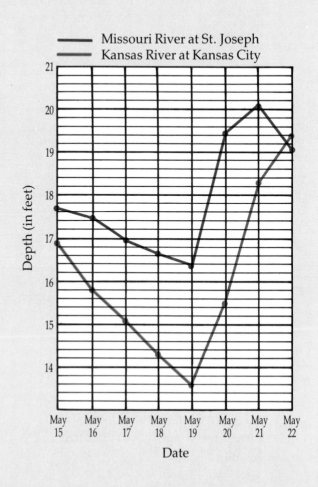

Using the Strategy

Solve each problem.

1. What was the depth of the Missouri River on May 19?

2. What was the depth of the Kansas River on May 20?

3. What was the depth of the Kansas River on May 15?

4. What was the depth of the Missouri River on May 21?

5. What was the difference in the depths of the Missouri River on May 20 and on May 21?

6. What was the difference in the depths of the Kansas River on May 19 and on May 20?

7. Between which 2 dates did the depth of the Missouri River change the most?

8. Between which 2 dates did the depth of the Kansas River change the most?

9. On which date was there the least difference in the depths of the rivers?

10. On which date was there the greatest difference in the depths of the rivers?

11. What do you think the weather conditions in the area were from May 15 to May 19?

12. On 1 date during the 8-day period, there was a heavy rainstorm. Which date do you think it was?

ACTIVITY

MAKING AND USING A DOUBLE LINE GRAPH

The table shows the growth of Kate and her twin brother, Matt, from birth to age 20. Using graph paper, make a double line graph to show their growth.

Using your graph, estimate each of the following.

	Height (in inches)	
Age	Kate	Matt
birth	21	19
5	45	42
10	56	52
15	63	67
20	64	70

1. Kate's height at age 8

2. Matt's height at age 8

3. Matt's height at age 17

4. Matt's age when he was 62 inches tall

5. Kate's age when she was 47 inches tall

Using an Inch Ruler

The **inch (in.)** is a unit used to measure length in the customary system.

This ruler is marked in inches and parts of an inch.

The needle is 2 inches long to the nearest inch.

It is $1\frac{1}{2}$ inches long to the nearest half-inch.

It is $1\frac{3}{4}$ inches long to the nearest quarter-inch.

It is $1\frac{5}{8}$ inches long to the nearest eighth-inch.

It is $1\frac{11}{16}$ inches long to the nearest sixteenth-inch.

Try These

Read the ruler at each place marked.

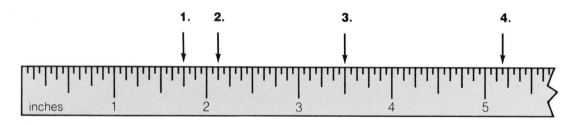

Measure to the nearest inch, half-inch, quarter-inch, and eighth-inch.

5.

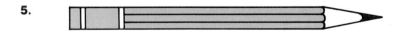

6.

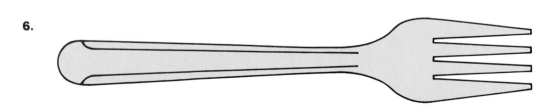

Exercises

Read the ruler at each place marked.

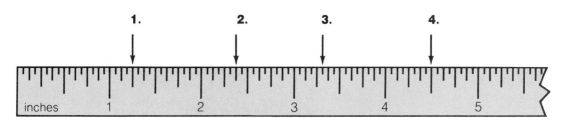

Measure to the nearest inch, half-inch, quarter-inch, and eighth-inch.

5.

6.

7.

Draw an arrow to show each length.

8. 2 inches

9. $1\frac{1}{2}$ inches

10. $\frac{3}{4}$ inch

11. $\frac{5}{8}$ inch

12. $2\frac{3}{8}$ inches

13. $\frac{11}{16}$ inch

 KEEPING IN SHAPE

Estimate each answer.

1. $\begin{array}{r} 186 \\ \times\ \ 8 \\ \hline \end{array}$

2. $\begin{array}{r} 616 \\ \times\ 49 \\ \hline \end{array}$

3. $\begin{array}{r} 704 \\ \times 385 \\ \hline \end{array}$

4. $\begin{array}{r} \$86.25 \\ \times\ \ \ \ 21 \\ \hline \end{array}$

5. $\begin{array}{r} 148.36 \\ \times\ \ \ \ 4.8 \\ \hline \end{array}$

6. $9\overline{)820}$

7. $29\overline{)2,358}$

8. $63\overline{)179.35}$

9. $56\overline{)41,879}$

10. 279×31

11. $11.56 \div 5$

12. 96.67×8.2

13. $24.21 \div 8$

14. $\$19.75 \times 62$

15. $721.63 \div 83$

Customary Units of Length

■ The **foot (ft)**, the **yard (yd)**, and the **mile (mi)** are units used to measure length.

> 1 foot = 12 inches
> 1 yard = 3 feet
> 1 yard = 36 inches
> 1 mile = 5,280 feet
> 1 mile = 1,760 yards

A piano key is about 1 inch wide.

A piano bench is about 1 foot wide.

A piano bench is about 1 yard long.

The highway distance between Washington, D.C., and New York City is about 230 miles.

■ Find the number of inches in 4 ft 6 in.

$$4 \text{ ft } 6 \text{ in.} = \blacksquare \text{ in.}$$
$$1 \text{ ft} = 12 \text{ in.}$$
$$4 \text{ ft} = 4 \times 12 \text{ in.}$$
$$4 \text{ ft} = 48 \text{ in.}$$
$$4 \text{ ft } 6 \text{ in.} = 48 \text{ in.} + 6 \text{ in.}$$
$$4 \text{ ft } 6 \text{ in.} = 54 \text{ in.}$$

■ Find the number of yards and feet in 22 ft.

$$22 \text{ ft} = \blacksquare \text{ yd } \blacksquare \text{ ft}$$
$$3 \text{ ft} = 1 \text{ yd}$$
$$22 \text{ ft} = 7 \text{ yd } 1 \text{ ft}$$

$$\begin{array}{r} 7 \text{ R1} \\ 3\overline{)22} \\ \underline{21} \\ 1 \end{array}$$

Try These

Write *in., ft, yd,* or *mi.*

1. The highway distance from New York to Chicago is about 800 ▓.

2. The height of a classroom might be about 10 ▓.

3. A dog may be about 35 ▓ high.

4. The length of this book is about 10 ▓.

5. The height of a chair is about 1 ▓.

6. Your arm is about 18 ▓ long.

Copy and complete.

7. 2 ft = ▓ in.

8. 60 in. = ▓ ft

9. 9 ft = ▓ yd

10. 3 mi = ▓ ft

11. 3 ft 9 in. = ▓ in.

12. 152 ft = ▓ yd ▓ ft

Exercises

Write *in., ft, yd,* or *mi.*

1. The width of this book is about 8 ▩.
2. The height of a room is about 3 ▩.
3. The distance from Albuquerque to Oklahoma City is about 540 ▩.
4. The distance around earth at the equator is about 24,900 ▩.
5. A television may be about 25 ▩ wide.
6. The height of a man may be about 6 ▩.

Choose the sensible measurement.

7. A rug may be ▩ long.   **a.** 12 ft   **b.** 12 in.   **c.** 12 mi
8. The distance from home plate to right field may be about ▩.   **a.** 330 in.   **b.** 330 ft   **c.** 330 mi
9. A barn may be ▩ wide.   **a.** 50 mi   **b.** 50 ft   **c.** 50 in.
10. The length of a football field is about ▩.   **a.** 100 in.   **b.** 100 yd   **c.** 100 mi
11. A train can travel about ▩ per hour.   **a.** 40 yd   **b.** 40 ft   **c.** 40 mi
12. The length of a car is about ▩.   **a.** 3 yd   **b.** 3 in.   **c.** 3 ft

Copy and complete.

13. 36 in. = ▩ ft
14. 4 mi = ▩ ft
15. 2 yd 1 ft = ▩ ft
16. 11 ft = ▩ yd ▩ ft
17. 144 in. = ▩ ft
18. 2 mi = ▩ yd
19. 5 ft 8 in. = ▩ in.
20. 2 yd 10 in. = ▩ in.
21. 50 in. = ▩ ft ▩ in.
22. 212 in. = ▩ ft ▩ in.
23. 1 mi 200 yd = ▩ yd
★ 24. 2 mi = ▩ in.

Solve each problem.

25. A baseball bat is 32 in. long. How many feet and inches is that?
26. A runner jogs 5.5 mi each day. How many yards is that?
27. A marathon race is 26 mi 385 yd long. How many yards is that?
28. The longest field goal kicked was 63 yd. How many feet is that?
29. The distance from home plate to first base is 90 ft. How many yards is that?
30. A track is 440 yd long. How many laps must a runner complete to run 1 mi?
31. Fran Tarkenton passed a football for a total of 47,003 yd in his career. How many miles and yards is that?
★ 32. Roy Carlyle hit the longest home run ever, 618 ft, in 1929. What part of a mile was that? Round to the nearest hundredth.

Customary Units of Capacity and Weight

■ The **fluid ounce (fl oz)**, the **cup (c)**, the **pint (pt)**, the **quart (qt)**, and the **gallon (gal)** are units of capacity.

> **1 cup = 8 fluid ounces**
> **1 pint = 2 cups**
> **1 quart = 2 pints**
> **1 gallon = 4 quarts**

A bottle of shoe polish contains about 3 fluid ounces.
A small container of yogurt is 1 cup.
A bottle of shampoo is about 1 pint.
Milk is often sold in 1-quart containers.
A fishbowl holds about 1 gallon of water.

■ The **ounce (oz)**, the **pound (lb)**, and the **ton** are units used to measure weight.

> **1 pound = 16 ounces**
> **1 ton = 2,000 pounds**

A letter may weigh about 1 ounce.
A package of butter may weigh 1 pound.
A small car weighs about 1 ton.

■ Find the number of quarts in 3 gal 2 qt.

$$3 \text{ gal } 2 \text{ qt} = \blacksquare \text{ qt}$$
$$1 \text{ gal} = 4 \text{ qt}$$
$$3 \text{ gal} = 3 \times 4 \text{ qt}$$
$$3 \text{ gal} = 12 \text{ qt}$$
$$3 \text{ gal } 2 \text{ qt} = 12 \text{ qt} + 2 \text{ qt}$$
$$3 \text{ gal } 2 \text{ qt} = 14 \text{ qt}$$

■ Find the number of pounds and ounces in 49 oz.

$$49 \text{ oz} = \blacksquare \text{ lb } \blacksquare \text{ oz}$$
$$16 \text{ oz} = 1 \text{ lb}$$
$$49 \text{ oz} = 3 \text{ lb } 1 \text{ oz}$$

$$\begin{array}{r} 3 \text{ R1} \\ 16\overline{)49} \\ \underline{48} \\ 1 \end{array}$$

Try These

Write *fl oz, c, pt, qt,* or *gal*.

1. A bottle of baby oil may contain 8 ▦.
2. A bucket contains about 2 ▦ of water.
3. Cream is often sold in 1-▦ containers.
4. A glass holds about 1 ▦ of liquid.

Write *oz, lb,* or *ton*.

5. A truck may weigh 2 ▦.
6. An iron weighs about 3 ▦.
7. A tennis ball weighs about 5 ▦.
8. A man weighs about 160 ▦.

Copy and complete.

9. 3 qt = ▦ pt
10. 2 gal = ▦ qt
11. 70 oz = ▦ lb ▦ oz
12. 6 qt = ▦ gal ▦ qt
13. 2 lb 3 oz = ▦ oz
14. 2 tons 500 lb = ▦ lb

Exercises

Choose the sensible measurement.

1. A jar of jelly weighs about ▦.
   a. 20 oz b. 20 lb c. 20 tons
2. A girl might drink ▦ of juice.
   a. 1 c b. 1 fl oz c. 1 gal
3. An elephant weighs about ▦.
   a. 6 oz b. 6 lb c. 6 tons
4. A bottle of hand lotion holds ▦.
   a. 12 fl oz b. 12 gal c. 12 qt
5. A stick of butter weighs ▦.
   a. 4 oz b. 4 lb c. 4 tons
6. A saucepan holds about ▦ of soup.
   a. 2 fl oz b. 2 qt c. 2 c
7. Mr. Evans weighs about ▦.
   a. 175 oz b. 175 lb c. 175 tons
8. Irene bought ▦ of gas.
   a. 9 fl oz b. 9 c c. 9 gal

Copy and complete.

9. 8 tons = ▦ lb
10. 32 fl oz = ▦ c
11. 1 gal = ▦ pt
12. 2 gal 3 qt = ▦ qt
13. 20 oz = ▦ lb ▦ oz
14. 9 pt = ▦ c
15. 51 oz = ▦ lb ▦ oz
16. 7,500 lb = ▦ tons ▦ lb
17. 26 qt = ▦ gal ▦ qt

Fluid ounces for liquid measure are different from weight ounces for dry measure.

Write *liquid* for liquid measure or *dry* for dry measure.

18. 15-oz box of raisins
19. 46-fl oz can of tomato juice
20. 8-oz can of sliced pineapples
21. 16-oz can of beans
22. 13-fl oz can of evaporated milk
23. 1-oz jar of onion flakes

Working with Measurements

■ Jennifer bought a guitar in the Notes 'N' Scales Music Store. The guitar weighs 6 lb 9 oz. Jennifer also bought a case for the guitar. The case weighs 2 lb 12 oz. What is the total weight of the guitar and the case?

To find the total weight, add.

Add the ounces.

```
  6 lb  9 oz
+ 2 lb 12 oz
       21 oz
```

Add the pounds.

```
  6 lb  9 oz
+ 2 lb 12 oz
  8 lb 21 oz
```

Rename the answer.

```
   21 oz = 1 lb 5 oz
8 lb 21 oz = 9 lb 5 oz
```

The total weight of the guitar and the case is 9 lb 5 oz.

■ How much heavier is the guitar than the case?

Subtract to find the difference in weights.

```
  6 lb  9 oz      9 oz < 12 oz
− 2 lb 12 oz      Rename 1 lb as 16 oz.
                  16 oz + 9 oz = 25 oz
```

```
   5    25
   6̸ lb  9̸ oz
 − 2 lb 12 oz
   3 lb 13 oz
```

The guitar is 3 lb 13 oz heavier than the case.

Try These

Add. Rename when necessary.

1.
```
  1 lb 12 oz
+ 2 lb  3 oz
```

2.
```
  2 ft 9 in.
+ 1 ft 6 in.
```

3.
```
  4 gal 1 qt
+ 2 gal 2 qt
```

4.
```
  7 gal 3 qt
+ 1 gal 3 qt
```

Subtract. Rename when necessary.

5.
```
  8 gal 3 qt
− 3 gal 1 qt
```

6.
```
  5 ft 6 in.
− 3 ft 4 in.
```

7.
```
  3 lb
− 1 lb 8 oz
```

8.
```
  5 qt
− 3 qt 1 pt
```

Exercises

Add. Rename when necessary.

1. 3 ft 1 in.
+ 1 ft 9 in.

2. 4 lb 12 oz
+ 1 lb 9 oz

3. 6 ft 8 in.
+ 1 ft 10 in.

4. 1 h 30 min
+ 2 h 15 min

5. 2 gal 1 qt
+ 5 gal 3 qt

6. 2 lb 8 oz
+ 2 lb 8 oz

7. 2 qt 1 pt
+ 3 qt 1 pt

8. 1 ton   500 lb
+ 2 ton 1,800 lb

Subtract. Rename when necessary.

9. 2 lb 8 oz
− 1 lb 2 oz

10. 7 ft
− 2 ft 9 in.

11. 5 gal 1 qt
− 2 gal 3 qt

12. 6 ft 3 in.
− 5 ft 9 in.

13. 2 h 2 min
− 1 h 30 min

14. 5 lb 6 oz
− 1 lb 3 oz

15. 3 c 4 fl oz
− 1 c 5 fl oz

16. 4 tons
− 2 tons 900 lb

Compute. Rename when necessary.

17. 6 lb 12 oz
+ 3 lb 12 oz

18. 4 h
− 2 h 15 min

19. 5 ft 7 in.
+ 3 ft 5 in.

20. 6 ft 10 in.
− 3 ft 6 in.

21. 4 c 3 fl oz
+ 1 c 6 fl oz

22. 3 lb
− 1 lb 4 oz

23. 4 qt 1 pt
− 2 qt 1 pt

24. 3 gal 3 qt
+ 2 gal 3 qt

Solve each problem.

25. Emily bought a flute that weighs 1 lb 6 oz. The case weighs 15 oz. What is the total weight of the flute and the case?

26. A western guitar is 3 ft 4 in. long. A student guitar is 2 ft 9 in. long. How much longer is the western guitar?

27. Notes 'N' Scales painted its practice rooms. On Monday, Mr. Granger used 3 qt of paint. On Tuesday, he used 1 gal of paint. How many quarts of paint were used in all?

28. The manager of Notes 'N' Scales worked with new employees for 1 h 45 min in the morning. Then he worked with them for 3 h 20 min in the afternoon. How much time did he spend with new employees?

29. The full-size electronic keyboard weighs 18 lb. The mini electronic keyboard weighs 8 lb 4 oz. How much more does the full-size electronic keyboard weigh?

★ **30.** A carton of harmonicas arrives at Notes 'N' Scales. The weight of the contents of the box is 27 lb. How many harmonicas weighing 1 lb 2 oz are in the box?

Problem Solving: Applications

READ
PLAN
DO
CHECK

USING A DOUBLE LINE GRAPH

This line graph shows the accumulated amount of rainfall in the towns of Derby and Rogers. The data are for an 8-hour period. A rain gauge was used to measure the rainfall. The gauge was read each hour.

How much more rain had fallen in Rogers than in Derby at 12 noon?

To find how much more, subtract 0.8 from 0.9.

$$\begin{array}{r} 0.9 \leftarrow \text{rainfall in Rogers} \\ -0.8 \leftarrow \text{rainfall in Derby} \\ \hline 0.1 \end{array}$$

0.1 inch more rain had fallen in Rogers than in Derby at 12 noon.

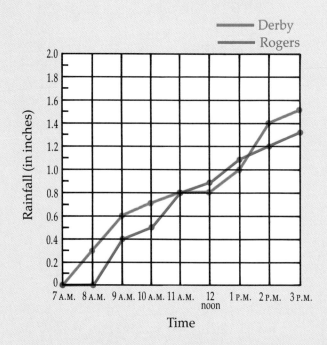

Try These

Solve each problem.

1. How much more rain had fallen in Derby than in Rogers at 2 P.M.?

2. How much rainfall was there in Rogers during this 8-hour period?

3. Which of these towns had more rain during this 8-hour period?

4. How much rain had fallen in Rogers at 12:30 P.M.?

5. Between which hours did the rainfall stop in Derby?

6. Between which hours did the greatest amount of rain fall in Derby?

Exercises

This graph shows the accumulated amount of snowfall in the cities of Loretts and Granger. The data are for a 24-hour period.

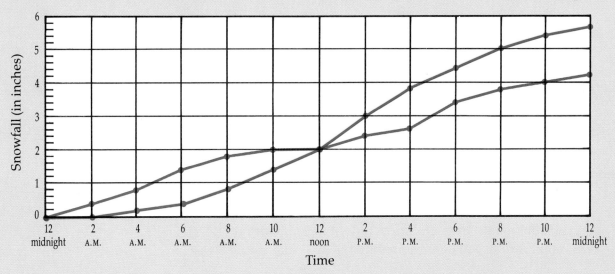

Solve each problem.

1. Between which hours did the snow begin falling in Granger?

2. How much snow had fallen in Loretts at 10 A.M.?

3. At what time had both Loretts and Granger received the same amount of snow?

4. How much more snow fell in Granger than in Loretts over this 24-hour period?

5. How much more snow fell in Granger than in Loretts at 2 P.M.?

6. Estimate how much snow had fallen in Loretts at 7 P.M.

7. Between which hours did the greatest amount of snow fall in Loretts?

8. Between which hours did the greatest amount of snow fall in Granger?

9. Between which hours did 0.4 in. of snow fall in Granger?

10. Between which hours did 0.6 in. of snow fall in Loretts?

11. Estimate how much snow had fallen in Granger at 3 P.M.

12. How much snow had fallen in Loretts at 9 A.M.?

13. The average amount of snowfall in Loretts during January is 14.65 in. The average amount in Granger during January is 5.5 in. more. What is the average amount of snowfall in Granger during January?

14. The average annual amount of snowfall in Granger is 77.3 in. The average annual amount of snowfall in Loretts is 18.65 in. less. What is the average annual amount of snowfall in Loretts?

CHAPTER CHECKPOINT

What time is it? (pp. 158–159)

1. 1 hour 18 minutes before 1:30 P.M.
3. 2 hours before 12:28 P.M.

2. 6 hours 49 minutes after 9:41 A.M.
4. 5 hours 50 minutes after 11:10 P.M.

Copy and complete. (pp. 160–161)

5. 2 days 5 hours = ▓ hours
7. 41 months = ▓ years ▓ months

6. 5 hours 2 minutes = ▓ minutes
8. 7 weeks 3 days = ▓ days

Measure the length of each line segment to the nearest centimeter and to the nearest millimeter. (pp. 162–163)

9. ●—————————————● **10.** ●————————————————●

Choose the sensible measurement. (pp. 162–163, 166–167)

	a.	**b.**	**c.**
11. A pencil is about ▓ long.	15 cm	15 mm	15 km
12. A canoe is about ▓ long.	3 m	3 dm	3 cm
13. A glass holds about ▓ of milk.	250 L	250 mL	5 L
14. A bag of potatoes weighs about ▓.	2 g	2 mg	2 kg

Copy and complete. (pp. 164–167)

15. 40 mm = ▓ cm
18. 80 mL = ▓ L

16. 5,400 m = ▓ km
19. 0.6 kg = ▓ g

17. 168 mm = ▓ m
20. 6.1 L = ▓ mL

Measure the pencil to the nearest inch, half-inch, and quarter-inch. (pp. 172–173)

21.

Choose the sensible measurement. (pp. 174–177)

	a.	**b.**	**c.**
22. The length of a car is about ▓.	15 in.	15 ft	15 mi
23. A pen is about ▓ long.	6 in.	6 ft	6 mi
24. This book weighs about ▓.	2 oz	2 lb	2 tons
25. A small bottle of juice may hold ▓.	6 fl oz	6 qt	6 gal

Copy and complete (pp. 174–177)

26. 36 in. = ▧ ft

27. 32 fl oz = ▧ c

28. 3 lb = ▧ oz

29. 6 ft 4 in. = ▧ in.

30. 68 oz = ▧ lb ▧ oz

31. 18 qt = ▧ gal ▧ qt

32. 16 qt = ▧ gal

33. 2 mi = ▧ ft

34. 3 mi = ▧ yd

35. 8,000 lb = ▧ tons

36. 2 tons 800 lb = ▧ lb

37. 2 lb 4 oz = ▧ oz

Compute. Rename when necessary. (pp. 178–179)

38.   3 ft 6 in.
       +2 ft 8 in.

39.   5 lb 8 oz
       −2 lb 3 oz

40.   6 h 10 min
       −2 h 30 min

41.   6 qt 1 pt
       +3 qt 1 pt

42.   5 gal 1 qt
       −2 gal 3 qt

43.   2 lb 14 oz
       +1 lb 6 oz

44.   5 ft 7 in.
       −2 ft 3 in.

45.   3 ton
       −2 ton 700 lb

Solve each problem. (pp. 158–181)

46. Betty had a meeting at 1:15 P.M. The meeting ended at 4:20 P.M. How long did the meeting last?

47. Betty and her staff sat around a table. The table was 11 ft 7 in. long. How many inches is that?

48. At the meeting, Mrs. Hughes poured 250 mL of water for each of 9 clients. How many liters of water were poured?

49. Betty videotaped her speech. It lasted 16 min 30 s. She cut 5 min 50 s from the tape. How long is Betty's speech now?

Sally grew two bean plants. She kept one in a dark room. She kept the other in the sun. After the beans sprouted, she measured the plants each day. Sally made this graph using her data for the first week.

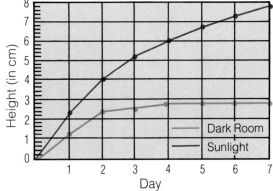

50. How tall was the plant in the sunlight at the end of the sixth day?

51. On the third day, how much taller was the plant in the sunlight than the one in the dark room?

52. What happened to the growth of the plant in the dark room from the fourth day to the seventh day?

COMPUTERS AND PROBLEM SOLVING

■ To solve a problem, the computer sometimes requires a specific input. How do you put a message in your program to tell the user what to do?

This program asks for the weights and prices of two items. The program computes the unit costs and tells you which item is a better buy.

```
NEW
10   INPUT "HOW MANY OUNCES IN PRODUCT1?"; O1
20   INPUT "HOW MUCH DOES PRODUCT1 COST?"; C1
30   INPUT "HOW MANY OUNCES IN PRODUCT2?"; O2
40   INPUT "HOW MUCH DOES PRODUCT2 COST?"; C2
50   LET U1 = C1 / O1
60   LET U2 = C2 / O2
70   IF U1 < U2 THEN GOTO 90
80   PRINT "PRODUCT2 IS THE BETTER BUY.": GOTO 100
90   PRINT "PRODUCT1 IS THE BETTER BUY."
100  END
```

Solve each problem.

1. What would happen if there were no GOTO in line 70?

2. How are the unit prices calculated by the program?

3. Change the variables in line 70 so that lines 50 and 60 are no longer needed for the program to work.

"VERY BERRY"
14 OZ
$1.26

■ This program will be more useful if lines are added to let the user input weights in pounds and ounces.

```
 5   INPUT "HOW MANY POUNDS IN PRODUCT1?"; P1
25   INPUT "HOW MANY POUNDS IN PRODUCT2?"; P2
```

The pound weights must be added to the ounce weights, but first they must be converted. Rewrite lines 50 and 60 so that the pound weights are multiplied by 16 and added to the ounce weights. The unit cost and price variables will stay the same.

```
50   LET U1 = C1 / (O1 + 16 * P1)
60   LET U2 = C2 / (O2 + 16 * P2)
```

The parentheses ( ) around the right-hand part of each expression tells the computer to complete that part of the calculation first.

Solve each problem.

1. Rewrite the program to compare the unit cost of liquids, using quarts and ounces.

2. Add lines to the program to have the computer print out the unit price of each item.

"MERRY BERRY"
18 OZ
$2.34

ENRICHMENT

FAHRENHEIT SCALE

Temperature can be measured in degrees Fahrenheit (°F). The Fahrenheit temperature scale is named after Gabriel Fahrenheit, a German scientist.

Pure water freezes at 32°F.
Pure water boils at 212°F.
The normal body temperature is 98.6°F.

The outside temperature on a very cold day can be below 0°F. A thermometer reading of ⁻10°F means the temperature is 10° below 0°.

The table shows the temperatures in one part of the Great Smoky Mountains in North Carolina.

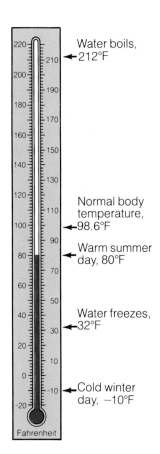

TEMPERATURE READINGS (°F)				
	Typical 24-Hour Day		Extremes in 35 Years	
Month	High	Low	High	Low
January	50	28	81	⁻9
February	54	29	80	⁻13
March	61	34	84	⁻2
April	72	43	93	19
May	79	50	99	28
June	86	58	102	36

Solve each problem.

1. What is the typical high temperature for April?

2. What is the typical low temperature for June?

3. What was the lowest temperature in March during the past 35 years?

4. What was the highest temperature in May during the past 35 years?

5. What is the difference between the typical high temperature and the typical low temperature in February?

6. What is the difference between the extreme high temperature and the extreme low temperature in February?

7. If the temperature were 36°F and then went down 9°, what would the new temperature be?

8. If the temperature were 5°F and then went down 8°, what would the new temperature be?

What does the digit 6 mean in each number?

1. 65,014 **2.** 6,709,000 **3.** 76,000,000,471

Write each number.

4. 85 thousand 215 **5.** 784 thousand 75
6. five hundred eleven million, three hundred thousand, twelve
7. sixty-one billion, six hundred thousand, three hundred

Write >, <, or =.

8. 5,461 ■ 4,516 **9.** 235,106 ■ 235,106
10. 35,064,815 ■ 35,046,851 **11.** 60,380,509,997 ■ 60,680,590,997

Round each number to the given place.

12. 786 to the nearest ten **13.** $16.63 to the nearest dollar

Add, subtract, or multiply. Estimate to check.

14.	**15.**	**16.**	**17.**	**18.**
98	$1.89	6,407	762	365
+37	× 6	−1,896	× 86	1,276
				+ 997

Divide.

19. 5)‾38 **20.** 3)‾369 **21.** 86)‾97,215 **22.** 40)‾$194.40

23. 9,108 ÷ 18 **24.** 24,415 ÷ 23 **25.** 159,516 ÷ 236

Write as a decimal.

26. 15 and 9 tenths **27.** 6 and 15 hundredths
28. 514 and 219 thousandths **29.** 83 and 6 hundredths

Round each number to the given place.

30. 9.5 to the nearest whole number **31.** 16.18 to the nearest tenth

(Continued)

Add or subtract.

32. $\begin{array}{r} 5.6 \\ +2.3 \\ \hline \end{array}$ **33.** $\begin{array}{r} 1.76 \\ -0.9 \\ \hline \end{array}$ **34.** $\begin{array}{r} 3.27 \\ +1.986 \\ \hline \end{array}$ **35.** $\begin{array}{r} 5.009 \\ -1.864 \\ \hline \end{array}$ **36.** $\begin{array}{r} 38.29 \\ 1.64 \\ +12.9 \\ \hline \end{array}$

Multiply.

37. $\begin{array}{r} 2.6 \\ \times\ \ 8 \\ \hline \end{array}$ **38.** $\begin{array}{r} 0.75 \\ \times\ 0.6 \\ \hline \end{array}$ **39.** $\begin{array}{r} 0.02 \\ \times\ \ \ 3 \\ \hline \end{array}$ **40.** $\begin{array}{r} 3.76 \\ \times\ 100 \\ \hline \end{array}$ **41.** $\begin{array}{r} 9.86 \\ \times\ 1.5 \\ \hline \end{array}$

Divide.

42. $3\overline{)27.75}$ **43.** $15\overline{)7.545}$ **44.** $0.09\overline{)2.817}$ **45.** $100\overline{)96.74}$

Copy and complete.

46. 4.9 cm = ▦ mm **47.** 9.6 m = ▦ cm **48.** 9,200 m = ▦ km
49. 30 mL = ▦ L **50.** 0.9 kg = ▦ g **51.** 36 mm = ▦ m
52. 48 in. = ▦ ft **53.** 6,000 lb = ▦ tons **54.** 32 qt = ▦ gal
55. 14 ft = ▦ yd ▦ ft **56.** 3 lb 3 oz = ▦ oz **57.** 19 qt = ▦ gal ▦ qt

Compute. Rename when necessary.

58. $\begin{array}{r} 4\text{ lb }6\text{ oz} \\ -2\text{ lb }9\text{ oz} \\ \hline \end{array}$ **59.** $\begin{array}{r} 5\text{ qt }1\text{ pt} \\ +1\text{ qt }1\text{ pt} \\ \hline \end{array}$ **60.** $\begin{array}{r} 9\text{ ft }6\text{ in.} \\ +3\text{ ft }8\text{ in.} \\ \hline \end{array}$ **61.** $\begin{array}{r} 9\text{ h }18\text{ min} \\ -3\text{ h }50\text{ min} \\ \hline \end{array}$

Solve each problem.

62. José bought a shirt for $12.98 and a tie for $6.59. The tax was $1.37. How much money did he spend?

63. There are 6,000 newspapers to deliver. Ed delivers 2,463. How many papers are left to deliver?

64. Each tray holds 18 necklaces. How many necklaces fit on 36 trays?

65. Elena's math test scores are 86, 93, 79, and 90. What is her average test score?

66. Eileen bought a record that cost $8.79. There is a sales tax of $.06 on a dollar. How much sales tax did Eileen pay?

67. Jerry paid $3.36 for 3 lb of chicken. What is the cost per pound?

7

**NUMBER
RELATIONSHIPS**

Divisibility

■ The whole numbers are 0, 1, 2, 3, 4, and so on. A number **is divisible by** a second number if the remainder is 0 when the first number is divided by the second.

$$\begin{array}{r} 5 \\ 3\overline{)15} \\ 15 \\ \hline 0 \end{array}$$
The remainder is 0.
15 is divisible by 3.

$$\begin{array}{r} 3 \text{ R3} \\ 4\overline{)15} \\ 12 \\ \hline 3 \end{array}$$
The remainder is not 0.
15 is not divisible by 4.

■ These rules for divisibility can help you divide mentally.

DIVISIBILITY BY 2
A number is divisible by 2 if the ones digit is 0, 2, 4, 6, or 8. Some numbers that are divisible by 2 are 40; 772; 984; 1,726; and 9,758.

Even numbers are divisible by 2.
Odd numbers are not divisible by 2.

DIVISIBILITY BY 5
A number is divisible by 5 if the ones digit is 0 or 5. Some numbers that are divisible by 5 are 25; 80; 105; and 6,790.

DIVISIBILITY BY 10
A number is divisible by 10 if the ones digit is 0. Some numbers that are divisible by 10 are 60; 200; and 7,770.

DIVISIBILITY BY 3
A number is divisible by 3 if the sum of its digits is divisible by 3.

Is 231 divisible by 3?

$$2 + 3 + 1 = 6$$

The sum, 6, is divisible by 3.
So 231 is divisible by 3.

DIVISIBILITY BY 9
A number is divisible by 9 if the sum of its digits is divisible by 9.

Is 243 divisible by 9?

$$2 + 4 + 3 = 9$$

The sum, 9, is divisible by 9.
So 243 is divisible by 9.

Try These

Is the first number divisible by the second? Write *yes* or *no*.

1. 10, 2
2. 17, 7
3. 53, 6
4. 15, 5
5. 41, 4
6. 426, 3
7. 45, 9
8. 123, 7
9. 655, 5
10. 64, 9
11. 153, 9
12. 408, 10
13. 40, 10
14. 5, 2
15. 105, 6

Exercises

Is the first number divisible by the second? Write *yes* or *no*.

1. 24, 8   **2.** 56, 7   **3.** 35, 6   **4.** 27, 10   **5.** 108, 9

6. 54, 4   **7.** 87, 3   **8.** 546, 9   **9.** 76, 4   **10.** 360, 10

11. 71, 3   **12.** 254, 9   **13.** 68, 4   **14.** 264, 3   **15.** 104, 8

16. 246, 3   **17.** 135, 5   **18.** 657, 9   **19.** 96, 6   **20.** 63, 2

 Is the first number divisible by the second? Divide the first number by the second. If the quotient is a whole number, the answer is yes. If the quotient is not a whole number, the answer is no.

21. 258, 6   **22.** 963, 7   **23.** 456, 8   **24.** 965, 13   **25.** 893, 3

26. 342, 4   **27.** 2,511; 9   **28.** 2,783; 11   **29.** 3,983; 7   **30.** 322, 14

Solve each problem mentally or with paper and pencil.

31. Can you divide 51 pencils equally among 3 people?

32. Can you divide 354 thumbtacks equally among 9 people?

33. Mr. Perkins has 3,252 papers on his desk. Can he put the papers into 2 equal piles? Into 3 equal piles? Into 5 equal piles?

34. Ms. Collins has 441 travel pamphlets. Can she put the pamphlets into 2 equal piles? Into 3 equal piles? Into 9 equal piles?

Any year that is divisible by 4 is a leap year except century years. Century years, such as 1600, 1700, and 1800, are leap years only if they are divisible by 400. For example, 1600 and 1604 were leap years, but 1700 was not.

Which of the following were leap years? Write *yes* or *no*.

★ **35.** 1776, the year the Declaration of Independence was signed

★ **36.** 800, the year Charlemagne became emperor of the Holy Roman Empire

★ **37.** 1798, the year smallpox vaccination was begun

★ **38.** 1492, the year Christopher Columbus discovered America

Multiples and Common Multiples

■ If you multiply 5 by any whole number, the product is a multiple of 5. Here are some of the multiples of 5:

0	5	10	15	20
↑	↑	↑	↑	↑
0×5	1×5	2×5	3×5	4×5

> 0 is a multiple of every whole number.

To say *is a multiple of* means the same as *is divisible by*.

18 is a multiple of 3.   18 is divisible by 3.

■ There are two lighthouse beacons. The beams of light are shining in the same direction. One beacon makes a complete turn in 3 seconds. The other takes 5 seconds. How soon will both beacons again be at the starting position at the same time?

This table can help you find the answer. It shows the times when each beacon is back at the starting position.

Seconds	1	2	3	4	5	6	7	8	9	10	11	12	13	14	15	16	17	18	19	20	21	22	23	24	25	26	27	28	29	30
First Beacon			▓			▓			▓			▓			▓			▓			▓			▓			▓			▓
Second Beacon					▓					▓					▓					▓					▓					▓

The times when the first beacon is back at the starting position are multiples of 3. The times when the second beacon is back at the starting position are multiples of 5.

After 15 seconds and after 30 seconds, both lights are shining in the starting direction. 15 and 30 are **common multiples** of 3 and 5.

Both beacons are back at the starting position after 15 seconds. 15 is the **least common multiple** of 3 and 5.

■ Find the least common multiple of 6 and 8.

Multiples of 6 greater than 0:   6, 12, 18, 24, 30, 36, 42, 48

Multiples of 8 greater than 0:   8, 16, 24, 32, 40, 48

24 and 48 are common multiples of 6 and 8. 24 is the least common multiple of 6 and 8.

Try These

Copy and complete.

1. multiples of 9: 0, 9, 18, ▓, ▓, ▓   **2.** multiples of 12: 0, 12, 24, ▓, ▓, ▓

Solve.

3. List the first ten multiples of 6 greater than 0.

4. List the first six multiples of 10 greater than 0.

5. List the two numbers that are on both lists.

6. What is the least common multiple of 6 and 10?

Exercises

Find the least common multiple of each pair of numbers.

1. 5, 4	**2.** 4, 8	**3.** 11, 7	**4.** 8, 12	**5.** 6, 14
6. 4, 12	**7.** 10, 15	**8.** 12, 6	**9.** 11, 13	**10.** 9, 36
11. 13, 1	**12.** 36, 48	**13.** 60, 90	★ **14.** 56, 36	★ **15.** 182, 143

Solve each problem.

16. Two boats cruise the lake. One boat passes the lighthouse every 18 min. The other boat passes every 45 min. They leave the lighthouse at the same time. How long will it be before both boats pass the lighthouse again at the same time?

★ **17.** Captain Matt's boat passes Hook's Landing every 35 min. Captain Ali's boat passes every 25 min. If both captains leave Hook's Landing at the same time, how long will it be before they meet there again? Give your answer in hours and minutes.

THINK AND TRY

USING CLUES

What number am I?

1. I am a 2-digit number. I am divisible by 9. My ones digit is 3.

2. I am the least number greater than 0 that is divisible by 8, by 12, and by 20.

3. I am a common multiple of 3, of 4, and of 8. I am less than 100. The sum of my digits is 9.

4. I am a 3-digit number. I am divisible by 9. My ones digit is 2. I am between 400 and 500.

Factors and Common Factors

■ Suppose that you wish to arrange 12 square stickers in a rectangular pattern. These are the choices you have:

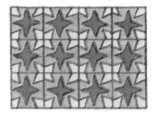

$1 \times 12 = 12$ $2 \times 6 = 12$ $3 \times 4 = 12$

The numbers shown in red are called factors of 12.
Each product shows two factors of 12.
Here is a complete list of the factors of 12:   1, 2, 3, 4, 6, 12.

■ You can divide to decide whether one number is a factor of another.

$$\begin{array}{r} 13 \\ 3\overline{)39} \end{array} \qquad\qquad \begin{array}{r} 5\ R4 \\ 7\overline{)39} \end{array}$$

The remainder is 0.   The remainder is 4.
3 is a factor of 39.   7 is not a factor of 39.

■ Here are three ways to say the same thing:

  3 is a factor of 39.   39 is divisible by 3.   39 is a multiple of 3.

■ The factors of 16 are 1, 2, 4, 8, and 16.
The factors of 28 are 1, 2, 4, 7, 14, and 28.

1, 2, and 4 are factors of both 16 and 28.
They are called **common factors** of 16 and 28.
The **greatest common factor** of 16 and 28 is 4.

■ The factors of 10 are 1, 2, 5, and 10.
The factors of 21 are 1, 3, 7, and 21.

The only common factor of 10 and 21 is 1.
So 1 is the greatest common factor of 10 and 21.

Try These

List the common factors of each pair of numbers. Then find their greatest common factor.

1. factors of 21:   1, 3, 7, 21
    factors of 18:   1, 2, 3, 6, 9, 18

2. factors of 12:   1, 2, 3, 4, 6, 12
    factors of 16:   1, 2, 4, 8, 16

Write each number as a product of two numbers in as many ways as possible. Then list all the factors of the number.

3. 6   **4.** 9   **5.** 14   **6.** 13   **7.** 22   **8.** 45

Exercises

List the factors of each number.

1. 15   **2.** 35   **3.** 25   **4.** 17   **5.** 32   **6.** 31
7. 50   **8.** 42   **9.** 24   **10.** 49   ★ **11.** 144   ★ **12.** 131

Find the greatest common factor of each pair of numbers.

13. 9, 12   **14.** 10, 15   **15.** 12, 8   **16.** 5, 7   **17.** 25, 20
18. 16, 36   **19.** 18, 22   **20.** 12, 6   **21.** 14, 21   **22.** 14, 15
23. 9, 18   **24.** 55, 77   **25.** 30, 36   ★ **26.** 150, 90   ★ **27.** 252, 468

Solve each problem.

28. Suppose you wish to arrange 18 square tiles in a rectangular pattern. Write a multiplication sentence for each choice you have.

★ **29.** Suppose you wish to arrange 72 square tiles in a rectangular pattern. Write a multiplication sentence for each choice you have.

KEEPING IN SHAPE

1. $8\overline{)75}$ **2.** $3\overline{)976}$ **3.** $6\overline{)2,767}$ **4.** $13\overline{)74}$ **5.** $30\overline{)280}$

6. $164 \div 39$ **7.** $765 \div 43$ **8.** $936 \div 113$ **9.** $6,958 \div 324$ **10.** $937 \div 52$

Prime and Composite Numbers

■ A **prime number** is a whole number with exactly two different factors, itself and 1.

$$13 = 1 \times 13$$

The factors of 13 are 1 and 13.
13 is a prime number.

A **composite number** is a whole number with more than two different factors.

$$6 = 1 \times 6$$
$$6 = 2 \times 3$$

The factors of 6 are 1, 2, 3, and 6.
6 is a composite number.

Is 1 a prime number or a composite number?

1 has just one factor, itself.
1 is neither prime nor composite.

■ Every composite number is the product of **prime factors**. Find the prime factors of 24. Use a **factor tree**.

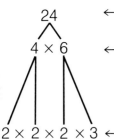

← Begin with 24.

← Choose any two factors whose product is 24.

Neither 4 nor 6 is prime. Find the factors of 4 and 6.

← All the factors are prime. Stop.

There are other factor trees for 24.

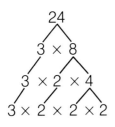

← Begin with 24. →

← Choose pairs of factors. →

Go on until all the factors are prime.

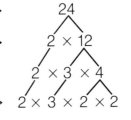

The prime factors are the same. Only the order is different.
The 2 appears three times and the 3 appears once.

Try These

Write *prime* or *composite*.

1. 2   **2.** 3   **3.** 4   **4.** 5   **5.** 8

6. 7   **7.** 9   **8.** 15   **9.** 19   **10.** 25

Show each number as a product of prime factors.

11. 6   **12.** 10   **13.** 20   **14.** 35   **15.** 48

Exercises

Write *prime* or *composite*.

1. 6   **2.** 10   **3.** 31   **4.** 47   **5.** 26

6. 11   **7.** 44   **8.** 29   **9.** 13   **10.** 37

11. 21   **12.** 58   **13.** 53   **14.** 75   **15.** 100

Copy and complete each factor tree.

16.
$$36 = 4 \times 9$$

17.
$$36 = 3 \times 12$$

18.
$$36 = 6 \times 6$$

19.

$$64 = 4 \times 16$$

20.
$$64 = 8 \times 8$$

21.
$$64 = 2 \times 32$$

22.

$$56 = 7 \times 8$$

23.

$$56 = 2 \times 28$$

24.
$$56 = 4 \times 14$$

Show each number as a product of prime factors.

25. 25   **26.** 45   **27.** 27   **28.** 32   **29.** 54

30. 48   **31.** 81   **32.** 40   **33.** 65   **34.** 72

35. 16   **36.** 100   **37.** 120   **38.** 150   **39.** 200

Two prime numbers that have a difference of 2 are called **twin primes**. For example, 17 and 19 are twin primes.

Solve each problem.

40. Find at least two more pairs of twin primes less than 20.

★ **41.** Find four pairs of twin primes greater than 20 and less than 100.

Problem Solving: Strategies

LOGICAL REASONING

- You can use **Venn diagrams** to show **sets** to help you solve problems.

Suppose set A is the set of all the factors of 10. The numbers that are factors of 10 are inside the circle. The numbers that are not factors of 10 are outside the circle. Not all of them can be shown. Only 8, 12, and 3 are shown here.

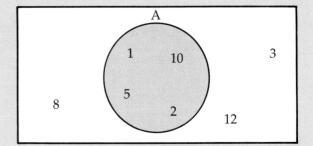

- Suppose you were told that set B is either the set of all prime numbers or the set of all odd numbers. How could you tell which it is?

Not all the numbers in set B are shown. Each number that is shown in set B is both a prime number and an odd number.

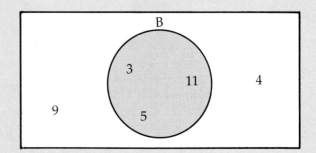

Look at the number 9 outside the circle. If set B were the set of odd numbers, then 9 would be inside set B. Therefore, set B must be the set of prime numbers.

Should the number 6 be inside or outside set B?

Because 6 is not a prime number, it should be outside the circle.

Using the Strategy

Set C is the set of all the factors of 42.

Write whether each number should be inside or outside set C.

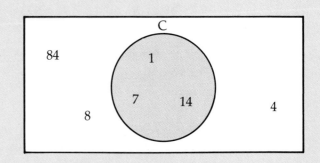

1. 11   2. 6   3. 3

4. 18   5. 21   6. 42

Set D is the set of all the multiples of 3.

Write whether each number should be *inside* or *outside* set D.

7. 6 **8.** 14 **9.** 51

10. 405 **11.** 137 **12.** 1,000

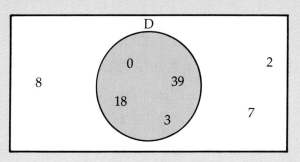

Solve each problem.

13. Which of the following could set E be?

  a. the set of all even numbers

  b. the set of all factors of 12

  c. the set of all multiples of 4

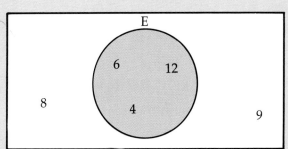

14. Which of the following could set F be?

  a. the set of all odd numbers

  b. the set of all prime numbers

  c. the set of all multiples of 3

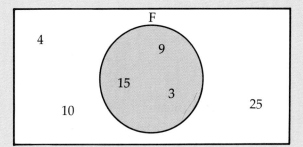

 ACTIVITY

EXPLORING NUMBER RELATIONSHIPS

Here is a famous unsolved problem in mathematics:
Can every even whole number greater than 2 be
written as a sum of two prime numbers?
No one knows the answer for sure.

This is the solution for the first five
even whole numbers greater than 2.

$4 = 2 + 2$ $10 = 3 + 7$ or $5 + 5$
$6 = 3 + 3$ $12 = 5 + 7$
$8 = 3 + 5$

Here is a list of all prime numbers
less than 40: 2, 3, 5, 7, 11, 13, 17,
19, 23, 29, 31, 37.

Write each even number from 14 through
40 as a sum of two prime numbers.

Problem Solving: Applications

USING A DOUBLE BAR GRAPH

This **double bar graph** compares the sales of the Earthmoving Equipment Company over a 4-year period inside and outside the United States. The graph shows sales in millions of dollars.

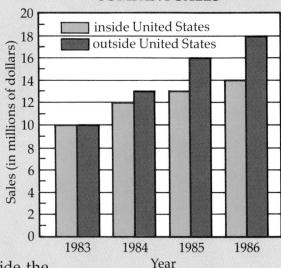

COMPANY SALES

The key above the graph shows what the different colors mean.

The green bars show sales inside the United States.
The brown bars show sales outside the United States.

In 1985, how much greater were sales outside the United States than sales inside the United States?

Sales outside the United States in 1985 were $16,000,000. Sales inside the United States in 1985 were $13,000,000.

Subtract $13,000,000 from $16,000,000 to find how much greater.

$$\begin{array}{r} \$16,000,000 \\ - \ \ 13,000,000 \\ \hline \$ \ \ 3,000,000 \end{array}$$

In 1985, sales outside the United States were $3,000,000 greater than sales inside the United States.

Try These

Solve each problem.

1. In 1986, how much less were sales inside the United States than sales outside the United States?

2. What were the total sales outside the United States for the 4-year period?

3. What were the total sales of the company in 1984?

4. How much greater were the total sales in 1985 than in 1984?

Exercises

This graph compares the average number of men and women who worked for the Earthmoving Equipment Company in various years. The graph shows the number of employees in thousands.

Solve each problem.

1. What was the average number of men working for the company in 1970?

2. How many more men than women worked for the company in 1950?

3. How many fewer men than women worked for the company in 1980?

4. What was the total number of employees in 1950?

5. What was the total number of employees in 1970?

6. What was the total number of employees in 1980?

7. In which years was the total number of employees over 13,000?

8. In which year was the difference between the number of men and the number of women the greatest?

9. Each employee receives about $2,000 in medical benefits. How much did these benefits cost the company in 1970?

10. In 1960, the company paid each employee an average of $8,934 for the year. Estimate the total amount the company paid its employees in 1960.

★ 11. In 1980, the company paid each employee an average of $12,234 for the year. Estimate the total amount the company paid its employees in 1980.

Is the first number divisible by the second? Write *yes* or *no*. (pp. 190–191)

1. 27, 3	**2.** 31, 5	**3.** 83, 9	**4.** 96, 8	**5.** 63, 3
6. 72, 6	**7.** 74, 7	**8.** 130, 10	**9.** 114, 6	**10.** 92, 13
11. 536, 3	**12.** 558, 9	**13.** 806, 9	**14.** 355, 5	**15.** 122, 3

For each number, list the first five multiples greater than 0. (pp. 192–193)

16. 6	**17.** 9	**18.** 7	**19.** 13	**20.** 10

Find the least common multiple of each pair of numbers. (pp. 192–193)

21. 5, 6	**22.** 9, 3	**23.** 4, 6	**24.** 7, 4	**25.** 3, 12
26. 6, 15	**27.** 16, 6	**28.** 14, 3	**29.** 9, 15	**30.** 20, 15

List the factors of each number. (pp. 194–195)

31. 7	**32.** 33	**33.** 4	**34.** 11	**35.** 34

Find the greatest common factor of each pair of numbers. (pp. 194–195)

36. 6, 9	**37.** 2, 6	**38.** 15, 5	**39.** 9, 21	**40.** 6, 18
41. 12, 18	**42.** 14, 21	**43.** 18, 24	**44.** 16, 4	**45.** 18, 27
46. 24, 18	**47.** 4, 18	**48.** 6, 54	**49.** 24, 40	**50.** 72, 9

Write *prime* or *composite*. (pp. 196–197)

51. 15	**52.** 9	**53.** 11	**54.** 51	**55.** 49
56. 7	**57.** 61	**58.** 81	**59.** 23	**60.** 93

Show each number as a product of prime factors. (pp. 196–197)

61. 14	**62.** 22	**63.** 49	**64.** 18	**65.** 60
66. 54	**67.** 75	**68.** 9	**69.** 33	**70.** 70

Solve each problem. (pp. 190–201)

71. Can you divide a sack of 76 walnuts equally among 3 people?

72. Can you divide 2,412 paper clips equally into 9 boxes?

73. Nicholas jogs every second day. He swims every third day. He started this exercise program by jogging and swimming on the same day. How many days will it be before Nicholas again jogs and swims on the same day?

74. Two cars start to go around a race track at the same time. One car goes around every 10 min. The other car goes around every 8 min. How long will it take before they are both at the starting line again at the same time?

75. Suppose you wish to arrange 12 square tiles in a rectangular pattern. Write a multiplication sentence for each choice you have.

76. Suppose you wish to arrange 24 square tiles in a rectangular pattern. Write a multiplication sentence for each choice you have.

The graph shows the number of bushels of alfalfa and soybeans Lisa Abbott grew on her farm. The data are for a 4-year period.

77. How many bushels of alfalfa did Lisa grow in 1984?

78. How many more bushels of soybeans than alfalfa did Lisa grow in 1982?

79. During the 4 years, which crop did Lisa produce more of? How much more?

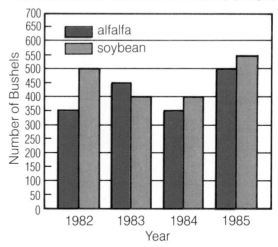

ALFALFA AND SOYBEAN PRODUCTION

80. During which year did Lisa grow more alfalfa than soybeans?

81. In which year was the total number of bushels over 900?

82. Did Lisa grow equal amounts of each crop in any year?

83. In which years was the alfalfa crop less than 400 bushels?

84. During which years was Lisa's total production the same? What was the total number of bushels harvested?

85. In 1983, Lisa sold a bushel of alfalfa for $2.43. How much was Lisa paid for her alfalfa crop in 1983?

COMPUTERS AND PROBLEM SOLVING

■ It is easy for you to use pencil and paper to find the least common multiple of a pair of small numbers. But, suppose you need to find the least common multiple of a pair of large numbers like 5,136 and 90,331.

A computer is most helpful for jobs that take too long or are too difficult because they involve repeated operations or large numbers.

In the following program, the computer finds the least common multiple of a pair of numbers.

```
NEW
10   PRINT "FIND THE LEAST COMMON MULTIPLE."
20   INPUT "WHAT IS THE FIRST NUMBER?"; A
30   LET A1 = A
40   INPUT "WHAT IS THE SECOND NUMBER?"; B
50   IF A1 / B = INT (A1 / B) THEN GOTO 80
60   LET A1 = A1 + A
70   GOTO 50
80   PRINT "THE LEAST COMMON MULTIPLE"
90   PRINT "OF "; A; " AND "; B; " IS "; A1;"."
100  END
```

Solve each problem.

1. Draw a flow chart of the program. How many loops are there?

2. What conditions are tested in this program?

■ One number is divisible by another if there is a remainder of 0 after the division. The INT function can be used to check for divisibility.

IF A1 / B = INT (A1 / B) THEN PRINT A; " IS DIVISIBLE BY "; B

If there is no decimal part in the quotient of A1 / B, then the IF statement is true.

In line 50 of the program, the computer checks to see if A1, a multiple of A, is divisible by B. If it is, the computer prints out the answer. If it is not, A1 is increased by A in line 60. Then, divisibility is tested again.

Solve each problem.

1. Is it necessary to input the larger number first? Why or why not?

3. What is the purpose of the INT function in line 50?

How many times will the program loop with the following inputs?

4. 5 then 9

5. 7 then 13

6. 8 then 15

2. When this program reaches line 90, the computer is ready to print the least common multiple of the two numbers. Change line 100 to LET A = A1. Add these lines.

```
110    GOTO 30
120    END
```

What does the program do now? What can you make the program do?

ENRICHMENT

THE SIEVE OF ERATOSTHENES

Eratosthenes was a Greek scientist and mathematician. In about 250 B.C., he discovered a way to find prime numbers. Here is how the method works for the whole numbers from 1 through 100.

Copy the table of numbers.

1. Cross out the number 1. (1 is not a prime number.)

2. Circle the number 2. (2 is a prime number.)

3. Cross out all the other multiples of 2. (They are not prime numbers.)

4. Circle the number 3. (3 is a prime number.)

1	2	3	4	5	6	7	8	9	10
11	12	13	14	15	16	17	18	19	20
21	22	23	24	25	26	27	28	29	30
31	32	33	34	35	36	37	38	39	40
41	42	43	44	45	46	47	48	49	50
51	52	53	54	55	56	57	58	59	60
61	62	63	64	65	66	67	68	69	70
71	72	73	74	75	76	77	78	79	80
81	82	83	84	85	86	87	88	89	90
91	92	93	94	95	96	97	98	99	100

5. Cross out all the other multiples of 3. Why have some of these already been crossed out?

6. Circle the number 5 and cross out all the other multiples of 5.

7. Circle the number 7 and cross out all the other multiples of 7.

8. Circle all the numbers that have not been crossed out.

9. The numbers that are crossed out are composite numbers. The numbers that are circled are "caught in the sieve." They are the prime numbers less than 100. List them.

10. Make a table of the whole numbers from 1 through 150. Use the same process to find all the prime numbers less than 150. (You will need to cross out all the other multiples of the numbers 2, 3, 5, 7, and 11.) Then list the prime numbers greater than 100 and less than 150.

Round to the nearest tenth.

1. 56.37   **2.** 16.49   **3.** 19.846   **4.** 1.551   **5.** 4.798

6. 39.429   **7.** 217.65   **8.** 28.263   **9.** 41.827   **10.** 85.06

Round to the nearest hundredth.

11. 0.0456   **12.** 1.781   **13.** 0.2356   **14.** 9.987   **15.** 7.055

16. 6.666   **17.** 3.554   **18.** 4.777   **19.** 0.7848   **20.** 5.335

Add or subtract. Estimate to check.

21. 63.42
+ 3.638

22. 62.05
− 19.555

23. 23.456
+ 19.287

24. 58.889
+ 1.8683

25. 10.3398
− 3.595

26. 26.587 − 16.598   **27.** 63.58 + 12   **28.** 4,562 − 1,789   **29.** 27 − 16.8

Multiply. Estimate to check.

30. 73.4
× 3.9

31. 62.7
× 1.07

32. 84.8
× 6.51

33. 34.6
× 15.78

34. 44.02
× 18.2

Divide.

35. $2.4\overline{)9.6}$ **36.** $0.07\overline{)49.7}$ **37.** $0.6\overline{)9.90}$ **38.** $2.1\overline{)0.8421}$ **39.** $0.009\overline{)5.4}$

Find the least common multiple of each pair of numbers.

40. 4, 7   **41.** 6, 9   **42.** 12, 6   **43.** 10, 14   **44.** 8, 5

Solve each problem.

45. A factory has 32,151 spark plugs. The factory uses 6 in each car. Estimate the number of cars that can be supplied with spark plugs.

46. On Monday, Ray put 13.4 gal of gas in his car. On Tuesday, he put in 8.9 gal. How much did he put in altogether?

47. How far will a man walk in 3 h if he is walking at an average speed of 2.8 mph?

48. Shirley left home at 9:30 A.M. She returned at 4:15 P.M. How long was she gone?

SKILLS CHECK

Choose the correct answer.

1. In 1,439.5687, which digit is in the thousandths place?

  a. 1
  b. 6
  c. 7
  d. NG

2. What is 2,587,894 rounded to the nearest ten-thousand?

  a. 2,500,000
  b. 2,580,000
  c. 2,590,000
  d. 2,600,000

3. $56.8 + 0.2399 + 154$

  a. 72.4399
  b. 111.0765
  c. 211.0399
  d. NG

4. Which decimal is equivalent to 0.4?

  a. 0.004
  b. 0.04
  c. 0.40
  d. 4.0

5. $5 - 0.2841$

  a. 0.2341
  b. 4.7159
  c. 7.841
  d. NG

6. Which number is one and six hundred forty thousandths?

  a. 0.164
  b. 1.064
  c. 1.604
  d. 1.640

7.   2 ft 8 in.
   $+$4 ft 7 in.

  a. 7 ft 3 in.
  b. 7 ft 4 in.
  c. 7 ft 5 in.
  d. NG

8. $0.015\overline{)7.05}$

  a. 0.47
  b. 4.7
  c. 47
  d. 470

9. What is the greatest common factor of 8 and 12?

  a. 2
  b. 4
  c. 24
  d. NG

10. The highest mountain in the United States, Mt. McKinley, is 6,187 m high. North Peak is 5,903 m high. How much higher is Mt. McKinley?

  a. 104 m
  b. 200 m
  c. 284 m
  d. 1,824 m

11. Jill bought an umbrella for $4.85 and a scarf for $11.33. Both prices include tax. How much change should she receive from $50.00?

  a. $33.82
  b. $38.67
  c. $45.15
  d. $66.18

12. Tim received the following marks on his math tests: 84, 73, 66, 81, 92, and 96. What was his average mark on the 6 tests?

  a. 62
  b. 72
  c. 82
  d. NG

Try These

Write two equivalent fractions for the part that is red.

1.

2.

Copy and complete.

3. $\frac{1}{3} = \frac{1 \times 2}{3 \times \blacksquare} = \frac{2}{\blacksquare}$

4. $\frac{2}{5} = \frac{2 \times \blacksquare}{5 \times 3} = \frac{\blacksquare}{15}$

5. $\frac{1}{2} = \frac{1 \times \blacksquare}{2 \times \blacksquare} = \frac{8}{\blacksquare}$

Exercises

Copy and complete. Do as many as you can mentally.

1. $\frac{3}{5} = \frac{3 \times \blacksquare}{5 \times 2} = \frac{\blacksquare}{10}$

2. $\frac{4}{7} = \frac{4 \times 4}{7 \times \blacksquare} = \frac{16}{\blacksquare}$

3. $\frac{3}{8} = \frac{3 \times 3}{8 \times \blacksquare} = \frac{9}{\blacksquare}$

4. $\frac{3}{7} = \frac{\blacksquare}{14}$

5. $\frac{2}{3} = \frac{6}{\blacksquare}$

6. $\frac{3}{4} = \frac{\blacksquare}{12}$

7. $\frac{2}{5} = \frac{6}{\blacksquare}$

8. $\frac{1}{3} = \frac{\blacksquare}{27}$

9. $\frac{1}{5} = \frac{\blacksquare}{10}$

10. $\frac{7}{8} = \frac{14}{\blacksquare}$

11. $\frac{4}{5} = \frac{\blacksquare}{20}$

12. $\frac{5}{8} = \frac{\blacksquare}{40}$

13. $\frac{5}{6} = \frac{\blacksquare}{18}$

14. $\frac{1}{2} = \frac{\blacksquare}{14}$

15. $\frac{4}{9} = \frac{20}{\blacksquare}$

 Copy and complete.

★ **16.** $\frac{7}{17} = \frac{\blacksquare}{5,508}$

★ **17.** $\frac{13}{43} = \frac{1,222}{\blacksquare}$

★ **18.** $\frac{11}{29} = \frac{627}{\blacksquare}$

★ **19.** $\frac{3}{35} = \frac{\blacksquare}{6,055}$

Solve each problem.

20. A piece of fabric is 10 yd long. 7 yd is needed for a curtain. What part of the fabric is needed for the curtain?

21. Lisa knitted a sweater. She used 3 balls of pink wool, 3 balls of blue wool, and 4 balls of white wool. What part of the sweater is white?

22. A piece of fabric is 6 yd long. Half of it is yellow. How many feet long is the whole piece of fabric?

★ **23.** David has 60 squares of fabric. $\frac{2}{3}$ of the squares are red. How many squares are not red?

Fractions in Lowest Terms

■ Another way to find equivalent fractions is to divide both terms by a common factor.

3 is a common factor of 6 and 24. $\frac{6}{24} = \frac{6 \div 3}{24 \div 3} = \frac{2}{8}$ $\frac{6}{24} = \frac{2}{8}$

6 is a common factor of 6 and 24. $\frac{6}{24} = \frac{6 \div 6}{24 \div 6} = \frac{1}{4}$ $\frac{6}{24} = \frac{1}{4}$

$\frac{6}{24}$, $\frac{2}{8}$, and $\frac{1}{4}$ are equivalent fractions.

When both terms have no common factors greater than 1, the fraction is in **lowest terms**.
$\frac{6}{24}$ in lowest terms is $\frac{1}{4}$.

■ To **simplify** a fraction is to write it in lowest terms.

> To simplify a fraction, divide the numerator and the denominator by the greatest common factor.

Write $\frac{12}{16}$ in lowest terms.

Factors of 12:   1, 2, 3, 4, 6, 12
Factors of 16:   1, 2, 4, 8, 16
Common factors of 12 and 16:   1, 2, 4
Greatest common factor of 12 and 16:   4

Divide both terms by 4.

$$\frac{12}{16} = \frac{12 \div 4}{16 \div 4} = \frac{3}{4}$$

$\frac{12}{16}$ in lowest terms is $\frac{3}{4}$.

Try These

Find the greatest common factor.

1. 12 and 18   **2.** 6 and 15   **3.** 8 and 14   **4.** 14 and 35

Copy and complete.

5. $\frac{15}{20} = \frac{15 \div 5}{20 \div 5} = \frac{\blacksquare}{\blacksquare}$

6. $\frac{6}{8} = \frac{6 \div 2}{8 \div \blacksquare} = \frac{\blacksquare}{\blacksquare}$

7. $\frac{6}{30} = \frac{6 \div \blacksquare}{30 \div 6} = \frac{\blacksquare}{\blacksquare}$

Exercises

Find the greatest common factor.

1. 4 and 12   **2.** 10 and 15   **3.** 9 and 15

4. 12 and 30   **5.** 20 and 24   **6.** 16 and 24

Simplify if possible. Do as many as you can mentally.

7. $\frac{6}{10}$ **8.** $\frac{4}{6}$ **9.** $\frac{10}{20}$ **10.** $\frac{4}{16}$ **11.** $\frac{5}{25}$ **12.** $\frac{10}{30}$

13. $\frac{6}{20}$ **14.** $\frac{3}{24}$ **15.** $\frac{9}{18}$ **16.** $\frac{21}{28}$ **17.** $\frac{50}{100}$ **18.** $\frac{75}{100}$

19. $\frac{12}{28}$ **20.** $\frac{18}{36}$ **21.** $\frac{3}{9}$ **22.** $\frac{15}{30}$ **23.** $\frac{10}{16}$ **24.** $\frac{18}{21}$

25. $\frac{4}{20}$ **26.** $\frac{12}{15}$ **27.** $\frac{14}{35}$ **28.** $\frac{21}{35}$ **29.** $\frac{30}{45}$ **30.** $\frac{40}{100}$

Solve each problem.
Simplify if possible.

31. You know that 1 lb is equal to 16 oz. What part of a pound is 2 oz? 8 oz? 12 oz?

32. A calculator weighs 3 oz. What part of a pound does it weigh?

33. The calculator is 4 in. long and 3 in. wide. What part of a foot is its width?

★ **34.** The price of the calculator was $7.95. The tax was $.08 on the dollar. What was the total price?

 THINK AND TRY

FINDING A PATTERN

Copy and complete each pattern. Write the fractions in lowest terms.

Think: $\frac{2}{8}$

1. $\frac{1}{8}$, $\frac{1}{4}$, $\frac{3}{8}$, $\frac{1}{2}$, ■, ■, ■, 1

2. $\frac{1}{6}$, $\frac{1}{3}$, $\frac{1}{2}$, ■, ■, ■, $1\frac{1}{6}$, ■, ■, ■, ■, 2

3. $\frac{1}{16}$, $\frac{1}{8}$, $\frac{3}{16}$, $\frac{1}{4}$, ■, ■, ■, ■, ■, ■, ■, $\frac{3}{4}$, ■, ■, ■, 1

Mixed Numbers

■ A number line can be marked in thirds.

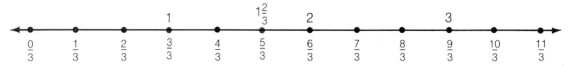

The fraction $\frac{3}{3}$ names the same number as 1. $\frac{3}{3} = 1$

The fraction $\frac{5}{3}$ is greater than 1.

$\frac{5}{3}$ names the same number as the **mixed number** $1\frac{2}{3}$.

$1\frac{2}{3}$ means $1 + \frac{2}{3}$: $1\frac{2}{3} = 1 + \frac{2}{3}$

Read: one and two-thirds

■ Write $\frac{8}{6}$ as a mixed number.

$\frac{8}{6}$ means $8 \div 6$.

Think:

$$\begin{array}{r} 1 \text{ R2, or } 1\frac{2}{6} \\ 6\overline{)8} \\ 6 \\ \hline 2 \end{array}$$

remainder
divisor

$\frac{8}{6} = 1\frac{2}{6}$

You can simplify $1\frac{2}{6}$.

$$\frac{2}{6} = \frac{2 \div 2}{6 \div 2} = \frac{1}{3}$$

$$1\frac{2}{6} = 1\frac{1}{3}$$

So $\frac{8}{6} = 1\frac{1}{3}$.

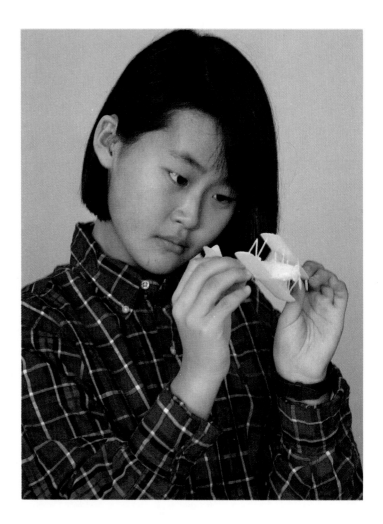

Try These

**Write each fraction as a whole number or as a mixed number.
Simplify if possible. Do as many as you can mentally.**

1. $\frac{6}{6}$ 2. $\frac{8}{3}$ 3. $\frac{40}{8}$ 4. $\frac{30}{9}$ 5. $\frac{39}{6}$ 6. $\frac{18}{2}$

Exercises

Write each fraction as a whole number or as a mixed number.
Simplify if possible. Do as many as you can mentally.

1. $\frac{8}{2}$
2. $\frac{13}{5}$
3. $\frac{12}{8}$
4. $\frac{0}{5}$
5. $\frac{17}{3}$
6. $\frac{22}{4}$

7. $\frac{6}{5}$
8. $\frac{21}{7}$
9. $\frac{22}{7}$
10. $\frac{23}{7}$
11. $\frac{28}{7}$
12. $\frac{15}{6}$

13. $\frac{3}{2}$
14. $\frac{12}{6}$
15. $\frac{19}{4}$
16. $\frac{39}{9}$
17. $\frac{35}{8}$
18. $\frac{35}{7}$

19. $\frac{54}{6}$
20. $\frac{35}{17}$
21. $\frac{15}{4}$
22. $\frac{23}{2}$
23. $\frac{274}{10}$
24. $\frac{496}{12}$

Divide. Write each quotient as a mixed number.
Simplify if possible. Do as many as you can mentally.

25. $8\overline{)23}$
26. $9\overline{)42}$
27. $5\overline{)18}$
28. $4\overline{)98}$
29. $7\overline{)68}$

30. $10\overline{)123}$
31. $6\overline{)232}$
32. $12\overline{)255}$
33. $20\overline{)146}$
34. $25\overline{)735}$

Solve each problem. Simplify if possible.

35. Sue bought $\frac{7}{4}$ oz of airplane paint. Write the number of ounces as a mixed number.

36. Ron built a model of a hangar. The model was 48 in., or $\frac{48}{12}$ ft, wide. Write the number of feet as a whole number.

37. Sue built an airplane model 15 in., or $\frac{15}{12}$ ft, long. Write the number of feet as a mixed number.

★ 38. Each container of fuel for the model airplane costs $4. How many containers can Sue buy for $14?

 THINK AND TRY

USING CLUES

What fraction am I?

1. I am a fraction equivalent to $4\frac{2}{5}$. I am in lowest terms.

2. I am a mixed number. I am $\frac{2}{3}$ greater than $1\frac{2}{3}$.

Adding and Subtracting Fractions

■ Sara Clark is a newspaper reporter. She drove $\frac{8}{10}$ of a mile from her apartment to do an interview. Then she drove $\frac{5}{10}$ of a mile to her office. How far did she drive altogether?

Add $\frac{8}{10}$ and $\frac{5}{10}$ to find how far.

Two fractions have **common denominators** when they have the same denominators.

To add fractions with common denominators:

1. Add the numerators.
2. Use the common denominator.
3. Simplify if possible.

$$\frac{8}{10} + \frac{5}{10} = \frac{13}{10}$$
$$= 1\frac{3}{10}$$

$$\begin{array}{r} \frac{8}{10} \\ +\frac{5}{10} \\ \hline \frac{13}{10} = 1\frac{3}{10} \end{array}$$

Sara drove $1\frac{3}{10}$ miles.

■ Subtract: $\frac{5}{8} - \frac{3}{8}$

To subtract fractions with common denominators:

1. Subtract the numerators.
2. Use the common denominator.
3. Simplify if possible.

$$\frac{5}{8} - \frac{3}{8} = \frac{2}{8}$$
$$= \frac{1}{4}$$

$$\begin{array}{r} \frac{5}{8} \\ -\frac{3}{8} \\ \hline \frac{2}{8} = \frac{1}{4} \end{array}$$

Try These

Add. Simplify if possible.

1. $\frac{1}{3} + \frac{1}{3}$ **2.** $\frac{3}{8} + \frac{5}{8}$ **3.** $\frac{3}{4} + \frac{3}{4}$ **4.** $\frac{3}{7} + \frac{6}{7}$

Subtract. Simplify if possible.

5. $\frac{3}{5} - \frac{1}{5}$ **6.** $\frac{5}{8} - \frac{1}{8}$ **7.** $\frac{5}{10} - \frac{3}{10}$ **8.** $\frac{7}{16} - \frac{3}{16}$

Exercises

Add or subtract. Simplify if possible.

1. $\frac{3}{5} + \frac{1}{5}$

2. $\frac{9}{11} - \frac{2}{11}$

3. $\frac{3}{4} - \frac{2}{4}$

4. $\frac{2}{6} + \frac{1}{6}$

5. $\frac{9}{12} - \frac{3}{12}$

6. $\frac{2}{7} + \frac{2}{7}$

7. $\frac{4}{5} - \frac{1}{5}$

8. $\frac{7}{8} - \frac{5}{8}$

9. $\frac{2}{3} + \frac{1}{3}$

10. $\frac{7}{10} - \frac{7}{10}$

11. $\frac{5}{6} + \frac{5}{6}$

12. $\frac{8}{9} - \frac{2}{9}$

13. $\frac{75}{80} - \frac{35}{80}$

14. $\frac{30}{100} + \frac{9}{100}$

★ **15.** $\frac{2}{3} + \frac{2}{3} + \frac{2}{3}$

★ **16.** $\frac{10}{22} + \frac{9}{22} + \frac{15}{22}$

17. $\begin{array}{r} \frac{4}{5} \\ + \frac{2}{5} \\ \hline \end{array}$

18. $\begin{array}{r} \frac{9}{10} \\ - \frac{8}{10} \\ \hline \end{array}$

19. $\begin{array}{r} \frac{5}{6} \\ + \frac{1}{6} \\ \hline \end{array}$

20. $\begin{array}{r} \frac{11}{18} \\ - \frac{3}{18} \\ \hline \end{array}$

21. $\begin{array}{r} \frac{24}{35} \\ - \frac{17}{35} \\ \hline \end{array}$

22. $\begin{array}{r} \frac{52}{100} \\ - \frac{18}{100} \\ \hline \end{array}$

23. $\begin{array}{r} \frac{2}{9} \\ + \frac{7}{9} \\ \hline \end{array}$

24. $\begin{array}{r} \frac{8}{15} \\ + \frac{12}{15} \\ \hline \end{array}$

Copy and complete.

★ **25.** $\frac{\blacksquare}{\blacksquare} - \frac{3}{5} = \frac{1}{5}$

★ **26.** $\frac{2}{10} + \frac{\blacksquare}{\blacksquare} = \frac{9}{10}$

★ **27.** $\frac{7}{8} - \frac{\blacksquare}{\blacksquare} = \frac{3}{4}$

★ **28.** $\frac{\blacksquare}{\blacksquare} + \frac{3}{7} = 1$

★ **29.** $\frac{5}{9} - \frac{\blacksquare}{\blacksquare} = \frac{2}{9}$

★ **30.** $\frac{\blacksquare}{\blacksquare} + \frac{5}{6} = 1\frac{2}{3}$

Solve each problem. Simplify if possible.

31. Ruth and Dan wrote ads. Ruth wrote $\frac{3}{8}$ of a page of ads. Dan wrote $\frac{7}{8}$ of a page. How much more did Dan write?

32. Beth covered a story. She wrote the story in $\frac{2}{3}$ h. She took $\frac{2}{3}$ h to type and edit it. How long did she take to prepare the story?

★ **33.** Sara spent $\frac{1}{4}$ h driving to city hall and back. She spent 1 h covering a press conference and $\frac{3}{4}$ h preparing her story. How much time did Sara spend on this story?

★ **34.** A ream of paper has 500 sheets. One month Ruth used $\frac{4}{5}$ of a ream. The second month she used $\frac{3}{5}$ of a ream. How many sheets of paper did Ruth use in these 2 months?

Least Common Denominator

- Compare $\frac{4}{5}$ and $\frac{3}{5}$.

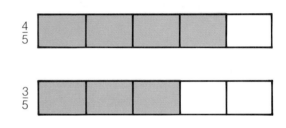

The fractions have a common denominator, so compare the numerators.

$$4 > 3$$

so $\quad \frac{4}{5} > \frac{3}{5} \quad$ or $\quad \frac{3}{5} < \frac{4}{5}$

- Compare $\frac{3}{4}$ and $\frac{5}{6}$.

The fractions have different denominators. First find equivalent fractions with a common denominator. Think of multiples of 4 and 6. The least common multiple of 4 and 6 is 12. 12 is called the **least common denominator** of $\frac{3}{4}$ and $\frac{5}{6}$.

Write equivalent fractions for $\frac{3}{4}$ and $\frac{5}{6}$ using 12 as a common denominator.

$\frac{3}{4} = \frac{\blacksquare}{12}$ $\qquad$ $\frac{5}{6} = \frac{\blacksquare}{12}$

$\frac{3}{4} = \frac{3 \times 3}{4 \times 3} = \frac{9}{12}$ $\qquad$ $\frac{5}{6} = \frac{5 \times 2}{6 \times 2} = \frac{10}{12}$

Compare. $\qquad \frac{9}{12} < \frac{10}{12} \quad$ so $\quad \frac{3}{4} < \frac{5}{6}$

- Compare $1\frac{3}{8}$ and $1\frac{4}{5}$.

Since the whole numbers are the same, compare the fractions. Find equivalent fractions. The least common multiple of 5 and 8 is 40. Use 40 as the least common denominator.

$\frac{3}{8} = \frac{3 \times 5}{8 \times 5} = \frac{15}{40}$ $\qquad$ $\frac{4}{5} = \frac{4 \times 8}{5 \times 8} = \frac{32}{40}$

$$\frac{15}{40} < \frac{32}{40}$$

so $\quad \frac{3}{8} < \frac{4}{5} \quad$ and $\quad 1\frac{3}{8} < 1\frac{4}{5}$

Try These

Find the least common denominator.
Then write equivalent fractions using that denominator.

1. $\frac{1}{2}, \frac{5}{6}$ **2.** $\frac{1}{4}, \frac{1}{5}$ **3.** $\frac{1}{5}, \frac{5}{10}$ **4.** $\frac{2}{8}, \frac{1}{6}$ **5.** $\frac{3}{4}, \frac{2}{9}$

Write >, <, or =.

6. $\frac{2}{5} \blacksquare \frac{5}{6}$ **7.** $1\frac{3}{8} \blacksquare 1\frac{4}{9}$ **8.** $\frac{7}{10} \blacksquare \frac{5}{8}$ **9.** $\frac{7}{8} \blacksquare \frac{6}{7}$ **10.** $\frac{1}{4} \blacksquare \frac{8}{9}$

Exercises

Find the least common denominator.
Then write equivalent fractions using that denominator.

1. $\frac{3}{4}, \frac{3}{8}$ **2.** $\frac{3}{4}, \frac{5}{6}$ **3.** $\frac{2}{6}, \frac{1}{9}$ **4.** $\frac{1}{2}, \frac{1}{3}$ **5.** $\frac{7}{8}, \frac{5}{6}$

6. $\frac{2}{3}, \frac{4}{5}$ **7.** $\frac{4}{7}, \frac{7}{8}$ ★ **8.** $\frac{1}{5}, \frac{3}{16}$ ★ **9.** $\frac{5}{9}, \frac{1}{8}$ ★ **10.** $\frac{3}{4}, \frac{4}{5}, \frac{5}{6}$

Write >, <, or =.

11. $\frac{3}{4} \blacksquare \frac{3}{8}$ **12.** $\frac{3}{4} \blacksquare \frac{5}{6}$ **13.** $\frac{3}{5} \blacksquare \frac{5}{10}$ **14.** $\frac{2}{6} \blacksquare \frac{2}{4}$ **15.** $\frac{2}{4} \blacksquare \frac{2}{5}$

16. $2\frac{1}{3} \blacksquare 2\frac{2}{6}$ **17.** $1\frac{4}{9} \blacksquare 1\frac{7}{9}$ ★ **18.** $\frac{13}{5} \blacksquare 2\frac{6}{10}$ ★ **19.** $3\frac{2}{3} \blacksquare \frac{21}{9}$ ★ **20.** $1\frac{7}{9} \blacksquare \frac{11}{7}$

Solve each problem. Simplify if possible.

21. Jim walked $\frac{1}{2}$ mi to school. Fran walked $\frac{2}{3}$ mi to school. Who walked farther?

22. The school is $\frac{3}{8}$ mi from Julie's house. The park is $\frac{1}{4}$ mi from her house. Which is closer?

23. Sharon walked $\frac{3}{5}$ mi in the morning and $\frac{2}{5}$ mi in the afternoon. How much farther did she walk in the morning?

24. Steve walked $\frac{2}{10}$ mi to Larry's house. Then Steve and Larry walked $\frac{3}{10}$ mi to the park. How far did Steve walk altogether?

25. Pat lives $1\frac{1}{2}$ mi from school. Ellen lives $1\frac{3}{5}$ mi from school. Who lives farther from school?

★ **26.** Bob walked $\frac{2}{3}$ mi. Jean walked $\frac{3}{4}$ mi. Howard walked $\frac{3}{5}$ mi. Who walked the farthest?

Adding with Different Denominators

■ David Barton manages a restaurant. He spent $\frac{1}{4}$ of his advertising budget for newspaper ads and $\frac{1}{2}$ of his advertising budget for radio commercials. How much of his advertising budget did he spend in all?

Add $\frac{1}{4}$ and $\frac{1}{2}$ to find the answer.

To add fractions with different denominators, find the least common denominator. Since 4 is a multiple of 2, 4 is the least common denominator. Write a fraction equivalent to $\frac{1}{2}$ using that denominator.

$$\frac{1}{2} = \frac{2}{4}$$

Add.

$$\frac{1}{4} + \frac{1}{2}$$
$$\downarrow$$
$$\frac{1}{4} + \frac{2}{4} = \frac{3}{4}$$

$$\frac{1}{4} = \frac{1}{4}$$
$$+\frac{1}{2} = +\frac{2}{4}$$
$$\overline{\quad\quad\ \frac{3}{4}}$$

David spent $\frac{3}{4}$ of his advertising budget.

■ Add: $\frac{2}{3} + \frac{1}{2}$

Find the least common denominator. The least common denominator is 6. Write equivalent fractions using that denominator.

$$\frac{2}{3} = \frac{4}{6} \qquad \frac{1}{2} = \frac{3}{6}$$

Add.

$$\frac{2}{3} + \frac{1}{2}$$
$$\downarrow \qquad \downarrow$$
$$\frac{4}{6} + \frac{3}{6} = \frac{7}{6}$$
$$= 1\frac{1}{6}$$

$$\frac{2}{3} = \frac{4}{6}$$
$$+\frac{1}{2} = +\frac{3}{6}$$
$$\overline{\quad\quad\ \frac{7}{6}} = 1\frac{1}{6}$$

Try These

Add. Simplify if possible.

1. $\frac{1}{3} + \frac{1}{2}$ **2.** $\frac{2}{6} + \frac{1}{4}$ **3.** $\frac{2}{3} + \frac{3}{4}$ **4.** $\frac{7}{9} + \frac{2}{3}$

Exercises

Add. Simplify if possible.

1. $\frac{3}{4} + \frac{1}{8}$ **2.** $\frac{4}{5} + \frac{2}{3}$ **3.** $\frac{11}{12} + \frac{7}{12}$ **4.** $\frac{2}{6} + \frac{7}{10}$

5. $\frac{3}{10} + \frac{1}{2}$ **6.** $\frac{1}{2} + \frac{3}{8}$ **7.** $\frac{2}{5} + \frac{1}{4}$ **8.** $\frac{4}{5} + \frac{3}{4}$

9. $\frac{1}{2} + \frac{3}{5}$ **10.** $\frac{4}{9} + \frac{8}{9}$ ★ **11.** $\frac{1}{2} + \frac{3}{7} + \frac{5}{8}$ ★ **12.** $\frac{3}{4} + \frac{5}{6} + \frac{1}{2}$

13. $\begin{array}{r} \frac{2}{3} \\ + \frac{1}{3} \\ \hline \end{array}$
14. $\begin{array}{r} \frac{1}{6} \\ + \frac{1}{2} \\ \hline \end{array}$
15. $\begin{array}{r} \frac{2}{3} \\ + \frac{4}{9} \\ \hline \end{array}$
16. $\begin{array}{r} \frac{2}{5} \\ + \frac{1}{2} \\ \hline \end{array}$
17. $\begin{array}{r} \frac{5}{9} \\ + \frac{5}{12} \\ \hline \end{array}$

18. $\begin{array}{r} \frac{2}{3} \\ + \frac{1}{8} \\ \hline \end{array}$
19. $\begin{array}{r} \frac{5}{6} \\ + \frac{3}{5} \\ \hline \end{array}$
20. $\begin{array}{r} \frac{9}{10} \\ + \frac{5}{6} \\ \hline \end{array}$
★ **21.** $\begin{array}{r} \frac{2}{3} \\ \frac{6}{15} \\ + \frac{2}{3} \\ \hline \end{array}$
★ **22.** $\begin{array}{r} \frac{7}{12} \\ \frac{2}{15} \\ + \frac{1}{9} \\ \hline \end{array}$

Solve each problem. Simplify if possible.

23. Each week David takes $\frac{1}{2}$ h to order paper products. He spends $\frac{3}{4}$ h reviewing his waiter schedule. How much time does David spend on the two jobs?

24. A delivery truck arrived filled with cases of vegetables. Artie unloaded $\frac{1}{2}$ of the cases. David unloaded $\frac{1}{6}$ of the cases. What part of the cases did they unload altogether?

25. The restaurant used $\frac{1}{2}$ of a case of tomato sauce one day and $\frac{5}{8}$ of a case the next day. How much did the restaurant use altogether in the 2 days?

★ **26.** This week David has used $\frac{1}{10}$ of his operating budget on repair work, $\frac{1}{5}$ on food, and $\frac{1}{2}$ on wages. What part of his operating budget does he have left?

Subtracting with Different Denominators

■ Sonia Fisher sells oil lamps in her store. One kind holds $\frac{1}{2}$ of a can of lamp oil. Another kind holds $\frac{6}{10}$ of a can. How much more does the second kind of oil lamp hold?

Subtract $\frac{1}{2}$ from $\frac{6}{10}$ to find the answer.

To subtract fractions with different denominators, find the least common denominator. Since 10 is a multiple of 2, 10 is the least common denominator. Write a fraction equivalent to $\frac{1}{2}$ using that denominator.

$$\frac{1}{2} = \frac{5}{10}$$

Subtract.

$$\frac{6}{10} - \frac{1}{2}$$

$$\downarrow$$

$$\frac{6}{10} - \frac{5}{10} = \frac{1}{10}$$

The second kind of oil lamp holds $\frac{1}{10}$ of a can more.

■ Subtract: $\frac{5}{6} - \frac{1}{8}$

Find the least common denominator. The least common denominator is 24. Write equivalent fractions using that denominator.

$$\frac{5}{6} = \frac{20}{24} \qquad \frac{1}{8} = \frac{3}{24}$$

Subtract.

$$\begin{array}{r} \frac{5}{6} = \frac{20}{24} \\ -\frac{1}{8} = -\frac{3}{24} \\ \hline \frac{17}{24} \end{array}$$

Try These

Subtract. Simplify if possible.

1. $\frac{3}{4} - \frac{1}{2}$

2. $\frac{7}{8} - \frac{1}{6}$

3. $\frac{3}{5} - \frac{1}{2}$

4. $\frac{5}{6} - \frac{5}{9}$

Exercises

Subtract. Simplify if possible.

1. $\dfrac{3}{4} - \dfrac{1}{3}$

2. $\dfrac{5}{7} - \dfrac{2}{7}$

3. $\dfrac{3}{4} - \dfrac{1}{10}$

4. $\dfrac{7}{10} - \dfrac{2}{5}$

5. $\dfrac{8}{9} - \dfrac{1}{3}$

6. $\dfrac{7}{10} - \dfrac{3}{20}$

7. $\dfrac{5}{6} - \dfrac{3}{7}$

8. $\dfrac{3}{8} - \dfrac{1}{8}$

9. $\dfrac{7}{8} - \dfrac{1}{3}$

10. $\dfrac{1}{2} - \dfrac{1}{5}$

11. $\dfrac{5}{8} - \dfrac{1}{3}$

12. $\dfrac{93}{100} - \dfrac{7}{10}$

13. $\begin{array}{r} \dfrac{2}{3} \\ -\dfrac{4}{9} \\ \hline \end{array}$

14. $\begin{array}{r} \dfrac{3}{4} \\ -\dfrac{1}{5} \\ \hline \end{array}$

15. $\begin{array}{r} \dfrac{13}{15} \\ -\dfrac{8}{15} \\ \hline \end{array}$

16. $\begin{array}{r} \dfrac{1}{10} \\ -\dfrac{1}{18} \\ \hline \end{array}$

17. $\begin{array}{r} \dfrac{14}{15} \\ -\dfrac{3}{12} \\ \hline \end{array}$

18. $\begin{array}{r} \dfrac{7}{8} \\ -\dfrac{3}{10} \\ \hline \end{array}$

19. $\begin{array}{r} \dfrac{5}{6} \\ -\dfrac{1}{4} \\ \hline \end{array}$

20. $\begin{array}{r} \dfrac{7}{8} \\ -\dfrac{2}{3} \\ \hline \end{array}$

21. $\begin{array}{r} \dfrac{9}{10} \\ -\dfrac{1}{4} \\ \hline \end{array}$

22. $\begin{array}{r} \dfrac{19}{20} \\ -\dfrac{3}{5} \\ \hline \end{array}$

Compute. Simplify if possible.

23. $\dfrac{3}{8} + \dfrac{1}{9}$

24. $\dfrac{2}{3} - \dfrac{4}{7}$

25. $\dfrac{5}{7} + \dfrac{3}{4}$

26. $\dfrac{5}{9} - \left(\dfrac{1}{3} - \dfrac{1}{9}\right)$

27. $\left(\dfrac{2}{5} + \dfrac{1}{4}\right) + \dfrac{1}{20}$

★ 28. $\dfrac{4}{5} - \left(\dfrac{3}{4} - \dfrac{1}{3}\right)$

Copy and complete. Simplify if possible.

★ 29. $\dfrac{\blacksquare}{\blacksquare} + \dfrac{1}{4} = \dfrac{3}{4}$

★ 30. $\dfrac{\blacksquare}{\blacksquare} - \dfrac{2}{5} = \dfrac{1}{4}$

★ 31. $\dfrac{3}{4} - \dfrac{\blacksquare}{\blacksquare} = \dfrac{1}{3}$

Solve each problem. Simplify if possible.

32. Sonia used $\dfrac{3}{4}$ pt of stain and $\dfrac{1}{3}$ pt of varnish. How much more stain did she use?

33. Sonia took $\dfrac{5}{6}$ h to sand a table and $\dfrac{1}{2}$ h to stain it. How much time did she spend altogether?

★ 34. Sonia has 1 yd of linen. She uses $\dfrac{5}{8}$ yd of the linen to replace the shade of an antique lamp. How much linen does Sonia have left?

★ 35. Sonia makes a cleaning solution for some brass oil lamps. She mixes $\dfrac{3}{4}$ c of water with $\dfrac{1}{8}$ c of lemon juice. She then uses $\dfrac{1}{2}$ c of the solution. How much solution is left?

Problem Solving: Strategies

GENERALIZING

Sometimes **finding a pattern** is a strategy that
helps to solve a problem.

Such fractions as $\frac{1}{2}$, $\frac{1}{3}$, $\frac{1}{8}$, and $\frac{1}{31}$ are called **unit fractions**.
The numerator of a unit fraction is 1.

Find a shortcut for adding unit fractions.

First, find each sum using a
common denominator.

Now, look at the circled digits.
Is there a pattern?

$$\begin{array}{r} \frac{1}{2} = \frac{3}{6} \\ +\frac{1}{3} = +\frac{2}{6} \\ \hline \frac{5}{6} \end{array} \qquad \begin{array}{r} \frac{1}{4} = \frac{7}{28} \\ +\frac{1}{7} = +\frac{4}{28} \\ \hline \frac{11}{28} \end{array}$$

$$\frac{1}{②} + \frac{1}{③} = \frac{⑤}{6} \qquad \frac{1}{④} + \frac{1}{⑦} = \frac{11}{㉘}$$

Do you see a shortcut for adding
unit fractions?

To find the numerator of the sum, add the denominators
of the addends. To find the denominator of the sum,
multiply the denominators of the addends.

$$\frac{1}{②} + \frac{1}{③} = \frac{⑤}{6} \qquad \begin{array}{l} 2 + 3 = 5 \\ 2 \times 3 = 6 \end{array} \qquad \frac{1}{④} + \frac{1}{⑦} = \frac{11}{㉘} \qquad \begin{array}{l} 4 + 7 = 11 \\ 4 \times 7 = 28 \end{array}$$

Using the Strategy

**Use the shortcut to add. Do as many as you can mentally.
Then check by adding using a common denominator.**

1. $\frac{1}{5} + \frac{1}{6}$ **2.** $\frac{1}{4} + \frac{1}{3}$ **3.** $\frac{1}{3} + \frac{1}{5}$ **4.** $\frac{1}{4} + \frac{1}{7}$ **5.** $\frac{1}{2} + \frac{1}{7}$

6. $\frac{1}{2} + \frac{1}{5}$ **7.** $\frac{1}{9} + \frac{1}{8}$ **8.** $\frac{1}{3} + \frac{1}{7}$ **9.** $\frac{1}{3} + \frac{1}{8}$ **10.** $\frac{1}{4} + \frac{1}{5}$

Find each difference. Look for a shortcut.

11. $\frac{1}{4} - \frac{1}{7}$ **12.** $\frac{1}{5} - \frac{1}{6}$ **13.** $\frac{1}{3} - \frac{1}{8}$ **14.** $\frac{1}{2} - \frac{1}{5}$ **15.** $\frac{1}{5} - \frac{1}{7}$

Copy and complete to describe the shortcut for subtracting unit fractions.

16. To find the numerator of the difference, subtract the ▦ of the first fraction from the ▦ of the second fraction.

17. To find the denominator of the difference, multiply the ▦ of the two fractions.

Use the shortcut to subtract. Do as many as you can mentally. Then check.

18. $\frac{1}{3} - \frac{1}{5}$ **19.** $\frac{1}{6} - \frac{1}{7}$ **20.** $\frac{1}{2} - \frac{1}{3}$ **21.** $\frac{1}{4} - \frac{1}{5}$ **22.** $\frac{1}{5} - \frac{1}{8}$

 ACTIVITY

USING A MODEL

Cut out six strips of paper.
Each strip should be 6 in. long and 1 in. wide.
Write the number 1 on one of the strips.

Cut another strip in half.
Write the fraction $\frac{1}{2}$ on each of the halves.

Cut another strip into thirds.
Write the fraction $\frac{1}{3}$ on each of the thirds.

Cut the three remaining strips into fourths, sixths, and eighths.
Write the correct fractions.

Now use the strips to find the sum of $\frac{1}{2} + \frac{1}{3}$.

1. Lay a strip labeled $\frac{1}{2}$ and a strip labeled $\frac{1}{3}$ end to end.

2. Use strips that all have the same denominator. Find how many laid end to end are the same length as the two strips laid end to end in exercise 1. Five strips labeled $\frac{1}{6}$ work.

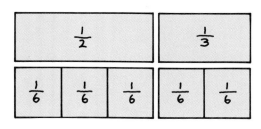

3. Since the five strips labeled $\frac{1}{6}$ stand for $\frac{5}{6}$, $\frac{1}{2} + \frac{1}{3} = \frac{5}{6}$.

Use the method above to find each of the following.

1. $\frac{1}{2} + \frac{1}{4}$ **2.** $\frac{1}{3} + \frac{1}{6}$ **3.** $\frac{3}{8} + \frac{1}{4}$ **4.** $\frac{1}{6} + \frac{2}{3}$

Adding and Subtracting Mixed Numbers

■ Joseph baked rye bread. He used $2\frac{1}{4}$ cups of whole wheat flour and $3\frac{1}{4}$ cups of rye flour. How much flour did he use in all?

To find the answer, add $2\frac{1}{4}$ and $3\frac{1}{4}$.

Add the fractions.	**Add the whole numbers.**	**Simplify the sum.**
$2\frac{1}{4}$	$2\frac{1}{4}$	$2\frac{1}{4}$
$+3\frac{1}{4}$	$+3\frac{1}{4}$	$+3\frac{1}{4}$
$\frac{2}{4}$	$5\frac{2}{4}$	$5\frac{2}{4} = 5\frac{1}{2}$

Joseph used $5\frac{1}{2}$ cups of flour.

■ Subtract: $6\frac{3}{4} - 2\frac{2}{3}$

Find the least common denominator. Write equivalent fractions.	**Subtract the fractions.**	**Subtract the whole numbers.**
$6\frac{3}{4} = 6\frac{9}{12}$	$6\frac{3}{4} = 6\frac{9}{12}$	$6\frac{3}{4} = 6\frac{9}{12}$
$-2\frac{2}{3} = -2\frac{8}{12}$	$-2\frac{2}{3} = -2\frac{8}{12}$	$-2\frac{2}{3} = -2\frac{8}{12}$
	$\frac{1}{12}$	$4\frac{1}{12}$

Try These

Add or subtract. Simplify if possible.

1. $4\frac{1}{3}$
$+1\frac{1}{3}$

2. $11\frac{9}{10}$
$-\ 9\frac{3}{10}$

3. $2\frac{2}{5}$
$+1\frac{1}{10}$

4. $7\frac{8}{9}$
$-3\frac{1}{3}$

5. $\frac{2}{3}$
$+5\frac{1}{4}$

6. $6\frac{3}{5} - 4\frac{1}{2}$

7. $13\frac{1}{4} - 4\frac{1}{4}$

8. $21\frac{1}{6} + 17\frac{2}{3}$

Exercises

Add or subtract. Simplify if possible.

1. $6\frac{2}{3}$
   $+7\frac{1}{6}$

2. $2\frac{1}{4}$
   $+1\frac{3}{8}$

3. $3\frac{5}{6}$
   $-2\frac{1}{6}$

4. $5\frac{1}{2}$
   $+\ \ \frac{3}{8}$

5. $8\frac{1}{2}$
   $-3\frac{1}{3}$

6. $13\frac{1}{2}$
   $+36\frac{2}{5}$

7. $4\frac{5}{12}$
   $-1\frac{1}{3}$

8. $16\frac{3}{5}$
   $+\ 8\frac{3}{8}$

9. $32\frac{3}{4}$
   $-\ \ \ \frac{3}{10}$

10. $16\frac{5}{12}$
    $+\ 9\frac{1}{8}$

11. $6\frac{1}{4} + 6\frac{1}{4}$

12. $13\frac{1}{6} + 11\frac{2}{9}$

13. $16\frac{2}{3} - 9\frac{1}{5}$

14. $12\frac{5}{6} - 5\frac{2}{3}$

15. $4\frac{3}{8} + 9\frac{1}{2}$

16. $17\frac{2}{5} - 9\frac{2}{5}$

Compute. Simplify if possible.

17. $\left(6\frac{3}{4} - \frac{1}{2}\right) + 3\frac{1}{4}$

18. $5\frac{3}{8} + \left(8\frac{1}{4} - 3\frac{1}{8}\right)$

19. $\frac{5}{8} + \left(18\frac{1}{4} - 11\frac{1}{8}\right)$

★ 20. $\left(1\frac{3}{5} + 6\frac{1}{5}\right) - 3\frac{3}{10}$

★ 21. $15\frac{3}{4} - \left(3\frac{1}{3} + 6\frac{1}{6}\right)$

★ 22. $14\frac{2}{5} + 8\frac{1}{2} + 36\frac{3}{8}$

Find the next number in each pattern.

23. $\frac{3}{6}, \frac{6}{6}, \frac{9}{6}, \frac{12}{6}, \frac{15}{6}, \blacksquare$

24. $\frac{20}{8}, \frac{18}{8}, \frac{16}{8}, \frac{14}{8}, \frac{12}{8}, \blacksquare$

25. $\frac{2}{12}, \frac{6}{12}, \frac{10}{12}, \frac{14}{12}, \frac{18}{12}, \blacksquare$

26. $\frac{15}{5}, \frac{13}{5}, \frac{14}{5}, \frac{12}{5}, \frac{13}{5}, \blacksquare$

Solve each problem. Simplify if possible.

27. Joseph made muffins. He used $\frac{1}{2}$ c of flour and $1\frac{3}{4}$ c of corn meal. How much more corn meal did he use?

28. Laura used $2\frac{1}{2}$ c of milk and $1\frac{1}{3}$ c of water to make a cream soup. How much liquid did Laura use?

29. Jackie buys 2 bags of onions and 2 bags of potatoes. Each bag of onions weighs $1\frac{1}{2}$ lb, and each bag of potatoes weighs $3\frac{1}{2}$ lb. What is the total weight of the bags of onions and potatoes?

★ 30. Scott takes $\frac{1}{2}$ h to drive to his cooking class from home. Cooking class is $2\frac{3}{4}$ h long. Then he drives home. If Scott leaves his house at 6:00 P.M., about what time should he arrive home?

More Adding Mixed Numbers

■ Sometimes when you add mixed numbers, the fraction in the answer is greater than or equal to 1. When that happens, you can simplify.

Louise Berg is a playground recreation director. She ran $2\frac{3}{4}$ laps this morning and $4\frac{1}{4}$ laps this afternoon. How many laps did she run today?

Add $2\frac{3}{4}$ and $4\frac{1}{4}$ to find the number of laps.

Add.

$$\begin{array}{r} 2\frac{3}{4} \\ +4\frac{1}{4} \\ \hline 6\frac{4}{4} \end{array}$$

Simplify the sum.

$$6\frac{4}{4} = 6 + \frac{4}{4}$$
$$= 6 + 1$$
$$= 7$$

Louise ran 7 laps today.

■ Add: $2\frac{2}{3} + 3\frac{3}{4}$

Add.

$$\begin{array}{r} 2\frac{2}{3} = \quad 2\frac{8}{12} \\ +3\frac{3}{4} = +3\frac{9}{12} \\ \hline 5\frac{17}{12} \end{array}$$

Simplify the sum.

$$5\frac{17}{12} = 5 + \frac{17}{12}$$
$$= 5 + 1\frac{5}{12}$$
$$= 6\frac{5}{12}$$

Try These

Add. Simplify if possible.

1. $\begin{array}{r} 5\frac{1}{3} \\ +5\frac{2}{3} \\ \hline \end{array}$

2. $\begin{array}{r} 4\frac{3}{5} \\ +5\frac{2}{3} \\ \hline \end{array}$

3. $\begin{array}{r} 14\frac{3}{4} \\ + 6\frac{1}{3} \\ \hline \end{array}$

4. $\begin{array}{r} 3\frac{1}{2} \\ +6\frac{3}{5} \\ \hline \end{array}$

5. $\begin{array}{r} 7\frac{3}{4} \\ +8\frac{5}{8} \\ \hline \end{array}$

6. $7\frac{3}{4} + 8\frac{3}{4}$

7. $5\frac{1}{5} + 9\frac{4}{5}$

8. $16\frac{3}{4} + 21\frac{2}{5}$

Exercises

Add. Simplify if possible.

1. $7\frac{1}{3}$ $+2\frac{5}{6}$

2. $9\frac{3}{4}$ $+4\frac{3}{8}$

3. $8\frac{5}{10}$ $+6\frac{3}{8}$

4. $3\frac{2}{5}$ $+2\frac{4}{5}$

5. $9\frac{1}{5}$ $+8\frac{5}{6}$

6. $6\frac{4}{9} + 5\frac{5}{9}$

7. $8\frac{1}{2} + 6\frac{1}{4}$

8. $9\frac{1}{2} + 15\frac{7}{10}$

9. $10\frac{7}{12} + 8\frac{4}{5}$

★ **10.** $1\frac{1}{3} + 12\frac{5}{6} + 8\frac{7}{9}$

★ **11.** $17\frac{1}{2} + 13\frac{3}{4} + 8\frac{5}{8}$

Compute. Simplify if possible.

12. $\left(5\frac{2}{3} + 6\frac{3}{4}\right) + 7\frac{4}{12}$

13. $\left(10\frac{4}{12} + 4\frac{1}{3}\right) + 6\frac{5}{8}$

★ **14.** $\left(5\frac{7}{8} + 3\frac{1}{3}\right) + \left(9\frac{5}{8} + 12\frac{4}{6}\right)$

Solve each problem.
If information is missing, tell what you need to know.

15. On weekends, Louise teaches tennis. She worked $4\frac{1}{2}$ h on Saturday and $5\frac{3}{4}$ h on Sunday. How many hours did she work on the weekend?

16. A handball tournament was played in three parts. The first part took $4\frac{3}{4}$ h to complete, and the second part took $2\frac{1}{2}$ h. How long did the tournament take altogether?

17. Louise is taking two college courses in management. One course is worth $2\frac{1}{2}$ credits. The other course is worth $3\frac{1}{2}$ credits. How many credits will Louise receive?

★ **18.** Louise has 12 cases of tennis balls to use in a month. She uses $3\frac{3}{4}$ cases the first week and $2\frac{1}{2}$ cases the second week. How many cases are left for the rest of the month?

KEEPING IN SHAPE

1. 2,842 $+ \ 960$

2. 8,295 $-6,878$

3. 982.5 $+ \ 63.7$

4. 39.5 -17.32

5. 15.369 $+ \ 2.397$

6. $28.42 + 9.6$

7. $9.32 - 2.7$

8. $29 + 6,845$

9. $5 - 2.338$

More Subtracting Mixed Numbers

■ Sometimes you must rename the mixed number to subtract.

A flight takes $4\frac{1}{4}$ hours. The plane has been traveling for $1\frac{3}{4}$ hours. How much longer will the trip take?

Subtract $1\frac{3}{4}$ from $4\frac{1}{4}$ to find the answer.

Because $\frac{3}{4} > \frac{1}{4}$, rename $4\frac{1}{4}$ to subtract.

$$4\frac{1}{4} = 3 + 1 + \frac{1}{4}$$
$$= 3 + \frac{4}{4} + \frac{1}{4}$$
$$= 3\frac{5}{4}$$

Subtract.

$$
\begin{array}{r}
4\frac{1}{4} = 3\frac{5}{4} \\
-1\frac{3}{4} = -1\frac{3}{4} \\
\hline
2\frac{2}{4} = 2\frac{1}{2}
\end{array}
$$

The trip will take another $2\frac{1}{2}$ hours.

■ Subtract: $9 - 6\frac{1}{3}$

Because $\frac{1}{3} > \frac{0}{3}$, rename 9 to subtract.

$$9 = 8 + 1$$
$$= 8 + \frac{3}{3}$$
$$= 8\frac{3}{3}$$

Subtract.

$$
\begin{array}{r}
9 = 8\frac{3}{3} \\
-6\frac{1}{3} = -6\frac{1}{3} \\
\hline
2\frac{2}{3}
\end{array}
$$

■ Subtract: $6\frac{1}{2} - 3\frac{2}{3}$

Find the least common denominator. Write equivalent fractions.

$$
\begin{array}{r}
6\frac{1}{2} = 6\frac{3}{6} \\
-3\frac{2}{3} = -3\frac{4}{6} \\
\hline
\end{array}
$$

Because $\frac{4}{6} > \frac{3}{6}$, rename $6\frac{3}{6}$ to subtract.

$$6\frac{3}{6} = 5 + 1 + \frac{3}{6}$$
$$= 5 + \frac{6}{6} + \frac{3}{6}$$
$$= 5\frac{9}{6}$$

Subtract.

$$
\begin{array}{r}
6\frac{1}{2} = 5\frac{9}{6} \\
-3\frac{2}{3} = -3\frac{4}{6} \\
\hline
2\frac{5}{6}
\end{array}
$$

Try These

Subtract. Simplify if possible.

1. $4\frac{1}{3}$
   $-1\frac{2}{3}$

2. 8
   $-5\frac{1}{4}$

3. $9\frac{3}{8}$
   $-6\frac{5}{8}$

4. $21\frac{2}{9}$
   $-8\frac{2}{3}$

5. $18\frac{1}{4}$
   $-9\frac{3}{8}$

6. $7 - 2\frac{3}{4}$

7. $12\frac{2}{5} - 5\frac{3}{5}$

8. $13\frac{1}{6} - 4\frac{2}{3}$

Exercises

Subtract. Simplify if possible.

1. $16\frac{2}{5}$
   $-8\frac{1}{2}$

2. $2\frac{3}{10}$
   $-1\frac{4}{5}$

3. 7
   $-2\frac{5}{6}$

4. $5\frac{3}{5}$
   $-\frac{4}{5}$

5. $24\frac{1}{3}$
   $-8\frac{4}{5}$

6. $26\frac{1}{2} - 6\frac{3}{4}$

7. $5\frac{1}{4} - 2\frac{2}{3}$

8. $21\frac{5}{6} - 4\frac{3}{4}$

9. $17 - 3\frac{7}{8}$

10. $12\frac{2}{9} - 4\frac{5}{6}$

11. $16\frac{1}{8} - 12\frac{1}{6}$

Copy and complete. Simplify if possible.

★ 12. $24 - \blacksquare = 12\frac{1}{2}$

★ 13. $3\frac{1}{4} + \blacksquare = 5\frac{3}{4}$

★ 14. $8\frac{1}{6} - \blacksquare = 7$

Solve each problem. Simplify if possible.

15. Alicia has two pieces of luggage. Her luggage weighs $36\frac{1}{2}$ lb. Ann's luggage weighs $27\frac{3}{4}$ lb. How much heavier is Alicia's luggage?

16. Mark's flight took $4\frac{1}{4}$ h. The taxi ride from the airport to the city took $\frac{2}{3}$ h. How much longer was the airplane flight?

17. On the flight from Chicago to New York, $6\frac{1}{3}$ cases of orange juice were used. Only $2\frac{3}{4}$ cases of tomato juice were used. How many cases of the two juices were used altogether?

18. Pete is taking a course on airplane maintenance. The course is worth $2\frac{1}{2}$ credits. He needs 5 credits to graduate. How many more credits will Pete need after he completes the course?

Fractions: Addition and Subtraction   231

Problem Solving: Applications

FORMULATING PROBLEMS

Jeff washes cars and mows lawns to
earn extra money during the summer.
He charges $4 per hour. Here is part
of the record he kept.

Day	Date	Job	Time (in hours)	Amount
Monday	7-14-86	Willis lawn	$1\frac{1}{2}$	$6
		Willis car	1	$4
Tuesday	7-15-86	Franklin lawn	$2\frac{3}{4}$	$11
		Avery 1st car	$\frac{3}{4}$	$3
		Avery 2nd car	$1\frac{1}{4}$	$5
Wednesday	7-16-86	Adams car	1	$4
		Romero car	$\frac{3}{4}$	$3
		Romero lawn	$3\frac{1}{2}$	$14

There are many questions you could
ask using this information.
For example, you could ask a question
that can be solved by subtracting.

How much longer did Jeff
take to mow the Franklin lawn
than the Willis lawn?

To find the answer, subtract $1\frac{1}{2}$
from $2\frac{3}{4}$.

$$
\begin{array}{r}
2\frac{3}{4} = 2\frac{3}{4} \\
-1\frac{1}{2} = -1\frac{2}{4} \\
\hline
1\frac{1}{4}
\end{array}
$$

Jeff took $1\frac{1}{4}$ hour longer to
mow the Franklin lawn.

Try These

**Write a question using the information in Jeff's record.
Then answer the question.**

1. Use the times for washing the Avery cars.

2. Use the amounts Jeff made on Tuesday.

3. Write a question that can be solved by subtracting.

4. Use $2\frac{1}{2}$ h as the answer.

Exercises

Here is a table that gives the number of hours Jeff worked each day during 2 weeks in August.

Day	August 4–9	August 11–16
Monday	$3\frac{3}{4}$	0
Tuesday	$4\frac{1}{4}$	$3\frac{1}{2}$
Wednesday	$1\frac{1}{2}$	$3\frac{3}{4}$
Thursday	$3\frac{1}{4}$	6
Friday	$4\frac{3}{4}$	$3\frac{3}{4}$
Saturday	$6\frac{3}{4}$	$5\frac{1}{2}$

**Write a question using the information in the table.
Then answer the question.**

1. Use the times Jeff worked on Monday and Tuesday of the first week.

2. Use the times Jeff worked on the two Tuesdays.

3. Write a question that requires addition of three or more numbers.

4. Write a question that can be solved by subtracting.

5. Write a question that requires finding the greatest number among several numbers.

★ 6. Write a question that requires putting five numbers in order from least to greatest.

★ 7. Use $5\frac{1}{4}$ h as the answer.

★ 8. Use $8\frac{1}{2}$ h as the answer.

CHAPTER CHECKPOINT

Copy and complete. (pp. 210–211)

1. $\frac{3}{8} = \frac{\blacksquare}{24}$

2. $\frac{4}{9} = \frac{8}{\blacksquare}$

3. $\frac{3}{4} = \frac{\blacksquare}{12}$

4. $\frac{2}{5} = \frac{10}{\blacksquare}$

5. $\frac{1}{10} = \frac{\blacksquare}{100}$

6. $\frac{2}{7} = \frac{\blacksquare}{35}$

7. $\frac{9}{11} = \frac{27}{\blacksquare}$

8. $\frac{4}{5} = \frac{\blacksquare}{20}$

9. $\frac{5}{6} = \frac{25}{\blacksquare}$

10. $\frac{1}{5} = \frac{5}{\blacksquare}$

Write each fraction in lowest terms. (pp. 212–213)

11. $\frac{3}{18}$

12. $\frac{4}{20}$

13. $\frac{8}{44}$

14. $\frac{9}{21}$

15. $\frac{36}{42}$

16. $\frac{7}{14}$

17. $\frac{5}{15}$

18. $\frac{8}{24}$

19. $\frac{18}{27}$

20. $\frac{24}{36}$

21. $\frac{18}{30}$

22. $\frac{21}{28}$

Write each fraction as a whole number or as a mixed number. (pp. 214–215)

23. $\frac{12}{4}$

24. $\frac{29}{7}$

25. $\frac{36}{9}$

26. $\frac{54}{12}$

27. $\frac{82}{9}$

28. $\frac{77}{11}$

Add or subtract. Simplify if possible. (pp. 216–217)

29. $\frac{5}{8} - \frac{3}{8}$

30. $\frac{9}{11} + \frac{9}{11}$

31. $\frac{2}{4} + \frac{3}{4}$

32. $\frac{9}{10} - \frac{3}{10}$

33. $\frac{5}{6} + \frac{1}{6}$

34. $\frac{4}{5} - \frac{1}{5}$

35. $\frac{7}{9} - \frac{5}{9}$

36. $\frac{7}{12} + \frac{11}{12}$

Write >, <, or =. (pp. 218–219)

37. $\frac{5}{8} \ \blacksquare \ \frac{5}{15}$

38. $\frac{5}{12} \ \blacksquare \ \frac{8}{12}$

39. $\frac{4}{5} \ \blacksquare \ \frac{5}{6}$

40. $\frac{5}{7} \ \blacksquare \ \frac{4}{7}$

41. $2\frac{1}{2} \ \blacksquare \ 2\frac{3}{4}$

42. $\frac{4}{9} \ \blacksquare \ \frac{3}{8}$

43. $\frac{9}{11} \ \blacksquare \ \frac{15}{30}$

44. $\frac{3}{4} \ \blacksquare \ \frac{2}{3}$

45. $4\frac{1}{5} \ \blacksquare \ 5\frac{1}{4}$

46. $3\frac{1}{4} \ \blacksquare \ 3\frac{2}{8}$

Add or subtract. Simplify if possible. (pp. 220–223)

47. $\frac{3}{4} + \frac{1}{2}$

48. $\frac{5}{6} + \frac{2}{3}$

49. $\frac{7}{8} - \frac{3}{4}$

50. $\frac{5}{9} - \frac{1}{3}$

51. $\frac{5}{8} - \frac{1}{3}$

52. $\frac{1}{6} + \frac{4}{9}$

53. $\frac{1}{5} + \frac{3}{10}$

54. $\frac{5}{6} - \frac{3}{8}$

Add or subtract. Simplify if possible. (pp. 226–231)

55. $5\frac{1}{2}$
$+3\frac{1}{3}$

56. $6\frac{1}{2}$
$-3\frac{2}{7}$

57. $16\frac{8}{10}$
$-\ 6\frac{2}{5}$

58. $9\frac{1}{3}$
$+7\frac{2}{9}$

59. $18\frac{7}{9}$
$-\ 6$

60. $8\frac{3}{4}$
$+5\frac{3}{8}$

61. 9
$-7\frac{1}{6}$

62. $7\frac{8}{11}$
$+12\frac{1}{2}$

63. $21\frac{1}{4}$
$-\ 7$

64. $16\frac{1}{2}$
$+\ 9\frac{3}{4}$

65. $18 - 4\frac{3}{8}$

66. $7\frac{1}{6} - 3\frac{4}{9}$

67. $7\frac{2}{8} + 6\frac{3}{5}$

Find the next number in each pattern. (pp. 224–225)

68. $\frac{28}{4}, \frac{24}{4}, \frac{20}{4}, \frac{16}{4}, \frac{12}{4},$ ▩

69. $\frac{6}{8}, \frac{9}{8}, \frac{12}{8}, \frac{15}{8}, \frac{18}{8},$ ▩

70. $\frac{1}{12}, \frac{5}{12}, \frac{9}{12}, \frac{13}{12}, \frac{17}{12},$ ▩

71. $\frac{17}{20}, \frac{15}{20}, \frac{13}{20}, \frac{11}{20}, \frac{9}{20},$ ▩

Solve each problem. Simplify if possible. (pp. 210–231)

72. Martina ran $\frac{7}{10}$ mi. Natalie ran $\frac{3}{4}$ mi. How much farther did Natalie run?

73. Mr. Cooke worked $3\frac{3}{4}$ h before lunch and $3\frac{1}{2}$ h after lunch. How many hours did he work altogether?

74. Paco bought $2\frac{1}{3}$ lb of chicken wings and $3\frac{1}{2}$ lb of chicken legs. Did he buy more pounds of wings or legs? How many more?

75. Ms. Baker had $8\frac{1}{4}$ qt of paint. After painting her living room, she had $3\frac{3}{4}$ qt left. How many quarts did she use?

Here is a price list of extra pieces for a model train set.

Write a question. Then answer the question. (pp. 232–233)

76. Use addition of three prices.

77. Use multiplication of a price by a number.

78. Use subtraction to compare two prices.

Model Train Pieces	
straight track	$ 4.95
curved track	$ 4.95
set of 4 figures	$ 9.95
water crane	$39.95
engine shed	$94.95

COMPUTERS AND PROBLEM SOLVING

Match each Logo command with its meaning. Use the examples to help you remember.

1. TEST
TEST :SIZE > 1

2. IFFALSE
IFFALSE [PR [NO]]

3. SETPOS
SETPOS [40 20]

4. READLIST
TEST READLIST = [YES]

5. HOME

6. LEFT
LEFT 45

7. REPEAT
REPEAT 4[FD 8 RT 90]

8. ROUND
ROUND 4.3

9. *
PRINT 6 * 5

10. /
PRINT 36 / 6

11. PU

12. CS

a. Turns the turtle to the left.

b. Tells the computer to read more than one word or number.

c. Determines if some condition has been met.

d. Sends the turtle to the center of the screen.

e. Tells the computer what to do if a condition has not been met.

f. Tells the computer to divide one number by another.

g. Tells the computer to round a decimal to the nearest whole number.

h. Tells the turtle to move without drawing a line.

i. Tells the turtle to repeat the commands inside the brackets a certain number of times.

j. Erases all lines from the screen.

k. Tells the computer to multiply two numbers.

l. Moves the turtle to a specific location on the grid.

■ A **procedure** is a set of commands to tell the computer how to do a task. When you type a procedure, the first line is the title line. It must contain the word TO and the name of the procedure. The last line of a procedure is the word END.

This procedure tells the turtle to draw a triangle.

TO TRI
REPEAT 3 [FD 30 RT 120]
END

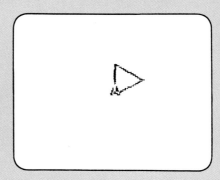

After you type a procedure, it stays in the computer's memory. Then you only have to type the procedure name to run the procedure.

■ Procedures can use other procedures. The procedure HEX uses TRI.

TO HEX
REPEAT 6 [TRI RT 60]
END

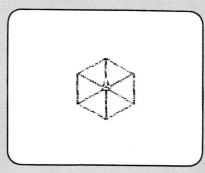

Now the procedure BIGHEX uses HEX.

TO BIGHEX
REPEAT 6 [HEX FD 30 RT 60]
END

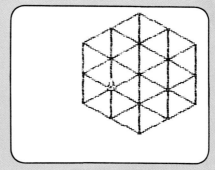

Solve each problem.

1. Trace the path of the turtle in BIGHEX. How many hexagons does the turtle draw? Include all sizes.

2. How many small triangles does the turtle draw in BIGHEX?

ENRICHMENT

DENSITY

■ Between any two fractions that are not equivalent, you can find another fraction. This property is called **density**.

Find a fraction between $\frac{1}{5}$ and $\frac{1}{3}$.

First find equivalent fractions with a common denominator. $\frac{1}{5} = \frac{3}{15}$ $\frac{1}{3} = \frac{5}{15}$

$\frac{4}{15}$ is between $\frac{3}{15}$ and $\frac{5}{15}$, since $\frac{3}{15} < \frac{4}{15}$ and $\frac{4}{15} < \frac{5}{15}$.
So $\frac{4}{15}$ is between $\frac{1}{5}$ and $\frac{1}{3}$.

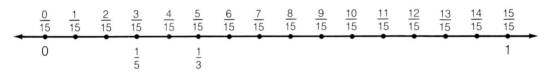

■ Find a fraction between $\frac{1}{2}$ and $\frac{2}{3}$.

First find equivalent fractions with a common denominator. $\frac{1}{2} = \frac{3}{6}$ $\frac{2}{3} = \frac{4}{6}$

What fraction is between $\frac{3}{6}$ and $\frac{4}{6}$? Use a greater common denominator to find equivalent fractions. $\frac{1}{2} = \frac{6}{12}$ $\frac{2}{3} = \frac{8}{12}$

$\frac{7}{12}$ is between $\frac{6}{12}$ and $\frac{8}{12}$. So $\frac{7}{12}$ is between $\frac{1}{2}$ and $\frac{2}{3}$.

Find a fraction between each pair of fractions.

1. $\frac{2}{3}, \frac{4}{5}$ 　　　　 **2.** $\frac{2}{5}, \frac{1}{2}$ 　　　　 **3.** $\frac{5}{8}, \frac{5}{6}$ 　　　　 **4.** $\frac{1}{2}, \frac{3}{4}$

5. $\frac{1}{3}, \frac{1}{2}$ 　　　　 **6.** $\frac{3}{5}, \frac{4}{4}$ 　　　　 **7.** $\frac{0}{10}, \frac{1}{10}$ 　　　　 **8.** $\frac{15}{3}, \frac{16}{3}$

Find a mixed number between each pair of numbers.

9. $5\frac{1}{2}, 5\frac{5}{6}$ 　　　 **10.** $4\frac{2}{3}, 5$ 　　　 **11.** $7\frac{3}{4}, 7\frac{4}{5}$ 　　　 **12.** $2, 2\frac{1}{5}$

Write each number.

1. eight and five tenths
2. thirty and seven hundredths
3. six hundred twelve
4. nine and twenty-two thousandths

Write >, <, or =.

5. 67.5 ▨ 6.75

6. $\frac{1}{4}$ ▨ $\frac{1}{3}$

7. 3.007 ▨ 3.07

8. 2.13 ▨ 2.130

9. 29.09 ▨ 29.90

10. $\frac{6}{7}$ ▨ $\frac{3}{4}$

Round to the given place.

11. 0.48 to the nearest tenth
12. 74.168 to the nearest hundredth
13. 24.26 to the nearest one
14. 82.55 to the nearest ten

Compute. Estimate to check.

15. 68.4 + 39.67
16. 198.79 − 12.8
17. 62.99 + 4.114
18. 98 − 76.5
19. 32.4 + 96.791
20. 394 + 29.5

Multiply. Estimate to check.

21. 96.2 × 3.4
22. 198.1 × 2.6
23. 76.38 × 0.98
24. 8 × $1.75
25. 90 × $8.23
26. $3.98 × 67

Divide.

27. 568 ÷ 2
28. $29.20 ÷ 4
29. 6,728 ÷ 8
30. $198.75 ÷ 5
31. 973 ÷ 7
32. $76.50 ÷ 50

Solve each problem.

33. Matthew's weekly earnings for July and August were $25, $40, $35, $43, $36, $45, $22, and $34. What were Matthew's average weekly earnings?

34. Scott made high-protein bread. He used $1\frac{1}{4}$ c of soy flour and $4\frac{1}{2}$ c of whole wheat flour. How much flour did he use?

35. A 24-oz box of detergent costs $3.36 at Bill's Supermarket. What is the cost per ounce?

36. Frances worked 6 h 55 min on Monday and 7 h 15 min on Tuesday. How long did she work altogether?

SKILLS CHECK

Choose the correct answer.

1. In 569.482, which number is in the hundredths place?

  a. 2
  b. 4
  c. 5
  d. 8

2. What is 54,658 rounded to the nearest thousand?

  a. 50,000
  b. 54,000
  c. 55,000
  d. 56,000

3. $62 - 25.9$

  a. 36.1
  b. 36.9
  c. 37.9
  d. 87.9

4. Which number is fifty-four and fifty-four thousandths?

  a. 54.054
  b. 54.540
  c. 54,054
  d. 54,540

5. $5\frac{2}{3} + 6\frac{1}{2}$

  a. $11\frac{1}{6}$ **b.** $11\frac{3}{5}$

  c. $12\frac{1}{6}$ **d.** NG

6. $7\frac{3}{4} - 3\frac{1}{2}$

  a. $3\frac{1}{4}$ **b.** $4\frac{1}{4}$

  c. 5   **d.** NG

7. Which number is divisible by 5?

  a. 1,598
  b. 2,574
  c. 5,551
  d. 9,870

8. Compute: 6^3

  a. 36
  b. 216
  c. 729
  d. NG

9. Estimate: 59×82

  a. 400
  b. 480
  c. 4,800
  d. 40,000

10. Monica bought 3 T-shirts for $2.79 each. She bought 2 pairs of slacks for $7.49 each. How much did she spend?

  a. $10.28
  b. $15.28
  c. $23.35
  d. $28.35

11. Julio bought $2\frac{1}{4}$ gal of cranberry juice and $3\frac{1}{2}$ gal of apple juice. How much did he buy altogether?

  a. $5\frac{1}{3}$ gal

  b. $5\frac{3}{8}$ gal

  c. $5\frac{3}{4}$ gal

  d. NG

12. A 12-kg bag of dog food costs $30. What is the cost per kilogram?

  a. $2.00
  b. $2.50
  c. $3.50
  d. $6.00

9

FRACTIONS:
MULTIPLICATION AND DIVISION

Mixed Numbers and Fractions

■ Find the point on the number line for the fraction $\frac{4}{2}$ and the whole number 2.

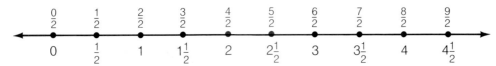

$\frac{4}{2}$ and 2 name the same number. $\frac{4}{2} = 2$

Find the point for the fraction $\frac{5}{2}$ and the mixed number $2\frac{1}{2}$. $\frac{5}{2}$ and $2\frac{1}{2}$ name the same number. $\frac{5}{2} = 2\frac{1}{2}$

■ There are several ways to write a fraction as a mixed number.

Write $\frac{9}{2}$ as a mixed number.

One way: Another way:

$\frac{9}{2} = \frac{8}{2} + \frac{1}{2}$ $\frac{9}{2}$ means $9 \div 2$.

$\quad = 4 + \frac{1}{2}$

$\quad = 4\frac{1}{2}$

$$\begin{array}{r} 4 \text{ R1, or } 4\frac{1}{2} \leftarrow \text{remainder} \\ 2\overline{)9} \quad\quad\quad \leftarrow \text{divisor} \\ \underline{8} \\ 1 \end{array}$$

■ You can also write a mixed number as a fraction.

Write $2\frac{1}{3}$ as a fraction.

One way: Another way:

$2\frac{1}{3} = 2 + \frac{1}{3}$ $2\frac{1}{3} = \dfrac{\blacksquare}{3}$

$\quad = \frac{6}{3} + \frac{1}{3}$ How many thirds?

$\quad = \frac{7}{3}$ Multiply: $3 \times 2 = 6$
            Add: $6 + 1 = 7$

$$2\frac{1}{3} = \frac{7}{3}$$

Try These

Write each fraction as a mixed number or as a whole number.

1. $\frac{7}{4}$ **2.** $\frac{12}{3}$ **3.** $\frac{9}{5}$ **4.** $\frac{11}{5}$ **5.** $\frac{15}{3}$ **6.** $\frac{22}{7}$

Write each mixed number as a fraction.

7. $1\frac{1}{2}$ **8.** $3\frac{2}{3}$ **9.** $1\frac{3}{4}$ **10.** $2\frac{1}{5}$ **11.** $3\frac{3}{5}$ **12.** $4\frac{3}{8}$

Exercises

Write each fraction as a mixed number or as a whole number.

1. $\frac{7}{3}$ **2.** $\frac{5}{4}$ **3.** $\frac{10}{2}$ **4.** $\frac{15}{4}$ **5.** $\frac{17}{5}$ **6.** $\frac{8}{3}$

7. $\frac{20}{4}$ **8.** $\frac{13}{10}$ **9.** $\frac{19}{6}$ **10.** $\frac{35}{3}$ **11.** $\frac{27}{5}$ **12.** $\frac{48}{7}$

13. $\frac{30}{5}$ **14.** $\frac{27}{2}$ **15.** $\frac{50}{4}$ **16.** $\frac{20}{10}$ **17.** $\frac{280}{40}$ **18.** $\frac{783}{100}$

Write each mixed number as a fraction.

19. $1\frac{7}{8}$ **20.** $4\frac{1}{5}$ **21.** $7\frac{1}{8}$ **22.** $10\frac{3}{4}$ **23.** $5\frac{4}{16}$ **24.** $3\frac{1}{6}$

25. $3\frac{1}{4}$ **26.** $2\frac{3}{8}$ **27.** $8\frac{1}{3}$ **28.** $4\frac{3}{4}$ **29.** $9\frac{7}{8}$ **30.** $3\frac{9}{13}$

31. $9\frac{9}{10}$ **32.** $2\frac{3}{7}$ **33.** $4\frac{3}{5}$ **34.** $9\frac{1}{2}$ **35.** $10\frac{6}{7}$ **36.** $8\frac{5}{9}$

Solve each problem.

37. Henry has 8 oranges. He cuts each orange into fourths. How many fourths is that?

38. 9 apples are shared equally by Jane, Henry, Nina, and Ramón. How many does each person have?

★ **39.** There are $2\frac{5}{6}$ melons in the refrigerator. How many people can Henry serve if each person gets $\frac{1}{6}$ of a melon?

★ **40.** Henry uses $\frac{1}{8}$ of his food budget for vegetables, $\frac{1}{4}$ for meat, and $\frac{1}{5}$ for canned goods. Does he have more than half of his budget left?

Multiplying Fractions

■ Mr. Friendly plowed $\frac{1}{4}$ of a field. Then he planted potatoes on $\frac{1}{2}$ of the part he had plowed. On what part of his field did he plant potatoes?

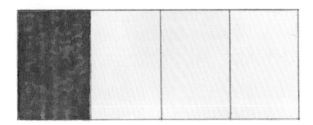

$\frac{1}{2}$ of $\frac{1}{4}$ is $\frac{1}{8}$

$\frac{1}{2} \times \frac{1}{4} = \frac{1}{8}$

Each of the smallest rectangles in the drawing is $\frac{1}{8}$ of the whole rectangle.

Mr. Friendly planted potatoes on $\frac{1}{8}$ of the field.

To multiply fractions:

1. Multiply the numerators. $\qquad \frac{1}{2} \times \frac{1}{4} = \frac{1 \times 1}{} = \frac{1}{}$

2. Multiply the denominators. $\qquad \frac{1}{2} \times \frac{1}{4} = \frac{1 \times 1}{2 \times 4} = \frac{1}{8}$

3. Simplify if possible.

■ Multiply: $\frac{2}{3} \times \frac{1}{4}$

$$\frac{2}{3} \times \frac{1}{4} = \frac{2 \times 1}{3 \times 4}$$
$$= \frac{2}{12}$$
$$= \frac{1}{6}$$

■ When one factor is a whole number, first write it as a fraction.

Multiply: $3 \times \frac{2}{5}$

Think: $3 = \frac{3}{1}$

$$3 \times \frac{2}{5} = \frac{3}{1} \times \frac{2}{5}$$
$$= \frac{3 \times 2}{1 \times 5}$$
$$= \frac{6}{5}$$
$$= 1\frac{1}{5}$$

Multiply: $\frac{2}{3} \times 6$

Think: $6 = \frac{6}{1}$

$$\frac{2}{3} \times 6 = \frac{2}{3} \times \frac{6}{1}$$
$$= \frac{2 \times 6}{3 \times 1}$$
$$= \frac{12}{3}$$
$$= 4$$

Try These

Study each figure. Then complete to find each product.

1.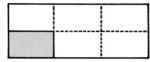

$$\frac{1}{2} \times \frac{1}{3} = \frac{\blacksquare}{\blacksquare}$$

2.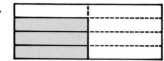

$$\frac{3}{4} \times \frac{1}{2} = \frac{\blacksquare}{\blacksquare}$$

3.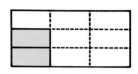

$$\frac{2}{3} \times \frac{1}{3} = \frac{\blacksquare}{\blacksquare}$$

Multiply. Simplify if possible.

4. $\frac{1}{2} \times \frac{7}{8}$　　**5.** $9 \times \frac{1}{2}$　　**6.** $\frac{1}{2} \times \frac{4}{5}$　　**7.** $\frac{1}{4} \times \frac{1}{2}$　　**8.** $\frac{4}{5} \times 6$

Exercises

Multiply. Simplify if possible.

1. $\frac{2}{3} \times \frac{4}{5}$　　**2.** $5 \times \frac{2}{3}$　　**3.** $\frac{1}{6} \times \frac{4}{5}$　　**4.** $3 \times \frac{1}{3}$　　**5.** $\frac{1}{5} \times 7$

6. $\frac{3}{4} \times 12$　　**7.** $\frac{2}{5} \times \frac{5}{8}$　　**8.** $\frac{3}{4} \times \frac{1}{3}$　　**9.** $\frac{3}{5} \times \frac{2}{3}$　　★ **10.** $\frac{6}{7} \times \frac{2}{3} \times \frac{7}{8}$

Solve each problem. Simplify if possible.

11. Mr. Friendly plowed $\frac{2}{3}$ of another field. Then he planted cotton on $\frac{3}{4}$ of the part that he had plowed. On what part of the field did he plant cotton?

12. Mr. Friendly planted cotton on $\frac{1}{4}$ of a field and potatoes on $\frac{1}{2}$ of the same field. He did not plant the rest of the field. What part of the field did he plant?

 THINK AND TRY

GUESSING AND CHECKING

There are four whole numbers. When the numbers are arranged in order from greatest to least, each number is half as much as the number before it. The sum of the numbers is 45. What are the four numbers?

More Multiplying Fractions

- You can use a shortcut when multiplying fractions:

  1. Divide the numerator and the denominator by a common factor.
  2. Then multiply.

Multiply: $\frac{3}{4} \times \frac{5}{6}$

$$\frac{3}{4} \times \frac{5}{6} = \frac{\overset{1}{\cancel{3}} \times 5}{4 \times \underset{2}{\cancel{6}}}$$

3 is a common factor of 3 and 6.

$$= \frac{1 \times 5}{4 \times 2}$$

$$= \frac{5}{8}$$

- Sometimes the shortcut can be used twice.

Multiply: $\frac{9}{10} \times \frac{5}{12}$

$$\frac{9}{10} \times \frac{5}{12} = \frac{\overset{3}{\cancel{9}} \times \overset{1}{\cancel{5}}}{\underset{2}{\cancel{10}} \times \underset{4}{\cancel{12}}}$$

3 is a common factor of 9 and 12.
5 is a common factor of 5 and 10.

$$= \frac{3 \times 1}{2 \times 4}$$

$$= \frac{3}{8}$$

- If the product of two numbers is 1, the numbers are **reciprocals** of each other.

The reciprocal of $\frac{2}{3}$ is $\frac{3}{2}$. $\frac{2}{3} \times \frac{3}{2} = \frac{6}{6} = 1$

The reciprocal of 5 is $\frac{1}{5}$. $\frac{5}{1} \times \frac{1}{5} = \frac{5}{5} = 1$

The reciprocal of $3\frac{1}{2}$ is $\frac{2}{7}$. $\frac{7}{2} \times \frac{2}{7} = \frac{14}{14} = 1$

Try These

Multiply. Simplify if possible.

1. $\frac{1}{2} \times \frac{2}{3}$ **2.** $\frac{3}{5} \times \frac{5}{8}$ **3.** $\frac{1}{2} \times \frac{4}{8}$ **4.** $\frac{5}{6} \times \frac{3}{5}$ **5.** $\frac{5}{8} \times \frac{6}{7}$

Write each reciprocal.

6. $\frac{2}{5}$ **7.** $\frac{1}{3}$ **8.** 6   **9.** $2\frac{1}{2}$ **10.** $5\frac{1}{4}$ **11.** $\frac{5}{9}$

Exercises

Multiply. Simplify if possible.

1. $\frac{2}{3} \times \frac{7}{8}$ 2. $\frac{3}{4} \times \frac{8}{9}$ 3. $\frac{3}{10} \times \frac{2}{5}$ 4. $\frac{4}{5} \times \frac{5}{8}$ 5. $\frac{3}{14} \times \frac{7}{18}$

6. $\frac{5}{6} \times \frac{2}{3}$ 7. $\frac{2}{3} \times \frac{5}{12}$ 8. $\frac{5}{6} \times \frac{2}{7}$ 9. $\frac{5}{8} \times \frac{4}{15}$ 10. $\frac{1}{2} \times \frac{8}{9}$

11. $\frac{2}{3} \times \frac{3}{8}$ 12. $\frac{2}{9} \times \frac{3}{4}$ 13. $\frac{7}{8} \times \frac{8}{9}$ 14. $\frac{3}{8} \times \frac{6}{7}$ 15. $\frac{4}{5} \times \frac{16}{20}$

16. $\frac{3}{7} \times \frac{5}{9}$ 17. $\frac{3}{4} \times \frac{4}{9}$ 18. $\frac{1}{2} \times \frac{3}{4}$ 19. $\frac{7}{16} \times \frac{4}{21}$ ★ 20. $\frac{4}{15} \times \frac{3}{5} \times 10$

Copy and complete.

21. $\frac{4}{5} \times \blacksquare = 1$ 22. $12 \times \blacksquare = 1$ 23. $1\frac{2}{3} \times \blacksquare = 1$

24. $2\frac{1}{2} \times \blacksquare = 1$ 25. $\blacksquare \times \frac{1}{10} = 1$ 26. $\blacksquare \times 100 = 1$

Solve each problem. Simplify if possible.

27. Jan is learning to play the tuba. She practices $\frac{3}{4}$ h 5 days a week. How many hours does she practice in a week?

28. $\frac{2}{3}$ of Mrs. Stroub's students take flute lessons. About $\frac{1}{4}$ of these students are beginners. What fraction are beginning flute students?

29. Fred practices his solo for $\frac{5}{6}$ h. Jan practices her solo for $\frac{1}{2}$ as long. What part of an hour does Jan spend practicing?

★ 30. On Friday, Jan practiced 3 h for the concert. $\frac{1}{4}$ of this time was spent playing chords. How many minutes did she spend playing chords?

KEEPING IN SHAPE

1. 546×58 2. $6{,}780 \div 5$ 3. 0.8×0.6
4. 8.03×3.72 5. $1{,}728 \div 36$ 6. $3.95 \div 5$
7. 2.06×8.5 8. $44.38 \div 0.7$ 9. $2.232 \div 1.8$

Dividing Fractions

- Joan Cortney works in a clothing factory. She uses $\frac{3}{4}$ foot of lace on each dress. She has 3 feet of lace. How many dresses can she put lace on?

To find the answer, divide 3 by $\frac{3}{4}$.

Find how many $\frac{3}{4}$s are in 3.

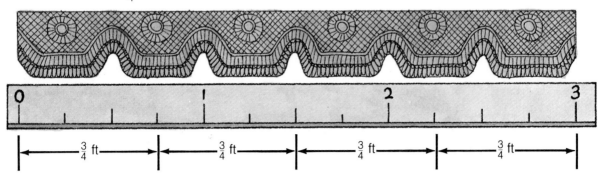

The diagram shows that there are four $\frac{3}{4}$s in 3.

> *To divide by a fraction, multiply by its reciprocal.*

Write 3 as a fraction.	**Show multiplication by the reciprocal of $\frac{3}{4}$.**	**Multiply. Simplify.**
$3 \div \frac{3}{4} = \frac{3}{1} \div \frac{3}{4}$	$\frac{3}{1} \times \frac{4}{3}$	$\frac{3}{1} \times \frac{4}{3} = \frac{12}{3}$
⤷ reciprocals ⤴		$= 4$

Joan can put lace on 4 dresses.

- Divide: $\frac{2}{3} \div \frac{3}{5}$

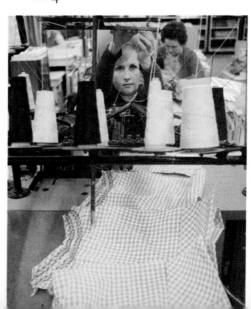

Show multiplication by the reciprocal of $\frac{3}{5}$.	**Multiply. Simplify.**
$\frac{2}{3} \div \frac{3}{5} = \frac{2}{3} \times \frac{5}{3}$	$\frac{2}{3} \times \frac{5}{3} = \frac{10}{9}$
	$= 1\frac{1}{9}$

Try These

Divide. Simplify if possible.

1. $\frac{5}{8} \div \frac{1}{4}$

2. $6 \div \frac{2}{3}$

3. $\frac{2}{3} \div \frac{1}{3}$

4. $\frac{5}{8} \div 5$

5. $\frac{4}{9} \div \frac{1}{2}$

6. $\frac{5}{6} \div \frac{2}{3}$

7. $\frac{7}{10} \div \frac{1}{5}$

8. $7 \div \frac{2}{3}$

9. $\frac{4}{7} \div \frac{2}{3}$

10. $\frac{5}{8} \div 2$

Exercises

Divide. Simplify if possible.

1. $\frac{3}{4} \div \frac{1}{2}$

2. $10 \div \frac{1}{2}$

3. $\frac{15}{16} \div \frac{1}{8}$

4. $\frac{1}{3} \div \frac{2}{5}$

5. $\frac{1}{9} \div \frac{2}{5}$

6. $\frac{2}{3} \div \frac{2}{9}$

7. $\frac{1}{3} \div 5$

8. $\frac{3}{4} \div \frac{3}{4}$

9. $\frac{3}{5} \div 6$

10. $\frac{2}{3} \div 4$

11. $4 \div \frac{1}{4}$

12. $\frac{1}{6} \div 2$

13. $\frac{4}{5} \div \frac{9}{10}$

14. $3 \div \frac{1}{2}$

15. $\frac{2}{3} \div \frac{1}{5}$

16. $\frac{2}{7} \div 6$

17. $\frac{5}{8} \div \frac{2}{3}$

18. $75 \div \frac{1}{2}$

19. $\frac{4}{9} \div \frac{4}{5}$

20. $\frac{4}{11} \div \frac{9}{10}$

Compute.

21. $\left(\frac{3}{4} \times \frac{7}{9}\right) \div \left(3 \times \frac{1}{4}\right)$

22. $\left(\frac{5}{16} + \frac{1}{4}\right) \times \left(\frac{11}{12} - \frac{1}{4}\right)$

23. $\left(16 \div \frac{1}{4}\right) + \left(\frac{5}{8} \times \frac{2}{5}\right)$

24. $\left(\frac{5}{8} - \frac{1}{4}\right) \times \left(4 \div \frac{1}{2}\right)$

25. $2\frac{9}{10} - \left(\frac{1}{2} \div \frac{4}{5}\right)$

★ 26. $\left(5\frac{1}{3} - 1\frac{1}{2}\right) + 2\frac{1}{4}$

Solve each problem.

27. Joan is making blouses. She uses $\frac{2}{3}$ yd of lace on each blouse. She has 8 yd of lace. How many blouses can she put lace on?

28. Joan used $\frac{1}{2}$ yd of blue ribbon and $\frac{3}{4}$ yd of green ribbon on a skirt. How much ribbon did she use altogether?

29. Joan walks $\frac{3}{4}$ mi altogether to work and back. How many times would she have to walk to work and back in order to walk 6 mi?

★ 30. Joan has a piece of fabric 5 yd long and 1 yd wide. Each tie requires a piece of fabric $\frac{5}{8}$ yd wide and 1 yd long. How many ties can she make?

Multiplying and Dividing Mixed Numbers

■ Pat Blum worked on her sculpture for $4\frac{1}{2}$ hours on Thursday. Ed Davis worked on his sculpture $1\frac{1}{2}$ times as long. How many hours did Ed work?

Multiply $4\frac{1}{2}$ by $1\frac{1}{2}$ to find the answer.

Write both mixed numbers as fractions.

$$4\frac{1}{2} = \frac{9}{2}$$

$$1\frac{1}{2} = \frac{3}{2}$$

Multiply. Simplify.

$$\frac{9}{2} \times \frac{3}{2} = \frac{27}{4}$$

$$= 6\frac{3}{4}$$

Ed worked $6\frac{3}{4}$ hours.

■ You can also divide mixed numbers.

Divide: $7\frac{1}{2} \div 1\frac{1}{2}$

Write both mixed numbers as fractions.

$$7\frac{1}{2} = \frac{15}{2}$$

$$1\frac{1}{2} = \frac{3}{2}$$

Divide. Simplify.

$$7\frac{1}{2} \div 1\frac{1}{2} = \frac{15}{2} \div \frac{3}{2}$$

$$= \frac{15}{2} \times \frac{2}{3}$$

$$= \frac{30}{6}$$

$$= 5$$

Try These

Multiply. Simplify if possible.

1. $3\frac{1}{2} \times 2\frac{1}{3}$ **2.** $\frac{3}{4} \times 1\frac{1}{2}$ **3.** $3 \times 1\frac{1}{2}$ **4.** $1\frac{1}{4} \times 4$

Divide. Simplify if possible.

5. $2\frac{1}{2} \div 1\frac{1}{4}$ **6.** $7 \div 1\frac{1}{3}$ **7.** $1\frac{1}{3} \div 1\frac{3}{5}$ **8.** $2\frac{3}{10} \div \frac{1}{2}$

Exercises

Multiply. Simplify if possible.

1. $\frac{3}{5} \times 2\frac{1}{3}$

2. $5 \times 3\frac{1}{2}$

3. $2\frac{3}{4} \times 1\frac{1}{10}$

4. $2\frac{1}{3} \times 1\frac{3}{5}$

5. $\frac{2}{3} \times 2\frac{1}{3}$

6. $\frac{3}{4} \times 2\frac{1}{2}$

7. $1\frac{3}{4} \times 1\frac{1}{3}$

8. $4 \times 1\frac{1}{2}$

9. $2\frac{1}{3} \times 6$

10. $4 \times 2\frac{1}{2}$

11. $1\frac{2}{5} \times \frac{1}{5}$

12. $3\frac{1}{3} \times 4\frac{1}{2}$

Divide. Simplify if possible.

13. $1\frac{1}{4} \div 1\frac{1}{2}$

14. $9\frac{1}{2} \div \frac{3}{4}$

15. $\frac{7}{8} \div 3\frac{3}{8}$

16. $6 \div 1\frac{1}{5}$

17. $5 \div 3\frac{1}{2}$

18. $6\frac{2}{3} \div 1\frac{3}{4}$

19. $3\frac{5}{6} \div 1\frac{2}{3}$

20. $3\frac{1}{4} \div 6$

21. $3\frac{1}{2} \div \frac{5}{8}$

22. $1\frac{7}{10} \div 3\frac{2}{5}$

23. $8 \div 2\frac{1}{2}$

24. $4\frac{2}{3} \div 1\frac{7}{9}$

Multiply or divide. Simplify if possible.

25. $1\frac{1}{3} \times 1\frac{1}{3}$

26. $3\frac{1}{2} \div 3\frac{1}{4}$

27. $6 \times 5\frac{1}{2}$

28. $3 \div 2\frac{1}{3}$

29. $2\frac{1}{2} \div \frac{5}{8}$

30. $\frac{1}{4} \times 9\frac{1}{2}$

31. $5\frac{1}{2} \times \frac{1}{4}$

32. $6\frac{3}{4} \div 2$

Solve each problem. Simplify if possible.

33. 1 box contains $2\frac{1}{4}$ lb of nuts and bolts. Ed used $3\frac{1}{2}$ boxes to make a large outdoor sculpture. How many pounds of nuts and bolts did he use?

34. Pat is working on a sculpture for an office building. She has $6\frac{1}{4}$ ft of pipe. She uses $3\frac{1}{2}$ ft in a sculpture. How many feet of pipe does she have left?

★ 35. Pat worked on a clay sculpture for $3\frac{1}{2}$ h this week. Ed worked on his clay sculpture $2\frac{1}{2}$ times as long. How many more hours did Ed work on his sculpture?

★ 36. A painter is using $13\frac{1}{2}$ in. of wire to hang each painting. He has $13\frac{1}{2}$ ft of wire. How many paintings can he hang?

Problem Solving: Strategies

LOGICAL REASONING

■ Sometimes you can solve a problem by **working backward**.

Beth had some flowers. She gave $\frac{1}{2}$ of them to her sister.
Then she had 8 left. How many flowers did she have
to begin with?

You can solve this problem by
working backward. You know that
Beth had 8 flowers after giving $\frac{1}{2}$ of
them to her sister.

Work backward.

$$2 \times 8 = 16$$

Check to see if 16 works.

$$\frac{1}{2} \times 16 = 8$$

Beth had 16 flowers to begin with.

■ If you add 13 to a number and then double the sum, you
get 34. What is the original number?

You know that when you double the sum, you get 34.

Work backward.   Check to see if 17 is the sum.

$$\frac{1}{2} \times 34 = 17$$ $$2 \times 17 = 34$$

The sum is 17.

You know that when you add 13 to the original number,
you get 17.

Work backward again.   Check to see if 4 works.

$$17 - 13 = 4$$ $$4 + 13 = 17$$

So the original number must be 4.

Using the Strategy

Solve each problem.

1. If you add 342 to a number, you get 511. What is the number?

2. If you subtract 13.2 from a number, you get 6.3. What is the number?

3. If you triple a number, you get 141. What is the number?

4. If you take $\frac{1}{4}$ of a number and add 12, you get 18. What is the number?

5. Laila has 3 errands to take care of. Each one will take her about $\frac{1}{2}$ h. She would like to be finished by noon. About what time should she start her errands?

6. Esther gave 13 of her stickers to Nicole. She gave $\frac{1}{2}$ of the remaining stickers to Rita. She then had 14 stickers. How many did she begin with?

7. Len Jacoby has a reservation for a flight that leaves at 9:30 A.M. He wants to arrive at the airport $\frac{1}{2}$ h early. It takes $\frac{3}{4}$ h to drive from his house to the airport. What time should he plan to leave his house?

8. Arnold left the farm with a sack of oranges. He met Alice and gave her $\frac{1}{2}$ of the oranges. He met Allen and gave him $\frac{1}{2}$ of what was left. He arrived home with 7 oranges. How many oranges did he have when he started?

ACTIVITY

USING FRACTIONS

This is a game for two players. To play, you need four number cubes with the faces on each cube numbered from 1 through 6. The players take turns rolling the cubes.

1. Roll the four number cubes. Using the numbers on the cubes, make up two fractions whose product is as great as possible. Write that product.

2. After each player has taken a turn, the player with the greater product gets 1 point. The first player to get 5 points wins.

One possible product:

$$\frac{2}{5} \times \frac{6}{3} = \frac{12}{15} = \frac{4}{5}$$

Can you think of at least one way to make a greater product?

Fractions and Decimals

■ You can find a decimal that is equivalent to a fraction.

Find a decimal that is equivalent to $\frac{1}{4}$.

Write $\frac{1}{4}$ as a fraction using 100 as the denominator.

$$\frac{1}{4} = \frac{1 \times 25}{4 \times 25} = \frac{25}{100}$$

Write $\frac{25}{100}$ as a decimal.

$$\frac{25}{100} = 0.25$$

■ You can also find a decimal that is equivalent to a mixed number.

Find a decimal that is equivalent to $2\frac{1}{4}$.

$$2\frac{1}{4} = 2 + \frac{1}{4}$$
$$= 2 + 0.25 = 2.25$$

■ You can find a fraction or a mixed number that is equivalent to a decimal.

Find a fraction that is equivalent to 0.8.

$$0.8 = \frac{8}{10} = \frac{4}{5}$$

Find a mixed number that is equivalent to 2.31.

$$2.31 = 2\frac{31}{100}$$

Try These

Write each fraction or mixed number as a decimal.

1. $\frac{1}{2}$　　**2.** $\frac{21}{25}$　　**3.** $3\frac{1}{4}$　　**4.** $\frac{9}{20}$　　**5.** $\frac{3}{5}$　　**6.** $4\frac{3}{4}$

Write each decimal as a fraction or as a mixed number. Simplify if possible.

7. 0.5　　**8.** 0.02　　**9.** 4.73　　**10.** 0.15　　**11.** 6.12　　**12.** 8.95

Exercises

Write each fraction or mixed number as a decimal.

1. $\frac{3}{20}$

2. $3\frac{1}{5}$

3. $\frac{3}{25}$

4. $9\frac{4}{5}$

5. $6\frac{3}{10}$

6. $\frac{2}{5}$

7. $\frac{1}{20}$

8. $3\frac{7}{10}$

9. $\frac{29}{50}$

10. $3\frac{11}{20}$

11. $4\frac{17}{100}$

12. $9\frac{1}{10}$

13. $\frac{49}{50}$

14. $2\frac{13}{25}$

15. $\frac{1}{25}$

16. $8\frac{2}{4}$

17. $1\frac{1}{2}$

18. $2\frac{1}{5}$

Write each decimal as a fraction or as a mixed number. Simplify if possible.

19. 0.6

20. 3.9

21. 0.44

22. 6.3

23. 0.72

24. 3.45

25. 3.4

26. 2.91

27. 0.39

28. 3.75

29. 15.1

30. 0.85

31. 0.42

32. 6.38

33. 7.2

34. 0.8

35. 6.4

36. 9.75

 A calculator display shows $\boxed{168.5}$.

Which of the following does that mean? $168\frac{1}{5}$ $168\frac{2}{10}$ $168\frac{1}{2}$

Think: $168.5 = 168\frac{5}{10} = 168\frac{1}{2}$ So 168.5 is the same as $168\frac{1}{2}$.

Choose the correct answer for each calculator display.

37. $\boxed{95.25}$

   a. $95\frac{2}{5}$

   b. $95\frac{1}{4}$

   c. $95\frac{4}{10}$

38. $\boxed{18.6}$

   a. $18\frac{6}{100}$

   b. $18\frac{3}{5}$

   c. $18\frac{1}{6}$

Solve each problem.

39. About $\frac{1}{4}$ of Enrico's customers use cash to pay for their purchases. What decimal could Enrico use for the fraction $\frac{1}{4}$?

40. About 0.35 of Enrico's customers use credit cards to pay for their purchases. What fraction could Enrico use for the decimal 0.35?

Fractions: Multiplication and Division   255

Problem Solving: Applications

READ
PLAN
DO
CHECK

USING FRACTIONS AND DECIMALS

Sometimes there is a decimal and a fraction in the same problem.

A paper mill produced paper at a rate of 3.4 tons per hour for $4\frac{1}{2}$ hours. How much paper did it produce during that time?

To find the answer, multiply $4\frac{1}{2}$ and 3.4.

USING DECIMALS

Change $4\frac{1}{2}$ to a decimal.
First, write $\frac{1}{2}$ as a decimal.

$$\frac{1}{2} = \frac{5}{10}$$
$$= 0.5$$

Then, add 4.

$$4\frac{1}{2} = 4 + 0.5$$
$$= 4.5$$

Multiply.

$$4\frac{1}{2} \times 3.4$$
$$\downarrow \qquad \downarrow$$
$$4.5 \times 3.4 = 15.3$$

The paper mill produced 15.3 tons of paper.

USING FRACTIONS

Change 3.4 to a mixed number.

$$3.4 = 3\frac{4}{10}$$
$$= 3\frac{2}{5}$$

Write $4\frac{1}{2}$ and $3\frac{2}{5}$ as fractions.

$$4\frac{1}{2} = \frac{9}{2}$$
$$3\frac{2}{5} = \frac{17}{5}$$

Multiply. Simplify.

$$4\frac{1}{2} \times 3\frac{2}{5}$$
$$\downarrow \qquad \downarrow$$
$$\frac{9}{2} \times \frac{17}{5} = \frac{153}{10} = 15\frac{3}{10}$$

The paper mill produced $15\frac{3}{10}$ tons of paper.

Since $15.3 = 15\frac{3}{10}$, these answers are the same.

Sometimes changing the fractions to decimals makes a problem easier. Sometimes changing the decimals to fractions makes a problem easier. Both ways give the same answer.

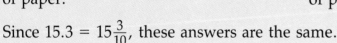

Try These

Solve each problem.

1. Ms. Prinsky works at the paper mill. She earns $9.50 per hour. How much does she earn in $7\frac{1}{2}$ h?

2. The mill produced $19\frac{1}{5}$ tons of paper one day and 18.7 tons the next day. How many tons did it produce altogether?

Exercises

Solve each problem.

1. Ms. Rambo earns $10.20 per hour as an assistant bookkeeper. She works $7\frac{3}{4}$ h per day. How much does she earn in a day?

2. One day the mill produced paper at a rate of 4.7 tons per hour for $6\frac{1}{2}$ h. How much paper did it produce?

3. Mr. Gertz makes $9.60 per hour. He works $7\frac{1}{2}$ h per day, 5 days per week. How much does he earn in a week?

4. Mrs. Miller earns $10.30 per hour. One day she worked $3\frac{3}{4}$ h before lunch and $4\frac{1}{4}$ h after lunch. How much did she earn that day?

5. Mr. Jordan's regular rate of pay is $8.70 per hour. When he works more than 40 h in a week, he is paid $1\frac{1}{2}$ times as much per hour for each hour of overtime. How much is that per hour?

6. One day a machine produced 4.7 tons of paper. Another machine produced $3\frac{3}{4}$ tons of paper. How much more paper did the first machine produce than the second machine?

This graph shows the number of people hired at the mill each month for the first 6 months of 1986. No one was hired in February and April.

7. What was the average number of people hired each month for the 6 months?

8. How many more people were hired from April through June than from January through March?

9. How many people were hired from January through June?

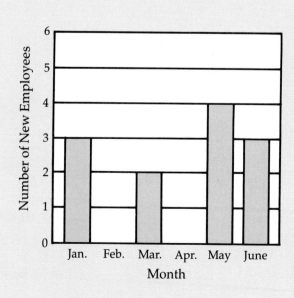

Fractions: Multiplication and Division   257

More about Fractions and Decimals

■ You can divide to find a decimal equivalent to a fraction.

Find a decimal that is equivalent to $\frac{1}{8}$.

Place the decimal point. Write a 0 in the dividend. Divide.

$$
\begin{array}{r}
0.1 \\
8\overline{)1.0} \\
\underline{8} \\
2
\end{array}
$$

Continue to write 0s in the dividend until the remainder is 0.

$$
\begin{array}{r}
0.125 \\
8\overline{)1.000} \\
\underline{8} \\
20 \\
\underline{16} \\
40 \\
\underline{40} \\
0 \leftarrow \text{remainder of 0}
\end{array}
$$

■ Sometimes when you divide, there is never a remainder of zero. The quotient is a **repeating decimal**.

Write $\frac{1}{3}$ as a decimal.   Write $\frac{3}{11}$ as a decimal.

The digits in the quotients repeat.

$$
\begin{array}{r}
0.3333 \\
3\overline{)1.0000} \\
\underline{9} \\
10 \\
\underline{9} \\
10 \\
\underline{9} \\
10 \\
\underline{9} \\
1
\end{array}
$$

$$
\begin{array}{r}
0.2727 \\
11\overline{)3.0000} \\
\underline{2\ 2} \\
80 \\
\underline{77} \\
30 \\
\underline{22} \\
80 \\
\underline{77} \\
3
\end{array}
$$

There is never a remainder of 0.

The quotient is 0.3333....   The quotient is 0.2727....

The dots (…) mean that the digits keep repeating forever. 0.3333… and 0.2727… are repeating decimals. To show that a digit repeats, write a bar over the repeating digit or digits.

$\frac{1}{3} = 0.\overline{3}$ $\frac{3}{11} = 0.\overline{27}$

Try These

Divide to write each fraction as a decimal.
Continue to write 0s in the dividend until the remainder is 0.

1. $\dfrac{4}{5}$

2. $\dfrac{3}{8}$

3. $\dfrac{3}{25}$

4. $\dfrac{2}{5}$

5. $\dfrac{19}{20}$

6. $\dfrac{2}{16}$

Write each fraction as a decimal.
Use a bar to show repeating digits.

7. $\dfrac{4}{9}$

8. $\dfrac{2}{3}$

9. $\dfrac{43}{99}$

10. $\dfrac{5}{27}$

11. $\dfrac{2}{11}$

12. $\dfrac{1}{9}$

Exercises

Divide to write each fraction as a decimal.
Continue to write 0s in the dividend until the remainder is 0.

1. $\dfrac{3}{10}$

2. $\dfrac{5}{8}$

3. $\dfrac{17}{10}$

4. $\dfrac{7}{8}$

5. $\dfrac{1}{20}$

6. $\dfrac{5}{4}$

7. $\dfrac{1}{25}$

8. $\dfrac{3}{20}$

9. $\dfrac{7}{50}$

10. $\dfrac{1}{50}$

11. $\dfrac{21}{25}$

★ 12. $\dfrac{96}{256}$

Write each fraction as a decimal.
Use a bar to show repeating digits.

13. $\dfrac{7}{9}$

14. $\dfrac{4}{11}$

15. $\dfrac{5}{33}$

16. $\dfrac{5}{9}$

17. $\dfrac{8}{11}$

18. $\dfrac{12}{37}$

19. $\dfrac{32}{99}$

20. $\dfrac{6}{11}$

21. $\dfrac{2}{9}$

22. $\dfrac{5}{12}$

23. $\dfrac{11}{15}$

★ 24. $\dfrac{3}{7}$

Solve each problem.

25. Scott plays baseball with his friends. In one game, he got 3 hits in 4 times at bat. What decimal could he use for the fraction $\dfrac{3}{4}$?

26. Mark plays baseball for the Tigers. The Tigers practice $1\dfrac{1}{2}$ h each day. How many hours do they practice in 6 days?

★ 27. The Bucks have won 0.275 of their games. The Tigers have won 9 games out of 38. Which team has the better record?

★ 28. Last year the Tigers played 40 games. They won 0.550 of them. How many games did they win last year?

CHAPTER CHECKPOINT

Write each fraction as a mixed number or as a whole number. (pp. 242–243)

1. $\frac{7}{2}$

2. $\frac{9}{4}$

3. $\frac{12}{3}$

4. $\frac{21}{7}$

5. $\frac{8}{5}$

6. $\frac{17}{5}$

7. $\frac{5}{2}$

8. $\frac{24}{7}$

9. $\frac{18}{3}$

10. $\frac{9}{5}$

11. $\frac{19}{4}$

12. $\frac{25}{5}$

Write each mixed number as a fraction. (pp. 242–243)

13. $1\frac{1}{4}$

14. $7\frac{2}{3}$

15. $2\frac{1}{3}$

16. $6\frac{3}{4}$

17. $9\frac{2}{5}$

18. $4\frac{2}{9}$

19. $8\frac{3}{5}$

20. $3\frac{3}{8}$

21. $4\frac{1}{2}$

22. $8\frac{1}{4}$

23. $5\frac{1}{6}$

24. $7\frac{3}{11}$

Multiply. Simplify if possible. (pp. 244–247, 250–251)

25. $\frac{3}{4} \times \frac{1}{2}$

26. $\frac{5}{6} \times \frac{11}{12}$

27. $\frac{7}{8} \times 4$

28. $\frac{2}{3} \times \frac{5}{6}$

29. $9 \times \frac{2}{3}$

30. $\frac{3}{5} \times \frac{2}{3}$

31. $\frac{2}{9} \times \frac{3}{4}$

32. $\frac{5}{8} \times \frac{4}{15}$

33. $3\frac{1}{2} \times \frac{3}{10}$

34. $1\frac{2}{3} \times 1\frac{3}{4}$

35. $3\frac{1}{3} \times 15$

36. $3 \times 2\frac{1}{3}$

Divide. Simplify if possible. (pp. 248–251)

37. $6 \div \frac{1}{2}$

38. $\frac{5}{6} \div \frac{3}{4}$

39. $\frac{7}{8} \div \frac{3}{4}$

40. $\frac{3}{4} \div 2$

41. $\frac{3}{5} \div \frac{2}{5}$

42. $\frac{2}{3} \div 3$

43. $\frac{3}{5} \div \frac{2}{3}$

44. $8 \div 2\frac{3}{4}$

45. $1\frac{5}{8} \div 1\frac{1}{2}$

46. $\frac{2}{3} \div 1\frac{1}{3}$

47. $2\frac{1}{2} \div \frac{1}{4}$

48. $6\frac{3}{4} \div 2\frac{1}{2}$

Write each fraction or mixed number as a decimal.
(pp. 254–255)

49. $\frac{1}{2}$

50. $\frac{3}{4}$

51. $6\frac{9}{20}$

52. $\frac{1}{10}$

53. $\frac{20}{25}$

54. $8\frac{3}{5}$

Write each decimal as a fraction or as a mixed number.
Simplify if possible. (pp. 254–255)

55. 2.8   **56.** 0.57   **57.** 7.15   **58.** 0.4   **59.** 9.88   **60.** 0.7

61. 6.3   **62.** 8.75   **63.** 0.66   **64.** 4.12   **65.** 5.2   **66.** 0.25

Divide to write each fraction as a decimal.
Continue to write 0s in the dividend until the remainder is 0. (pp. 258–259)

67. $\frac{1}{2}$ **68.** $\frac{3}{5}$ **69.** $\frac{7}{10}$ **70.** $\frac{11}{20}$ **71.** $\frac{9}{40}$ **72.** $\frac{37}{50}$

Write each fraction as a decimal.
Use a bar to show repeating digits. (pp. 258–259)

73. $\frac{8}{9}$ **74.** $\frac{5}{11}$ **75.** $\frac{2}{9}$ **76.** $\frac{7}{33}$ **77.** $\frac{59}{99}$ **78.** $\frac{7}{11}$

Solve each problem. Simplify if possible. (pp. 242–259)

79. Ann cut 3 apples into fourths. How many fourths was that?

80. How many pieces $\frac{3}{4}$ ft long can be cut from a wire $10\frac{1}{2}$ ft long?

81. Leslie had $\frac{3}{4}$ qt of juice. She drank $\frac{1}{3}$ of it. How much juice did she drink?

82. Pete works $3\frac{1}{2}$ h a day. How many hours does he work in 5 days?

83. Juan's guitar cost $150. He practices $\frac{1}{2}$ h every day. How many hours does he practice each week?

84. About $\frac{2}{5}$ of Mrs. Barrister's students take flute lessons. What decimal could Mrs. Barrister use for the fraction $\frac{2}{5}$?

85. Gwen bought $3\frac{1}{2}$ lb of bananas. The bananas cost $.20 per pound. How much did she spend?

86. Chang earns $13.60 per hour as an electrician. How much would he earn for working $38\frac{1}{4}$ h?

87. Sue is baking muffins. She has $4\frac{1}{2}$ c of bran. She uses $\frac{3}{4}$ c of bran for each batch. How many batches of muffins can Sue make?

88. Paul has a board that is 10 ft long. He wants to cut it into pieces that are $\frac{2}{3}$ ft long. How many pieces will Paul have?

COMPUTERS AND PROBLEM SOLVING

■ A fraction can be changed to a decimal. One way is to multiply the denominator so that the new denominator is 100. Another way is to divide the numerator by the denominator.

The computer handles non-integer numbers as decimals. It is very easy to use the computer to change fractions to decimals.

Type PRINT 3/4. The computer will display .75.

Any time the computer uses a number for math, it uses the decimal version of the number.

■ Below are three procedures that work together to display a list of fractions and their decimal equivalents. The SENTENCE command puts this output together when it is displayed.

```
TO EQU
MAKE "DENOMINATOR 1
REPEAT 10 [EQU2]
END

TO EQU2
MAKE "NUMERATOR 1
REPEAT 10 [EQU3]
MAKE "DENOMINATOR :DENOMINATOR + 1
END

TO EQU3
PRINT (SENTENCE :NUMERATOR "/ :DENOMINATOR "=
    :NUMERATOR / :DENOMINATOR)
MAKE "NUMERATOR :NUMERATOR + 1
END
```

Solve each problem.

1. How many times does each procedure run when you type EQU?

2. Where does the output occur in these three procedures?

■ All three of the EQU procedures use the MAKE command to change the value of a **variable** while the procedure is running. The first time the variable appears after MAKE, it has quotation marks in front of it. In that form, it stands for the variable name.

When the variable appears a second time, it is preceded by a colon and stands for the value that it contains. Each time one of these MAKE commands is executed, the value in "NUMERATOR or "DENOMINATOR is increased by 1. The SENTENCE command in EQU3 causes all of the other items in the parentheses to be printed together.

What will be printed after each series of commands?

1. MAKE "SUM 3 + 7 + 5
   PRINT :SUM

2. MAKE "NAME [GEORGE WASHINGTON]
   PRINT :NAME

★ 3. MAKE "NUMBER "34
   PRINT "NUMBER

★ 4. MAKE "1776 "FAMOUS
   MAKE "NUMBER :1776
   PRINT :NUMBER

ENRICHMENT

USING FRACTIONS WITH A CALCULATOR

■ You may want to use a calculator to add, subtract, multiply, and divide fractions and mixed numbers. You only have to change the fractions to decimals.

Add: $\frac{3}{4} + \frac{1}{2}$

Use your calculator and divide to find decimals equivalent to $\frac{3}{4}$ and $\frac{1}{2}$.

$$3 \div 4 = 0.75 \qquad 1 \div 2 = 0.5$$
$$\frac{3}{4} = 0.75 \qquad \frac{1}{2} = 0.5$$

Add: 0.75 + 0.5

$$0.75 + 0.5 = 1.25 \qquad \text{So } \frac{3}{4} + \frac{1}{2} = 1.25.$$

■ Multiply: $1\frac{2}{5} \times 2\frac{1}{4}$

Find decimals equivalent to $1\frac{2}{5}$ and $2\frac{1}{4}$.

First, find decimals equivalent to $\frac{2}{5}$ and $\frac{1}{4}$.

$$2 \div 5 = 0.4 \qquad 1 \div 4 = 0.25$$

Then, add the whole number parts of the mixed numbers.

$$1\frac{2}{5} = 1 + 0.4 = 1.4 \qquad 2\frac{1}{4} = 2 + 0.25 = 2.25$$

Multiply: 1.4 × 2.25

$$1.4 \times 2.25 = 3.15 \qquad \text{So } 1\frac{2}{5} \times 2\frac{1}{4} = 3.15.$$

Use your calculator to compute.

1. $\frac{3}{5} + \frac{1}{4}$

2. $\frac{1}{2} - \frac{2}{5}$

3. $2\frac{1}{2} \times 3\frac{1}{2}$

4. $3\frac{1}{2} + 1\frac{3}{4}$

5. $4\frac{2}{5} \div 2\frac{1}{5}$

6. $15\frac{3}{4} + 7\frac{3}{5}$

7. $8\frac{7}{10} \times 5$

8. $21\frac{1}{5} - 16\frac{1}{4}$

PLANNING A BIKE TRIP

You and some friends are going to go on a 1-day bike trip. There is much preparation involved. What things should you consider in planning the trip?

Some Questions to Explore
- Where will you go?
- How long will it take to get there and back?
- What should you bring along?

Some Strategies to Explore
Consider the first two questions. You can use a combination of strategies to answer the questions.

- Find information on a map to determine what places you should consider.
- Make a list of these places and their distances. Decide on a place.
- Make a detailed map of the routes/trails you will take in order to complete your trip in 1 day.
- Make a schedule of planned stops and the length of your stops.

Decide what strategy you will use to answer the other question above. List other questions and strategies you need to explore. Then solve the problem.

SKILLS CHECK

Choose the correct answer.

1. Round 86 to the nearest ten.

  a. 80   **b.** 85
  c. 90   **d.** NG

2.
$$\begin{array}{r} 2,347 \\ 1,201 \\ 896 \\ +\quad 15 \\ \hline \end{array}$$

  a. 3,869   **b.** 4,178
  c. 4,459   **d.** 5,316

3.
$$\begin{array}{r} 914 \\ \times\,207 \\ \hline \end{array}$$

  a. 14,658   **b.** 24,678
  c. 188,188   **d.** NG

4. $80\overline{)403}$

  a. 5 R3
  b. 41
  c. 50 R3
  d. 503

5. Which is the decimal for sixty-one and forty-two thousandths?

  a. 0.6142
  b. 61.0042
  c. 61.042
  d. 61.42

6.
$$\begin{array}{r} 12.43 \\ -\;\;9.726 \\ \hline \end{array}$$

  a. 2.704
  b. 3.314
  c. 22.156
  d. NG

7. $8,000 \text{ g} = \blacksquare \text{ kg}$

  a. 8
  b. 80
  c. 800
  d. NG

8. Estimate: $36,031 \div 7$

  a. 500
  b. 2,000
  c. 5,000
  d. 50,000

9. $5\frac{3}{8} + 3\frac{1}{4}$

  a. $2\frac{1}{8}$ **b.** $7\frac{5}{8}$

  c. $8\frac{1}{2}$ **d.** $8\frac{5}{8}$

10. A florist had 368 daisies. She divided them into bunches of 8 each. How many bunches did she make?

  a. 38 bunches
  b. 46 bunches
  c. 52 bunches
  d. NG

11. Tim ran 2,000 m around a track. Jeff ran 1,750 m around the same track. How much farther did Tim run?

  a. 250 m
  b. 750 m
  c. 3,750 m
  d. NG

12. Jan had $\frac{7}{8}$ yd of wrapping ribbon. She used $\frac{3}{4}$ yd. How much ribbon was left?

  a. $\frac{1}{8}$ yd   **b.** $\frac{1}{4}$ yd

  c. $\frac{1}{2}$ yd   **d.** $\frac{2}{3}$ yd

10

RATIO AND PERCENT

Ratio

■ A **ratio** is used to compare two numbers.

The ratio of jump ropes to weights is 2 to 4.
The ratio of weights to jump ropes is 4 to 2.
The ratio of jump ropes to gym
equipment is 2 to 6.

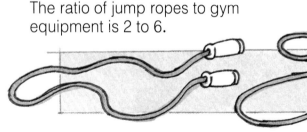

■ Here are three ways to write a ratio:

Write: 2 to 4 or 2 : 4 or $\frac{2}{4}$

Read: two to four

2 is the first term of the ratio.
4 is the second term of the ratio.

■ The ratio of basketballs to hoops
is 6 to 2, 6 : 2, or $\frac{6}{2}$.
The ratio of hoops to equipment
is 2 to 8, 2 : 8, or $\frac{2}{8}$.
The ratio of basketballs to dollars
is 6 to 90, 6 : 90, or $\frac{6}{90}$.

What is the ratio of hoops to
basketballs?
What is the ratio of dollars to
basketballs?

$90.00

Try These

Write each ratio.

1. boys to girls
2. girls to mats
3. mats to students
4. girls to boys
5. boys to mats
6. students to girls

Exercises

Write each ratio.

1. lockers to books
2. books to caps
3. sneakers to footballs
4. caps to sneakers
5. basketballs to caps
6. lockers to footballs
7. caps to footballs and basketballs

This table shows the inventory of gym equipment.

Write each ratio.

8. volleyballs to volleyball nets
9. basketballs to volleyballs
10. 1-lb weights to 5-lb weights
11. 5-lb weights to 2-lb weights
12. 10-lb weights to all the weights
13. volleyball nets to stopwatches
14. basketballs to 2-lb weights
★ 15. volleyballs to basketballs to stopwatches

INVENTORY	
Equipment	Quantity
basketball	12
volleyball	6
volleyball net	3
1-lb weight	20
2-lb weight	16
5-lb weight	10
10-lb weight	8
stopwatch	4

Solve each problem.

16. The gym teacher received 4 more 1-lb weights. What is the ratio of 1-lb weights to 5-lb weights now?

17. The basketball team uses $\frac{3}{4}$ of the basketballs during practice. How many basketballs do they use?

18. 1 volleyball net is badly torn. The gym teacher decides to throw it out. 2 new volleyball nets are bought. What is the ratio of volleyballs to volleyball nets now?

19. There are 145 students in the school sports program. 25 students are on the track team. 18 students are on the swim team. Write a ratio of students on the track team to all the students in the sports program.

★ 20. Each basketball costs $25. Each volleyball costs $22. Write a ratio of the value of the basketball inventory to the value of the volleyball inventory.

★ 21. 3 students are using 2-lb weights. Each of them is using 2 weights. Write a ratio of the number of 2-lb weights being used to the number of 2-lb weights not being used.

Equal Ratios

■ Lionel and Karen are making fruit punch for a pool party. The recipe says to mix 6 cups of orange juice with 3 cups of pineapple juice.

The ratio of orange juice to pineapple juice is $6 : 3$, or $\frac{6}{3}$.

Lionel and Karen have 12 cups of orange juice. How many cups of pineapple juice do they need to make fruit punch?

Multiply to find the amount of pineapple juice.

$$\text{orange juice} \longrightarrow \frac{6}{3} = \frac{6 \times 2}{3 \times 2} = \frac{12}{6} \longleftarrow \text{pineapple juice}$$

They need 6 cups of pineapple juice.

$\frac{6}{3}$ and $\frac{12}{6}$ are **equal ratios**. $\frac{6}{3} = \frac{12}{6}$

■ Lionel and Karen have 1 cup of pineapple juice left. How many cups of orange juice do they need to make fruit punch?

Divide to find the amount of orange juice.

$$\text{orange juice} \longrightarrow \frac{6}{3} = \frac{6 \div 3}{3 \div 3} = \frac{2}{1} \longleftarrow \text{pineapple juice}$$

They need 2 cups of orange juice.

$\frac{6}{3}$ and $\frac{2}{1}$ are equal ratios. $\frac{6}{3} = \frac{2}{1}$

Try These

Copy and complete to make equal ratios.

1. $\frac{3}{4} = \frac{3 \times 5}{4 \times 5} = \frac{\blacksquare}{20}$

2. $\frac{8}{12} = \frac{8 \div 4}{12 \div 4} = \frac{2}{\blacksquare}$

3. $\frac{6}{30} = \frac{6 \div 6}{30 \div 6} = \frac{\blacksquare}{5}$

4. $\frac{9}{25} = \frac{36}{\blacksquare}$

5. $\frac{18}{15} = \frac{\blacksquare}{5}$

6. $\frac{16}{40} = \frac{2}{\blacksquare}$

7. $\frac{1}{4} = \frac{\blacksquare}{16}$

Exercises

Copy and complete to make equal ratios.

1. $\frac{5}{7} = \frac{25}{\blacksquare}$ **2.** $\frac{20}{12} = \frac{5}{\blacksquare}$ **3.** $\frac{1}{3} = \frac{6}{\blacksquare}$ **4.** $\frac{18}{27} = \frac{\blacksquare}{3}$

5. $\frac{3}{5} = \frac{\blacksquare}{30}$ **6.** $\frac{7}{12} = \frac{35}{\blacksquare}$ **7.** $\frac{15}{9} = \frac{\blacksquare}{3}$ **8.** $\frac{35}{45} = \frac{\blacksquare}{9}$

9. $\frac{4}{15} = \frac{20}{\blacksquare}$ **10.** $\frac{100}{30} = \frac{\blacksquare}{3}$ **11.** $\frac{140}{1,000} = \frac{\blacksquare}{100}$ **12.** $\frac{9}{20} = \frac{45}{\blacksquare}$

13. $\frac{48}{60} = \frac{\blacksquare}{5}$ **14.** $\frac{3}{4} = \frac{\blacksquare}{100}$ **15.** $\frac{98}{200} = \frac{\blacksquare}{400}$ **16.** $\frac{150}{400} = \frac{3}{\blacksquare}$

Are the ratios equal? Write *yes* or *no*.

17. $\frac{15}{18}$ and $\frac{2}{3}$ **18.** $\frac{20}{30}$ and $\frac{4}{6}$ **19.** $\frac{4}{5}$ and $\frac{12}{15}$ **20.** $\frac{3}{11}$ and $\frac{7}{22}$

21. $\frac{21}{32}$ and $\frac{7}{8}$ **22.** $\frac{1}{\$1.50}$ and $\frac{2}{\$3}$ ★ **23.** $\frac{5}{40}$ and $\frac{9}{72}$ ★ **24.** $\frac{3}{30}$ and $\frac{4}{45}$

Solve each problem.

25. The ratio of orange slices to pineapple chunks is 5 to 3. Lionel cut 20 orange slices. How many pineapple chunks does he need?

26. The ratio of cheese snacks to meat snacks is 8 to 5. Karen made 15 meat snacks. How many cheese snacks should she make?

27. Karen and Lionel shop for supplies. A package of 100 paper plates costs $2.80. How much would a package of 25 plates cost if the cost per plate is the same?

★ **28.** There will be 8 people at the pool party. Lionel and Karen want each person to have 3 c of punch. How many quarts of punch should they make?

KEEPING IN SHAPE

Copy and complete.

1. 8 cm = $\blacksquare$ mm   **2.** 230 mg = $\blacksquare$ g   **3.** 0.4 L = $\blacksquare$ mL

4. 5,000 g = $\blacksquare$ kg   **5.** 3 km = $\blacksquare$ m   **6.** 700 cm = $\blacksquare$ m

7. 6 L = $\blacksquare$ mL   **8.** 8.2 dm = $\blacksquare$ cm   **9.** 45 g = $\blacksquare$ kg

10. 1,275 m = $\blacksquare$ km   **11.** 0.095 kg = $\blacksquare$ g   **12.** 0.36 g = $\blacksquare$ mg

Proportions

■ A statement that two ratios are equal is called a **proportion**.

$\frac{3}{4} = \frac{9}{12}$ is a proportion.

Find the **cross products** of $\frac{3}{4}$ and $\frac{9}{12}$.

$$\frac{3}{4} \bowtie \frac{9}{12}$$

$$3 \times 12 \qquad 4 \times 9$$
$$36 \quad = \quad 36$$

The cross products of a proportion are equal.

■ Do the ratios $\frac{7}{8}$ and $\frac{3}{4}$ form a proportion?

Find the cross products.

$$\frac{7}{8} \bowtie \frac{3}{4}$$

$$7 \times 4 \qquad 8 \times 3$$
$$28 \quad \neq \quad 24$$
$$\underset{\text{is not equal to}}{\curvearrowleft}$$

The cross products are not equal, so $\frac{7}{8} \neq \frac{3}{4}$. The ratios are not equal. $\frac{7}{8}$ and $\frac{3}{4}$ do not form a proportion.

■ Sometimes one term of a proportion is missing. Use cross products to find the missing term.

Solve for n.

$$\frac{4}{10} = \frac{6}{n}$$
$\left[\begin{array}{l}\text{This is another way of writing } \frac{4}{10} = \frac{6}{\blacksquare}.\\ \text{The letter } n \text{ represents the number we want to find.}\end{array}\right.$

$\left.\begin{array}{l}4n \\ \text{means} \\ 4 \times n\end{array}\right\}$
$$4 \times n = 10 \times 6$$
$$4n = 60$$
$$\frac{4n}{4} = \frac{60}{4}$$
$\left[\begin{array}{l}\text{Divide both sides of}\\ \text{the equal sign by 4.}\end{array}\right.$
$$n = 15$$

Try These

**Do the ratios form a proportion? Write *yes* or *no*.
Use cross products to check.**

1. $\frac{5}{2}$ and $\frac{15}{10}$

2. $\frac{2}{4}$ and $\frac{5}{10}$

3. $\frac{6}{8}$ and $\frac{15}{20}$

4. $\frac{3}{6}$ and $\frac{6}{9}$

Solve for *n*.

5. $\frac{2}{8} = \frac{3}{n}$

6. $\frac{6}{3} = \frac{n}{5}$

7. $\frac{3}{9} = \frac{n}{15}$

8. $\frac{8}{12} = \frac{10}{n}$

Exercises

**Do the ratios form a proportion? Write *yes* or *no*.
Use cross products to check.**

1. $\frac{4}{8}$ and $\frac{6}{12}$

2. $\frac{3}{12}$ and $\frac{2}{6}$

3. $\frac{9}{12}$ and $\frac{6}{8}$

4. $\frac{2}{6}$ and $\frac{6}{9}$

5. $\frac{3}{15}$ and $\frac{4}{10}$

6. $\frac{8}{5}$ and $\frac{10}{6}$

7. $\frac{2}{10}$ and $\frac{3}{15}$

8. $\frac{12}{8}$ and $\frac{9}{6}$

9. $\frac{8}{20}$ and $\frac{6}{15}$

10. $\frac{6}{10}$ and $\frac{12}{18}$

11. $\frac{12}{15}$ and $\frac{15}{25}$

12. $\frac{16}{12}$ and $\frac{8}{4}$

Solve for *n*.

13. $\frac{4}{20} = \frac{5}{n}$

14. $\frac{2}{12} = \frac{3}{n}$

15. $\frac{21}{3} = \frac{n}{2}$

16. $\frac{12}{28} = \frac{n}{21}$

17. $\frac{6}{14} = \frac{n}{21}$

18. $\frac{10}{4} = \frac{15}{n}$

19. $\frac{15}{21} = \frac{n}{14}$

20. $\frac{4}{32} = \frac{3}{n}$

21. $\frac{10}{25} = \frac{n}{20}$

22. $\frac{15}{9} = \frac{25}{n}$

★ **23.** $\frac{2.7}{1.2} = \frac{1.8}{n}$

★ **24.** $\frac{1.5}{1.8} = \frac{n}{2.4}$

Solve each problem.

25. Mr. Reid repairs clocks. He repairs an average of 12 clocks in 8 h. About how many clocks can he repair in 30 h?

26. A package contains 4 large gears and 3 small gears. Mr. Reid orders 20 large gears. How many small gears will he receive?

27. Mr. Reid repaired 15 clocks. $\frac{2}{3}$ of the clocks he repaired were overwound. How many clocks were overwound?

28. Mr. Reid works 6 days per week. He is paid $350 per week. At that rate, how much does he make in 27 days?

Problem Solving: Applications

USING PROPORTIONS

■ Julie's shadow is 42 cm long. She is 140 cm tall. The shadow of a meter stick is 30 cm long. The meter stick is 100 cm tall. The shadows are measured at the same time.

Write the ratio of the lengths of the shadows and the ratio of the heights of the objects.

	length of shadows	height of objects
Julie ⟶	$\dfrac{42}{30}$	$\dfrac{140}{100}$
meter stick ⟶		

Do the ratios form a proportion?

Find the cross products.

$$\dfrac{42}{30} \underset{}{\overset{}{\times}} \dfrac{140}{100}$$

$$42 \times 100 \qquad 30 \times 140$$
$$4{,}200 \;=\; 4{,}200$$

The cross products are equal. The ratios form a proportion.

> These ratios always form a proportion when the shadows are measured at the same time of day.

■ At a certain time of day, Mark's shadow was 0.6 m long. He is 1.8 m tall. The shadow of a flagpole was 2.4 m long. How high is the flagpole?

Write a proportion to find the height of the flagpole.

	length of shadows	height of objects
Mark ⟶	$\dfrac{0.6}{2.4}$ =	$\dfrac{1.8}{n}$
flagpole ⟶		

$$0.6 \times n = 2.4 \times 1.8$$
$$\dfrac{0.6n}{0.6} = \dfrac{4.32}{0.6}$$
$$n = 7.2$$

The flagpole is 7.2 m high.

Try These

For each problem, the shadows were measured at the same time of day.

Solve each problem.

1. What is the height of the lighthouse?

2. What is the height of the tree?

Exercises

For each problem, the shadows were measured at the same time of day.

Solve each problem.

1. What is the height of the beach umbrella?

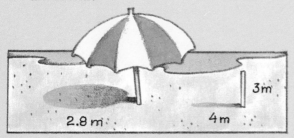

2. What is the height of the lifeguard's chair?

3. For every 10 pails sold, the beach shop sold 6 shovels. The shop sold 75 pails. How many shovels did it sell?

4. The shadow of a water fountain is 0.6 m long. The fountain is 1.5 m high. The shadow of a fence is 1.4 m long. How high is the fence?

5. The beach shop sold 56 beach balls in 7 days. At that rate, how many beach balls will be sold in 12 days?

6. Pat is a lifeguard. She earns $250 in 5 days. How many days will it take for Pat to earn $1,000?

7. Gary's shadow is 1.2 m long. He is 1.8 m tall. The shadow of the basketball backboard is 2.8 m long. How high is the backboard?

★ **8.** The shadow of a sign is 2 m long. The sign is 1.5 m high. The shadow of the snack bar is 3 m long. What is the height of the snack bar?

Scale Drawings

This is a **scale drawing** of a playground. 1 cm on the drawing represents 5 m in the actual playground.

The **scale** is 1 cm to 5 m. The scale gives the ratio between the distances on the drawing and the actual distances.

The drawing is 10 cm long. How long is the actual playground?

Write a proportion to find the answer.

$$\frac{1}{5} = \frac{10}{n} \quad \begin{array}{l} \longleftarrow \text{ length of drawing in centimeters} \\ \longleftarrow \text{ actual length in meters} \end{array}$$

$$1 \times n = 5 \times 10$$

$$n = 50$$

The playground is 50 m long.

Try These

Solve each problem.

1. Measure the width of the playground. Find the width of the actual playground.

2. Measure the top bar of the swings. What is the length of the actual swings?

3. Measure the length of the skating rink. What is the length of the actual skating rink?

4. Measure the width of the skating rink. What is the width of the actual skating rink?

Exercises

This is a scale drawing of Jim's neighborhood. The scale is 2 cm to 1 km.

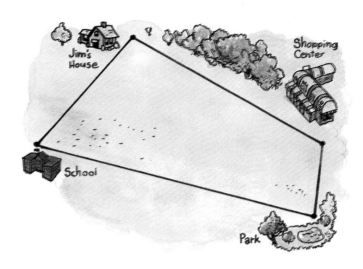

Measure the map distance to the nearest centimeter. Then find the actual distance.

1. Jim's house to the school

2. the park to the shopping center

3. Suppose Jim could walk in a straight line from home to the park. How far would he walk on that shortcut?

4. Jim walked from home to school. From school, he walked to the park. Then he took the shortcut home. How far did he walk altogether?

Some points of interest in Washington, D.C., are shown on this map. 1 cm on the map stands for 400 m.

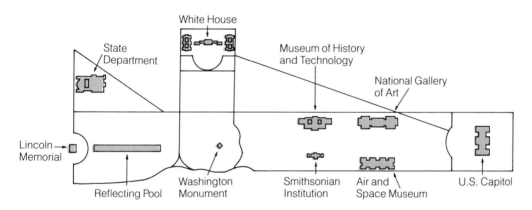

Measure the map distance to the nearest centimeter. Use that distance to estimate the actual distance.

5. the White House to the U.S. Capitol

6. the State Department to the White House

7. the National Gallery of Art to the Air and Space Museum

8. the Lincoln Memorial to the Washington Monument

9. Estimate the actual distance from the Lincoln Memorial to the U.S. Capitol. Find the answer in kilometers.

★ 10. Arlington National Cemetery is about 2.4 km from the Lincoln Memorial. Estimate the map distance between these two points.

Problem Solving: Strategies

ORGANIZING INFORMATION

Making a diagram is a way to organize information to help you solve a problem.

French trappers and traders came to the United States before it became an independent nation. They traveled in large canoes on the lakes and rivers of such states as Wisconsin, Michigan, and Illinois.

These are entries from the log of the trader Pierre Chouteau.

August 18: We paddled 60 km due east from the mouth of the Marais River to La Croix.

August 19: From La Croix, we paddled 30 km due north to the tribe's village.

August 20: There was a strong southwest wind, so we paddled 20 km due west to North Point. Then we paddled 50 km due south to the shore where Marc's supplies were stored. On this day, we crossed the same spot we crossed on August 18.

How did Pierre know they crossed the same spot they had crossed on the first leg of this trip?

Draw a diagram to discover how he could be sure. The scale of the drawing is 1 cm = 10 km.

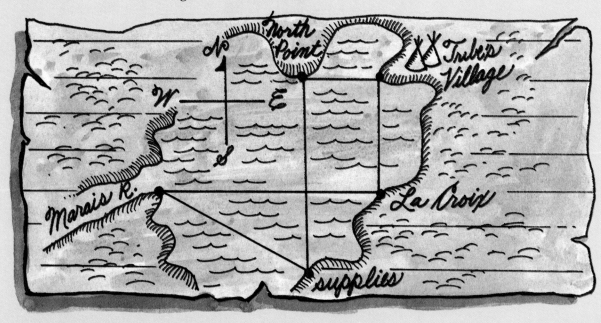

Using the Strategy

**Draw a diagram of each of these four journeys. Use the scale
1 cm = 10 km. Which routes cross the same spot twice?**

1. from *M* 30 km due west to *N*,
from *N* 20 km due south to *P*,
from *P* 10 km due east to *Q*,
from *Q* 40 km due north to *R*

2. from *G* 40 km due north to *H*,
from *H* 20 km due east to *I*,
from *I* 10 km due south to *J*,
from *J* 10 km due west to *K*

3. from *A* 40 km due east to *B*,
from *B* 10 km due north to *C*,
from *C* 20 km due east to *D*

4. from *W* 50 km due east to *X*,
from *X* 10 km due north to *Y*,
from *Y* 30 km southwest to *Z*

Suppose you have a pirate's map of a
Caribbean island. In a ship's log, you
find these directions to buried treasure:
"Stand in the arch facing the pyramid.
Walk 30 paces forward. Turn left. Walk
120 paces. Now walk half the distance
on a line to the palm tree. Dig there."

Solve each problem. (Hint: 1 cm = 30 paces)

5. One of the letters on the map
marks the treasure. Which
letter is it?

6. Write a set of directions that
would take you from the
pyramid to point *E*.

ACTIVITY

MAKING A DIAGRAM

**Make a diagram that shows the order of the letters in each of
the following. Use the clues.**

1. The letters are *A*, *B*, and *C*.
B is to the left of *C*.
A is between *B* and *C*.

2. The letters are *D*, *E*, *F*, and *G*.
G is to the left of *D*.
G is to the right of *F*.
E is between *F* and *G*.

Percents and Fractions

The symbol for percent is %.

■ **Percent** means per hundred, or hundredths. Think of a percent as a ratio of some number to 100.

A circus stand has 100 balloons. 60 of the balloons are red. The ratio of red balloons to all the balloons is 60 to 100.

$$\text{red balloons} \longrightarrow \frac{60}{100} \longleftarrow \text{all the balloons}$$

60% of the balloons are red.

There are 40 balloons that are not red. The ratio of balloons that are not red to all the balloons is 40 to 100.

$$\text{balloons not red} \longrightarrow \frac{40}{100} \longleftarrow \text{all the balloons}$$

40% of the balloons are not red.

■ It is easy to write a fraction that names hundredths as a percent.

$$\frac{30}{100} = 30\% \qquad \frac{9}{100} = 9\% \qquad \frac{100}{100} = 100\%$$

If the denominator does not name hundredths, rename the fraction.

Write $\frac{4}{5}$ as a percent.

Rename the fraction as hundredths.

$$\frac{4}{5} = \frac{4 \times 20}{5 \times 20} = \frac{80}{100}$$

Write $\frac{80}{100}$ as a percent.

$$\frac{4}{5} = \frac{80}{100} = 80\%$$

■ You can also write a percent as a fraction.

Write 50% as a fraction.

Write 50% as hundredths.

$$50\% = \frac{50}{100}$$

Simplify $\frac{50}{100}$.

$$\frac{50}{100} = \frac{50 \div 50}{100 \div 50} = \frac{1}{2}$$

Try These

Write each fraction as a percent.

1. $\frac{92}{100}$
2. $\frac{3}{4}$
3. $\frac{1}{50}$
4. $\frac{3}{20}$
5. $\frac{3}{5}$
6. $\frac{8}{25}$

Write each percent as a fraction. Simplify if possible.

7. 3%
8. 10%
9. 8%
10. 25%
11. 45%
12. 38%

Exercises

Write each fraction as a percent.

1. $\frac{37}{100}$ 2. $\frac{2}{4}$ 3. $\frac{1}{5}$ 4. $\frac{49}{50}$ 5. $\frac{2}{10}$ 6. $\frac{19}{20}$

7. $\frac{21}{50}$ 8. $\frac{49}{100}$ 9. $\frac{1}{2}$ 10. $\frac{2}{5}$ 11. $\frac{1}{100}$ 12. $\frac{1}{4}$

13. $\frac{7}{100}$ 14. $\frac{7}{20}$ 15. $\frac{5}{10}$ 16. $\frac{27}{50}$ 17. $\frac{2}{2}$ ★ 18. $\frac{6}{8}$

Write each percent as a fraction. Simplify if possible.

19. 27% 20. 12% 21. 60% 22. 30% 23. 47% 24. 92%

25. 19% 26. 66% 27. 16% 28. 86% 29. 55% 30. 48%

31. 68% 32. 3% 33. 90% 34. 36% 35. 85% 36. 18%

Solve each problem. Simplify if possible.

37. The circus has 50 animals. 15 of them are elephants. What percent of the animals are elephants?

38. 40% of the circus performers are clowns. What fraction of the performers are clowns?

39. There are 500 people at the circus. $\frac{3}{5}$ of them are children. What percent of the people at the circus are children?

★ 40. 200 souvenirs were sold. 45% of the souvenirs sold were balloons. What fraction were balloons? How many balloons were sold?

 THINK AND TRY

WRITING PERCENTS AS MIXED NUMBERS

Percents greater than 100% represent numbers greater than 1.

Write 175% as a fraction.

Write 175% as hundredths.

$$175\% = \frac{175}{100}$$

Write $\frac{175}{100}$ in lowest terms.

$$\frac{175}{100} = 1\frac{75}{100} = 1\frac{3}{4}$$

Write each percent as a mixed number.

1. 125% 2. 250% 3. 375% 4. 160% 5. 115% 6. 210%

Percents, Fractions, and Decimals

■ You can write a percent as a decimal.

Write 36% as a decimal.
36% means 36 hundredths.

$$36\% = 0.36$$

Write 9% as a decimal.
9% means 9 hundredths.

$$9\% = 0.09$$

■ You can also write a decimal as a percent.

Write 0.08 as a percent.

$$0.08 = 8 \text{ hundredths}$$
$$8 \text{ hundredths} = 8\%$$

Write 0.27 as a percent.

$$0.27 = 27 \text{ hundredths}$$
$$27 \text{ hundredths} = 27\%$$

Write 0.2 as a percent.

Write tenths as hundredths.

$$0.2 = 0.20$$

Write hundredths as a percent.

$$0.20 = 20\%$$

■ You can write a fraction as a percent.
First divide to write the fraction as a decimal.

Write $\frac{1}{8}$ as a percent.

$$\begin{array}{r} 0.125 \\ 8\overline{)1.000} \\ \underline{8} \\ 20 \\ \underline{16} \\ 40 \\ \underline{40} \\ 0 \end{array}$$

$$0.125 = \frac{125}{1{,}000}$$

$$\frac{125}{1{,}000} = \frac{125 \div 10}{1{,}000 \div 10} = \frac{12.5}{100}$$

$$0.125 = 12.5\%$$

$$\frac{1}{8} = 12.5\%$$

Try These

Write each percent as a decimal.

1. 45% **2.** 60% **3.** 4% **4.** 99% **5.** 1% **6.** 16%

Write each decimal or fraction as a percent.

7. 0.68 **8.** 0.5 **9.** 0.02 **10.** $\frac{12}{40}$ **11.** $\frac{5}{8}$ **12.** $\frac{6}{15}$

Exercises

Write each percent as a decimal.

1. 66% **2.** 80% **3.** 25% **4.** 3% **5.** 74% **6.** 35%
7. 7% **8.** 46% **9.** 12% **10.** 24% **11.** 10% **12.** 58%

Write each decimal as a percent.

13. 0.25 **14.** 0.05 **15.** 0.3 **16.** 0.73 **17.** 0.66 **18.** 0.42
19. 0.06 **20.** 0.4 **21.** 0.71 **22.** 0.2 **23.** 0.27 **24.** 0.14

Write each fraction as a percent.

25. $\frac{3}{12}$ **26.** $\frac{3}{8}$ **27.** $\frac{12}{16}$ **28.** $\frac{12}{30}$ **29.** $\frac{4}{8}$ **30.** $\frac{9}{60}$

31. $\frac{15}{24}$ **32.** $\frac{56}{80}$ **33.** $\frac{21}{35}$ **34.** $\frac{7}{8}$ **35.** $\frac{21}{70}$ **36.** $\frac{6}{48}$

 You can use a calculator to write a fraction as a percent.

Write $\frac{2}{3}$ as a percent to the nearest tenth of a percent.

Remember: $\frac{2}{3}$ means 2 ÷ 3. $\frac{2}{3}$ = 0.6666. . .

Round 0.6666 to the nearest thousandth.   **Write 0.667 as a percent.**

　　0.6666 ⟶ 0.667   　　0.667 = 66.7%

Write each fraction as a percent to the nearest tenth of a percent.

37. $\frac{5}{6}$ **38.** $\frac{2}{11}$ **39.** $\frac{5}{9}$ **40.** $\frac{6}{7}$ **41.** $\frac{8}{15}$ **42.** $\frac{5}{12}$

Finding a Percent of a Number

■ Steve owns a boat-rental shop. He needs more rowboats. A $350 rowboat is on sale for 20% off. How much money can Steve save if he buys the rowboat on sale?

Find 20% of $350.

Write the percent as a decimal.

$$20\% = 0.20$$

Multiply.

$$
\begin{array}{r}
\$350 \longleftarrow \text{original price} \\
\times 0.20 \longleftarrow \text{percent saved} \\
\hline
\$70.00
\end{array}
$$

Steve can save $70.

What is the sale price of the rowboat?

$$
\begin{array}{r}
\$350 \longleftarrow \text{regular price} \\
- \quad 70 \longleftarrow \text{amount saved} \\
\hline
\$280
\end{array}
$$

The sale price is $280.

■ Sometimes using a fraction instead of a decimal makes it easier to find the percent of a number.

Steve has 24 rowboats at his boat-rental shop. One day 75% of the rowboats were rented. How many rowboats were rented that day?

Find 75% of 24.

Write the percent as a fraction in lowest terms.

$$75\% = \frac{75}{100} = \frac{3}{4}$$

Multiply.

$$\frac{3}{\underset{1}{4}} \times \overset{6}{24} = \frac{18}{1} = 18$$

18 rowboats were rented that day.

Try These

Use a decimal to find each answer.

1. 25% of 24

2. 16% of 52

3. 90% of $35

Use a fraction to find each answer.

4. 50% of 68

5. 25% of 12

6. 20% of 45

Exercises

Use a decimal to find each answer.

1. 98% of 60

2. 15% of 200

3. 25% of $4.60

4. 27% of $42

5. 35% of 80

6. 52% of 150

7. 8% of 125

8. 44% of $24

9. 68% of 300

10. 55% of 80

11. 62% of 250

12. 84% of 175

Use a fraction to find each answer.

13. 50% of 82

14. 40% of 60

15. 25% of 76

16. 5% of $30

17. 10% of 70

18. 50% of 36

19. 75% of 48

20. 45% of 300

21. 30% of 120

22. 20% of 90

23. 25% of 148

24. 80% of 320

Solve each problem. You may use a calculator to check.

25. A canoe costs $400. It is on sale for 15% off. How much money can Steve save? What is the sale price of the canoe?

26. An average of 480 people visit Highland Lake each day. 70% of the people go swimming. How many people go swimming?

27. 52 people are boating. 75% of these people own their boats. How many people own their boats?

28. Steve has 40 life jackets. 30% of the life jackets are for children. How many life jackets are for children?

29. A sailboat costs $760. It is on sale for 25% off. How much money can Steve save? What is the sale price of the sailboat?

30. Steve spent $7,000 to repair the boat dock. 60% of the money was spent on supplies. How much did Steve spend on supplies?

31. The boat-rental shop earns an average of $1,050 in 7 days. At that rate, how much does the shop earn in 30 days?

★ **32.** Steve buys 18 life jackets. Each life jacket costs $15. There is a sales tax of 7% on the dollar. What is the total cost of the life jackets?

Problem Solving: Applications

PERCENTS AND BANKING

■ Percents are used in banking in many ways.
When customers borrow money from a bank, they must
repay the loan and a percent of the loan called **interest**.

Ms. Bonetti borrowed $2,000 for 2 years at an interest rate
of 17% per year. Her agreement with the bank was that
she would repay the entire loan at the end of 2 years.
How much interest will she have to pay?

Write the percent as a decimal.

$$17\% = 0.17$$

Multiply the amount of the loan by the interest rate.

$$
\begin{array}{r}
\$2,000 \\
\times\ \ 0.17 \\
\hline
140\ 00 \\
200\ 0 \\
\hline
\$340.00
\end{array}
$$

Multiply the result by the time in years.

$$
\begin{array}{r}
\$340 \\
\times\ \ \ 2 \\
\hline
\$680
\end{array}
$$

Ms. Bonetti will have to pay $680 in interest.

How much will she owe the bank at the end of the 2
years? Add the amounts of the loan and the interest.

$$
\begin{array}{r}
\$2,000 \\
+\ \ \ 680 \\
\hline
\$2,680
\end{array}
$$

Ms. Bonetti will owe $2,680 at the end of the 2 years.

■ Banks also use percents to pay interest to customers
who have money in savings accounts.

Suppose Mr. Sullivan deposits $1,500 in a savings
account. The bank pays interest of 6% per year.
How much interest will his money earn in 2 months?

Write the percent as a decimal.

$$6\% = 0.06$$

Multiply the amount of the deposit by the interest rate.

$$
\begin{array}{r}
\$1,500 \\
\times\ \ 0.06 \\
\hline
\$90.00
\end{array}
$$

Multiply the result by the time in years.

2 months = $\frac{1}{6}$ year

$\frac{1}{6} \times \$90 = \$15$

Mr. Sullivan will earn $15 in interest in 2 months.

Try These

Solve each problem.

1. Mr. Goldman borrowed $3,500 for 4 years at an interest rate of 18% per year. He agreed to repay the entire loan at the end of 4 years. What will the interest be on his loan?

2. Catherine deposited $476 in her savings account. The bank pays interest at a rate of 5% per year. How much interest will her money earn in 3 months?

Exercises

Solve each problem. For each loan, the entire loan will be repaid at the end of the loan period.

1. Ms. White borrowed $11,000 for 3 years at an interest rate of 16% per year. What will the interest be on her loan? How much will she owe the bank at the end of the 3 years?

2. Randy has $2,540 in his savings account. The bank pays interest at a rate of 6% per year. How much interest will Randy's money earn in 1 month?

3. Mrs. Duncan borrowed $781.20 from a bank for 1 year at an interest rate of 19% per year. What will the interest be on her loan? Round your answer to the nearest cent.

4. Mr. York deposited $17,630 in a savings account. The bank pays interest at a rate of 7% per year. How much interest will his money earn in 2 months? Round to the nearest cent.

5. Mr. Hobbs has $450 in his savings account. The money earns 6% interest in 1 year. How much interest will it earn in 3 months? How much will be in Mr. Hobbs's account then?

6. Ms. Stanowski borrowed $1,200 for 6 months at an interest rate of 18% per year. How much will the interest be on her loan? How much will she owe the bank at the end of the 6 months?

Solve each problem.

★ **7.** Steve deposited $1,500 in his savings account. The bank pays interest at a rate of 4% per year. After 1 month, he deposited another $600 in his account. How much interest will he have earned altogether after another month has passed?

★ **8.** Mr. Lerner borrowed $1,000 at an interest rate of 18% per year. At the end of the first month, he repaid $500 of the loan. At the end of the second month, he was able to repay another $500. How much interest did he owe the bank then?

Write each ratio. (pp. 268–269)

1. robins to blue jays

2. blue jays to goldfinches

3. goldfinches to all the birds

Copy and complete to make equal ratios. (pp. 270–271)

4. $\dfrac{15}{35} = \dfrac{\blacksquare}{7}$

5. $\dfrac{3}{5} = \dfrac{\blacksquare}{30}$

6. $\dfrac{4}{7} = \dfrac{12}{\blacksquare}$

7. $\dfrac{42}{56} = \dfrac{6}{\blacksquare}$

Do the ratios form a proportion? Write *yes* or *no*.
Use cross products to check. (pp. 272–273)

8. $\dfrac{2}{4}$ and $\dfrac{7}{14}$

9. $\dfrac{6}{9}$ and $\dfrac{10}{15}$

10. $\dfrac{3}{6}$ and $\dfrac{4}{12}$

11. $\dfrac{6}{16}$ and $\dfrac{15}{40}$

Solve for *n*. (pp. 272–273)

12. $\dfrac{4}{8} = \dfrac{6}{n}$

13. $\dfrac{12}{8} = \dfrac{n}{10}$

14. $\dfrac{3}{9} = \dfrac{n}{21}$

15. $\dfrac{16}{4} = \dfrac{20}{n}$

16. $\dfrac{15}{18} = \dfrac{n}{12}$

17. $\dfrac{28}{7} = \dfrac{12}{n}$

18. $\dfrac{27}{12} = \dfrac{18}{n}$

19. $\dfrac{6}{10} = \dfrac{n}{25}$

Write each fraction as a percent. (pp. 280–281)

20. $\dfrac{1}{4}$

21. $\dfrac{9}{20}$

22. $\dfrac{2}{5}$

23. $\dfrac{6}{25}$

24. $\dfrac{7}{10}$

25. $\dfrac{43}{50}$

Write each percent as a fraction. Simplify if possible. (pp. 280–281)

26. 10%

27. 16%

28. 50%

29. 69%

30. 84%

31. 75%

Write each percent as a decimal. (pp. 282–283)

32. 36%

33. 87%

34. 4%

35. 24%

36. 50%

37. 9%

Write each decimal as a percent. (pp. 282–283)

38. 0.14

39. 0.72

40. 0.06

41. 0.38

42. 0.7

43. 0.95

Write each fraction as a percent. (pp. 282–283)

44. $\frac{6}{8}$ **45.** $\frac{3}{6}$ **46.** $\frac{3}{8}$ **47.** $\frac{7}{28}$ **48.** $\frac{10}{16}$ **49.** $\frac{12}{15}$

Use a decimal to find each answer. (pp. 284–285)

50. 4% of 50 **51.** 20% of $68 **52.** 3% of 150
53. 22% of 85 **54.** 30% of 520 **55.** 65% of 250

Use a fraction to find each answer. (pp. 284–285)

56. 50% of 36 **57.** 75% of 24 **58.** 25% of $48
59. 100% of 54 **60.** 40% of 180 **61.** 15% of 160

Solve each problem. (pp. 268–287)

62. The ratio of apples to peaches is 3 to 5. There are 15 peaches. How many apples are there?

63. Bob buys 8 ft of wire for $3.40. How much would 10 ft of wire cost?

64. Marie has 50 coupons. 35 of them are for food. What percent of the coupons are for food?

65. Kathy has 40 stamps. 25% of them are for postcards. How many of the stamps are for postcards?

66. The shadow of a post is 36 cm long. The post is 120 cm tall. At the same time, the shadow of a building is 4.5 m long. How tall is the building?

67. A refrigerator costs $950. It is on sale for 15% off. How much money can be saved? What is the sale price of the refrigerator?

68. Laura has $575 in her savings account. The bank pays interest at the rate of 8% per year. How much interest will Laura earn in 3 months?

69. Rick borrowed $800 for 1 year at an interest rate of 13% per year. What was the total amount of interest he paid?

1 cm on this drawing stands for 4 m in the actual yard.

70. Measure the length of the yard. What is the length of the actual yard?

71. Measure the width of the yard. What is the width of the actual yard?

COMPUTERS AND PROBLEM SOLVING

A ratio compares two numbers. Equal ratios are two ratios with the same relationship. This relationship can be expressed as a factor.

These procedures take a number and multiply it by a certain factor. The ratio of the original number and the product is shown by the proportions of a rectangle.

```
TO EQUALRATIO :WIDTH :FACTOR
MAKE "HEIGHT :WIDTH * :FACTOR
RECTANGLE :HEIGHT :WIDTH
END

TO RECTANGLE :HEIGHT :WIDTH
REPEAT 2 [FD :HEIGHT RT 90 FD :WIDTH RT 90]
END
```

There are two variables on the title line of each procedure. The user decides what values to give these variables when the procedure is run. The variable :WIDTH is the first number of the ratio. The variable :FACTOR sets the ratio. :HEIGHT and :WIDTH determine the dimensions of the rectangle drawn.

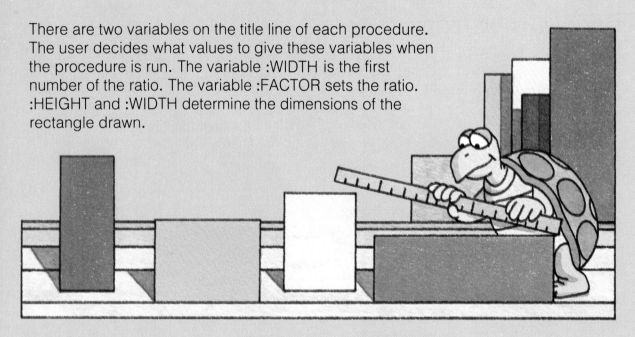

Solve each problem.

1. What are the dimensions of the rectangle if the user types EQUALRATIO 10 5?

2. What value entered for :FACTOR would draw a square?

3. Add a line to RECTANGLE to move the turtle to the right after drawing, so that the user can run the procedure several times in a row and compare the resulting rectangles.

The procedure SPIRAL draws a rectangular spiral. The proportions of the spiral are determined by the variable :RATIO. :SIDE1 has a length of 6 at first. Each time the procedure INCREASE repeats, it adds 6 to :SIDE1 and multiplies :SIDE1 by :RATIO to get a new value for :SIDE2.

```
TO SPIRAL :RATIO
MAKE "SIDE1 6
MAKE "SIDE2 :SIDE1 * :RATIO
REPEAT 20 [ FD :SIDE1 RT 90 FD :SIDE2 RT 90
   INCREASE :RATIO]
END

TO INCREASE :RATIO
MAKE "SIDE1 :SIDE1 + 6
MAKE "SIDE2 :SIDE1 * :RATIO
END
```

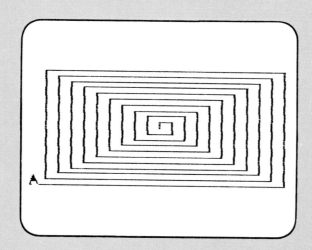

Solve each problem.

1. The user types SPIRAL 20/10. What is the length of the second line that the turtle draws? The last line?

2. What happens if you type SPIRAL 1/1? What does SPIRAL look like when the ratio you enter is greater than 1? What does SPIRAL look like when you enter a ratio that is less than 1?

3. Would SPIRAL still work if you changed the second line to REPEAT 20 [FD :SIDE1 RT 60 FD :SIDE2 RT 120 INCREASE :RATIO]? What would the output look like?

ENRICHMENT

THE PERCENT ONE NUMBER IS OF ANOTHER

■ What percent of 20 is 15?
Let n be the percent.

> What percent of 20 is 15?
> $n \times 20 = 15$

Write an equation.	$n \times 20 = 15$
Solve for n.	$\frac{20n}{20} = \frac{15}{20}$ ← ⌈Divide both sides ⌊by 20.
	$n = 0.75$
Write the percent.	$n = 75\%$

$$
\begin{array}{r}
0.75 \\
20\overline{)15.00} \\
14\ 0 \\
\hline
1\ 00 \\
1\ 00 \\
\hline
0
\end{array}
$$

15 is 75% of 20.

■ 25 is what percent of 40?

Write an equation.	$25 = n \times 40$
Solve for n.	$\frac{25}{40} = \frac{40n}{40}$ ← ⌈Divide both sides ⌊by 40.
	$0.625 = n$
	$\frac{0.625}{1,000} = \frac{62.5}{100}$
Write the percent.	$62.5\% = n$

$$
\begin{array}{r}
0.625 \\
40\overline{)25.000} \\
24\ 0 \\
\hline
1\ 00 \\
80 \\
\hline
200 \\
200 \\
\hline
0
\end{array}
$$

25 is 62.5% of 40.

Solve for n. Write n as a percent.

1. $n \times 24 = 18$ **2.** $n \times 50 = 16$ **3.** $n \times 150 = 90$

4. $40 = n \times 200$ **5.** $20 = n \times 160$ **6.** $15 = n \times 50$

Write each equation. Then solve.

7. What percent of 125 is 25?   **8.** What percent of 96 is 72?

9. What percent of 110 is 9.9?   **10.** What percent of 136 is 51?

11. 39 is what percent of 60?   **12.** 147 is what percent of 150?

13. 23 is what percent of 50?   **14.** 1.3 is what percent of 26?

Find the least common multiple of each pair of numbers.

1. 7, 5   **2.** 2, 7   **3.** 3, 6   **4.** 8, 6   **5.** 4, 10

6. 5, 10   **7.** 6, 9   **8.** 6, 10   **9.** 7, 9   **10.** 9, 12

Find the greatest common factor of each pair of numbers.

11. 4, 8   **12.** 6, 12   **13.** 16, 20   **14.** 3, 5   **15.** 10, 20

16. 14, 21   **17.** 5, 7   **18.** 18, 27   **19.** 4, 16   **20.** 24, 18

Show each number as a product of prime factors.

21. 25   **22.** 27   **23.** 40   **24.** 35   **25.** 30

Copy and complete.

26. $\dfrac{2}{5} = \dfrac{\blacksquare}{15}$ **27.** $\dfrac{3}{6} = \dfrac{\blacksquare}{18}$ **28.** $\dfrac{4}{7} = \dfrac{12}{\blacksquare}$ **29.** $\dfrac{5}{8} = \dfrac{\blacksquare}{32}$ **30.** $\dfrac{4}{6} = \dfrac{28}{\blacksquare}$

Simplify if possible.

31. $\dfrac{8}{14}$ **32.** $\dfrac{12}{24}$ **33.** $\dfrac{27}{45}$ **34.** $\dfrac{7}{21}$ **35.** $\dfrac{20}{30}$

Write >, <, or =. (pp. 218–219)

36. $\dfrac{4}{7} \ \blacksquare \ \dfrac{3}{4}$ **37.** $\dfrac{5}{6} \ \blacksquare \ \dfrac{1}{4}$ **38.** $\dfrac{5}{6} \ \blacksquare \ \dfrac{7}{9}$ **39.** $\dfrac{3}{4} \ \blacksquare \ \dfrac{9}{12}$ **40.** $\dfrac{1}{3} \ \blacksquare \ \dfrac{2}{5}$

Compute. Simplify if possible.

41. $\dfrac{3}{4} + \dfrac{1}{4}$ **42.** $\dfrac{3}{8} - \dfrac{1}{8}$ **43.** $\dfrac{4}{5} + \dfrac{3}{5}$ **44.** $\dfrac{6}{7} - \dfrac{4}{7}$

45. $\dfrac{5}{6} - \dfrac{1}{2}$ **46.** $\dfrac{3}{4} + \dfrac{1}{6}$ **47.** $\dfrac{7}{8} + \dfrac{3}{4}$ **48.** $\dfrac{6}{12} - \dfrac{1}{3}$

49. $\begin{array}{r} 9\frac{1}{10} \\ +\ 8\frac{5}{6} \\ \hline \end{array}$ **50.** $\begin{array}{r} \frac{9}{10} \\ -\ \frac{1}{2} \\ \hline \end{array}$ **51.** $\begin{array}{r} 6\frac{3}{4} \\ +\ 2\frac{1}{3} \\ \hline \end{array}$ **52.** $\begin{array}{r} 9 \\ -\ 1\frac{1}{8} \\ \hline \end{array}$ **53.** $\begin{array}{r} 2\frac{2}{3} \\ +\ 1\frac{5}{6} \\ \hline \end{array}$

(Continued)

Multiply. Simplify if possible.

54. $\frac{2}{3} \times \frac{1}{4}$
$\qquad$
55. $\frac{1}{5} \times 7$
$\qquad$
56. $2\frac{1}{3} \times 6$
$\qquad$
57. $3\frac{1}{8} \times 1\frac{1}{5}$

Divide. Simplify if possible.

58. $\frac{5}{8} \div \frac{1}{4}$
$\qquad$
59. $6 \div \frac{2}{3}$
$\qquad$
60. $5\frac{1}{4} \div \frac{7}{10}$
$\qquad$
61. $3 \div 1\frac{7}{8}$

Do the ratios form a proportion? Write *yes* or *no*.
Use cross products to check.

62. $\frac{10}{12}$ and $\frac{15}{24}$
$\qquad$
63. $\frac{2}{4}$ and $\frac{5}{10}$
$\qquad$
64. $\frac{6}{10}$ and $\frac{9}{15}$
$\qquad$
65. $\frac{6}{9}$ and $\frac{8}{12}$

Solve for *n*.

66. $\frac{3}{6} = \frac{n}{8}$
$\qquad$
67. $\frac{21}{9} = \frac{14}{n}$
$\qquad$
68. $\frac{6}{4} = \frac{n}{10}$
$\qquad$
69. $\frac{15}{18} = \frac{20}{n}$

Write each fraction as a percent.

70. $\frac{2}{5}$
$\qquad$
71. $\frac{9}{12}$
$\qquad$
72. $\frac{9}{10}$
$\qquad$
73. $\frac{6}{16}$
$\qquad$
74. $\frac{2}{8}$
$\qquad$
75. $\frac{6}{15}$

Compute.

76. 12% of 75
$\qquad$
77. 50% of 480
$\qquad$
78. 6% of 58

79. 25% of 24
$\qquad$
80. 8% of 450
$\qquad$
81. 80% of 150

Solve each problem.

82. A coat sells for $90. It is on sale for 20% off. What is the sale price of the coat?

83. Connie had $3\frac{1}{2}$ yd of lace. She used $1\frac{5}{8}$ yd. How much lace did Connie have left?

84. A recipe calls for $1\frac{1}{4}$ c of flour. Jack is making the recipe 4 times. How much flour will he need?

85. There are 870 students. 40% of them are in a sports program. How many students are in a sports program?

86. Juanita's test scores in science are 86, 91, 99, 78, 95, and 97. What is her average?

87. Randy bought 3 shirts for $15.95 each. The tax was $2.87. What was the total cost of his purchase?

GEOMETRY

11

Basic Geometric Figures

■ Some special words are used in geometry.

Term	Figure	Symbol
A **point** is a position in space.	• *A*	point *A*
A **line** is a set of points that continues without end in two opposite directions.	*P* *Q*	line *PQ* ($\overleftrightarrow{PQ}$) or line *QP* ($\overleftrightarrow{QP}$)
A **line segment** is part of a line. It has two **endpoints**.	*P* *Q* endpoints	segment *PQ* ($\overline{PQ}$) or segment *QP* ($\overline{QP}$)
A **ray** is part of a line. It has only one endpoint.	*A* *B*	ray *AB* ($\overrightarrow{AB}$)
An **angle** is formed when two rays have the same endpoint. The endpoint is the **vertex** of the angle.	*A* *B* *C* vertex	angle *ABC* (∠*ABC*) or angle *CBA* (∠*CBA*) or angle *B* (∠*B*)

■ A **plane** can be thought of as a flat surface that goes on and on in all directions.

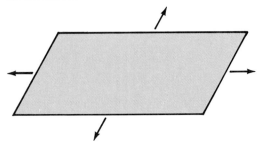

■ If two line segments have the same measurement, then they are **congruent.** $\overline{CD}$ **is congruent to** $\overline{EF}$. Their measurement is 2.5 cm.

Try These

Use this figure to answer exercises 1–6.

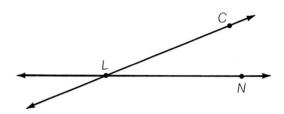

1. Name three points.
2. Name two lines.
3. Name two line segments.
4. Name four rays.
5. Name an angle.
6. Is $\overline{LC}$ congruent to $\overline{LN}$?

Exercises

Use this figure to answer exercises 1–6.

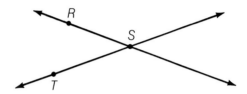

1. Name three points.
2. Name two lines.
3. Name two line segments.
4. Name four rays.
5. Name an angle.
6. Is $\overline{RS}$ congruent to $\overline{SR}$?

Write *true* or *false*.

7. $\overline{BC}$ is the same as $\overline{CB}$.

8. $\overleftrightarrow{BD}$ is the same as $\overleftrightarrow{DB}$.

9. $\overrightarrow{CB}$ is the same as $\overrightarrow{BC}$.

10. $\angle CBD$ is the same as $\angle DBC$.

Do the segments look congruent? Write *yes* or *no*.
Use a ruler or tracing paper to check.

11.

12.

13.

14.

15.

16.

Draw each figure. Then label it.

17. $\overline{XY}$

18. $\overrightarrow{SH}$

19. $\angle ADB$

20. $\overleftrightarrow{BC}$

Measuring and Classifying Angles

■ A **protractor** is used to measure angles. It is marked in units of measure called **degrees (°)**. To measure an angle, follow these steps:

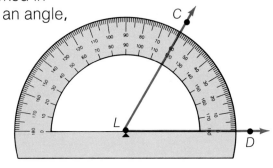

1. Place the center point of the protractor on the vertex of the angle.
2. Place the 0° mark on one ray of the angle.
3. Read the number of degrees where the other ray goes through the scale.

Read: 60 degrees
Write: 60°

The measure of ∠CLD is 60°.

■ Angles have special names.

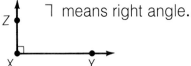

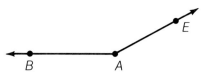

∠ZXY is a **right** angle. Its measure is 90°.

∠BAC is an **acute** angle. Its measure is less than 90°.

∠BAE is an **obtuse** angle. Its measure is greater than 90°.

■ Angles are congruent if they have the same measure. The measure of ∠E is 30°. The measure of ∠Q is 30°. ∠E is congruent to ∠Q.

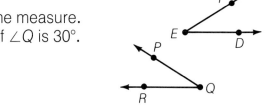

■ You can draw an angle using a ruler and a protractor. Here is how to draw a 120° angle.

Draw one ray.

Place the protractor as if you were measuring. Make a mark at 120°.

Draw the other ray.

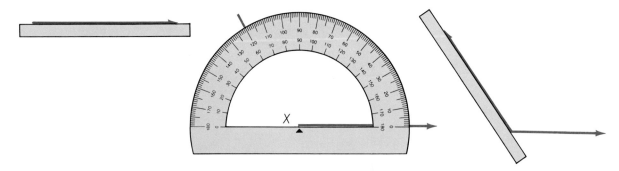

Try These

Find the measure of each angle. Write *right*, *acute*, or *obtuse*.

1.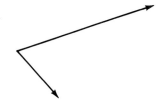

2.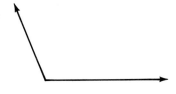

3.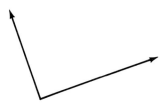

Draw an angle with each measure.

4. 30°   **5.** 90°   **6.** 170°   **7.** 65°   **8.** 115°

Exercises

Find the measure of each angle. Write *right*, *acute*, or *obtuse*.

1.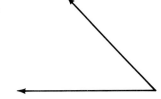

2.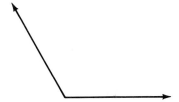

3.

4.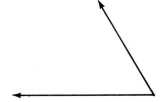

5.

6.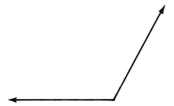

7. In exercises 1–6, which angles are congruent?

Draw an angle with each measure.

8. 165°   **9.** 55°   **10.** 145°   **11.** 47°   ★ **12.** 200°

Draw an angle that is congruent to each angle shown.

13.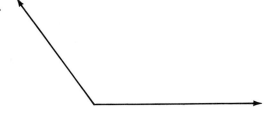

14.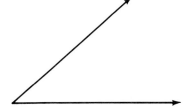

Perpendicular and Parallel Lines

- When two lines meet at a common point, we say they **intersect**. Four angles are formed when two lines intersect.

    $\overleftrightarrow{LD}$ intersects $\overleftrightarrow{JM}$ at point K.

- Two lines that intersect and form right angles are **perpendicular** lines.

    $\overleftrightarrow{RS}$ is perpendicular to $\overleftrightarrow{MT}$.
    In symbols: $\overleftrightarrow{RS} \perp \overleftrightarrow{MT}$

- Two lines in a plane that do not intersect are **parallel** lines.

    $\overleftrightarrow{XY}$ is parallel to $\overleftrightarrow{ZW}$.
    In symbols: $\overleftrightarrow{XY} \parallel \overleftrightarrow{ZW}$

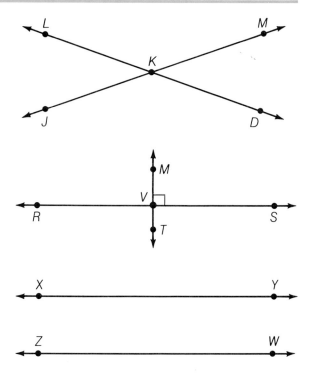

Try These

Use this figure to answer exercises 1–6.

1. Name two lines that intersect and are not perpendicular.

2. Name two lines that are perpendicular.

3. Name two lines that are parallel.

4. Name two right angles.

5. Name three acute angles.

6. Name three obtuse angles.

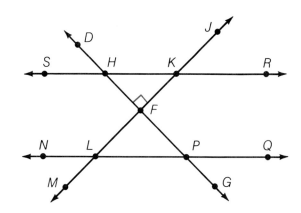

Exercises

Use this figure to answer exercises 1–6.

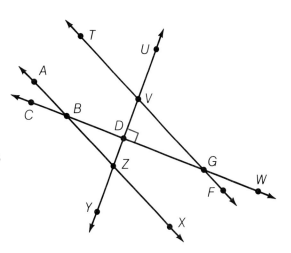

1. Name two lines that intersect and are not perpendicular.

2. Name two lines that are perpendicular.

3. Name two lines that are parallel.

4. Measure ∠UDW, ∠CDU, ∠CDY, and ∠YDW. What is true about the four angles formed by perpendicular lines?

5. Find the measures of ∠UVT and ∠FVY. Are these angles congruent?

6. Find the measures of ∠TVY and ∠UVF. Are these angles congruent?

Solve each problem. Use the map to answer each question.

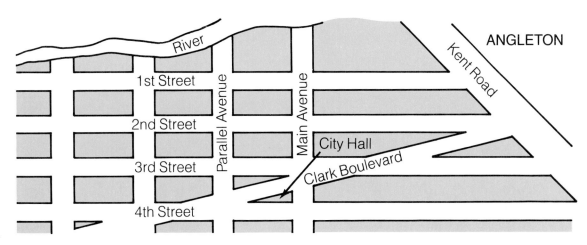

7. Name two streets that appear to be parallel.

8. Name two streets whose intersection forms an obtuse angle.

9. Name two streets that appear to be perpendicular to Main Avenue.

10. What is true of two streets that are perpendicular to the same avenue?

11. Find the measure of the obtuse angle formed by 3rd Street and Clark Boulevard.

12. Find the measure of the acute angle formed by 1st Street and Kent Road.

13. Find the measure of the acute angle formed by 2nd Street and Kent Road.

14. How do the angles in exercises 12 and 13 compare?

Polygons

■ These figures are **polygons**. Each side is a line segment.

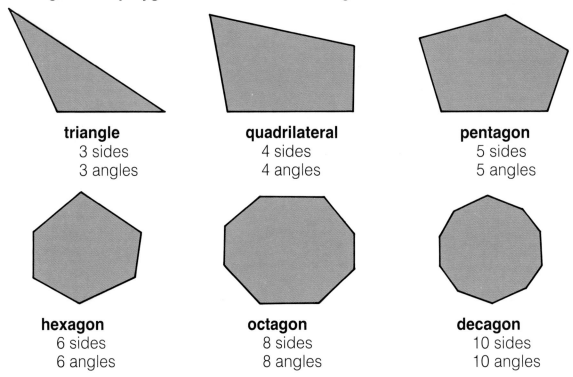

triangle	**quadrilateral**	**pentagon**
3 sides	4 sides	5 sides
3 angles	4 angles	5 angles

hexagon	**octagon**	**decagon**
6 sides	8 sides	10 sides
6 angles	8 angles	10 angles

■ A **regular polygon** has all sides congruent and all angles congruent.

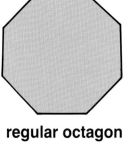

regular pentagon   **regular octagon**

■ The vertex of an angle of a polygon is called a vertex of the polygon. The plural of *vertex* is *vertices*.

The vertices of this pentagon are the points *A*, *B*, *C*, *D*, and *E*. We can call the figure pentagon *ABCDE*.

A **diagonal** of a polygon is a line segment that connects vertices that are not next to each other. The diagonal $\overline{AD}$ is shown in red.

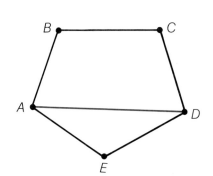

Try These

Name each polygon.

1.

2.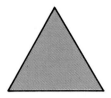

3.

4.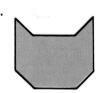

5. In exercises 1–4, which polygons are regular?

Exercises

Name each polygon.

1.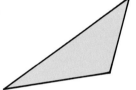

2.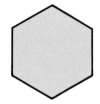

3.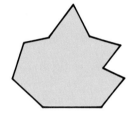

4.

5. In exercises 1–4, which polygons are regular?

How many angles does each polygon have?

6. pentagon

7. hexagon

8. octagon

9. quadrilateral

10. triangle

11. decagon

Use this figure to answer exercises 12–15.

12. Name one quadrilateral.

13. Name two diagonals.

★ **14.** Name eight triangles.

★ **15.** Name four pentagons.

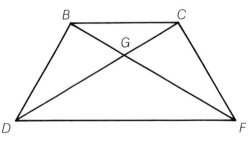

16. Draw and name all the diagonals of pentagon *PQRST*. How many are there?

★ **17.** Draw and name all the diagonals of hexagon *ABCDEF*. How many are there?

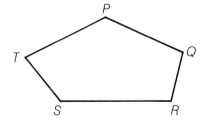

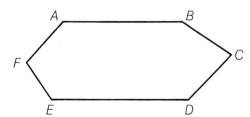

Congruent Polygons

■ Polygons are congruent when they have the same size and shape.

Is triangle *GHF* congruent to triangle *KLM*?

Trace triangle *GHF*. **Slide** the tracing to see how the points and sides match triangle *KLM*.

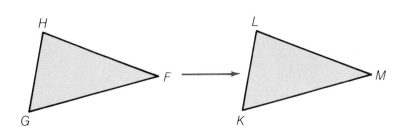

Triangle *GHF* is congruent to triangle *KLM*. Their matching parts, or **corresponding parts**, are congruent.

Corresponding Sides	Corresponding Angles
$\overline{GH}$ and $\overline{KL}$	∠*G* and ∠*K*
$\overline{HF}$ and $\overline{LM}$	∠*H* and ∠*L*
$\overline{GF}$ and $\overline{KM}$	∠*F* and ∠*M*

■ Is triangle *PQR* congruent to triangle *ABC*?

Trace triangle *PQR*. **Turn** the tracing to see how the points and sides match triangle *ABC*.

Triangle *PQR* is congruent to triangle *ABC*.

Can you name the corresponding sides and the corresponding angles?

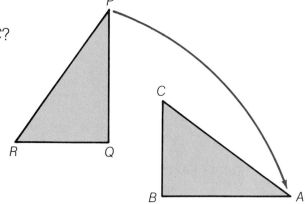

■ Is quadrilateral *MNPQ* congruent to quadrilateral *ABCD*?

Trace quadrilateral *MNPQ*. **Flip** the tracing over to see how the points and sides match quadrilateral *ABCD*.

Quadrilateral *MNPQ* is congruent to quadrilateral *ABCD*.

Can you name the corresponding sides and the corresponding angles?

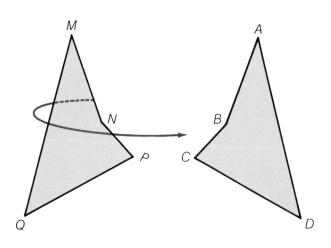

Try These

Are the polygons congruent? Write *yes* or *no*.

1. 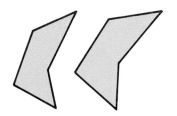　**2.** 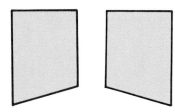　**3.**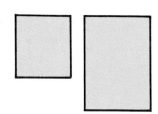

Triangle *QRS* is congruent to triangle *DEF*.

Copy and complete.

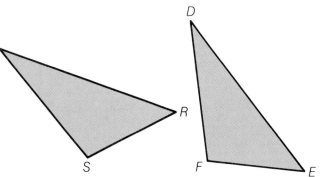

4. Angle *Q* is congruent to angle ▦.

5. Angle *S* is congruent to angle ▦.

6. $\overline{RS}$ is congruent to ▦.

7. $\overline{SQ}$ is congruent to ▦.

Exercises

Are the polygons congruent? Write *yes* or *no*.

1. 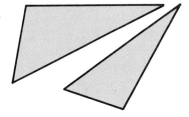　**2.** 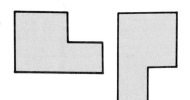　**3.**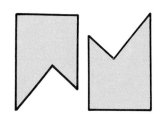

Hexagon *JKLMNO* is congruent to hexagon *ABCDEF*.

Copy and complete.

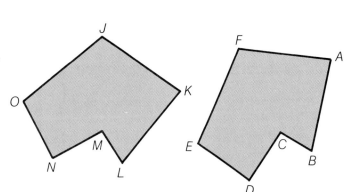

4. Angle *O* is congruent to angle ▦.

5. Angle *L* is congruent to angle ▦.

6. Angle *J* is congruent to angle ▦.

7. $\overline{JK}$ is congruent to ▦.

8. $\overline{MN}$ is congruent to ▦.

9. $\overline{OJ}$ is congruent to ▦.

Quadrilaterals

Some quadrilaterals have special names.

A **trapezoid** is a quadrilateral with exactly one pair of parallel sides.

$\overline{GH}$ is parallel to $\overline{KJ}$.

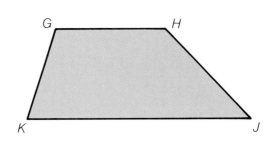

A **parallelogram** is a quadrilateral whose opposite sides are parallel and congruent.

$\overline{AB}$ is parallel to and congruent to $\overline{CD}$.
$\overline{AC}$ is parallel to and congruent to $\overline{BD}$.

Opposite angles of a parallelogram are also congruent.

$\angle C$ is congruent to $\angle B$.
$\angle A$ is congruent to $\angle D$.

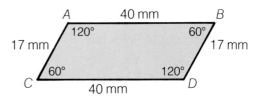

A **rectangle** is a parallelogram with four right angles.

A **square** is a rectangle with all sides congruent.

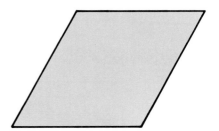

A **rhombus** is a parallelogram with all sides congruent.

If the angles of a rhombus are right angles, then it is a square.

Try These

Write a special name for each quadrilateral.

1.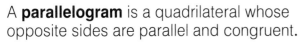

2.

3.

4.

Exercises

Use the figures to answer exercises 1–6.

a. 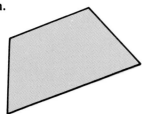 b. 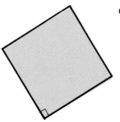 c.  d.

1. Which figures are quadrilaterals?

2. Which figures are rhombuses?

3. Which figures are parallelograms?

4. Which figures are rectangles?

5. Which figure is a trapezoid?

6. Which figure is a square?

Use this parallelogram to answer exercises 7–12.

7. Name two pairs of parallel sides.

8. Name the side opposite $\overline{RS}$.

9. Name the angle opposite $\angle QTS$.

10. What is the measure of $\overline{QT}$?

11. What is the measure of $\angle QRS$?

★ **12.** What is the sum of the measures of the four angles of parallelogram *QRST*? Is this true for all parallelograms?

Write *true* or *false*.

13. All squares are rectangles.

14. All rectangles are squares.

15. All parallelograms are rectangles.

16. All rectangles are parallelograms.

17. All squares are rhombuses.

18. All rhombuses are squares.

Solve each problem.

19. A restaurant's patio has five congruent sides. What shape is the patio?

20. A swimming pool has four congruent sides but is not a square. What shape is the pool?

Triangles

■ Triangles have special names that depend on the number of their sides that are congruent.

equilateral triangle
Three sides are congruent.

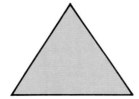

isosceles triangle
At least two sides are congruent.

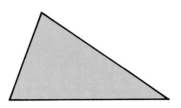

scalene triangle
No sides are congruent.

■ Triangles have special names that depend on the measures of their angles.

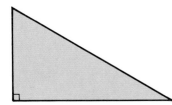

right triangle
One angle is 90°. It is a right angle.

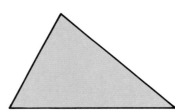

acute triangle
Every angle is less then 90°. All angles are acute.

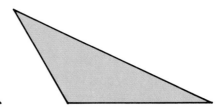

obtuse triangle
One angle is greater than 90°. It is an obtuse angle.

■ Find the sum of the measures of the angles of these triangles.

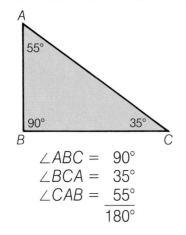

$$\angle ABC = 90°$$
$$\angle BCA = 35°$$
$$\angle CAB = \underline{55°}$$
$$180°$$

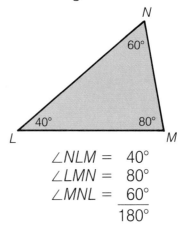

$$\angle NLM = 40°$$
$$\angle LMN = 80°$$
$$\angle MNL = \underline{60°}$$
$$180°$$

> *The sum of the measures of the angles of a triangle is always 180°.*

Try These

Name each triangle as *equilateral, isosceles,* or *scalene.*
Then name each as *right, acute,* or *obtuse.*

1.    2.    3. 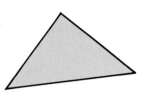   4.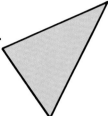

Exercises

Name each triangle as *equilateral, isosceles,* or *scalene.*
Then name each as *right, acute,* or *obtuse.*

1. 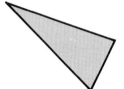   2. 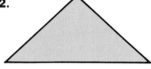   3. 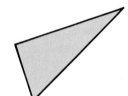   4.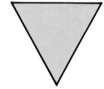

Measure each angle of the triangle.
Then find the sum of the angles.

5.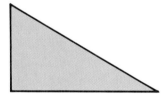

6.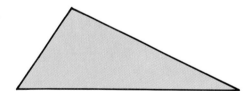

Solve each problem.

7. Could a triangle have angles with
   measures of 47°, 58°, and 75°?

8. Could a triangle have angles with
   measures of 35°, 49°, and 106°?

 THINK AND TRY

USING LOGICAL REASONING

One angle of a right triangle is twice the measure of the
smallest angle. What is the measure of the smallest angle?

Problem Solving: Strategies

LOGICAL REASONING

■ If you know the measures of two
angles of a triangle, you can find the
measure of the third angle.

The measures of two of the angles of
this triangle are shown. Find the
measure of the third angle.

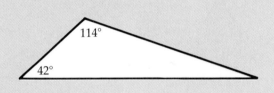

You know that the sum of the measures of all three angles
of the triangle is 180°. If you add the measure of the third
angle to 42° and 114°, the sum will be 180°.

First, add 42° and 114°.

$$
\begin{array}{r}
114° \\
+\ \ 42° \\
\hline
156°
\end{array}
$$

Then, subtract 156° from 180°.

$$
\begin{array}{r}
180° \\
-156° \\
\hline
24°
\end{array}
$$

So the measure of the third angle is 24°.

To check, add the measures of the
three angles. The sum should be 180°.

$$
\begin{array}{r}
114° \\
42° \\
+\ \ 24° \\
\hline
180° \quad \blacktriangleright
\end{array}
$$

■ Sometimes you are given the measure of only one angle.
Suppose you know that ∠ABC and ∠ACB are congruent.
Find the measures of ∠ACB and ∠BAC.

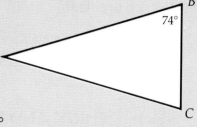

Since ∠ABC and ∠ACB are congruent, their
measures are the same. The measure of ∠ABC is
74°. Therefore, the measure of ∠ACB is also 74°.

To find the measure of ∠BAC, add the measures of
the two other angles. Then subtract the sum from 180°.

$$
\begin{array}{r}
74° \\
+74° \\
\hline
148°
\end{array}
\qquad
\begin{array}{r}
180° \\
-148° \\
\hline
32°
\end{array}
$$

The measure of ∠BAC is 32°.

Using the Strategy

For each triangle, find the measure of the angle that is not shown.

1.

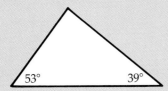

53°   39°

2.

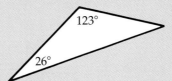

123°

26°

3.

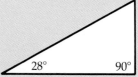

28°   90°

Solve each problem.

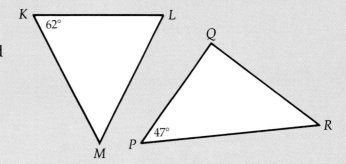

K   62°   L

M   P   47°   Q   R

4. Look at triangle *KLM.* ∠*KLM* and ∠*LKM* are congruent. Find the measures of ∠*KLM* and ∠*KML.*

5. Look at triangle *PQR.* ∠*PQR* is a right angle. Find the measures of ∠*PQR* and ∠*PRQ.*

6. In triangle *STU,* the measure of ∠*STU* is 49° and the measure of ∠*TSU* is 55°. Find the measure of ∠*SUT.* (Hint: Make a sketch.)

7. In triangle *DEF,* the measure of ∠*DEF* is 113° and the measure of ∠*EDF* is 36°. Find the measure of ∠*DFE.* (Hint: Make a sketch.)

ACTIVITY

EXPERIMENTING WITH ANGLES

1. Draw a triangle and cut it out.

2. Tear off the corners of the triangle.

3. Can you fit the three corners together so that they form a line?

4. Draw a triangle that is not similar to the first one. Cut it out and tear the corners off.

5. Can you fit the three corners together so that they form a line?

6. What can you conclude about the measure of an angle whose rays are on the same line, as shown?

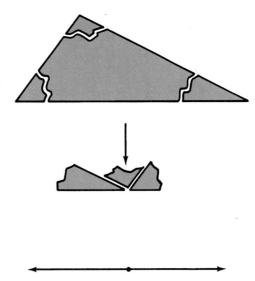

Similar Figures

■ Figures that have the same shape are called **similar figures**.

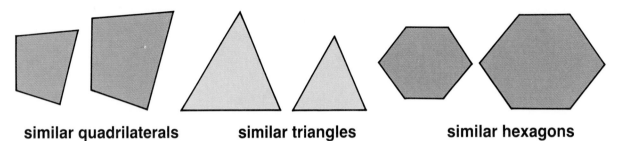

similar quadrilaterals   **similar triangles**   **similar hexagons**

■ In similar figures, the corresponding angles are congruent.

These triangles are similar.

> Corresponding Angles
> $\angle J$ and $\angle R$
> $\angle K$ and $\angle S$
> $\angle L$ and $\angle T$

Find the measures of $\angle R$, $\angle S$, and $\angle T$.

> $\angle J = 35°$, so $\angle R = 35°$
> $\angle K = 90°$, so $\angle S = 90°$
> $\angle L = 55°$, so $\angle T = 55°$

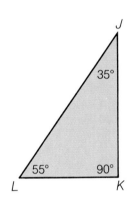

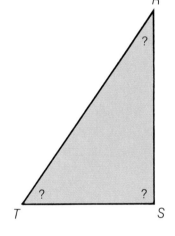

■ In similar figures, the ratios of corresponding sides are equal.

The rectangles shown are similar.

Find the length of side $\overline{XY}$.

Write a <u>proportion</u> to find the length of side $\overline{XY}$.

Corresponding Sides
$\overline{AB}$ and $\overline{WX}$ $\overline{BC}$ and $\overline{XY}$
$\overline{CD}$ and $\overline{YZ}$ $\overline{DA}$ and $\overline{ZW}$

$$\frac{CD}{YZ} = \frac{BC}{XY}$$

$$\frac{4}{10} = \frac{6}{n}$$

$$4 \times n = 10 \times 6$$

$$\frac{4n}{4} = \frac{60}{4}$$

$$n = 15$$

The length of side $\overline{XY}$ is 15 cm.

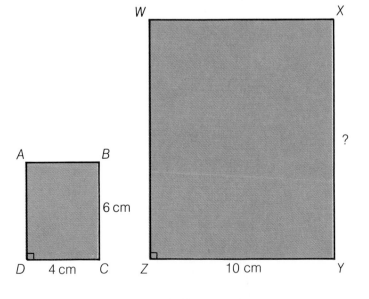

Try These

Are the figures similar? Write *yes* or *no*.

1.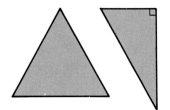

2.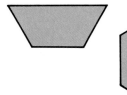

3.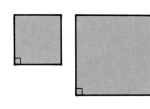

Triangle *WXY* is similar to triangle *KLM*.

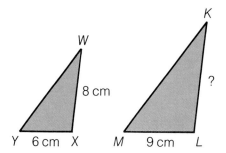

4. Name three pairs of corresponding sides.

5. Name three pairs of corresponding angles.

6. Find the length of *KL*.

Exercises

Are the figures similar? Write *yes* or *no*.

1.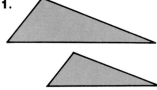

2.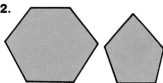

3.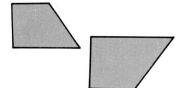

Triangle *STU* is similar to triangle DEF.

4. Find the length of $\overline{FE}$.

5. Find the length of $\overline{ST}$.

6. Find the measure of ∠*T*.

7. Find the measure of ∠*F*.

8. Find the measure of ∠*S*.

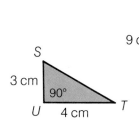

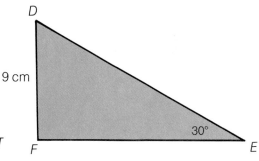

A photo and an enlargement are similar figures.

Solve each problem.

9. Josh is enlarging a photo that is 12 cm long and 8 cm wide. The enlargement will be 20 cm wide. How long will the enlargement be?

10. Josh enlarged another photo to 24 cm long and 18 cm wide. The original photo was 20 cm long. How wide was the original photo?

Circles

■ All the points of a circle are the same distance from the **center** of the circle. Point O is the center of the circle.

A **radius** is a line segment that connects a point on the circle with the center. The plural of *radius* is *radii*. Line segment *OM* is a radius of the circle.

A **chord** is a line segment that connects two points on the circle. Line segment *RQ* is a chord of the circle.

A **diameter** is a chord that passes through the center of the circle. Chord *PN* is a diameter of the circle.

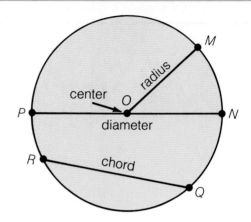

■ You can use a compass to draw a circle.

Put the metal tip on a point. Move the pencil around to draw the circle.

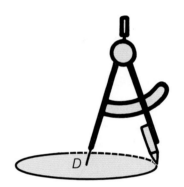

Try These

Use the circle to answer exercises 1–6. The center of the circle is point *F*.

1. Name a diameter.

2. Name three radii.

3. Is $\overline{RA}$ a diameter? Why?

4. Find the length of each radius in centimeters. Are they all the same length?

5. Find the length of the diameter. How does the length of a diameter compare to the length of a radius?

6. Find the length of $\overline{RA}$. Is it longer or shorter than a diameter?

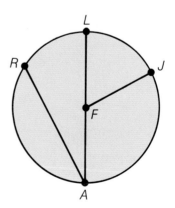

Exercises

Use the circle to answer exercises 1–7.
The center of the circle is point G.

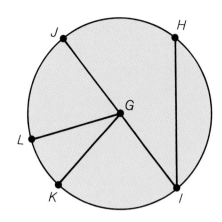

1. Name a diameter.

2. Name four radii.

3. Is $\overline{JI}$ a diameter? Why?

4. Find the length of the diameter.

5. Find the lengths of $\overline{GL}$ and $\overline{GK}$.

6. How does the length of the diameter compare to the sum of the lengths of the two radii?

7. Find the length of $\overline{HI}$. Is the diameter the longest chord in the circle?

8. Draw a circle with each of the following.
   a. point D as the center
   b. $\overline{CF}$ as a diameter
   c. $\overline{DR}$ as a radius
   d. $\overline{ST}$ as a chord

Solve each problem.

9. Caroline has a round tablecloth that has a diameter of 150 cm. She wants to cover the top of a round table that has a radius of 95 cm. Will the tablecloth cover the top of the table?

★ 10. A circular table has a radius of 65 cm. Betty wants to buy a tablecloth that hangs 15 cm below the edge of the table. What is the diameter of the tablecloth Betty should buy?

KEEPING IN SHAPE

Compute. Simplify if possible.

1. $\dfrac{2}{5}$ $+\dfrac{3}{5}$

2. $9\dfrac{5}{6}$ $-3\dfrac{1}{6}$

3. $5\dfrac{2}{3}$ $+5\dfrac{1}{4}$

4. $10\dfrac{3}{4}$ $+12\dfrac{3}{5}$

5. $9\dfrac{3}{7}$ $-4\dfrac{2}{7}$

6. $11\dfrac{9}{10}$ $-4\dfrac{1}{10}$

7. $14\dfrac{5}{6}$ $+7\dfrac{3}{4}$

8. $13\dfrac{5}{8}$ $-7\dfrac{3}{16}$

9. $4\dfrac{2}{7}$ $+9\dfrac{5}{14}$

10. $11\dfrac{2}{5}$ $+15\dfrac{1}{2}$

Symf/metry

■ When a figure is folded along
a **line of symmetry**, the two
parts match.

The red lines are lines of symmetry.

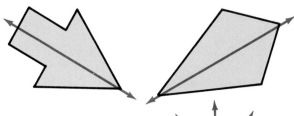

■ Some figures have more
than one line of symmetry.

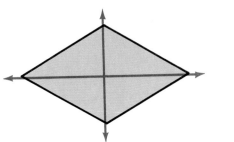
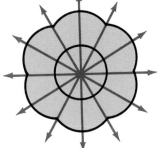

■ Sometimes a figure does not have a line
of symmetry.

Trace the parallelogram.
Does it have a line of symmetry?
Check by folding the tracing.

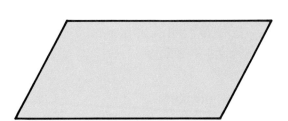

■ Flipping a figure over a line of symmetry gives a **mirror image**.

Each figure is a **reflection** of the other.

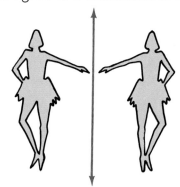

Try These

Is the red line a line of symmetry? Write *yes* or *no*.

1.
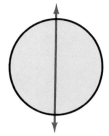

2.
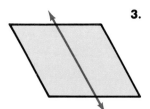

3.
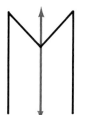

4.

Exercises

Trace each figure. Draw as many lines of symmetry as you can. Tell how many lines of symmetry each figure has.

1.

2.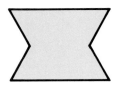

3.

4.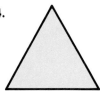

5.

6.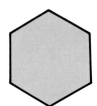

7.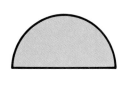

8.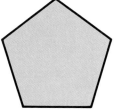

The red line is a line of symmetry.

Copy and complete.

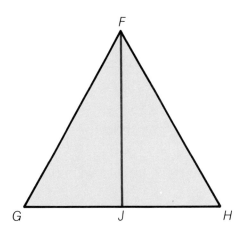

9. Triangle *FGJ* is congruent to triangle ▦.

10. Angle *G* is congruent to angle ▦.

11. Angle *GFJ* is congruent to angle ▦.

12. Angle *GJF* is congruent to angle ▦.

13. $\overline{FG}$ is congruent to ▦.

14. $\overline{GJ}$ is congruent to ▦.

Find each answer. Draw a diagram if you need to.

15. How many lines of symmetry does a square have?

★ 16. How many lines of symmetry does a circle have?

Some of the digits shown below have lines of symmetry.

1 2 3 4 5 6 7 8 9 0

17. Which digits have horizontal lines of symmetry?

18. Which digits have vertical lines of symmetry?

Space Figures

■ A **cube** is a **space figure**.
Each **face** is a square. A cube has
6 faces. Each **edge** is a line segment.
A cube has 12 edges. Point *W* is a vertex.
A cube has 8 vertices.

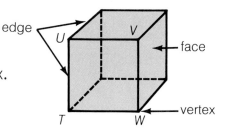

■ These space figures are **prisms**.

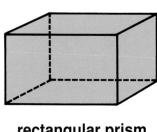 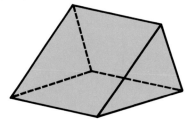 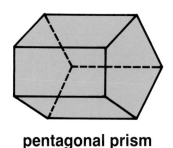

rectangular prism   **triangular prism**   **pentagonal prism**

■ These space figures are **pyramids**.

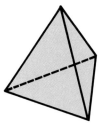 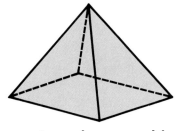 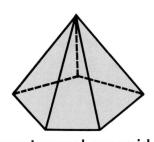

triangular pyramid   **rectangular pyramid**   **pentagonal pyramid**

■ These are space figures without straight edges.

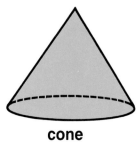 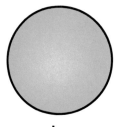 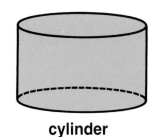

cone   **sphere**   **cylinder**

A cone has
one face that
is curved and
one face that
is flat.

A cylinder has
one face that
is curved and
two faces that
are flat.

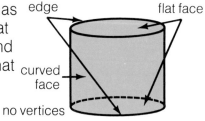

Try These

Name the shape of each object.

1.
2.
3.
4.

Exercises

Name the shape of each object.

1.
2.
3.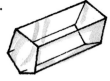
4.

Each pattern could be folded to make a space figure.
Name the shape of each figure.

5.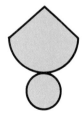
6.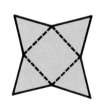
7.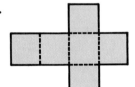
8.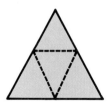

Copy and complete the table.

	9.	10.	11.	12.	13.	14.
Number of Faces						
Number of Vertices						
Number of Edges						

Solve each problem.

★ **15.** How many faces, edges, and vertices does a hexagonal prism have?

★ **16.** How many faces, edges, and vertices does a hexagonal pyramid have?

Graphing Ordered Pairs

■ (4, 2) is an **ordered pair** of numbers. An ordered pair names a point on a graph.

The point where the two number lines intersect is called the **origin**. To graph an ordered pair, start at the origin. The first number tells you how many units to move to the right. The second number tells you how many units to move up.

■ Graph (4, 2).

> Start at the origin.
> Count 4 units to the right.
> Then count 2 units up.

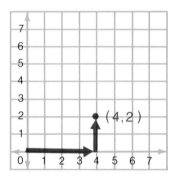

■ The order of the numbers is important. (2, 4) is different from (4, 2).

Graph (2, 4).

> Start at the origin.
> Count 2 units to the right.
> Then count 4 units up.

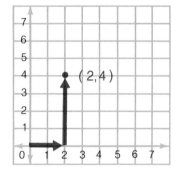

Try These

Name the point for each ordered pair.

1. (4, 7)   2. (7, 4)
3. (2, 5)   4. (5, 0)
5. (0, 0)   6. (0, 2)

Name the ordered pair for each point.

7. D   8. E
9. F   10. H
11. J   12. K

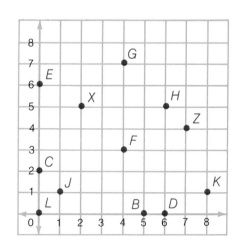

Exercises

Name the point for each ordered pair.

1. (3, 6)   **2.** (5, 3)   **3.** (3, 5)

4. (4, 0)   **5.** (0, 4)   **6.** (2, 3)

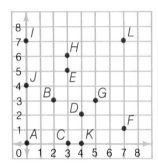

Name the ordered pair for each point.

7. *A*   **8.** *D*   **9.** *L*

10. *C*   **11.** *F*   **12.** *I*

Make a pair of axes on graph paper. Graph each ordered pair. Label each with its letter.

13. *M*(2, 4)   **14.** *N*(1, 5)   **15.** *P*(0, 3)   **16.** *Q*(6, 0)

17. *R*(3, 1)   **18.** *S*(5, 2)   **19.** *T*(5, 5)   **20.** *V*(0, 0)

THINK AND TRY

DRAWING SIMILAR FIGURES

You can draw similar figures using graph paper. To draw an enlargement of triangle *ABC* with sides twice as long, multiply each number in the ordered pairs for the vertices by 2. Graph the new ordered pairs, and then connect them.

Original Triangle	Enlargement
A(1, 1) ⟶	*P*(2, 2)
B(3, 1) ⟶	*Q*(6, 2)
C(4, 3) ⟶	*R*(8, 6)

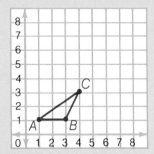

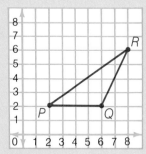

1. Write the ordered pair for each vertex of triangle *MNP*.

2. Multiply each number in the ordered pairs by 3.

3. Make a pair of axes on graph paper. Graph the new ordered pairs, and then connect them.

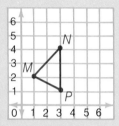

Problem Solving: Applications

READ
PLAN
DO
CHECK

USING A CIRCLE GRAPH

This **circle graph** shows the results of an election for mayor in Brant Rock. In this election, a candidate must have a majority of the votes to win. Having a majority means receiving more than half of the votes. Did any candidate have a majority?

You can look at the circle graph and easily see that no candidate had a majority. Ms. Rossetti received the most votes, and she received less than half.

Brant Rock Election Results

The total number of votes cast was 296. How many votes did Ms. Rossetti receive?

Look at the graph. Ms. Rossetti received $\frac{3}{8}$ of the votes.

Find $\frac{3}{8}$ of 296.

$$\frac{3}{8} \times \frac{296}{1} = \frac{3 \times \overset{37}{\cancel{296}}}{\underset{1}{\cancel{8}} \times 1}$$

$$= \frac{111}{1}$$

$$= 111$$

Ms. Rossetti received 111 of the votes.

How many more votes did Ms. Rossetti receive than Mr. Walker?

First, find $\frac{1}{4}$ of 296.   Then, subtract.

$$\frac{1}{4} \times \frac{296}{1} = \frac{1 \times \overset{74}{\cancel{296}}}{\underset{1}{\cancel{4}} \times 1}$$

$$= 74$$

$$\begin{array}{r} 111 \\ -\ 74 \\ \hline 37 \end{array}$$

Ms. Rossetti received 37 more votes than Mr. Walker.

Try These

Use the circle graph on page 322 to solve each problem.

1. How many votes did Mr. Jones receive?

2. How many votes did Ms. Adams receive?

3. Which two candidates received the same number of votes?

4. How many more votes did Ms. Adams receive than Mr. Jones?

Exercises

Use the circle graphs to solve each problem.

This circle graph shows the results of the Falls Village election. The total number of votes cast was 387.

1. Did any candidate have a majority? Who?

2. How many votes did Mr. Brown receive?

3. How many votes did Mr. Williams receive?

4. How many more votes did Mr. Williams receive than Ms. Davis?

Falls Village Election Results

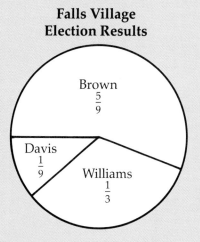

This circle graph shows Mr. Brown's campaign expenses. Altogether $4,300 was spent.

5. How much was spent for advertising?

6. How much was spent for telephones?

7. How much was spent for printing?

★ 8. What percent of the total was spent for telephones?

Brown Campaign Expenses

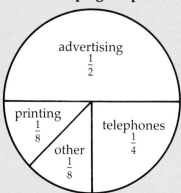

Candidate	Votes
Bell	45
O'Malley	18
Levin	9

★ 9. Draw a circle graph that shows the information in the table above. These are the results of the election of a sixth-grade representative to the student council.

Use this figure to answer exercises 1–8. (pp. 296–301)

1. Name five points.
2. Name four lines.
3. Name two line segments.
4. Name two intersecting lines.
5. Name two parallel lines.
6. Name two perpendicular lines.
7. Name three rays.
8. Name one right angle.

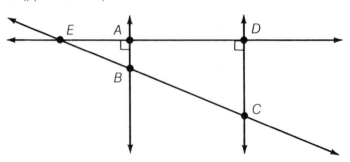

Find the measure of each angle. Write *right*, *acute*, or *obtuse*. (pp. 298–299)

9.  10. 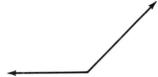 11.

Name each polygon. Give a special name for each triangle. (pp. 302–303, 308–309)

12. 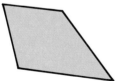 13.  14.   15.

Write a special name for each quadrilateral. (pp. 306–307)

16.  17.   18. 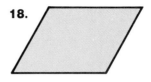 19.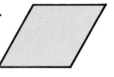

Are the figures similar? Write *yes* or *no*. (pp. 312–313)

20.  21. 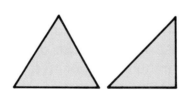 22.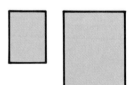

Use the circle to answer exercises 23–26.
The center of the circle is point P. (pp. 314–315).

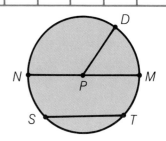

23. Name three radii.   **24.** Name a diameter.

25. Name a chord.   **26.** Find the length of a diameter.

Is the line a line of symmetry?
Write *yes* or *no*. (pp. 316–317)

Name the shape of each object.
(pp. 318–319)

27. 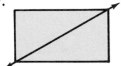   **28.** 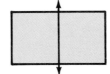   **29.**    **30.**

Name the point for each ordered pair. (pp. 320–321)

31. (3, 4)   **32.** (0, 0)   **33.** (5, 0)

Name the ordered pair for each point. (pp. 320–321)

34. D   **35.** E   **36.** F

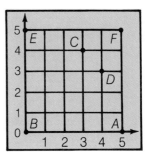

Solve each problem. (pp. 296–323)

37. A photo is being enlarged. The photo is 9 cm long and 6 cm wide. The enlargement is 15 cm long. How wide is it?

Nadine earned $80 during the month of May. This circle graph shows how she earned the money.

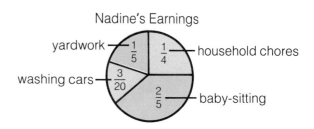

Nadine's Earnings

38. How did Nadine earn the most money?

39. How much did Nadine earn doing household chores?

40. How much did Nadine earn baby-sitting?

COMPUTERS AND PROBLEM SOLVING

■ An angle that measures exactly 90° is a right angle. Angles that measure less than 90° are acute angles. Those that measure more than 90° are obtuse angles.

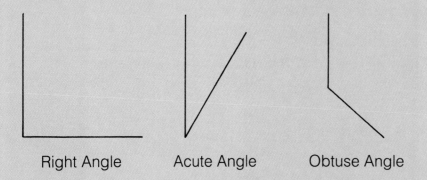

Right Angle   Acute Angle   Obtuse Angle

The procedure below uses this information to label an angle right, acute, or obtuse.

```
TO ANGLES :SIZE
IF :SIZE = 90 [PRINT[THAT IS A RIGHT ANGLE]STOP]
IF :SIZE < 90 [PRINT[THAT IS AN ACUTE ANGLE]STOP]
IF :SIZE > 90 [PRINT[THAT IS AN OBTUSE ANGLE]STOP]
END
```

The variable on the title line lets the user specify the angle to be tested. Then the computer tests the variable :SIZE against the three angle definitions.

Solve each problem.

1. What will the computer display if you type ANGLES 178?

2. What will the computer display if you type ANGLES 89?

3. What does the command STOP in the first, second, and third lines mean?

4. How many conditionals are tested in this procedure?

■ There are two ways to describe the corner of a polygon. You can measure the interior angle, the angle inside the polygon. Or you can measure the exterior angle. The exterior angle is always the same as the turn the turtle makes to form the corner.

Find the sum of exterior angles for each of these shapes.

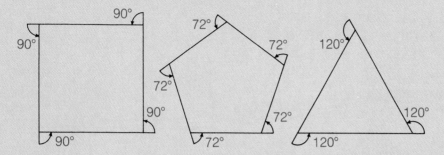

The exterior angles of any polygon add up to 360 degrees.

The procedure below divides 360 degrees by a number of angles and creates any polygon with sides 50 units long.

```
TO POLYGON :ANGLES
REPEAT :ANGLES [FD 50 LT 360 / :ANGLES]
END
```

Solve each problem.

1. How many left turns will the turtle make when drawing a hexagon? Is the number of turns always equal to the number of sides?

2. What would be the measure of each exterior angle in the case of a hexagon? Would you want the turtle to turn left six times by that amount?

ENRICHMENT

USING A COMPASS

Follow these instructions to make a design using a compass. In addition to a compass, you will need a piece of paper at least 8 inches wide and 8 inches long.

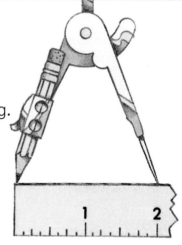

1. Set the distance between the point of the compass and the tip of the pencil at 2 inches.

   Draw all the circles in steps 2–5 without changing this distance.

2. Place the point of the compass in the center of the piece of paper. Draw a circle.

3. Place the point of the compass on any point of the circle. Draw another circle.

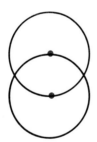

4. Place the point of the compass on one of the points where the two circles intersect. Draw another circle.

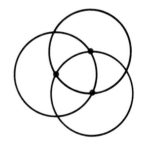

5. Continue drawing circles with centers at the points where the new circles intersect the first circle.

6. When you finish, you can color your design.

Try making other designs using a compass. You can also use a ruler.

Compute. Write each quotient as a mixed number or as a whole number.

1. $864 + 92 + 358$
2. $6,002 - 1,496$
3. 845×926
4. $658 \div 10$
5. $\$2.69 \times 75$
6. $19,038 \div 48$

Write >, <, or =.

7. $507 \,\blacksquare\, 570$
8. $6,521 \,\blacksquare\, 6,251$
9. $2,416,709 \,\blacksquare\, 2,146,907$
10. $1.049 \,\blacksquare\, 1.904$
11. $356.9 \,\blacksquare\, 365.9$
12. $18.020 \,\blacksquare\, 18.02$

Compute.

13. 5.6×0.5
14. $7 \div 1.4$
15. $3 - 0.096$
16. $4.5 + 7.98$

Copy and complete.

17. $40 \text{ mm} = \blacksquare \text{ cm}$
18. $6,000 \text{ mL} = \blacksquare \text{ L}$
19. $7,400 \text{ m} = \blacksquare \text{ km}$
20. $0.7 \text{ m} = \blacksquare \text{ cm}$
21. $9 \text{ dm} = \blacksquare \text{ cm}$
22. $5.6 \text{ km} = \blacksquare \text{ m}$
23. $2 \text{ gal} = \blacksquare \text{ qt}$
24. $6 \text{ yd} = \blacksquare \text{ ft}$
25. $3 \text{ lb} = \blacksquare \text{ oz}$

Find the least common multiple of each pair of numbers.

26. $3, 5$
27. $6, 8$
28. $11, 7$
29. $5, 4$
30. $10, 15$

Compute. Simplify if possible.

31. $\frac{7}{12} - \frac{4}{12}$
32. $2\frac{1}{4} \times 5$
33. $4\frac{7}{8} + 8\frac{1}{4}$
34. $3\frac{1}{2} \div 1\frac{1}{2}$

Solve each problem.

35. Jerry drove 80.5 km on Saturday and 156.9 km on Sunday. How many kilometers did he drive in the 2 days?

36. Chico weighed two bags of fertilizer. One bag weighed 4 lb 12 oz, and the other weighed 15 lb 7 oz. How much did they weigh altogether?

37. Angela is making half of a recipe that calls for $3\frac{1}{2}$ c of flour. How much flour should she use?

38. Terry worked from 1:45 P.M. to 5:30 P.M. How long did she work this afternoon?

SKILLS CHECK

Choose the correct answer.

1. Which is the number for 28 thousands?

- **a.** 2,800
- **b.** 28,000
- **c.** 28,000,000
- **d.** NG

2.   1,648
   $\times$ 35

- **a.** 13,184
- **b.** 57,680
- **c.** 60,880
- **d.** 502,680

3. $4,521 \div 9$

- **a.** 52 R3
- **b.** 62
- **c.** 502 R3
- **d.** NG

4. $7.6 - 0.327$

- **a.** 6.213
- **b.** 7.183
- **c.** 7.245
- **d.** NG

5. $7\overline{)52.64}$

- **a.** 7.36
- **b.** 7.52
- **c.** 8.09
- **d.** 9.26

6. Compute: 3^4

- **a.** 12
- **b.** 64
- **c.** 81
- **d.** NG

7. Find the least common multiple of 2 and 9.

- **a.** 6
- **b.** 18
- **c.** 24
- **d.** 36

8. $\dfrac{5}{6} = \dfrac{\blacksquare}{24}$

- **a.** 18
- **b.** 20
- **c.** 30
- **d.** 48

9. $3\dfrac{2}{3} \div \dfrac{2}{3}$

- **a.** $\dfrac{2}{11}$
- **b.** $2\dfrac{4}{9}$
- **c.** $2\dfrac{2}{3}$
- **d.** $5\dfrac{1}{2}$

10. Mrs. Valdez buys a dress for $34.88. She gives the clerk $50. How much change should Mrs. Valdez receive?

- **a.** $6.88
- **b.** $14.12
- **c.** $15.12
- **d.** $84.88

11. Mr. Delia orders 8 crates of tomatoes. Each crate weighs 16.85 kg. What is the total weight of his order?

- **a.** 129.56 kg
- **b.** 134.8 kg
- **c.** 138.98 kg
- **d.** 156.2 kg

12. Georgia has 50 books. $\dfrac{1}{5}$ of them are mystery books. How many of the books are mysteries?

- **a.** 5 books
- **b.** 10 books
- **c.** 25 books
- **d.** 40 books

12

PERIMETER, AREA, AND VOLUME

Perimeter

- The **perimeter** of a polygon is the distance around it. To find the perimeter of a polygon, add the lengths of its sides.

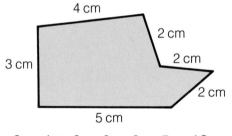

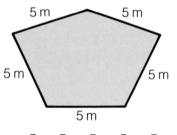

$$3 + 4 + 2 + 2 + 2 + 5 = 18$$

The perimeter is 18 cm.

$$5 + 5 + 5 + 5 + 5 = 25$$

The perimeter is 25 m.

- To find the perimeter of a rectangle, you can add the lengths of its sides. Since the opposite sides are the same length, you can use this rule to find the perimeter:

> *To find the perimeter (P) of a rectangle, add twice the length (l) and twice the width (w).*
>
> $$P = (2 \times l) + (2 \times w)$$

Find the perimeter of this rectangle.

$$
\begin{aligned}
P &= (2 \times l) + (2 \times w) \\
&= (2 \times 7) + (2 \times 3) \\
&= 14 + 6 \\
&= 20
\end{aligned}
$$

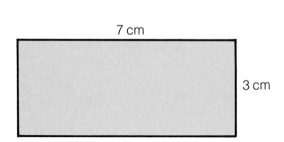

The perimeter is 20 cm.

Try These

Find the perimeter of each polygon.

1.

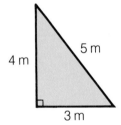

2.

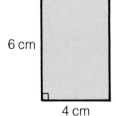

3.

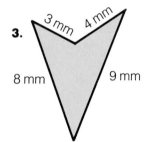

Exercises

Find the perimeter of each polygon.

1.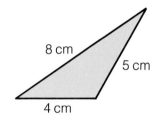

8 cm

5 cm

4 cm

2.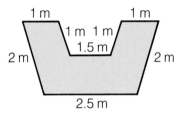

1 m 1 m

1 m 1 m

1.5 m

2 m 2 m

2.5 m

3.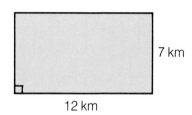

7 km

12 km

Find the perimeter of each rectangle with the given length and width.

4. 18 cm and 8 cm

5. 30 m and 16 m

6. 26 km and 13 km

7. 9.5 mm and 1.7 mm

8. $1\frac{1}{4}$ cm and $\frac{1}{2}$ cm

9. 42.8 m and 25.2 m

Find each missing measurement.

★ **10.** perimeter = 7.4 cm

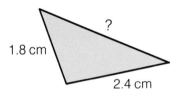

?

1.8 cm

2.4 cm

★ **11.** perimeter = 20 cm

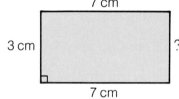

7 cm

3 cm

?

7 cm

★ **12.** perimeter = 42 m

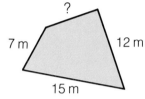

?

7 m

12 m

15 m

Solve each problem.

13. Pete's home is on this piece of land. What is the perimeter of Pete's land?

14. What is the perimeter of Pete's swimming pool?

15. Pete wants to put a fence around his garden. How much fencing does he need?

★ **16.** The perimeter of Pete's house is 150 m. What is the length of the front of Pete's house?

★ **17.** A neighbor's house has a rectangular shape. The front of the house measures 30 m. The perimeter is 90 m. How long is each side of the house?

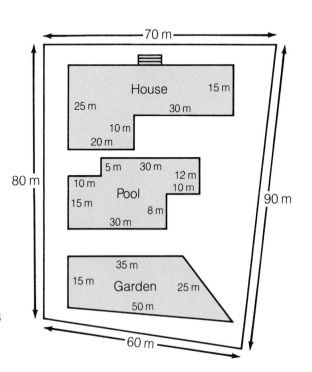

70 m

House

15 m

25 m

30 m

10 m

20 m

80 m

5 m   30 m

10 m

Pool

12 m

10 m

15 m

8 m

30 m

90 m

35 m

15 m

Garden

25 m

50 m

60 m

Area of a Rectangle and a Parallelogram

■ The **area** of a region is the number of square units needed to cover the region. A **square centimeter (cm²)** is a unit used to measure area.

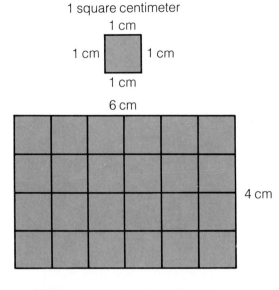

1 square centimeter

You can count the square centimeters to find the area of this rectangle. The area is 24 square centimeters (cm²).

You can also multiply to find the area.

Think: 4 rows
6 square centimeters in each row
$6 \times 4 = 24$

The area is 24 cm².

> To find the area (A) of a rectangle, multiply the length (l) and the width (w).
>
> $$A = l \times w$$

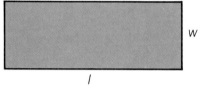

The **square meter (m²)**, the **square millimeter (mm²)**, and the **square kilometer (km²)** are also units used to measure area.

■ A parallelogram can be rearranged to form a rectangle.

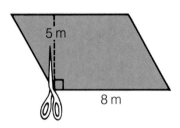

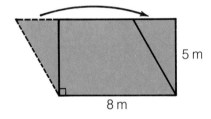

The **base** is 8 m. The **height** is 5 m.

The length is 8 m. The width is 5 m.

> To find the area (A) of a parallelogram, multiply the base (b) and the height (h).
>
> $$A = b \times h$$

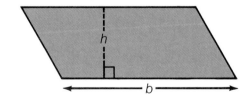

Find the area of the parallelogram.

The area is 40 m².

$A = b \times h$
$= 8 \times 5$
$= 40$

Try These

Find the area of each polygon.

1.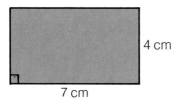

4 cm
7 cm

2.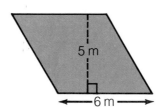

5 m
6 m

3.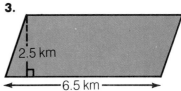

2.5 km
6.5 km

Exercises

Find the area of each polygon.

1.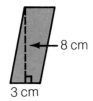

8 cm
3 cm

2.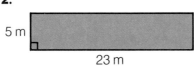

5 m
23 m

3.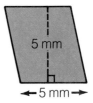

5 mm
5 mm

4. a rectangle 0.9 m long and 0.4 m wide

5. a parallelogram with base of 15 mm and height of 17 mm

6. a rectangle with width of 8.6 cm and length of 1.2 cm

Copy and complete the table.

	Rectangle			
	length	width	perimeter	area
7.	8 m	8 m	▨	▨
8.	16 cm	4 cm	▨	▨
9.	32 mm	9.5 mm	▨	▨

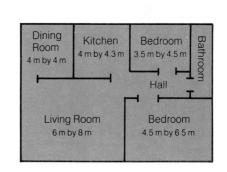

Dining Room 4 m by 4 m · Kitchen 4 m by 4.3 m · Bedroom 3.5 m by 4.5 m · Bathroom · Hall · Living Room 6 m by 8 m · Bedroom 4.5 m by 6.5 m

Solve each problem. Find each area.

The floor plan shows the measurements of each room.

10. the kitchen   **11.** the dining room

12. the living room   **13.** the larger bedroom

The map shows fields planted with corn.

★ **14.** How many square meters have been planted altogether?

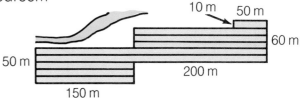

10 m · 50 m · 60 m · 50 m · 200 m · 150 m

Problem Solving: Strategies

ORGANIZING INFORMATION

Experimenting by **making a drawing** is a strategy that can help you solve a problem.

Cindy is planning a rectangular garden. She has 100 meters of material to build a fence around the garden. She wants the garden to have the greatest possible area.

Cindy experiments with diagrams. Here is one of them.

The perimeter is 100 meters.
What is the area?

$$A = l \times w$$
$$= 48 \times 2$$
$$= 96$$

48 m

2 m

The area is 96 square meters.

Here is another diagram.

45 m

5 m

The perimeter is 100 meters.
What is the area?

Is the area greater or less than the area of the first diagram?

Using the Strategy

Find the perimeter and the area of each figure.

1.
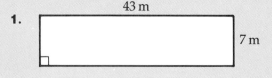
43 m
7 m

2.
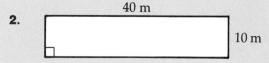
40 m
10 m

3.
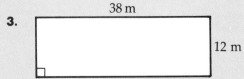
38 m
12 m

4.
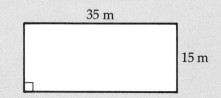
35 m
15 m

5.
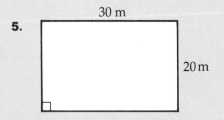
30 m
20 m

6.
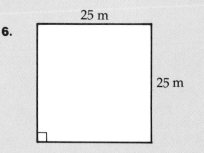
25 m
25 m

Solve each problem.

7. Draw a few more diagrams of a rectangular garden with a perimeter of 100 m. Find the area of each rectangular garden.

8. Copy and complete the table. Use the widths, lengths, and areas of all rectangles for which you have found the area.

9. Which rectangle has the greatest possible area?

10. Which rectangle has the least possible area?

Rectangles with Perimeter of 100 m		
width (in meters)	length (in meters)	area (in square meters)
2	48	96
5	45	225
7	43	
10	40	
12	38	
15	35	
20	30	
25	25	

Suppose Cindy has only 80 m of fencing.

11. Guess which rectangle with a perimeter of 80 m would have the greatest possible area.

12. Check your guess by experimenting and making a table.

ACTIVITY

EXPERIMENTING WITH PERIMETERS

Use a sheet of graph paper. 1 unit is the width of one of the squares on the graph paper. 1 square unit is the area of one of these squares.

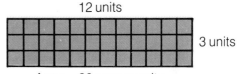

12 units

3 units

Area: 36 square units
Perimeter: 30 units

1. Cut out several rectangles that have an area of 36 square units each. Then find the perimeter of each rectangle.

2. Make a table to record your results.

3. Guess which rectangle would have the smallest perimeter.

4. Repeat the experiment for rectangles with an area of 16 square units. Guess which rectangle would have the smallest perimeter.

Area of a Triangle

■ A parallelogram can be cut into two congruent triangles.

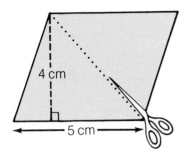

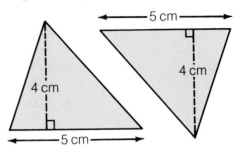

Find the area of the parallelogram.

$$A = b \times h$$
$$= 5 \times 4$$
$$= 20$$

The area of the parallelogram is 20 cm².

Find the area of each of the triangles.

$$A = \frac{1}{2} \times 20$$
$$= 10$$

The area of each triangle is $\frac{1}{2}$ the area of the parallelogram.

The area of each triangle is 10 cm².

> To find the area (A) of a triangle, multiply the length of a base (b) and the height (h). Then multiply by $\frac{1}{2}$.
>
> $$A = \frac{1}{2} \times b \times h$$

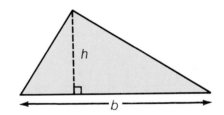

■ Find the area of each triangle.

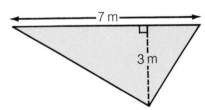

$$A = \frac{1}{2} \times b \times h$$
$$= \frac{1}{2} \times 7 \times 3$$
$$= 10\frac{1}{2}$$

The area is $10\frac{1}{2}$ m².

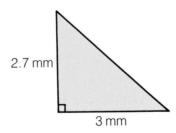

$$A = \frac{1}{2} \times b \times h$$
$$= \frac{1}{2} \times 3 \times 2.7$$
$$= 4.05$$

The area is 4.05 mm².

Try These

Find the area of each figure.

1.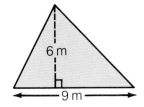

6 m
9 m

2.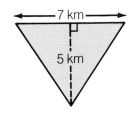

7 km
5 km

3.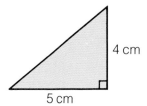

4 cm
5 cm

Exercises

Find the area of each figure.

1.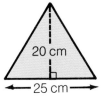

20 cm
25 cm

2.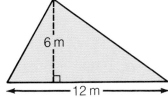

6 m
12 m

3.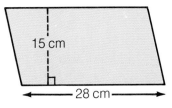

15 cm
28 cm

4.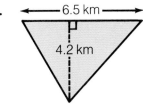

6.5 km
4.2 km

5.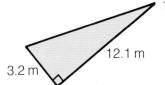

12.1 m
3.2 m

★ **6.**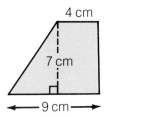

4 cm
7 cm
9 cm

Use the distances shown to estimate each area.

7. pond A **8.** pond B **9.** pond C

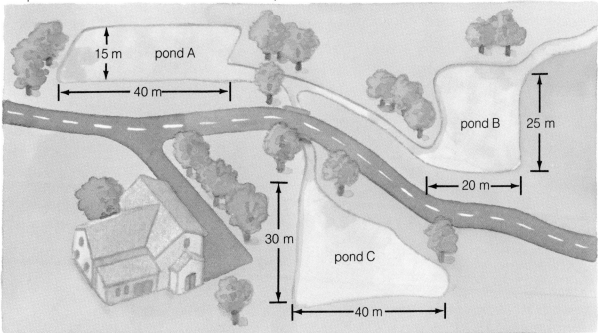

Circumference of a Circle

- The distance around a circle is the **circumference** of the circle.

  There is a relationship between the circumference of a circle and its diameter.

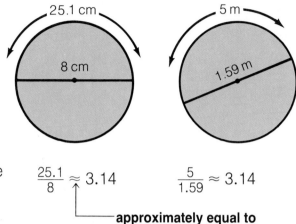

Find the ratio of the circumference of each circle to its diameter.

$$\frac{25.1}{8} \approx 3.14 \qquad \frac{5}{1.59} \approx 3.14$$

approximately equal to

The ratio of the circumference of any circle to its diameter is always the same. It is called **pi (π)**. To the nearest ten-thousandth, π is 3.1416. You can use 3.14 as an **approximation** for π.

> To find the circumference (C) of a circle, multiply π and the diameter (d).
> $$C = \pi \times d$$
> $$C \approx 3.14 \times d$$

- Find the circumference of each circle.

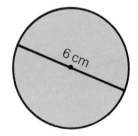

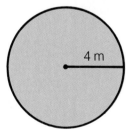

The diameter of a circle is twice the radius. So the diameter is 8 m.

$$C = \pi \times d$$
$$\approx 3.14 \times d$$
$$\approx 3.14 \times 6$$
$$\approx 18.84$$

The circumference is approximately 18.84 cm.

$$C = \pi \times d$$
$$\approx 3.14 \times d$$
$$\approx 3.14 \times 8$$
$$\approx 25.12$$

The circumference is approximately 25.12 m.

Try These

Find the circumference of each circle. Use 3.14 for π.

1.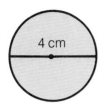
4 cm

2.
5 mm

3.
23 m

Exercises

Find the circumference of each circle. Use 3.14 for π.

1.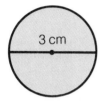
3 cm

2.
11.7 m

3.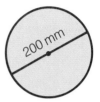
200 mm

4. a circle with diameter of 8 cm

5. a circle with diameter of 126 m

6. a circle with radius of 5 cm

7. a circle with radius of 10.3 m

Solve each problem. Use 3.14 for π.

8. A bicycle wheel has a diameter of 21 cm. Find its circumference.

9. The radius of Ali's tricycle wheel is 8.5 cm. Find the circumference of the wheel.

10. Matt rides his bicycle around a circular track. The radius of the track is 29 m. What is the distance around the track?

★ **11.** Strawberry Pond Park has a circular bicycle path with a circumference of 671.96 m. Find the diameter of the bicycle path.

KEEPING IN SHAPE

1. $\frac{1}{2} \times \frac{3}{4}$

2. $\frac{2}{4} \times 1\frac{11}{22}$

3. $6\frac{1}{2} \div 1\frac{1}{2}$

4. $8 - \frac{2}{3}$

5. $7\frac{2}{9} \div 1\frac{1}{4}$

6. $5\frac{2}{3} + 6\frac{1}{9}$

7. $3\frac{1}{2} - 1\frac{1}{4}$

8. $9\frac{1}{5} \times 1\frac{2}{3}$

Area of a Circle

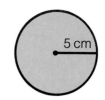

- Suppose you want to find the area of a circle with a radius of 5 cm.

Draw a square using two radii that are perpendicular. Make three more squares just like that using two more radii.

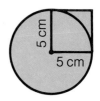

The area of each of the small squares is 25 cm², the radius multiplied by itself.

The area of the large square is 4 times the area of each of the small squares. So the area of the large square is 100 cm², or 4 times the radius multiplied by itself.

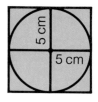

The area of the circle is less than 4 times the radius multiplied by itself. But the area is more than 2 times the radius multiplied by itself.

To estimate the area of the circle, you can multiply 3 times the radius multiplied by itself. So the area of the circle is about 75 cm².

The area of a circle is actually a little more than 3 times the radius multiplied by itself.

> To find the area (A) of a circle, multiply the radius (r) by itself. Then multiply the result by π.
>
> $A = \pi \times r \times r$　　or　$A = \pi \times r^2$
> $A \approx 3.14 \times r \times r$　or　$A \approx 3.14 \times r^2$

Find the area of the circle.

$$A = \pi \times r \times r$$
$$\approx 3.14 \times r \times r$$
$$\approx 3.14 \times 5 \times 5$$
$$\approx 3.14 \times 25$$
$$\approx 78.5$$

The area is approximately 78.5 cm².

- Find the area of the top of a merry-go-round of radius 7.1 m.

$$A = \pi \times r \times r$$
$$\approx 3.14 \times r \times r$$
$$\approx 3.14 \times 7.1 \times 7.1$$
$$\approx 3.14 \times 50.41$$
$$\approx 158.2874$$

The area is approximately 158.2874 m².

Try These

Find the area of each circle. Use 3.14 for π.

1.
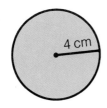
4 cm

2.
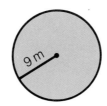
9 m

3.

14 km

Exercises

Find the area of each circle. Use 3.14 for π.

1.
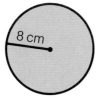
8 cm

2.
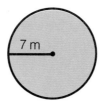
7 m

3.

16 mm

4.

6.6 m

★ **5.**
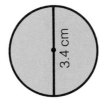
3.4 cm

★ **6.**

206 km

7. a circle with radius of 9.4 km

8. a circle with radius of 19 m

★ **9.** a circle with diameter of 6.4 cm

★ **10.** a circle with diameter of 22.2 m

Solve each problem. Use 3.14 for π.

11. A circular room has a radius of 7 m. What is the area of the room?

★ **12.** Ann painted the top of a round table. The diameter is 7.2 m. What area did she paint?

THINK AND TRY

USING A DIAGRAM

A record has a radius of 8.7 cm. The label has a radius of 2.9 cm. Find the area of the record that is not covered by the label. Round to the nearest 10 square centimeters. Use 3.14 for π.

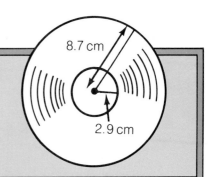
8.7 cm
2.9 cm

Surface Area

■ The total **surface area** of a space figure is the sum of the areas of all the faces.

The figure shown is a rectangular prism.
Next to it is a pattern for the rectangular prism.
Find the total surface area of the prism.

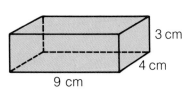

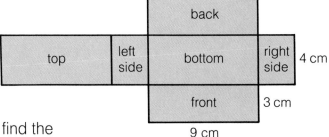

You can use a table to make sure you find the area of each face of the rectangular prism.

Face	Area of Face
top	$9 \times 4 = 36$
bottom	$9 \times 4 = 36$
front	$9 \times 3 = 27$
back	$9 \times 3 = 27$
left side	$4 \times 3 = 12$
right side	$4 \times 3 = 12$
Total:	150

The total surface area of the rectangular prism is 150 cm^2.

■ The figure to the right is a cube.
Below it is a pattern for the cube.
Find its total surface area.

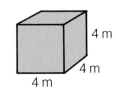

A cube has 6 faces.
All the faces of a cube have the same area.

To find the surface area of a cube, find the area of one face and then multiply by 6.

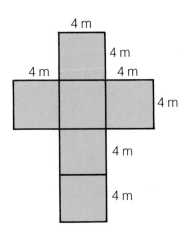

Area of one face: $4 \times 4 = 16$ m^2
Total surface area: $6 \times 16 = 96$ m^2

The total surface area of the cube is 96 m^2.

Try These

Find the total surface area of each figure.

1.
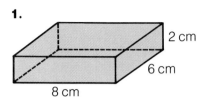
2 cm
6 cm
8 cm

2.
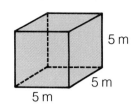
5 m
5 m
5 m

3.
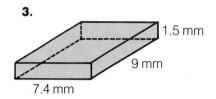
1.5 mm
9 mm
7.4 mm

Exercises

Find the total surface area of each figure.

1.
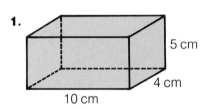
5 cm
4 cm
10 cm

2.
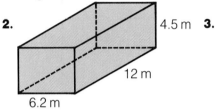
4.5 m
12 m
6.2 m

3.
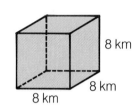
8 km
8 km
8 km

4.

9 cm
16 cm
32 cm

5.

25 cm
6.5 cm
18 cm

6.
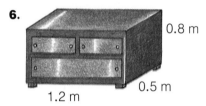
0.8 m
1.2 m
0.5 m

★ 7.
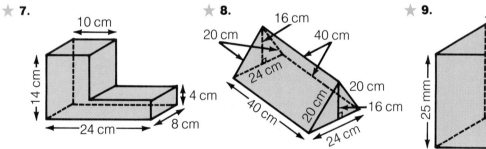
10 cm
14 cm
4 cm
24 cm
8 cm

★ 8.
16 cm
20 cm
40 cm
24 cm
40 cm
20 cm
20 cm
16 cm
24 cm

★ 9.
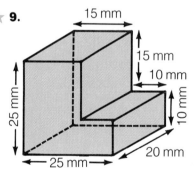
15 mm
15 mm
10 mm
25 mm
10 mm
25 mm
20 mm

Solve each problem. You may use a calculator to check.

10. What is the total surface area of a cardboard box that is 1.2 m long, 0.6 m wide, and 0.3 m high?

11. Find the total surface area of a number cube. Each edge measures 2.1 cm.

★ 12. What is the total surface area of a cardboard box that is 61 cm long, 40 cm wide, 50 cm high, and has no top?

★ 13. The total surface area of a cube is 150 m². What is the length of each edge of the cube?

Volume

- The **volume** of a space figure is the number of cubic units needed to fill it. A **cubic centimeter (cm³)** is a unit used to measure volume.

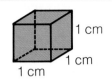

1 cubic centimeter

To find the volume of this rectangular prism, think of filling it with cubic centimeters.

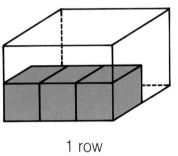

1 row
3 cubes

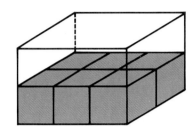

1 layer
3 × 2 cubes

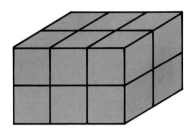

2 layers
3 × 2 × 2 cubes

The volume of the rectangular prism is 12 cm³.

- You can multiply to find the volume of any rectangular prism.

> *To find the volume (V) of a rectangular prism, multiply the length (l) and the width (w) and the height (h).*
>
> $V = l \times w \times h$

The **cubic meter (m³)**, the **cubic millimeter (mm³)**, and the **cubic kilometer (km³)** are also units used to measure volume.

Find the volume of this rectangular prism.

$V = l \times w \times h$
$\quad = 5 \times 4 \times 3$
$\quad = 60$

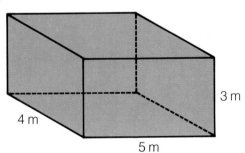

The volume of the rectangular prism is 60 m³.

- Find the volume of this cube.

$V = l \times w \times h$
$\quad = 10 \times 10 \times 10$
$\quad = 1{,}000$

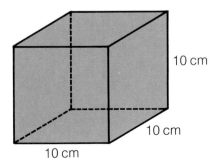

The volume of the cube is 1,000 cm³.

Try These

Find the volume of each rectangular prism.

1.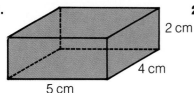
5 cm | 4 cm | 2 cm

2.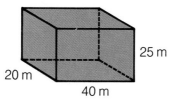
20 m | 40 m | 25 m

3.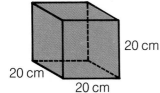
25 mm | 20 mm | 10 mm

Exercises

Find the volume of each rectangular prism.

1.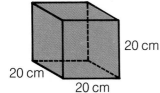
20 cm | 20 cm | 20 cm

2.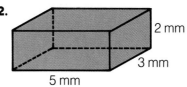
5 mm | 3 mm | 2 mm

3.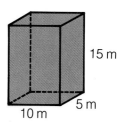
10 m | 5 m | 15 m

Alice has a new aquarium. It is 30 cm long and 20 cm wide. She filled it with water to a depth of 20 cm.

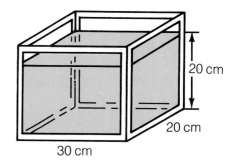
20 cm | 20 cm | 30 cm

Solve each problem.

4. Find the volume of the water.

★ **5.** What is the volume of the water in cubic meters?

THINK AND TRY

USING RELATIONSHIPS

1 cm³ holds 1 mL of water.
    1,000 mL = 1 L
A cube that is 10 cm on each side holds 1 L.

10 cm → | 10 cm → | 10 cm | 1 cm | 1 cm | 1 cm

1. How many milliliters of water are in Alice's aquarium?

2. How many liters of water is that?

1 mL of water weighs about 1 g.

3. About how much does the water in Alice's aquarium weigh in grams?

4. About how much does the water in Alice's aquarium weigh in kilograms?

Customary Units

■ The **square inch (in.²)**, the **square foot (ft²)**, and the **square yard (yd²)** are used to measure area.

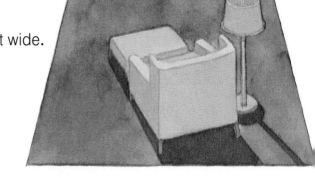

Find the area of a rug that is 8 ft long and 12 ft wide.

$$A = l \times w$$
$$= 8 \times 12$$
$$= 96$$

The area of the rug is 96 ft².

■ The **cubic inch (in.³)**, the **cubic foot (ft³)**, and the **cubic yard (yd³)** are used to measure volume.

Find the volume of a box that measures 20 in. long, 15 in. wide, and 12 in. high.

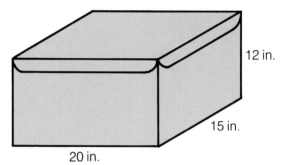

$$V = l \times w \times h$$
$$= 20 \times 15 \times 12$$
$$= 3,600$$

The volume of the box is 3,600 in.³.

Try These

Find the area of each figure. Use 3.14 for π when necessary.

1.

14 ft

2.

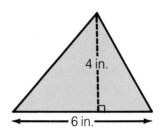

4 in.

6 in.

3.

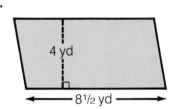

4 yd

8½ yd

Find the volume of each rectangular prism.

4.

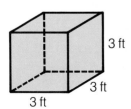

3 ft

3 ft

3 ft

5.

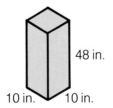

48 in.

10 in.   10 in.

6.

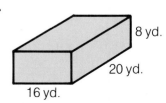

8 yd.

20 yd.

16 yd.

Exercises

Find the area of each figure.

1.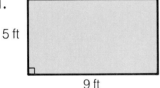
5 ft
9 ft

2.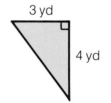
3 yd
4 yd

3.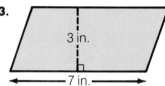
3 in.
7 in.

4.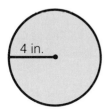
4 in.

5.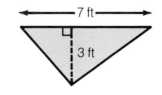
7 ft
3 ft

6.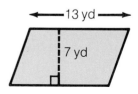
13 yd
7 yd

Find the circumference and the area of each circle. Use 3.14 for π.

7. a circle of radius 11 in.

★ **8.** a circle of diameter 12 ft

Find the volume of each rectangular prism.

9.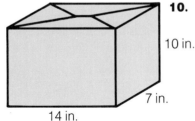
10 in.
7 in.
14 in.

10.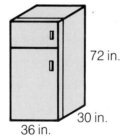
72 in.
36 in.
30 in.

★ **11.**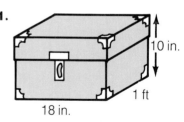
10 in.
1 ft
18 in.

Solve each problem.

12. Helen's house measures 55 ft by 40 ft. Helen wants to build a rectangular patio 36 ft long and 12 ft wide. What area will Helen's patio cover?

★ **13.** The long side of the patio is next to the house. Leo will build a fence around the other three sides of the patio. How many feet of fencing will Leo need?

★ **14.** Helen is going to cover the patio with tiles. There are tiles that measure 6 in. on each side. How many would Helen need? Use your answer to exercise 12 to solve this problem.

★ **15.** 6 tiles that measure 6 in. on each side cost $3.45. 6 tiles that measure 12 in. on each side cost $13.50. Which tiles should Helen buy to save money?

Problem Solving: Applications

MULTISTEP PROBLEMS

Becky and Janet are going to open an orange juice stand. They plan to sell freshly squeezed orange juice. They will use 8 ounces of juice for each serving. They want to know what their total cost per serving will be.

This is the information they gather:

> Juice oranges cost $.10 each. It takes 5 of these oranges to make about 8 ounces of juice. A package of 25 paper cups costs $1.00.

Step 1 Multiply to find how much 5 oranges will cost.

$$5 \times \$.10 = \$.50$$

5 oranges will cost $.50.

Step 2 Divide to find how much each paper cup will cost.

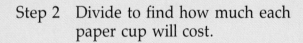

$$
\begin{array}{r}
\$\,.04 \\
25\overline{)\$1.00} \\
\underline{1\;00} \\
0
\end{array}
$$

Each paper cup will cost $.04.

Step 3 Add to find their total cost per serving.

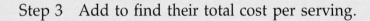

$$
\begin{array}{r}
\$.50 \\
+\;.04 \\
\hline
\$.54
\end{array}
$$

Their total cost per serving will be $.54.

Try These

Solve each problem.
Use the information given on page 350 if necessary.

1. Becky and Janet bought 2 packages of paper cups and 250 oranges. They bought materials to make a sign for $4.88. What was the total cost of their purchases?

2. Becky and Janet sold 50 servings of orange juice the first day. They charged $.75 per serving. How much money did they collect?

3. How much money did the girls have left after they subtracted their expenses? (You will need to use the answers to exercises 1 and 2.)

4. Becky and Janet divided the money they had left equally. How much did each of them take?

Exercises

Solve each problem. Explain the way you solved each problem.
Use the information given on page 350 if necessary.

1. On the second day, Becky and Janet bought 3 packages of paper cups and 400 oranges. What was the total cost of their purchases?

2. Becky and Janet sold 63 servings of orange juice the second day. They charged $.75 per serving. How much money did they collect?

3. How much money did Becky and Janet have left after they subtracted their expenses for the second day?

4. How much more money would the girls have collected the second day if they had charged $.85 per serving?

5. At the beginning of the third day, the girls raised the price to $.85 per serving. They sold 59 servings. How much money did they collect?

6. How much more money did Becky and Janet collect on the third day than on the second day?

7. Becky and Janet kept the price at $.85 per serving the fourth and fifth days. The graph shows how many servings of orange juice were sold on each of the first 5 days. How much money did they collect altogether?

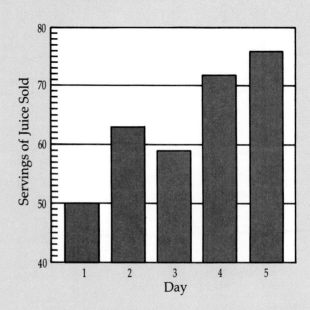

Find the perimeter of each polygon. (pp. 332–333)

1.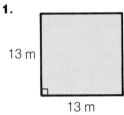
13 m
13 m

2.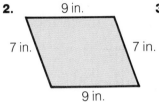
9 in.
7 in.
7 in.
9 in.

3.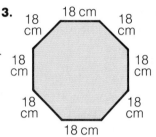
18 cm
18 cm
18 cm
18 cm
18 cm
18 cm
18 cm
18 cm

4.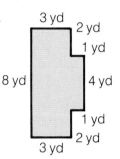
3 yd
2 yd
1 yd
8 yd
4 yd
1 yd
3 yd
2 yd

Find the area of each polygon. (pp. 334–335, 338–339)

5.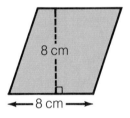
8 cm
8 cm

6.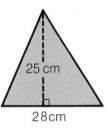
25 cm
28 cm

7.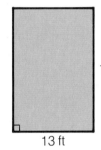
19 ft
13 ft

8.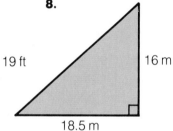
16 m
18.5 m

Find the circumference of each circle. Use 3.14 for π. (pp. 340–341)

9.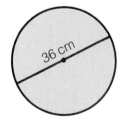
36 cm

10.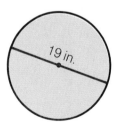
19 in.

11.
52 mm

12.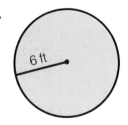
6 ft

Find the area of each circle. Use 3.14 for π. (pp. 342–343)

13.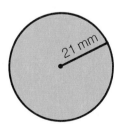
21 mm

14.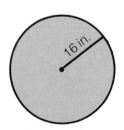
16 in.

15.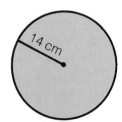
14 cm

Find the volume and the total surface area of each rectangular prism. (pp. 344–347)

16.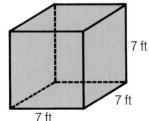
7 ft
7 ft
7 ft

17.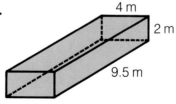
4 m
2 m
9.5 m

18.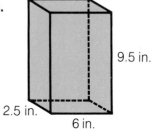
9.5 in.
2.5 in.
6 in.

Solve each problem. (pp. 332–351)

19. A rectangular lot is 60 m long and 35 m wide. There is a fence around the lot. How long is the fence?

20. A triangular piece of metal has a base of 15 cm and a height of 7 cm. What is its area?

21. The top of a drum has a radius of 7 in. What is the area of the top of the drum?

22. A sheet of paneling for a living room measures 4 ft by 8 ft. What is its area?

23. Jennifer is going to panel one wall of her room. The wall is 16 ft long and 8 ft high. What is the area of the wall?

24. How many 4-ft by 8-ft sheets of paneling will Jennifer need to cover her wall? Use the answers to exercises 22 and 23.

25. Derek is wrapping a gift for his father. The gift box is 45 cm long, 30 cm wide, and 25 cm high. What is the total surface area of the gift box?

26. Gloria is packing a storage box with winter clothes. The box is 5 ft long, 3 ft wide, and 2 ft high. What is the volume of the storage box?

27. A farmer is building a corral along a river. He has 60 yd of fencing. The river will be the fourth side of the corral. Experiment with rectangles for which the sum of the length and twice the width is 60 yd. Copy and complete the table for at least 4 rectangles. What measurements gave the greatest possible area?

Length (in yd)	Width (in yd)	Length Plus Twice Width	Area (in yd²)
50	5	60	250
40	10	▦	▦
30	15	▦	▦
▦	▦	60	▦

COMPUTERS AND
PROBLEM SOLVING

Use this procedure to get the turtle to draw a circle.

```
TO CIRCLE :SIZE
REPEAT 360 [FD :SIZE RT 1]
END
```

It takes 360 one-degree turns to complete the circle. The size of the circle is determined by the distance the turtle travels between turns.

The turtle needs to know the circumference of the circle. To specify a circle of a certain radius, you must add lines to the program that will calculate the circumference from the radius.

```
TO CIRCLE :RADIUS
SPLITSCREEN
PRINT SENTENCE [THE RADIUS IS] :RADIUS
PRINT SENTENCE [THE CIRCUMFERENCE IS]
    2 * :RADIUS *    3.14
PRINT SENTENCE [THE AREA IS] 3.14 * :RADIUS *
    :RADIUS
REPEAT 360 [FD 2 * :RADIUS * 3.14 / 360 RT 1]
END
```

The three PRINT command lines show the relationship between the radius, circumference, and area. The operation SENTENCE is used after each PRINT command to combine the rest of each line into a single list.

Solve each problem.

1. In the fourth line of the procedure, what does 2 * :RADIUS * 3.14 calculate?

2. What is the final calculation of the sixth line of the procedure?

If you divide a square into four smaller squares, it's easy to tell that each small square is one-fourth of the area of the large square.

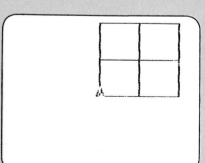

```
TO DIVIDESQUARE
REPEAT 4 [FD 80 RT 90]
REPEAT 4 [REPEAT 4 [FD 40 RT 90] FD 80 RT 90]
END
```

The procedure below uses CIRCLE three times to draw a large circle and divide it into four equal areas.

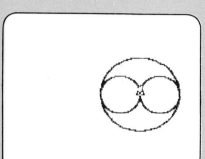

```
TO DIVIDECIRCLE
CIRCLE 40
CIRCLE 20
PU RT 90 FD 40 PD LT 90
CIRCLE 20
END
```

Solve each problem.

1. The top and bottom sections of the large circle are not the same shape as the circular side areas. Are they the same area? How do you know?

2. What happens in the fourth line of the procedure DIVIDECIRCLE?

ENRICHMENT

SURFACE AREA OF A CYLINDER

The can of tomatoes is shaped like a cylinder.
The top and bottom of the can are circles. When cut and
laid out flat, the curved face forms a rectangle whose
length is the circumference of each of the circles.

To find the surface area of the can, add the areas of
the top circle, the bottom circle, and the rectangle.

1. Find the area of the top.

$$A = \pi \times r \times r$$
$$\approx 3.14 \times r \times r$$
$$\approx 3.14 \times 6 \times 6$$
$$\approx 3.14 \times 36$$
$$\approx 113.04$$

The area of the top is approximately
113.04 cm². The area of the bottom
is also approximately 113.04 cm².

2. Find the area of the rectangle.

First find the circumference of each
of the circles. The diameter of each
of the circles is 12 cm.

$$C = \pi \times d$$
$$\approx 3.14 \times d$$
$$\approx 3.14 \times 12$$
$$\approx 37.68$$

The circumference is 37.68 cm.

Find the area of the rectangle.

$$A = l \times w$$
$$\approx 37.68 \times 15$$
$$\approx 565.2$$

The area of the rectangle is
approximately 565.2 cm².

3. Add the surface areas.

top	113.04 cm²
bottom	113.04 cm²
rectangle	+565.2 cm²
total	791.28 cm²

The surface area of the cylinder is
approximately 791.28 cm².

Find the surface area of each object. Use 3.14 for π.

1.
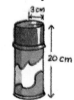

2.

3.

4.
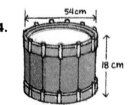

Multiply or divide. Write each quotient as a whole number or as a decimal.

1. 5.8×7.2 **2.** $7.5 \div 0.15$ **3.** 39.1×20.1

4. $0.8 \div 0.25$ **5.** 39.86×0.7 **6.** $172.08 \div 3.6$

Write each fraction or mixed number as a decimal.

7. $\frac{9}{10}$ **8.** $\frac{13}{20}$ **9.** $\frac{3}{4}$ **10.** $\frac{39}{50}$ **11.** $\frac{18}{25}$ **12.** $\frac{17}{100}$

13. $28\frac{1}{2}$ **14.** $\frac{1}{4}$ **15.** $\frac{4}{5}$ **16.** $7\frac{17}{20}$ **17.** $8\frac{2}{5}$

Write >, <, or =.

18. $39.5 \blacksquare 39.50$ **19.** $18.62 \blacksquare 81.26$ **20.** $107.1 \blacksquare 170.1$

21. $229.01 \blacksquare 229.10$ **22.** $56.3 \blacksquare 56.300$ **23.** $92.70 \blacksquare 90.72$

Compute. Rename when necessary.

24. $\begin{array}{r} 5 \text{ ft } 7 \text{ in.} \\ + 4 \text{ ft } 2 \text{ in.} \\ \hline \end{array}$ **25.** $\begin{array}{r} 6 \text{ lb } 8 \text{ oz} \\ - 2 \text{ lb } 3 \text{ oz} \\ \hline \end{array}$ **26.** $\begin{array}{r} 3 \text{ yd } 1 \text{ ft} \\ + 4 \text{ yd } 2 \text{ ft} \\ \hline \end{array}$ **27.** $\begin{array}{r} 4 \text{ h } 30 \text{ min} \\ - 1 \text{ h } 40 \text{ min} \\ \hline \end{array}$

Solve for n.

28. $\frac{5}{9} = \frac{10}{n}$ **29.** $\frac{12}{16} = \frac{n}{12}$ **30.** $\frac{15}{6} = \frac{n}{16}$ **31.** $\frac{8}{14} = \frac{12}{n}$

Find the area of each polygon.

32. a rectangle with length of 9 ft and width of 4 ft

33. a triangle with base of 5 cm and height of 3 cm

Solve each problem.

34. Jim bought 2 kg of watermelon at $.98 per kg, 1.5 kg of peaches at $2.50 per kg, and 3.25 kg of cherries at $1.80 per kg. How much did Jim spend?

35. Find the perimeter of a rectangular postage stamp that is 2.5 cm long and 2.2 cm wide.

SKILLS CHECK

Choose the correct answer.

1. 5,000
    × 42

 a. 21,000
 b. 30,000
 c. 201,000
 d. NG

2. 199 ÷ 9

 a. 21
 b. 21 R1
 c. 22 R1
 d. 23

3. 4,893 + 26,507

 a. 21,290
 b. 31,290
 c. 31,400
 d. NG

4. Which sentence is correct?

 a. $6\frac{1}{4} > 6\frac{1}{3}$
 b. $6\frac{1}{4} < 6\frac{1}{3}$
 c. $6\frac{1}{4} = 6\frac{1}{3}$

5. Round 47,871 to the nearest hundred.

 a. 47,800
 b. 47,870
 c. 47,900
 d. 48,000

6. Find the greatest common factor of 12 and 24.

 a. 6
 b. 12
 c. 24
 d. NG

7. $3.4\overline{)42.84}$

 a. 1.26
 b. 1.36
 c. 12.6
 d. 126

8. $\frac{5}{16} + 2\frac{1}{4}$

 a. $2\frac{3}{10}$
 b. $2\frac{9}{16}$
 c. $2\frac{3}{4}$
 d. NG

9. Find the decimal for $8\frac{6}{100}$.

 a. 8.006
 b. 8.06
 c. 8.6
 d. 8.60

10. Find the average of the following amounts: $31.45, $28.29, $7.32, $65.70.

 a. $30.69
 b. $32.94
 c. $33.19
 d. NG

11. Find the perimeter.

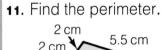
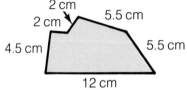

 a. 26 cm
 b. 30.5 cm
 c. 31.5 cm
 d. NG

12. What is $\frac{1}{2}$ of $3\frac{1}{2}$ c of flour?

 a. $1\frac{1}{2}$ c
 b. $1\frac{3}{4}$ c
 c. 7 c
 d. NG

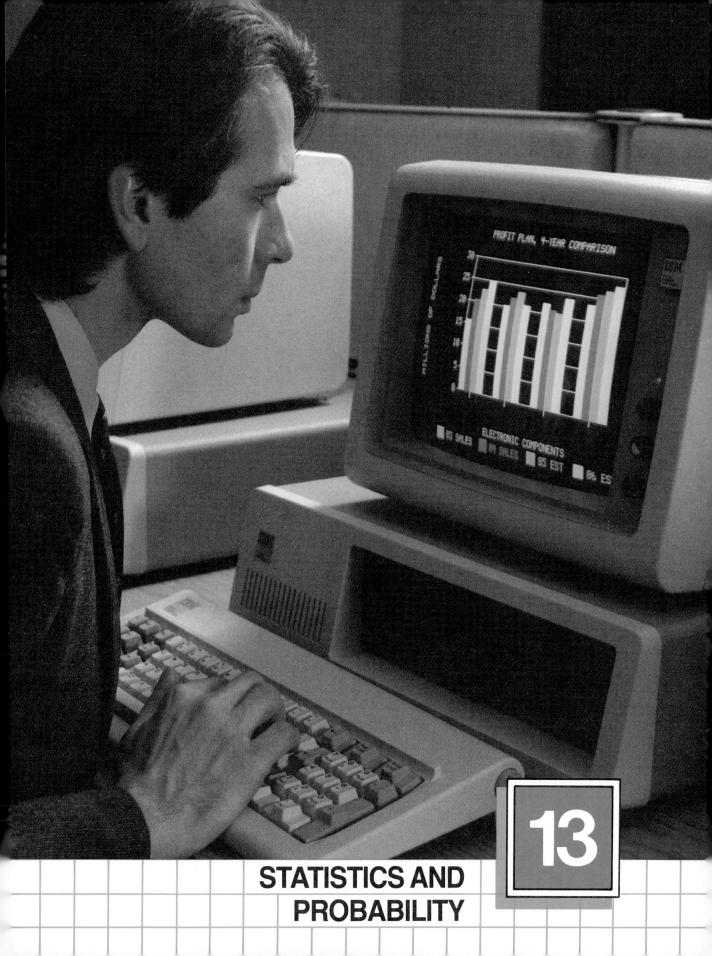

On the screen: PROFIT PLAN, 4-YEAR COMPARISON

MILLIONS OF DOLLARS

ELECTRONIC COMPONENTS

83 SALES   84 SALES   85 EST   86 ES

13

STATISTICS AND PROBABILITY

Collecting Data

■ Mary was on a trip. She decided to keep a record of the colors of the cars she saw. She made this **tally**, or count, of the first 60 cars.

Each mark stands for 1 car that Mary saw. ǁǁ stands for 5 cars.

The **frequency** is the number of cars of each color that Mary counted.

Facts like these are called **data**.

Car Color	Tally	Frequency
red	ǁǁ ǀ	6
green	ǁǁ ǁǁ ǁ	12
blue	ǁǁ ǁǁ ǁǁ	
white	ǁǁ ǁǀǀ	
black	ǁǀǀ	
gold	ǁǁ ǁǀǀ	
brown	ǁǁ ǀ	

■ You can divide the frequency of a color by 60 to find what part that color is of the whole. The part can be written as a fraction, as a decimal, or as a percent.

6 of the 60 cars that Mary saw were red. You can write the part as follows:

Fraction	Decimal	Percent
$\frac{6}{60}$, or $\frac{1}{10}$	0.1	10%

Try These

Solve each problem.

1. Copy and complete the table above.

2. Which color had the greatest frequency?

3. Which color had the least frequency?

4. Which colors had the same frequency?

5. List the colors in order from greatest frequency to least frequency.

6. 12 of the 60 cars counted were green. What fraction of the cars were green? Simplify if possible.

7. Write the fraction of cars that were green as a decimal.

8. What percent of the cars counted were green?

9. 15 of the 60 cars counted were blue. What fraction of the cars were blue? Simplify if possible.

10. Write the fraction of cars that were blue as a decimal.

Exercises

Solve each problem.

These are the votes from a class election that Mary was in.

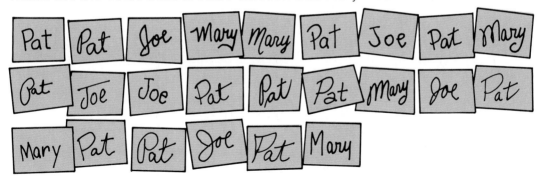

1. Make a tally of the votes for each candidate.

2. What was the frequency of the votes for Pat? For Joe? For Mary?

3. Who won the election?

4. What was the total number of votes?

5. Did the winner receive more than half of the votes?

6. Which two candidates received the same number of votes.

7. Copy and complete the table.

Vote	Frequency	Fraction of Total	Equivalent Decimal	Equivalent Percent
Pat	▨	$\frac{1}{2}$	▨	▨
Joe	▨	▨	0.25	▨
Mary	▨	▨	▨	25%

This table shows the type of books students like to read.

Type of Book	Tally	Frequency
mystery	ЖЖ ЖЖ ЖЖ ЖЖ ЖЖ ЖЖ ЖЖ I	▨
sports	ЖЖ ЖЖ ЖЖ ЖЖ III	▨
science fiction	ЖЖ ЖЖ IIII	▨
romance	ЖЖ ЖЖ ЖЖ ЖЖ ЖЖ II	▨

8. Copy and complete the table.

9. Find the total number of students in the survey.

10. What fraction of the students like to read mysteries? Science fiction?

11. What percent of the students like to read mysteries? Science fiction?

Range and Mean

■ Erica Nelson is a school secretary. She keeps a record of the number of students who are absent.

The **range** for this set of data is the difference between the greatest number and the least number of absences.

Day				M	T	W	T	F
Number Absent				24	20	18	16	22

greatest number: 24
least number: 16

$24 - 16 = 8$

The range is 8.

■ The **mean** for this set of data is the average number of absences for the 5 days.

Add to find the total number of absences.

```
   24
   20
   18
   16
 + 22
 ────
  100
```

Divide by the number of days, 5.

```
      20
  5) 100
     10
     ──
      0
      0
      ─
```

The mean number of absences was 20.

■ Sometimes a mean is not a whole number.

Find the mean of the numbers 4, 6, and 7 to the nearest tenth. To round to the nearest tenth, you need to know the hundredths place in the quotient.

Add the 3 numbers.

```
   4
   6
 + 7
 ──
  17
```

Divide the sum by 3.

```
     5.66 → 5.7
  3) 17.00
     15
     ──
      2 0
      1 8
      ───
        20
        18
        ──
         2
```

To the nearest tenth, the mean is 5.7.

Try These

Find the range and the mean for each set of data.

1. 7, 4, 6, 10, 13

2. $25, $19, $18, $30

Find the mean to the nearest tenth.

3. 43, 66, 51, 35, 76, 41, 40, 56, 66, 48

4. 50, 63, 48, 79, 86, 93, 108

Exercises

Find the range and the mean for each set of data.

1. 5, 7, 9, 8, 9, 4

2. 15, 17, 25, 18, 20

3. 21, 22, 23, 24, 25

4. 76, 24, 5, 47

5. $38, $45, $52

6. $112, $103, $115, $126

Find the mean to the nearest tenth.

7. 15, 11, 27

8. 9, 4, 7, 13, 30

9. 38, 47, 86, 23, 5, 103

10. 6, 48, 82, 13, 47

★ **11.** 5.7, 7, 6.3, 9.1, 3

★ **12.** 31.26, 15.87, 6.2, 8.23

 Find the range for each set of data. Find the mean for each set of data to the nearest tenth.

13. the scores that some students received on a test: 79, 94, 90, 84, 91, 76, 80, 91, 97, 87, 86, 81, 91, 81, 88

14. the ages of some students (given in months): 140, 141, 143, 141, 143, 142, 141, 139, 142, 143, 141, 144, 140

Solve each problem. You may choose paper and pencil or a calculator.

15. These are the number of absences each school day for 2 weeks: 27, 32, 43, 35, 20, 31, 20, 14, 25, 23. Find the mean number of absences.

16. These are the scores that some students received on a test: 75, 67, 100, 83, 91, 84, 93, 79. Find the range and the mean.

17. There are 5 sixth grades in the school. Here are the number of students in each class: 25, 28, 26, 23, 28. Find the mean number of students.

★ **18.** A student organization made $61.20, $38.72, and $46.38 on the last 3 bake sales. Find the average to the nearest cent.

Median and Mode

■ A school nurse measured the heights of some students to the nearest centimeter.

Name	Height (in cm)
Dave	153
Marie	142
Joe	151
Ann	148
Hal	151
José	149
Sue	148
Sam	151
Beth	139

The **median** for this set of data is the middle number when the heights are listed in order.

List the heights in order from least to greatest. Write each number as often as you see it in the nurse's chart.

139, 142, 148, 148, 149, 151, 151, 151, 153
↑
middle

The median height is 149 cm.

■ The **mode** for this set of data is the height that occurs most often.

Three students are 151 cm tall. The mode is 151 cm, because that height is listed most often.

What is the mean for this set of data?

■ Find the median and the mode for 13, 9, 18, 12, 10, 17, 20, and 17.

List the numbers in order from least to greatest.

9, 10, 12, 13, 17, 17, 18, 20
↑
middle

Since there is no middle number, the median is the average of the middle numbers, 13 and 17. The average of 13 and 17 is 15.

$13 + 17 = 30$
$30 \div 2 = 15$

The median of the set of numbers is 15. The mode is 17, because it is listed most often.

Try These

Find the median and the mode for each set of data.

1. 3, 4, 8, 3, 5   **2.** 15, 21, 27, 37, 13, 37

3. 192, 455, 145, 722, 682, 363, 455, 145, 93, 455

4. 173, 408, 129, 326, 209, 533, 615, 87, 326, 250

Exercises

Find the median and the mode for each set of data.

1. 21, 17, 72, 23, 72   **2.** 11, 15, 11, 12, 15, 11, 20

3. 41, 52, 43, 43, 57, 51   **4.** 2, 3, 5, 3, 1, 6, 3, 6, 7, 2

5. 113, 182, 201, 416, 98, 201, 332, 76, 101

★ **6.** 4.1, 4.29, 9.2, 7.4, 11.26, 4.1, 12.7, 7.9, 4.1, 11.3

Find the mean, the median, and the mode for each set of data.

7. 1, 7, 6, 5, 6, 5, 8, 2, 5   **8.** 15, 19, 11, 39, 19, 9, 5, 19

9. 33, 39, 35, 50, 35, 35, 33, 30, 43   **10.** 23, 19, 18, 21, 18, 3, 24

Compare the mean, the median, and the mode in exercises 7–10.

11. Are they ever all the same number?   **12.** Are they always all the same number?

Solve each problem.

13. These are the weights in kilograms of 9 students: 45, 50, 42, 40, 45, 48, 45, 42, 48. Find the range, the mean, the median, and the mode.

14. These are the heights in centimeters of 6 students: 142, 153, 150, 142, 152, 154. Find the range, the mean to the nearest tenth, the median, and the mode.

KEEPING IN SHAPE

Compute. Write each quotient as a mixed number.

1. $15 \div 8$ **2.** $13\frac{1}{2} + 24\frac{3}{4}$ **3.** $17.6 - 0.89$ **4.** 4.5×7.26

5. $46\frac{2}{3} - 21\frac{1}{2}$ **6.** $5.71 + 13.6$ **7.** $4\frac{3}{4} \times 5\frac{2}{3}$ **8.** $\frac{7}{9} \div \frac{2}{3}$

Problem Solving: Applications

ESTIMATING FROM A SAMPLE

Scientists use **sampling** to estimate wildlife populations.

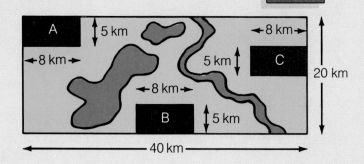

The wildlife preserve shown in the diagram is shaped like a rectangle. The giraffes were counted in all 3 sample areas at about the same time. (Sample areas are shaded.)

> In area A, 3 giraffes were counted.
> In area B, 4 giraffes were counted.
> In area C, 2 giraffes were counted.

So 9 giraffes were counted altogether in the sample areas.

Estimate the number of giraffes in the entire preserve.

First find the total area of the preserve.

$$A = l \times w$$
$$= 40 \times 20$$
$$= 800$$

The total area of the preserve is 800 km^2.

Each sample area is 5 × 8, or 40, km^2. The total sample area is 3 × 40, or 120, km^2. So the ratio of the sample area to the total area is $\frac{120}{800}$.

9 giraffes were counted in the sample areas. You can write a proportion to estimate the number of giraffes in the entire preserve.

$$\frac{120}{800} = \frac{9}{n}$$
$$120n = 7,200$$
$$n = 60$$

You can estimate that there are 60 giraffes in the entire preserve.

Try These

Solve each problem.

1. Last year only 6 giraffes were counted in the sample areas in the preserve. Estimate the total number of giraffes that were in the entire preserve last year.

2. Another preserve measures 15 km by 30 km. The total sample area is 60 km². 14 giraffes were counted in the sample areas. Estimate the total number of giraffes in the entire preserve.

Exercises

Solve each problem.

The diagram shows a state forest. Foresters photograph the area from airplanes. Then they pick sample areas to count the varieties of trees. The total area is 1,000 acres. Counts are taken in 2 areas. Each sample area is 5 acres.

1. Copy and complete the table below.

2. In 3 sample areas of another forest, foresters counted 680 pines, 475 pines, and 540 pines. What was the total number of pines in the sample areas?

3. Those 3 sample areas have a total area of 3 acres. The area of the whole forest is 100 acres. What is the ratio of the sample area to the total area?

4. Estimate the number of pines in the whole forest using your answers to exercises 2 and 3.

5. A forest is in the shape of a rectangle that measures 6 km by 10 km. 2 sample areas, each 2 km by 3 km, were chosen for a count of maples. In one, 343 maples were counted. In the other, 235 were counted. Estimate the number of maples in the forest.

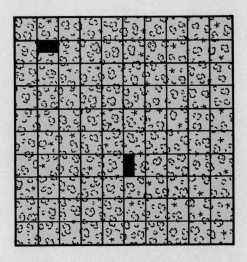

Kind of Tree	Number in Sample	Estimated Total
white oak	515	51,500
black walnut	87	
southern pine	789	
yellow poplar	236	
maple	125	

Probability

■ Jeff and Gina are playing a game with a spinner. The possible **outcomes** are red, blue, and green. The pointer is **equally likely** to stop on any one of the sections.

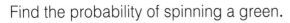

The **probability** of an event is the chance of its occurring.

Find the probability of spinning a green.

The probability of spinning a green is

$$\frac{\text{number of green sections}}{\text{total number of sections}} = \frac{1}{4}$$

The probability of spinning a green is $\frac{1}{4}$.

■ Find the probability of spinning a red.

The probability of spinning a red is

$$\frac{\text{number of red sections}}{\text{total number of sections}} = \frac{2}{4}$$
$$= \frac{1}{2}$$

The probability of spinning a red is $\frac{1}{2}$.

■ Find the probability of spinning a red or a blue.

$$\frac{\text{number of sections that are red or blue}}{\text{total number of sections}} = \frac{3}{4}$$

The probability of spinning a red or a blue is $\frac{3}{4}$.

■ Find the probability of spinning a red, a blue, or a green.

The number of sections that are red, blue, or green is 4. So the probability of spinning red, blue, or green is

$$\frac{4}{4}, \text{ or } 1$$

The probability of a certain event is 1.

Find the probability of spinning an orange.

The number of sections that are orange is 0. So the probability of spinning an orange is

$$\frac{0}{4}, \text{ or } 0$$

The probability of an impossible event is 0.

Try These

You are going to mix the cards and then choose one without looking.

Find the probability of choosing each of the following.

1. a green card

2. a red card

3. a blue card

4. an orange card

5. a red or blue card

6. a red, blue, or green card

Exercises

Find the probability of spinning each of the following.

1. 1

2. 2

3. 3

4. 4

5. 1 or 2

6. 1 or 4

7. 2 or 4

8. 1, 2, or 4

You are going to roll a cube that has 2 red faces, 2 blue faces, and 2 orange faces.

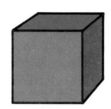

Find the probability that each color will end up on top.

9. red

10. blue

11. orange

12. green

All the marbles are the same size. You are going to shake the jar and then choose a marble without looking.

Find the probability of choosing each of the following.

13. red

14. blue

15. green

16. red or green

17. blue or green

18. blue or red

19. orange

20. red, blue, or green

★ **21.** Choose one of the experiments in the exercises above. Gather the needed materials. Do the experiment 50 times. Keep a record of the results. Are the results what you expected?

Probability and Prediction

■ Suppose there are 20 students in your class and you are holding a drawing. Each student's name is put on 1 slip of paper. The 20 slips are mixed, and someone chooses 1 slip without looking.

There are 20 possible outcomes.
The probability that you will win is $\frac{1}{20}$.
The probability that you will not win is $\frac{19}{20}$.

You can also find the probability that you will not win by subtracting the probability that you will win from 1.

$$1 - \frac{1}{20} = \frac{20}{20} - \frac{1}{20}$$
$$= \frac{19}{20}$$

Is it more likely that you will win or that you will not win?

$$\frac{1}{20} < \frac{19}{20}$$

It is more likely that you will not win.
The best **prediction** is that you will not win.

You can write probabilities as percents.

$$\frac{1}{20} = \frac{5}{100} \qquad \frac{19}{20} = \frac{95}{100}$$
$$= 5\% \qquad\qquad = 95\%$$

The probability that you will win is 5%.
The probability that you will not win is 95%.

■ Weather reports often give probabilities as percents. Suppose you heard this on the radio: "There is a 70% chance of rain tomorrow." This means that the probability of rain is $\frac{70}{100}$, or $\frac{7}{10}$.

What would you predict?
The best prediction is that it is going to rain.

Try These

Each probability is given as a percent. Write it as a fraction. Simplify if possible. Then write whether *rain* or *no rain* is more likely or whether both outcomes are *equally likely*.

1. There is a 10% chance of rain.

2. There is a 50% chance of rain.

3. There is a 60% chance of rain.

4. There is a 90% chance of rain.

For each situation, give the probability of choosing red as a fraction, as a decimal, and as a percent.

5. There are 4 marbles in a jar: 1 red and 3 clear. You shake the jar and choose one without looking.

6. There are 5 cards: 2 red, 2 blue, and 1 green. You mix them and choose one without looking.

Exercises

Each probability is given as a percent. Write it as a fraction. Simplify if possible. Then write whether *snow* or *no snow* is more likely or whether both outcomes are *equally likely*.

1. There is an 80% chance of snow.

2. There is a 40% chance of snow.

3. There is a 50% chance of snow.

★ **4.** There is a 100% chance of snow.

For each spinner, give the probability of spinning a 2 as a fraction, as a decimal, and as a percent. Simplify each fraction if possible.

5.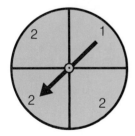

6.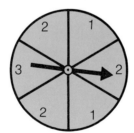

7.

THINK AND TRY

FINDING PROBABILITIES

Give the probability of winning each drawing as a fraction, as a decimal rounded to the nearest hundredth, and as a percent. Use a calculator.

1. There are 37 slips of paper. 4 of them have your name.

2. There are 86 slips of paper. 3 of them have your name.

Problem Solving: Strategies

GENERALIZING

You can draw conclusions about a large set of data by using a **sample**, or part of the set.

Are the numbers 0, 1, 2, 3, 4, 5, 6, 7, 8, and 9 equally likely to be the last digit in a telephone number? If they are, then the fraction of telephone numbers that end in each digit should be about $\frac{1}{10}$, or 10%.

A sample from a telephone book is shown here.

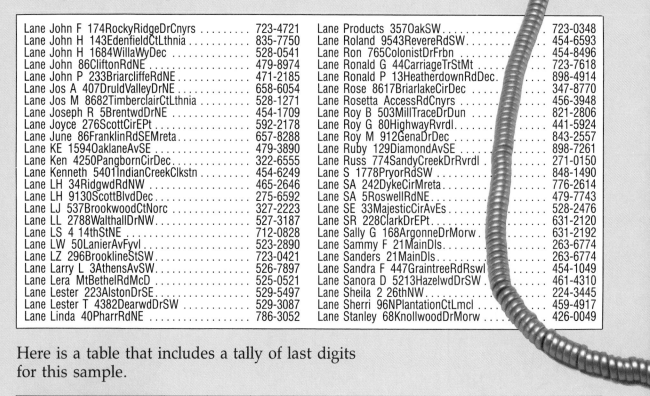

Lane John F 174RockyRidgeDrCnyrs	723-4721	Lane Products 357OakSW.................	723-0348
Lane John H 143EdenfieldCtLthnia	835-7750	Lane Roland 9543RevereRdSW.........	454-6593
Lane John H 1684WillaWyDec	528-0541	Lane Ron 765ColonistDrFrbn	454-8496
Lane John 86CliftonRdNE	479-8974	Lane Ronald G 44CarriageTrStMt	723-7618
Lane John P 233BriarcliffeRdNE	471-2185	Lane Ronald P 13HeatherdownRdDec.	898-4914
Lane Jos A 407DruldValleyDrNE	658-6054	Lane Rose 8617BriarlakeCirDec	347-8770
Lane Jos M 8682TimberclairCtLthnia	528-1271	Lane Rosetta AccessRdCnyrs	456-3948
Lane Joseph R 5BrentwdDrNE	454-1709	Lane Roy B 503MillTraceDrDun	821-2806
Lane Joyce 276ScottCirEPt	592-2178	Lane Roy G 80HighwayRvrdl.........	441-5924
Lane June 86FranklinRdSEMreta	657-8288	Lane Roy M 912GenaDrDec	843-2557
Lane KE 1594OaklaneAvSE	479-3890	Lane Ruby 129DiamondAvSE	898-7261
Lane Ken 4250PangbornCirDec	322-6555	Lane Russ 774SandyCreekDrRvrdl	271-0150
Lane Kenneth 5401IndianCreekClkstn	454-6249	Lane S 1778PryorRdSW	848-1490
Lane LH 34RidgwdRdNW	465-2646	Lane SA 242DykeCirMreta	776-2614
Lane LH 9130ScottBlvdDec	275-6592	Lane SA 5RoswellRdNE.........	479-7743
Lane LJ 537BrookwoodCtNorc	327-2223	Lane SE 33MajesticCirAvEs	528-2476
Lane LL 2788WalthallDrNW.............	527-3187	Lane SR 228ClarkDrEPt............	631-2120
Lane LS 4 14thStNE	712-0828	Lane Sally G 168ArgonneDrMorw .	631-2192
Lane LW 50LanierAvFyvl	523-2890	Lane Sammy F 21MainDls.........	263-6774
Lane LZ 296BrooklineStSW.............	723-0421	Lane Sanders 21MainDls.........	263-6774
Lane Larry L 3AthensAvSW.............	526-7897	Lane Sandra F 447GraintreeRdRswl	454-1049
Lane Lera MtBethelRdMcD	525-0521	Lane Sanora D 5213HazelwdDrSW .	461-4310
Lane Lester 223AlstonDrSE	529-5497	Lane Sheila 2 26thNW............	224-3445
Lane Lester T 4382DearwdDrSW	529-3087	Lane Sherri 96NPlantationCtLmcl	459-4917
Lane Linda 40PharrRdNE	786-3052	Lane Stanley 68KnollwoodDrMorw	426-0049

Here is a table that includes a tally of last digits for this sample.

Digit	0	1	2	3	4	5	6	7	8	9
Tally	卌 III	卌 I	III	III	卌 II	III	IIII	卌 I	卌 I	IIII
Frequency	8	6	3	3	7	3	4	6	6	4
Fraction of Total	$\frac{8}{50}$	$\frac{6}{50}$	$\frac{3}{50}$							
Equivalent Decimal	0.16	0.12	0.06							
Equivalent Percent	16%	12%	6%							

Since this sample is not very large, some of these percents are not that close to 10%. In general, the larger the sample, the closer the percent will be to 10%.

Using the Strategy

Solve each problem.

1. Copy and complete the table on page 372.

2. Here is another sample of 50 numbers from the same directory. Find the frequency for each last digit.

464-8981	896-0077	545-4586	592-7130	357-7995
740-3659	896-6052	786-0134	592-7130	429-4732
357-4750	739-0811	353-8280	712-2965	479-0021
479-8873	639-0739	767-9445	429-4136	978-7482
458-2601	528-2699	229-2065	358-3433	565-9845
886-5757	423-6644	592-8578	464-1568	464-6961
699-1466	445-4262	454-3606	457-2242	386-1902
544-0158	353-8379	497-1184	740-9762	886-4765
268-1302	565-6947	591-5736	225-7660	762-5963
767-6035	445-7050	626-7424	847-9670	464-1486

3. Combine the two samples to produce a larger sample of 100 numbers. Make a table similar to the one on page 372. (It does not need to show the tally.)

4. Check by adding the percents. Do they add up to 100%? Are some of the percents for the larger sample closer to 10% than the percents for the first sample? Are any of the percents farther from 10%?

ACTIVITY

USING A SAMPLE

Open a telephone directory to a page at random. Choose a column.

1. Count the number of telephone numbers in the column.

2. Make a table like the one on page 372. You could use a calculator to help you find the equivalent decimals. Round each decimal to the nearest hundredth. Change each rounded decimal to a percent.

3. Compare the percents to 10%. Are they close to 10%?

Combine your data with that of four or five classmates. Repeat steps 2 and 3.

4. Are the percents closer to 10%?

5. Predict what will happen if you combine data with data from the whole class. Check your prediction.

Using Tree Diagrams

■ Think about tossing a penny.

There are 2 possible
outcomes, heads and tails.
They are equally likely.

The probability of tossing heads is $\frac{1}{2}$.

The probability of tossing tails is $\frac{1}{2}$.

■ Think about tossing a penny and a nickel.

What is the probability of tossing heads
on both coins?

You can use a **tree diagram** to help you list the possible
outcomes. Use H for heads and T for tails.

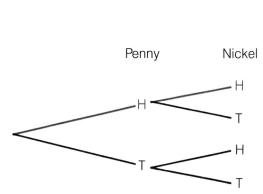

	OUTCOMES	
	Penny	Nickel
	H	H
	H	T
	T	H
	T	T

Each path through the tree gives a possible outcome.
The red path gives the outcome HH, heads on both coins.

There are 4 possible outcomes: HH, HT, TH, and TT.

Since each of these outcomes is equally likely,
the probability of tossing heads on both coins is $\frac{1}{4}$.

■ What is the probability of tossing 1 head and 1 tail?

The diagram shows that there are 2 possible outcomes with
1 head and 1 tail: HT and TH.

So the probability of tossing 1 head and 1 tail is $\frac{2}{4}$, or $\frac{1}{2}$.

Try These

2 brown socks and 2 green socks are in a drawer. They are not in pairs. You are going to pull out 2 socks without looking.

Solve each problem.

1. Copy and complete this tree diagram. B means brown and G means green.

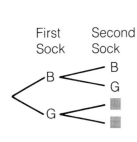

First Sock	Second Sock
B	B
B	▓
▓	▓
▓	▓

2. What is the probability of pulling out 2 brown socks?

3. What is the probability of pulling out 2 green socks?

4. What is the probability of pulling out 2 socks that match (both brown or both green)?

Exercises

Solve each problem.

You are going to spin this spinner twice.

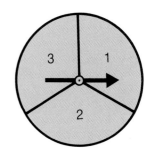

1. Copy and complete this tree diagram and table.

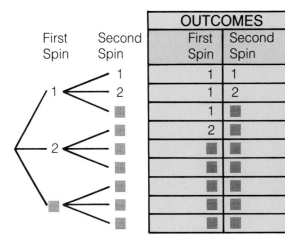

First Spin	Second Spin
1	1
1	2
1	▓
2	▓
▓	▓
▓	▓
▓	▓
▓	▓
▓	▓

2. What is the probability of spinning 1 both times?

3. What is the probability of spinning the same number both times?

4. What is the probability of spinning 2 numbers with a sum of 3 (a 1 and then a 2 or a 2 and then a 1)?

5. What is the probability of spinning 2 numbers with a sum of 4?

You are going to spin the spinner once and then toss a penny. One possible outcome is 2H, spinning a 2 and tossing heads.

6. List all the possible outcomes.

★ **7.** What is the probability of each of the possible outcomes?

CHAPTER CHECKPOINT

Find the range, the mean, the median, and the mode for each set of numbers. (pp. 362–365)

1. $19, $17, $24, $21, $24

3. 33, 35, 33, 37, 45, 39

2. 6, 7, 2, 7, 5, 7, 8

4. $32, $28, $21, $32, $56

Find the mean to the nearest tenth. (pp. 362–363)

5. 5, 8, 3, 4, 6, 2, 3

6. 17, 6, 23, 6, 18, 42

Find the probability of spinning each of the following. (pp. 368–369)

7. 1

8. 2

9. 1 or 2

10. 4

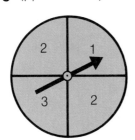

Write whether *rain* or *no rain* is more likely. (pp. 370–371)

11. The probability of rain is 30%.

12. The probability of rain is 80%.

For each jar, give the probability of choosing a red marble as a fraction, as a decimal, and as a percent. (pp. 370–371)

13.

14.

15.

Solve each problem. (pp. 360–375)

This is a tally of the students' pets.

Pet	Tally	Frequency
dogs	ЖЖ II	12
cats	Ж IIII	9
fish	III	3

16. Which pet is the most popular?

17. What fraction of the students have cats? Simplify if possible.

18. What percent of the students have fish?

Norman tossed a penny 20 times. Here is a tally of his results.

Heads	Tails
ⅢⅡ ⅢⅠ ⅡⅠ	ⅢⅠ Ⅲ

19. Copy and complete the table.

Outcome	Frequency	Fraction of Total	Equivalent Decimal	Equivalent Percent
heads	12	$\frac{3}{5}$		
tails				

20. A wildlife refuge has an area of 100 acres. 6 bears are counted in the sample areas. The total sample area is 8 acres. Estimate the total number of bears in the entire refuge.

21. Another wildlife refuge is 10 km by 20 km. The total sample area is 60 km². 15 deer were counted in the sample areas. Estimate the total number of deer in the entire refuge.

Suppose you spin this spinner twice.

22. Copy and complete the tree diagram and table to show the four possible outcomes. B means blue, and R means red.

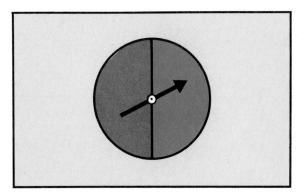

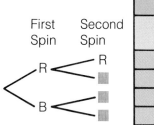

OUTCOMES	
First Spin	Second Spin
R	R
R	▩
▩	▩
▩	▩

23. What is the probability of spinning red twice?

24. What is the probability of spinning each color once?

25. What is the probability of spinning a red or a blue?

26. What is the probability of spinning a green once?

COMPUTERS AND PROBLEM SOLVING

■ Each time you flip a coin, heads is as likely an outcome as tails. You cannot predict the result.
The RANDOM command also gives you an outcome you cannot predict.

RANDOM X tells the computer to pick an integer between 0 and one less than X. Type PRINT RANDOM 7 and the computer displays a number between 0 and 6.
In the procedure below, the computer "flips a coin" 6 times.
0 stands for heads and 1 stands for tails.

```
TO FLIPS
REPEAT 6 [PRINT RANDOM 2]
END
```

```
?FLIPS
1
0
0
0
0
1
```

How many times did heads come up?

For each "flip", heads and tails have an equal probability of occurring. If you flip a coin often enough, it comes up heads half the time and tails half the time.

A tree diagram can represent the possible outcome of the coin toss.

```
TO TREE :BRANCH
RT 30 FD :BRANCH BK :BRANCH
LT 60 FD :BRANCH BK :BRANCH
RT 30
END
```

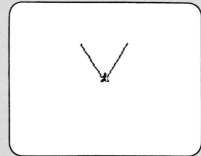

The fork represents one event with two possible outcomes. For each added event, a new fork must be created at the end of each old branch.
Use the command TREE after each FD :BRANCH command. Each time the computer comes to the TREE command, it will begin the TREE procedure again. You must limit the number of times that the computer restarts TREE to the number of events you want to represent in your tree diagram.

```
TO TREE :BRANCH
IF :BRANCH < 6 [ STOP ]
RT 30 FD :BRANCH
    TREE :BRANCH / 2
    BK :BRANCH
LT 60 FD :BRANCH
    TREE :BRANCH / 2
    BK :BRANCH RT 30
END
```

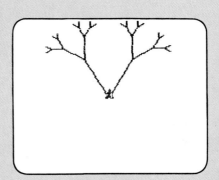

Solve each problem.

1. What is the shortest branch that is drawn when you type TREE 50? How is the limit set?

2. How many possible outcomes will TREE display when you type TREE 50?

3. Draw a flowchart that shows all the steps in TREE 8.

ENRICHMENT

NUMBER OF POSSIBLE COMBINATIONS

A family is trying to name a new daughter. They have chosen 3 possible first names: Evelyn, Kirsten, and Marjorie. They have chosen 2 possible middle names: Louise and Gail. How many possible combinations are there?

You can make a tree diagram to show all the possible combinations.

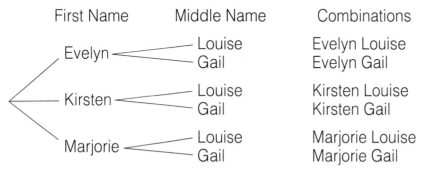

First Name	Middle Name	Combinations
Evelyn	Louise	Evelyn Louise
	Gail	Evelyn Gail
Kirsten	Louise	Kirsten Louise
	Gail	Kirsten Gail
Marjorie	Louise	Marjorie Louise
	Gail	Marjorie Gail

There are 6 possible combinations.

You can also get the same answer by multiplying.

Number of Choices for First Name		Number of Choices for Middle Name		Number of Possible Combinations
3	×	2	=	6

There are 6 possible combinations.

Solve each problem.

1. Eve is going to school. She has 6 skirts and 7 blouses in her closet. She is going to choose a skirt and a blouse. How many different outfits could she wear?

2. Fritz has 6 shirts, 2 pairs of pants, and 3 sweaters. He is going to choose a shirt, a pair of pants, and a sweater. How many different outfits could he wear?

3. How many different 2-letter combinations are there whose first letter is from the first half of the alphabet (A–M) and whose second letter is from the second half of the alphabet (N–Z)?

★ 4. How many different ways are there to arrange 4 books on a shelf? (Hint: How many choices are there for the first book? After you choose the first book, how many choices are there for the second book?)

PROBLEM SOLVING: SITUATIONS

PLANNING A SCIENCE FAIR

You are in charge of a student group that is planning the science fair. The science fair will be held in the gym. You will use lunchroom tables to display the exhibits. How will you set up the gym?

Some Questions to Explore
- How many lunchroom tables will fit in the gym?
- How will the tables be arranged?
- How many exhibits will there be?

Some Strategies to Explore
Consider the first two questions. You can use the strategies of finding information and making a scale drawing to help answer the questions.

- Find information about the useable area in the gym.
- Find information about the size of the tabletops.
- Make a scale drawing to show possible arrangements of the tables. Remember to allow for aisle space.
- Decide which arrangement makes the best use of the available floor space.

Decide what strategy you will use to answer the other question above. List other questions and strategies you need to explore. Then solve the problem.

SKILLS CHECK

Choose the correct answer.

1. 4,001
  −2,863

   a. 1,148
   b. 2,248
   c. 2,862
   d. NG

2. Round 135.891 to the nearest tenth.

   a. 135.8
   b. 135.9
   c. 135.89
   d. NG

3. $38\overline{)5,621}$

   a. 138 R16
   b. 147 R35
   c. 148 R3
   d. 1,470 R35

4. Compute: 3^5

   a. 15
   b. 81
   c. 125
   d. 243

5. Simplify: $\frac{30}{24}$

   a. $1\frac{1}{4}$
   b. $1\frac{1}{3}$
   c. $1\frac{1}{2}$
   d. NG

6. Which number is 13,461 divisible by?

   a. 2
   b. 3
   c. 5
   d. 9

7. Write 0.35 as a fraction.

   a. $\frac{3}{10}$
   b. $\frac{7}{20}$
   c. $\frac{3}{5}$
   d. NG

8. 3 h 15 min = ▇ min

   a. 135 minutes
   b. 195 minutes
   c. 315 minutes
   d. NG

9. Find the median for 4, 7, 13, 3, 5, 1, and 9.

   a. 4
   b. 5
   c. 6
   d. 7

10. Find the area of a rectangle 3.5 ft long and 2 ft wide.

   a. 3.5 ft²
   b. 5.5 ft²
   c. 7 ft²
   d. 11 ft²

11. The ratio of boys to girls is 3 to 4. There are 12 boys. How many girls are there?

   a. 9 girls
   b. 16 girls
   c. 144 girls
   d. NG

12. 34 children are going on a trip. At most, 4 will be in each car. How many cars are needed?

   a. 7 cars
   b. 8 cars
   c. 9 cars
   d. NG

14

INTEGERS

Integers

■ Branco Resources mines phosphates
at 2 km above sea level. The distance
above sea level can be shown with a
positive integer: $^+2$ km

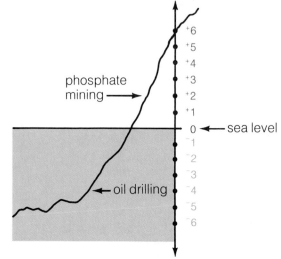

Casco Oil drills for oil at 4 km
below sea level. The distance
below sea level can be shown with
a **negative integer:** $^-4$ km

Integers can be listed this way:

$$\ldots, \ ^-5, \ ^-4, \ ^-3, \ ^-2, \ ^-1, \ 0, \ ^+1, \ ^+2, \ ^+3, \ ^+4, \ ^+5, \ \ldots$$

$^+1$ is another name for 1; $^+2$ is another name for 2; $^+3$ is
another name for 3; and so on. The dots mean that the
numbers continue forever in both directions.

■ Integers can be shown on a number line.

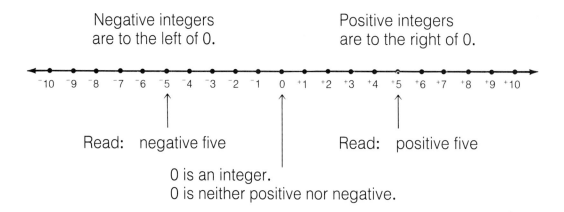

Negative integers
are to the left of 0.

Positive integers
are to the right of 0.

Read: negative five

Read: positive five

0 is an integer.
0 is neither positive nor negative.

■ Each integer has an **opposite**.

$^+3$ is three units to the right of 0. $^-3$ is three units to the left of 0.

$^+3$ is the opposite of $^-3$. $^-3$ is the opposite of $^+3$.

The opposite of 0 is 0.

Try These

Use the number line. Identify the integer named by each letter.

1. L
2. C
3. N
4. S
5. J
6. D

Write the opposite of each integer.

7. $^+7$
8. $^-3$
9. 0
10. $^+12$
11. $^-6$
12. $^-100$

Exercises

Use the number line. Identify the letter named by each integer.

1. $^-2$
2. $^+3$
3. $^+9$
4. $^-12$
5. $^-7$
6. $^+13$

Write each integer.

7. negative five
8. positive two
9. negative ten
10. positive six
11. negative seven
12. positive eleven

Use an integer to describe each situation.

13. 250 m above sea level
14. 20°F below 0
15. a loss of 8 points
16. down 4 flights
17. a gain of $19
18. 4 km below sea level
19. a gain of 3 yd
20. 5°F above 0
21. lost $6

Write the opposite of each integer.

22. $^+4$
23. $^-6$
24. $^-4$
25. 0
26. $^-84$
27. $^+218$

Solve each problem.

28. Casco Oil discovered oil at 1 km below sea level. The well produced 127,000 barrels in the first week. At that rate, how many barrels would it produce in 4 weeks?

★ 29. The outside temperature at a Branco Resources mine was 3°F at noon. By 8 P.M., it had fallen 7°F. What was the temperature at 8 P.M.?

Comparing and Ordering Integers

■ A meteorologist keeps weather records. The temperatures are recorded in degrees Celsius (°C).

On Saturday, the recorded temperature was ⁻3°C, 3°C below 0. On Sunday, the recorded temperature was ⁺2°C. On which day was it warmer?

You can use a number line to help you compare the temperatures.

$$^+2 \text{ is to the right of } ^-3.$$
$$^+2 > ^-3$$
Read: ⁺2 is greater than ⁻3

It was warmer on Sunday.

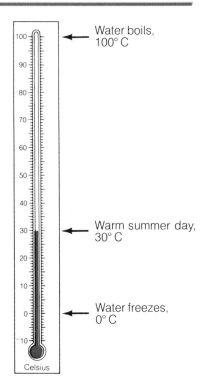

Water boils, 100° C

Warm summer day, 30° C

Water freezes, 0° C

Celsius

■ Compare ⁺5 and ⁺3.

$$^+5 \text{ is to the right of } ^+3.$$
$$^+5 > ^+3$$

Compare ⁻2 and 0.

$$^-2 \text{ is to the left of } 0.$$
$$^-2 < 0$$

Compare ⁻5 and ⁻3.

$$^-5 \text{ is to the left of } ^-3.$$
$$^-5 < ^-3$$
Read: ⁻5 is less than ⁻3

Compare ⁺1 and ⁻1.

$$^+1 \text{ is to the right of } ^-1.$$
$$^+1 > ^-1$$

■ You can use the number line to help you write integers in order from least to greatest.

Write ⁻2, ⁻6, and ⁺4 in order from least to greatest.

⁻2 and ⁺4 are to the right of ⁻6.
⁻6 is the least.

⁺4 is to the right of ⁻2.
⁺4 is the greatest.

The order from least to greatest is ⁻6, ⁻2, ⁺4.

Try These

Write > or <. Draw a number line that includes the integers from ⁻10 to ⁺10.

1. ⁻3 ▦ ⁺3
2. ⁺2 ▦ ⁻1
3. ⁻3 ▦ ⁺1
4. ⁻4 ▦ ⁻3
5. ⁻1 ▦ ⁻2
6. ⁺5 ▦ ⁺2
7. 0 ▦ ⁻4
8. 0 ▦ ⁺4

Write in order from least to greatest.

9. ⁺3, 0, ⁻5
10. ⁺1, ⁻9, ⁻4
11. ⁻2, ⁺3, ⁻6
12. ⁺2, ⁻3, 0, ⁻5
13. ⁺5, ⁻2, ⁺3, ⁻1
14. ⁻7, ⁻2, ⁻1, ⁻5

Exercises

Write > or <.

1. ⁻1 ▦ 0
2. ⁺3 ▦ 0
3. ⁻7 ▦ ⁻8
4. ⁻3 ▦ ⁺1
5. ⁻4 ▦ ⁺2
6. 0 ▦ ⁻6
7. ⁺8 ▦ ⁻6
8. ⁺10 ▦ ⁻9
9. ⁺8 ▦ ⁻8
10. ⁻5 ▦ 0
11. ⁺7 ▦ ⁺5
12. ⁻8 ▦ ⁺3
★ **13.** ⁻19 ▦ ⁺26
★ **14.** 0 ▦ ⁻86
★ **15.** ⁻64 ▦ ⁻62
★ **16.** ⁺106 ▦ ⁻160

Write in order from least to greatest.

17. ⁺4, 0, ⁻2
18. ⁻6, ⁺10, ⁻9
19. ⁺7, ⁻8, ⁺5
20. ⁺10, ⁻6, ⁺2, ⁻4
21. ⁻9, 0, ⁺1, ⁻6
22. ⁻8, ⁺7, ⁺3, ⁻4
★ **23.** ⁻68, ⁺59, ⁺67, ⁻64, ⁺68
★ **24.** ⁻91, ⁻98, ⁺37, ⁺42, ⁻12, ⁻9

This chart shows one day's high and low temperatures in several cities.

Solve each problem.

City	Temperature (°C)	
	High	Low
Cincinnati	0	⁻15
Chicago	⁻2	⁻22
Denver	⁻10	⁻20
Detroit	⁻8	⁻18
Memphis	⁺5	⁻10

25. Which city had the highest high temperature for the day?

26. Which city had the lowest high temperature?

27. Which city had the lowest low temperature?

28. Which city had the highest low temperature?

★ **29.** What was the change in degrees from the low to the high for Denver?

★ **30.** What was the change in degrees from the low to the high for Detroit?

Adding Integers

■ Billy spun $^+4$ points in the first round of a game. He spun $^+2$ points in the second round. What was his score after two rounds?

Add $^+4$ and $^+2$ to find the answer.

You can use a number line to add integers. Move to the *right* for a positive integer. Move to the *left* for a negative integer.

Start at 0.
Move 4 units to the right, to $^+4$.
Then move 2 more units to the right.

$$^+4 + {}^+2 = {}^+6$$

Billy's score was $^+6$.

■ Add: $^-1 + {}^-3$

Start at 0.
Move 1 unit to the left, to $^-1$.
Then move 3 more units to the left.

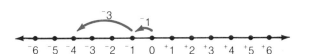

$$^-1 + {}^-3 = {}^-4$$

■ Add: $^+2 + {}^-5$

Start at 0.
Move 2 units to the right, to $^+2$.
Then move 5 units to the left.

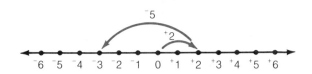

$$^+2 + {}^-5 = {}^-3$$

■ Add: $^-4 + {}^+6$

Start at 0.
Move 4 units to the left, to $^-4$.
Then move 6 units to the right.

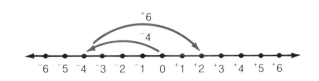

$$^-4 + {}^+6 = {}^+2$$

Add. Use the number line to help you.

1. $^+3 + {}^-5$

2. $^-3 + {}^-2$

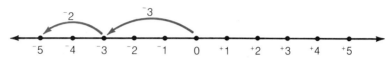

Add. Think of a number line.

3. $^+5 + {}^+3$

4. $^-3 + {}^+4$

5. $^-7 + {}^+3$

6. $^-3 + {}^-3$

Exercises

Add. Think of a number line.

1. $^+2 + {}^+1$	2. $^+1 + {}^-3$	3. $^-2 + {}^+2$	4. $^+5 + {}^-5$
5. $^+5 + {}^-7$	6. $^+7 + {}^+8$	7. $^+7 + {}^-8$	8. $^-8 + {}^-3$
9. $^+6 + {}^+6$	10. $^+4 + {}^-9$	11. $^+9 + {}^+1$	12. $^-9 + {}^-9$
13. $^-7 + {}^+9$	14. $^+9 + {}^+2$	15. $^-9 + {}^-8$	16. $^-1 + {}^-9$
17. $^+5 + {}^-8$	18. $^-3 + {}^+8$	19. $^+8 + {}^+6$	20. $^+7 + {}^-7$

21. $(^+5 + {}^-7) + {}^-3$

22. $(^-3 + {}^-7) + {}^-2$

23. $(^+18 + {}^-21) + {}^-19$

Solve each problem.

24. In the first round of a game, Billy spun $^+5$ points. In the second round, he spun $^-2$ points. What was his score after two rounds?

★ 25. Phil started the fourth round with a score of $^-12$. After the fourth round, he had a total score of $^-7$. What did he spin in the fourth round?

KEEPING IN SHAPE

Find the perimeter and the area of each polygon.

1. a rectangle with length of 25 mm and width of 12 mm

2. a square with sides of length 8.9 cm

3. a rectangle with length of 2.5 cm and width of 2.8 cm

4. a rectangle with length of 14.3 cm and width of 8.6 cm

Problem Solving: Strategies

GENERALIZING

Sometimes you can solve a problem
by **finding and extending a pattern**.

Imagine this machine. The machine adds
a certain integer to each input. The sum
of the two integers is the output. The
machine is called a "function machine."

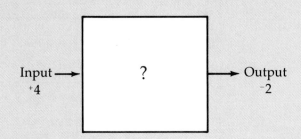

Input→ $^+4$?   → Output $^-2$

Here is an input-output table for this
machine. What is the integer that is
added to each input?

Look at the third line of the table.
What integer can you add to $^+8$ to give $^+2$?

$$^+8 + {}^-6 = {}^+2$$

Input	Output
$^+4$	$^-2$
$^-1$	$^-7$
$^+8$	$^+2$
$^+10$	
$^-3$	
$^+2$	

Now check to see whether $^-6$ works for the
integers in the first two lines of the table.

$$^+4 + {}^-6 = {}^-2 \; \blacktriangleright \qquad ^-1 + {}^-6 = {}^-7 \; \blacktriangleright$$

$^-6$ works. $^-6$ is the integer that is added to each input.

Using the Strategy

**Copy and complete the table. Then use the same machine to
find the output for each of the following inputs.**

1. 0
2. $^+6$
3. $^-2$
4. $^-4$
5. $^+9$

**For each machine, find the integer that is added.
Then complete each table.**

6.

Input	Output
$^-3$	$^+2$
$^+4$	$^+9$
$^-6$	$^-1$
0	
$^-4$	
$^+2$	

7.

Input	Output
$^-1$	$^-3$
$^+1$	$^-1$
$^+6$	$^+4$
$^+3$	
$^-6$	
$^+2$	

8.

Input	Output
$^+2$	$^+2$
$^-1$	$^-1$
$^-3$	$^-3$
$^+2$	
$^-8$	
$^-6$	

Imagine a machine that has the machines in exercises 6 and 7 inside. The output from the machine in exercise 6 then becomes the input for the machine in exercise 7.

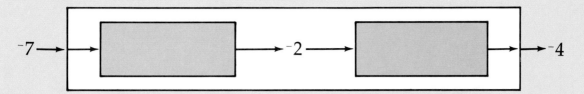

Using this machine, find the output for each of the following inputs.

9. $^+4$ **10.** $^-5$ **11.** $^-2$ **12.** 0 **13.** $^-10$

14. For this machine, find the integer that is added to the input to give the output.

ACTIVITY

MAKING A MODEL

Here is how to make a model of a machine that adds $^-6$ to inputs:

1. Cut out a piece of paper or thin cardboard. Use the dimensions shown.

2. Cut slots and label them with the words "Input" and "Output" as shown.

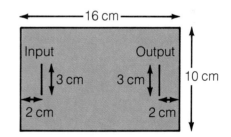

3. Cut a strip of paper 2 cm wide and 30 cm long. Draw a vertical line every 2 cm. Label each box with an integer as shown.

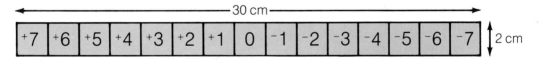

4. Place the strip of paper through the slots. Place $^+5$ at the input slot. Input $^+5$ by sliding the strip one box to the right. $^-1$ should appear at the output slot. Check other inputs in the same way.

Subtracting Integers

- The addition and subtraction of whole numbers are related operations. To find a difference, you can think of a missing addend.

  Subtract: $7 - 3$

  > $7 - 3 = \blacksquare$ can be thought of as $3 + \blacksquare = 7$.
  > What do you add to 3 to get 7?

  $7 - 3 = 4$

- The addition and subtraction of integers are also related. To find a difference, think of a missing addend.

  Subtract: $^+3 - {}^-2$

  > $^+3 - {}^-2 = \blacksquare$ can be thought of as $^-2 + \blacksquare = {}^+3$.
  > What do you add to $^-2$ to get $^+3$?
  > Use the number line to count.
  > You add $^+5$ to $^-2$ to get $^+3$.

  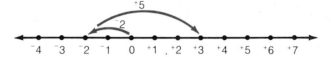

  $^-2 + {}^+5 = {}^+3$, so $^+3 - {}^-2 = {}^+5$.

- Notice that the answers are the same in these two examples:

  $$^+3 - {}^-2 = {}^+5 \qquad {}^+3 + {}^+2 = {}^+5$$

  > $^-2$ and $^+2$ are opposites.

  Compare these examples. Each subtraction problem has been rewritten as an addition problem using opposites.

Subtraction		Addition
$^+6 - {}^+4 = {}^+2$	$\longrightarrow$	$^+6 + {}^-4 = {}^+2$
$^+6 - {}^-4 = {}^+10$	$\longrightarrow$	$^+6 + {}^+4 = {}^+10$
$^-6 - {}^+4 = {}^-10$	$\longrightarrow$	$^-6 + {}^-4 = {}^-10$
$^-6 - {}^-4 = {}^-2$	$\longrightarrow$	$^-6 + {}^+4 = {}^-2$

  > $^+4$ and $^-4$ are opposites.

  > *Subtracting an integer is the same as adding its opposite.*

Try These

Copy and complete.

1. $^+7 - ^+8 = ^+7 + ^-8 = $ ▦
2. $^+3 - ^-1 = ^+3 + ^+1 = $ ▦
3. $^-4 - ^+1 = ^-4 + $ ▦ $ = $ ▦
4. $^-9 - ^-5 = ^-9 + $ ▦ $ = $ ▦
5. $^+5 - ^-4 = ^+5 + $ ▦ $ = $ ▦
6. $^-8 - ^-2 = ^-8 + $ ▦ $ = $ ▦

Exercises

Copy and complete.

1. $^+7 - ^-6 = ^+7 + $ ▦ $ = $ ▦
2. $^-8 - ^-3 = ^-8 + $ ▦ $ = $ ▦
3. $^+5 - ^+9 = ^+5 + $ ▦ $ = $ ▦
4. $^-4 - ^+6 = ^-4 + $ ▦ $ = $ ▦

Subtract.

5. $^-3 - ^+2$
6. $^-3 - ^-1$
7. $^+4 - ^-2$
8. $^-1 - ^-6$
9. $^+5 - ^-2$
10. $0 - ^+4$
11. $^-2 - 0$
12. $0 - ^-3$
13. $^+7 - ^+9$
14. $^+8 - ^-7$
15. $^-4 - ^+8$
16. $^+9 - ^-9$
17. $^+6 - ^-4$
18. $^-7 - ^-6$
19. $^+3 - ^+9$
20. $^-5 - ^+8$

 Using a calculator, you can subtract one positive integer from a second, even if the second is greater than the first.

Subtract: $^+5 - ^+8$

The answer will look like this: -3 . $^+5 - ^+8 = ^-3$

Subtract.

21. $^+9 - ^+17$
22. $^+37 - ^+14$
23. $^+27 - ^+49$
24. $^+126 - ^+278$
25. $^+175 - ^+58$
26. $^+235 - ^+400$
27. $^+34 - ^+207$
28. $^+221 - ^+1,625$

Solve each problem. You may choose paper and pencil or a calculator.

29. A research submarine is 8 m below sea level. It dives 5 m deeper. Use an integer to describe where the submarine is then.

30. At 15 m below sea level, the ocean temperature was 14°C. At the surface, the ocean temperature was 1.75° warmer. What was the temperature at the surface?

★ 31. What is the difference in temperature between 5°C and −7°C?

★ 32. What is the difference in temperature between −3°C and −7°C?

Problem Solving: Applications

USING INTEGERS

■ A share of stock is a share of a business. Active stocks change in value during a day's trading on the stock market.

Stockbrokers buy and sell stocks for their customers. A broker received this report showing the dollar value of a share of stock for five companies.

Stock	Opening Price	Change	Closing Price
Atlantic	$41	$^+5$	$46
Benefit	$26	$^-3$	$23
Redco	$25	$^-2$	■
Pacific	$14	$^+1$	■
STS	$37	$^-5$	■

The opening price is the cost of a share when the stock market opens each day. The closing price is the cost of a share when the market closes each day. The change column shows the number of points, or dollars, gained or lost.

A positive number means points gained.
A negative number means points lost.

■ What was the closing price of Redco?

From the report, you can see that the opening price was $25 and the change was $^-2$ points, or $^-$$2.
Add $^+25$ and $^-2$ to find the closing price. $^+25 + {}^-2 = {}^+23$

The closing price was $23.

■ What was the difference between the greatest gain and the greatest loss?

The greatest gain reported was $^+5$.
The greatest loss was $^-5$.
Find the difference between the two numbers. $^+5 - {}^-5 = {}^+10$

The difference between the greatest gain and the greatest loss was 10 points.

Try These

Solve each problem.

1. Copy and complete the table to find the closing prices for Redco, Pacific, and STS.

2. Renée owns 50 shares of Atlantic stock. How much was her stock worth when the market opened?

Exercises

For each stock, the opening price on Tuesday was equal to the closing price on Monday.

Solve each problem. Use the information in this table.

Stock	Opening Price on Monday	Change on Monday	Change on Tuesday
Northport	$32	$^+6$	$^-4$
Cowdy	$48	$^-3$	$^-2$
JFM	$34	$^-2$	$^+8$
Delray	$29	$^+2$	$^+5$

1. What was the closing price of Northport on Monday?

2. What was the closing price of Cowdy on Monday? What was its opening price on Tuesday?

3. What was the difference between the greatest gain and the greatest loss on Monday?

4. What was the difference between the greatest gain and the greatest loss on Tuesday?

5. How much more did Northport gain on Monday than Delray?

6. What was the closing price of JFM on Monday? On Tuesday?

7. What was the total change for the 2 days for Northport?

8. What was the total change for the 2 days for Cowdy?

9. What was the total change for the 2 days for JFM?

10. What was the total change for the 2 days for Delray?

11. Barry owns 75 shares of Northport stock. How much was his stock worth when the stock market opened on Monday?

12. Glenda owns 65 shares of JFM stock. How much was her stock worth when the stock market opened on Monday?

13. Nancy owns 105 shares of Delray stock. How much was her stock worth when the market opened on Monday? How much was her stock worth when the market closed on Tuesday? Did Nancy gain or lose money? How much money?

14. Earl owns 90 shares of Cowdy stock. How much was his stock worth when the market opened on Monday? How much was his stock worth when the market closed on Tuesday? Did Earl gain or lose money? How much money?

★ 15. When the market opened on Monday, Jason owned 500 shares of Delray. He sold $\frac{1}{2}$ of his shares at 2 P.M. How much was the rest of his stock worth when the market closed on Monday?

★ 16. Alicia owns 400 shares of Cowdy stock. On Thursday, it opened at $43\frac{1}{2}$. (This means $43.50.) The stock gained $1\frac{3}{4}$ points. What was her stock worth when the market closed on Thursday?

Graphing Ordered Pairs

■ You can graph ordered pairs of integers.

Graph ($^+2$, $^-3$).

Start at the origin.
$^+2$ tells you to count
2 units to the *right*.

$^-3$ tells you to then count
3 units *down*.

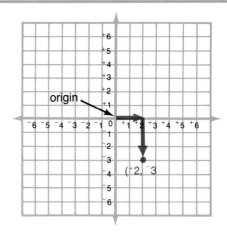

■ Graph ($^-3$, $^+4$).
Label the point A.

Start at the origin.
Count *left* 3.
Then count *up* 4.

Graph ($^-2$, $^-5$).
Label the point B.

Count *left* 2.
Then count *down* 5.

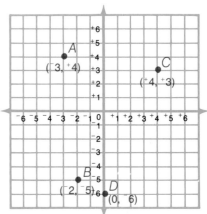

Graph ($^+4$, $^+3$).
Label the point C.

Count *right* 4.
Then count *up* 3.

Graph (0, $^-6$).
Label the point D.

Count *down* 6
from the origin.

Try These

Name the ordered pair for each point.

1. A
2. B
3. C
4. D
5. E
6. F

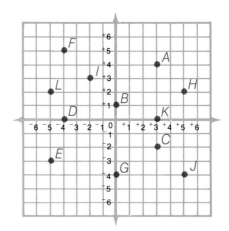

Name the point for each ordered pair.

7. (0, $^-4$)
8. ($^+5$, $^-4$)
9. ($^+3$, 0)
10. ($^+5$, $^+2$)
11. ($^-2$, $^+3$)
12. ($^-5$, $^+2$)

Exercises

Name the ordered pair for each point.

1. *M*
2. *N*
3. *P*
4. *R*
5. *S*
6. *T*
7. *V*
8. *X*
9. *Z*
10. *G*

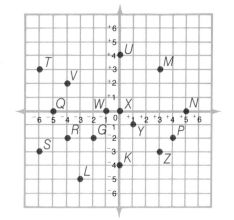

Name the point for each ordered pair.

11. $(0, {}^+4)$
12. $({}^-5, 0)$
13. $(0, {}^-4)$
14. $({}^-3, {}^-5)$
15. $({}^+1, {}^-1)$
16. $({}^-1, 0)$
17. $({}^+4, {}^-2)$
18. $({}^-4, {}^+2)$
19. $({}^-6, {}^+3)$
20. $({}^-4, {}^-2)$
21. $({}^+3, {}^-3)$
22. $({}^+3, {}^+3)$

**Make a pair of axes on graph paper. Graph each ordered pair.
Then draw a line segment connecting them. What word do you spell?**

23. Graph $({}^-3, {}^-2)$ and $({}^-3, {}^-6)$.
24. Graph $({}^-1, {}^-2)$ and $({}^-1, {}^-6)$.
25. Graph $({}^-3, {}^-4)$ and $({}^-1, {}^-4)$.
26. Graph $(1, {}^-2)$ and $(3, {}^-2)$.
27. Graph $(1, {}^-6)$ and $(3, {}^-6)$.
28. Graph $(2, {}^-2)$ and $(2, {}^-6)$.

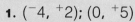

THINK AND TRY

GRAPHING GEOMETRIC FIGURES

Make a pair of axes on graph paper.
Graph point *A* through point *F* as
shown. Then draw line segments
that connect each of the following.
Name and label each geometric
figure formed.

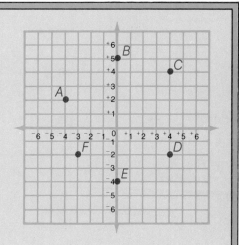

1. $({}^-4, {}^+2); (0, {}^+5)$
2. $({}^+4, {}^+4); ({}^+4, {}^-2); (0, {}^-4)$
3. $({}^-3, {}^-2); ({}^+4, {}^-2); (0, {}^-4); ({}^-3, {}^-2)$
4. $(0, {}^+5); ({}^+4, {}^+4); ({}^+4, {}^-2); (0, {}^-4); (0, {}^+5)$

CHAPTER CHECKPOINT

Use the number line. Identify the integer named by each letter. (pp. 384–385)

1. L **2.** S **3.** M **4.** R **5.** A **6.** D

Write the opposite of each integer. (pp. 384–385)

7. $^+3$ **8.** $^-6$ **9.** 0 **10.** $^-1$ **11.** $^+4$ **12.** $^-2$

13. $^+5$ **14.** $^+10$ **15.** $^-8$ **16.** $^+6$ **17.** $^+3$ **18.** $^-9$

Write > or <. (pp. 386–387)

19. $^-7$ ▨ $^+3$ **20.** $^-9$ ▨ $^-6$ **21.** $^+8$ ▨ $^+2$ **22.** $^-3$ ▨ 0

23. $^-2$ ▨ $^+1$ **24.** $^+3$ ▨ $^+4$ **25.** $^-5$ ▨ $^-7$ **26.** 0 ▨ $^-2$

27. $^-5$ ▨ $^+5$ **28.** $^+6$ ▨ $^+2$ **29.** $^+7$ ▨ $^-9$ **30.** $^-3$ ▨ $^+2$

Write in order from least to greatest. (pp. 386–387)

31. $^+2, 0, ^-4$ **32.** $^+3, ^-6, ^-5$ **33.** $^+3, ^-1, ^-6$

34. $^+5, ^-5, 0, ^-1$ **35.** $^+3, ^-4, ^+1, ^-6$ **36.** $^-7, ^+8, ^-1, ^+4$

37. $^-6, ^+1, ^+5, ^-8$ **38.** $^+9, ^-6, 0, ^+7, ^-8$ **39.** $^-6, ^+5, ^-3, ^-7$

Add. (pp. 388–389)

40. $^+5 + ^-2$ **41.** $^-3 + ^-1$ **42.** $^+2 + ^+3$ **43.** $^-2 + ^+3$

44. $^-3 + ^+1$ **45.** $^+4 + ^+3$ **46.** $^-1 + ^-4$ **47.** $^-3 + ^+1$

48. $^-2 + ^+1$ **49.** $^+2 + ^-2$ **50.** $0 + ^-2$ **51.** $^-4 + ^+4$

52. $^+6 + ^-3$ **53.** $^+5 + ^+3$ **54.** $^-9 + ^+6$ **55.** $^-7 + ^-2$

Subtract. (pp. 392–393)

56. $^+7 - ^+2$ **57.** $^-6 - ^-3$ **58.** $^+5 - ^+1$ **59.** $^-4 - ^-2$

60. $^-5 - ^+2$ **61.** $^+3 - ^-4$ **62.** $^-3 - ^+4$ **63.** $^+3 - ^-2$

64. $^+6 - ^+1$ **65.** $^-5 - ^-2$ **66.** $^+7 - ^+1$ **67.** $^-9 - ^-3$

68. $^-7 - ^+3$ **69.** $^+2 - ^-2$ **70.** $^-5 - ^+3$ **71.** $^+9 - ^+3$

Name the ordered pair for each point. (pp. 396–397)

72. *A* **73.** *C* **74.** *E*
75. *F* **76.** *B* **77.** *I*

Name the point for each ordered pair. (pp. 396–397)

78. ($^+$4, $^+$2) **79.** (0, $^-$4)
80. ($^-$4, $^+$2) **81.** ($^-$2, $^-$4)

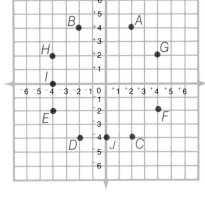

Solve each problem. (pp. 384–397)

82. The high temperature in Detroit one day was $^-$8°C. The high temperature in Chicago was $^-$3°C. Which city had the warmer temperature?

83. In the first round of a game, Don won 4 points. In the second round, he lost 5 points. What was his score after the second round?

84. A submarine at 6 m below sea level dives 4 m deeper. Use an integer to describe its new position.

85. The temperature was $^-$5°C at 8 A.M. It rose 3° by noon. It fell 4° by 10 P.M. What was the temperature at 10 P.M.?

This chart shows the number of points each player spun in a spinner game in each of two rounds. Each player began the game with 0 points.

86. What was Andrea's score after two rounds?

87. What was José's score after two rounds?

88. After the first round, what was the difference between Tammy's score and Bob's score?

89. After the first round, what was the difference between Ralph's score and José's score?

Player	First Round	Second Round
Ralph	$^+$4	$^-$6
Tammy	$^+$8	$^+$6
Bob	$^-$9	$^+$3
José	$^-$7	$^-$2
Andrea	$^+$9	$^-$3

90. Here is an input-output table for a machine. The machine adds the same integer every time you input an integer. Find the integer. Then copy and complete the table.

Input	Output
$^+$2	$^-$2
$^+$5	$^+$1
$^-$3	$^-$7
$^+$3	▦
$^+$6	▦
0	▦

COMPUTERS AND PROBLEM SOLVING

In the grid below, the turtle's HOME position is at (0, 0). Use the SETPOS command to move the turtle around the grid. Type SETPOS [30 −70] to move the turtle to the point labeled by the ordered pair (30, −70) on the grid. The SETPOS command gives the turtle a position specified by the ordered pair. The first number tells the turtle how far to move right or left. The second number indicates how far towards the top or bottom of the screen the turtle should travel.

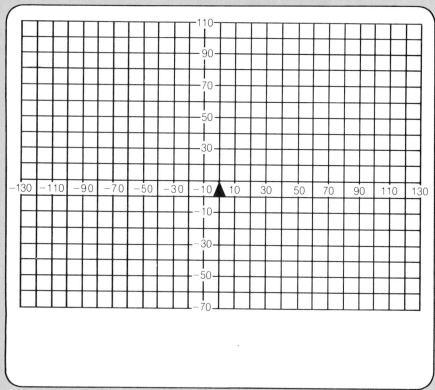

Solve each problem.

1. Write a procedure to teach the turtle to draw a square. Use five SETPOS commands. Three of the square's corners are points named by these ordered pairs:

  (80, 20) (60, 20) (60, 0)

Remember: use the PENUP or PU command if you want to keep the turtle from drawing while you move it.

2. Write a procedure to teach the turtle to draw a triangle. Put one corner at (−10, −30) and one corner at (−10, 30). Use four SETPOS commands.

3. Write a procedure to teach the turtle to draw an "H" by graphing points named by ordered pairs.

■ The DOT command is similar to SETPOS. It uses an ordered pair to place a dot on the screen at the intersection of the **coordinate numbers.**

The procedure below uses DOT to explore the relationship between pairs of numbers. The OUTPUT command in the procedure GIVE relays the user's input to the DOT command in GRAPH.

```
TO GRAPH
DOT GIVE
GRAPH
END

TO GIVE
PRINT [TYPE IN A PAIR OF
    NUMBERS TO GRAPH]
OUTPUT READLIST
END
```

Solve each problem.

1. What would the graph look like for these number pairs: (4, 9), (25, 30), (67, 72), (1, 6)?

2. Change the procedure so that it outputs connecting lines instead of just dots.

ENRICHMENT

SETS OF ORDERED PAIRS

In this table, $^+3$ is added to the first number to find the
second number.

First Number	Second Number
$^-4$	$^-1$
$^+2$	$+5$
$^-1$	■
$^-2$	■
0	■
$^-3$	■

Ordered Pairs

$(^-4,\ ^-1)$
$(^+2,\ ^+5)$
$(^-1,\ ■)$
$(^-2,\ ■)$
$(0,\ ■)$
$(^-3,\ ■)$

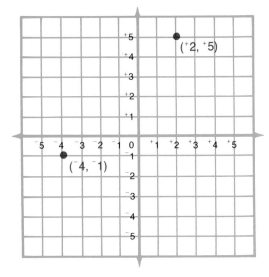

You can make an ordered pair using each row of the table.
The first two ordered pairs have been graphed.

Solve each problem.

1. Copy and complete the table and
   the list of ordered pairs.

2. Copy and complete the graph of the
   ordered pairs listed above.

3. Can you draw a straight line that
   goes through all the points? If so,
   draw the line.

4. Find another point on the line. Write
   the ordered pair for that point.

5. In exercise 4, what is the relationship
   between the first number and the
   second number in the ordered pair?

6. Find another point on the line. Does
   adding $^+3$ to the first number in the
   ordered pair give the second
   number in the ordered pair?

7. Make a table of at least six ordered
   pairs of integers that have a sum of
   0. Then locate points for the ordered
   pairs on a graph. Do they lie on a
   straight line?

First Number	Second Number
$^+3$	$^-3$
$^-3$	■
■	■

List the greatest common factor of each pair of numbers.

1. 6, 9 **2.** 10, 15 **3.** 12, 18 **4.** 9, 18 **5.** 5, 7

Copy and complete.

6. $\dfrac{2}{9} = \dfrac{12}{\blacksquare}$ **7.** $1 = \dfrac{\blacksquare}{7}$ **8.** $\dfrac{3}{4} = \dfrac{\blacksquare}{80}$ **9.** $\dfrac{25}{100} = \dfrac{1}{\blacksquare}$

Compute. Simplify if possible.

10. $\dfrac{1}{2} + \dfrac{5}{8}$ **11.** $3\dfrac{2}{9} + 5\dfrac{1}{6}$ **12.** $\dfrac{7}{8} - \dfrac{1}{2}$ **13.** $9\dfrac{1}{2} - 3\dfrac{3}{4}$

14. $\dfrac{2}{3} \times \dfrac{1}{2}$ **15.** $4\dfrac{1}{5} \times 2\dfrac{1}{2}$ **16.** $8 \div \dfrac{1}{4}$ **17.** $3\dfrac{3}{4} \div 2\dfrac{1}{8}$

Write each fraction as a percent.

18. $\dfrac{1}{4}$ **19.** $\dfrac{2}{5}$ **20.** $\dfrac{9}{10}$ **21.** $\dfrac{6}{15}$ **22.** $\dfrac{4}{5}$ **23.** $\dfrac{1}{2}$

Write each percent as a decimal.

24. 81% **25.** 9% **26.** 19% **27.** 60% **28.** 95% **29.** 2%

Use the figure to answer exercises 30–36.

30. Name five points.

31. Name two intersecting lines.

32. Name two rays.

33. Name four right angles.

34. Name two parallel lines.

35. Name figure *EFGH*.
  a. square **b.** rectangle **c.** parallelogram **d.** quadrilateral

36. Describe triangle *GFH*. (More than one answer is possible.)
  a. scalene **b.** isosceles **c.** equilateral **d.** right

(Continued)

Find the area of each polygon.

37. a rectangle 12 cm long
and 9.4 cm wide

38. a square with sides
of 6.8 m

39.

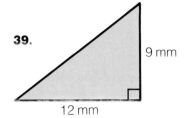

9 mm

12 mm

Add or subtract.

40. $^+3 + {^-6}$ **41.** $^+9 - {^+7}$ **42.** $^-7 - {^-7}$ **43.** $^+6 + {^+7}$

44. $^-6 - {^-5}$ **45.** $^-8 + {^-2}$ **46.** $^-1 + {^+4}$ **47.** $^+2 - {^-3}$

Name the ordered pair for each point.

48. B **49.** F **50.** G

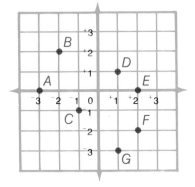

Name the point for each ordered pair.

51. $(^+1, {^+1})$ **52.** $(^-1, {^-1})$

53. $(^-3, 0)$ **54.** $(^+2, 0)$

Solve each problem.

55. Wyeth practices the trumpet $\frac{2}{3}$ h
each day. How many hours does
she practice each week?

56. On a map with the scale 2 cm =
25 km, a road is 6 cm long. How
long is the actual road?

57. Jan has 6 goldfish. Mel has 8
guppies. What is the ratio of
goldfish to guppies as a fraction
in lowest terms? As a percent?

58. Lois had dinner at a restaurant.
The bill was $18. She wants to
leave a 15% tip. How much should
she leave?

The Natural Grains Company bakes
1,200 loaves of bread each day. The
circle graph shows the fraction for each
kind of bread the company bakes.

59. Which two kinds of bread does the
company bake the most of?

60. How many loaves of whole wheat
bread does the company bake each
day?

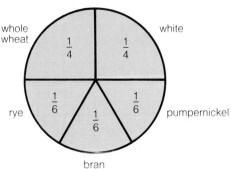

Bread Production

To the student:

In each chapter of this book, you studied a new problem solving strategy. These pages of Problem Solving: Extensions give you a chance to use those strategies to solve challenging real-life problems and interesting problems. There may be many ways to solve each problem. It is up to you to decide which strategy or strategies to use.

For some problems, you will have to conduct an experiment and do some measurements to get the data you need. For other problems, you may have to find necessary information in reference books.

We hope you find these Extensions interesting.

Good luck!

The authors

Problem Solving: Extensions

READING A CONTOUR MAP

This is a contour map. It shows how steeply land rises.

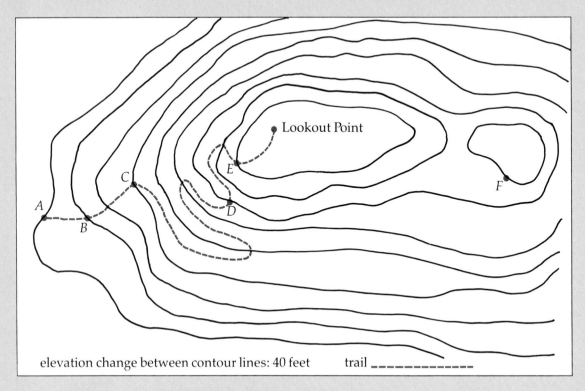

elevation change between contour lines: 40 feet   trail _ _ _ _ _ _ _ _ _ _ _ _

The elevation of point E is 6,680 feet.
What is the elevation of point A?

To solve this problem, count the number of spaces
between the contour lines from E to A. How many feet
are there between each set of contour lines?

Solve each problem.

1. How much higher is point E than
   point D?

2. How much higher is point C than
   point B?

3. Is the rise steeper from D to E or
   from B to C? How can you tell?

4. What is the elevation of point D?

5. What is the elevation of point F?

6. What point is at an elevation of
   6,480 ft?

7. What is the highest possible
   elevation for Lookout Point?
   How do you know?

8. Zigzag sections of the trail are
   called switchbacks. Why are there
   switchbacks from point C to the top?

Problem Solving: Extensions

ARRANGING A SCHEDULE

Each team in the Pony League plays every other team exactly once. How many games will be played altogether?

One way to solve this problem is to make a list of the teams in the Pony League. Then determine the number of games each team plays.

PONY LEAGUE	
Mustangs	Truckers
Giants	Pyramids
Bobcats	Sailors
Jays	Tornadoes

When counting the number of league games, be careful not to count a game between the same two teams twice.

Solve each problem.

1. Suppose each Pony League team plays exactly 1 game per week. How many weeks would their season last?

2. Suppose only 2 league games were played each week. How many weeks would the season last?

The South Side League has 6 teams. Each team plays every other team exactly once.

3. How many games will be played in the South Side League?

4. Each South Side team plays exactly 1 game per week. How many weeks does their season last?

5. The Harbor League is having an elimination tournament with 8 teams. If a team loses a game, they are out of the tournament. How many games must be played to have a winner?

6. The Hillsdale League has 7 teams. Each team plays every other team exactly once. Give names to the Hillsdale League teams. Make up a schedule for the season with 3 games played each week. Schedule no team for more than 1 game per week.

Problem Solving: Extensions

PATTERNS

Study this group of words:

river, ocean, swimming pool, lake, bay

Which word does not belong in this group? Explain why it does not belong.

To solve this problem, look for a pattern. All these words are related because they are all bodies of water. Find a characteristic that sets one word apart from the others.

Which word does not belong in each group? Why?

1. triangle, square, line, rectangle

2. Germany, Cuba, England, Italy

3. potato, steak, chicken, lamb

4. rose, carnation, daffodil, oak

5. Kansas, New York, California, Dallas

6. food, beef, bitter, school

7. 9, 12, 14, 30

8. September, spring, August, summer

9. Kennedy, Reagan, Washington, Lincoln, Einstein

10. flute, amplifier, violin, harp, tuba

11. leaf, root, stem, soil, flower

12. 36, 4, 9, 12, 15

13. glasses, shirt, hat, coat, pants

14. stomach, brain, digestive, heart, kidney

15. 4.5, 4.50, 4.05, 4.500

16. $\frac{2}{4}$, $\frac{4}{8}$, $\frac{3}{6}$, $\frac{5}{10}$, $\frac{2}{3}$

Problem Solving: Extensions

COMPARING CHECKING ACCOUNT FEES

Banks often charge a fee for the checks written on a checking account. These fees can vary from bank to bank.

COUNTY BANK

At County Bank, you pay only $.40 per check. No monthly service charge. Enroll now and receive a free gift. Gift offer limited.

FIRST BANK

Open a First Bank checking account and pay only $.15 per check, plus a $3.00 monthly service fee. Come in now and enjoy the savings.

HOME BANK

No fee for checks. Now you can write unlimited checks and pay only a $6.00 monthly service fee. Sign up now for this bill-payer special.

You write an average of 8 checks per month. Which bank offers the best checking account terms for you?

To solve this problem, compare the monthly fee for 8 checks at each bank.

Solve each problem.

1. Joseph writes about 15 checks per month. Which bank offers the best checking account terms for him?

2. Karen writes about 25 checks per month. Which bank offers the best checking account terms for her?

3. What is the greatest number of checks you could write at County Bank and not pay more than you would at First Bank?

4. What is the greatest number of checks you could write at First Bank and not pay more than you would at Home Bank?

Visit a bank in your neighborhood. Find out how the bank charges for a checking account.

5. If you write 8 checks in 1 month, how much will you pay in checking account fees at your neighborhood bank?

6. If you write 15 checks in 1 month, how much will you pay in checking account fees at your neighborhood bank?

Banks usually offer more than one kind of checking account. Investigate the terms of other checking accounts offered by your bank.

Problem Solving: Extensions

ESTIMATING OCEAN DEPTH

A depth recorder sends sound waves to the ocean bottom.
It measures the time it takes the sound waves to reach
bottom and return.

Suppose sound waves take
6 seconds to reach bottom
and return. How deep is the
ocean at that point?

To solve this problem, you
must first find how long it
takes the sound waves to
reach the bottom.

What other information do
you need? Where might you
look for this information?

Solve each problem.

1. What is the ocean depth if sound
   waves reach bottom and return in
   8 seconds? In 10 seconds?

2. What is the ocean depth if sound
   waves reach bottom and return in
   5 seconds? In 7 seconds?

3. The Mariana Trench in the Pacific
   Ocean is the deepest point known.
   It takes sound waves about 15
   seconds to reach bottom and
   return. What is the depth to the
   nearest 1,000 meters?

4. The Puerto Rico Trench is the
   deepest known point in the
   Atlantic Ocean. It is about
   8,600 meters in depth. To the
   nearest second, about how long
   would it take sound waves to
   reach bottom and return?
   (Suggestion: Use a calculator.)

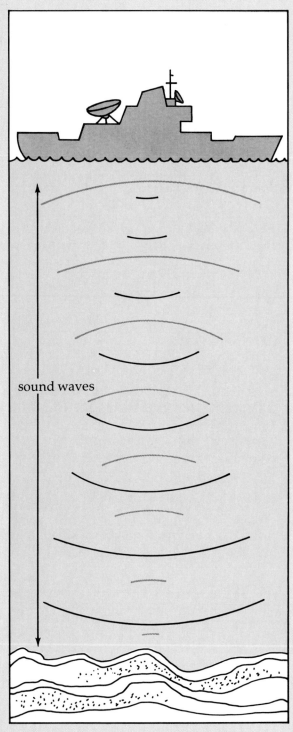

sound waves

Problem Solving: Extensions

ESTIMATING BOARD FEET

A board that is 1 foot square and 1 inch thick measures 1 board foot. You can use this table to estimate the number of board feet in a log.

A 14-ft log has this cross section. How many board feet are there in the log?

Length of Log (in feet)	Average Diameter of Log (in inches)					
	10	12	14	16	18	20
8	29	44	62	84	110	138
10	37	57	80	108	130	174
12	45	70	98	131	169	212
14	54	83	117	156	201	251
16	64	97	136	181	232	290

ESTIMATED BOARD FEET IN A LOG

To solve this problem, find the average diameter by averaging 8 in. and 12 in. Then use the table.

Estimate the number of board feet in each log.

1. log length: 10 ft

2. log length: 16 ft

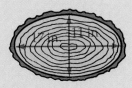

3. log length: 11 ft

4. Two logs are each 8 ft long. The average diameter of the smaller log is 12 in. The average diameter of the larger log is 18 in. The smaller log has what fraction of the board feet of the larger log?

5. An 11-ft log has an average diameter of 14 in. Which is the best estimate of the number of board feet?
a. 70　　　**b.** 80　　　**c.** 90　　　**d.** 100

6. A 16-ft log has an average diameter of 15 in. Which is the best estimate of the number of board feet?
a. 120　　　**b.** 140　　　**c.** 160　　　**d.** 180

7. A 9-ft log has an average diameter of 19 in. Which is the best estimate of the number of board feet?
a. 120　　　**b.** 140　　　**c.** 160　　　**d.** 180

Problem Solving: Extensions

EXPERIMENTING WITH COINS

Which is worth more, a pile of dimes weighing 2 kilograms or a pile of quarters weighing 1 kilogram?

One way to solve this problem is to simplify it. Experiment to find how many dimes are in a pile weighing about 10 grams. Then determine how many dimes are in piles weighing about 1 kilogram and about 2 kilograms.

Use the same method to find how many quarters are in a pile weighing about 10 grams. Then you can determine how many quarters are in a pile weighing about 1 kilogram.

Solve each problem.

1. Which is worth more, a pile of dimes weighing 1 kilogram or a pile of nickels weighing 3 kilograms?

2. Which is worth more, a pile of quarters weighing 2 kilograms or a pile of nickels weighing 5 kilograms?

3. Which is worth more, a pile of dimes weighing 6 kilograms or a pile of quarters weighing 3 kilograms?

4. Which is worth more, a pile of nickels weighing 4 kilograms or a pile of dimes weighing 2 kilograms?

A row of dimes placed edge to edge is 1 meter long. A row of quarters placed edge to edge is also 1 meter long.

5. Which row contains more coins?

6. About how many coins are there in each row?

7. Which is worth more, the row of dimes or the row of quarters?

Problem Solving: Extensions

PLANE REASONING

A checkerboard has 64 squares.
A domino will cover 2 squares.
32 dominoes will cover the
checkerboard without overlapping
or without extending beyond the
edges of the checkerboard.

Suppose you remove the square
in each corner of the checkerboard.
Could you cover the remaining
squares exactly with dominoes?
Give a logical reason for your answer.

Think: How would you describe the squares covered by
1 domino? How could you describe the squares
that were removed?

Solve this problem.

1. Suppose you remove only the 2 red squares from
the corners of the checkerboard. Could you cover
the remaining squares exactly with dominoes?
Give a logical reason for your answer.

This figure is a right triomino.
It can be turned in any direction.

**Can you fill each of the following checkerboards exactly with
right triominoes? If not, explain why.**

2. a 2-square by 3-square board

3. a 6-square by 6-square board

4. a 6-square by 9-square board

5. a 5-square by 6-square board

6. a 5-square by 8-square board

7. Suppose you remove the square in each corner of a
6-square by 6-square board. Could you cover the
remaining squares exactly with right triominoes?
Explain why or why not.

Problem Solving: Extensions

DEDUCTIVE REASONING

All birds have feathers.
All eagles are birds.
Therefore, ...

What conclusion can be drawn from these two statements?

Birds, feathers, and eagles are the terms of these two statements. Find the terms that are used only once in the two statements. Use them to draw a conclusion.

Can each conclusion be drawn from the two statements given? Write *yes* or *no*.

1. All collies are dogs.
   Max is a collie.
   Therefore, Max is a dog.

2. All kittens are cats.
   Missy is not a kitten.
   Therefore, Missy is not a cat.

3. All rectangles are quadrilaterals.
   ABCD is a rectangle.
   Therefore, *ABCD* is a quadrilateral.

4. All the gloves are green.
   Fran has a glove.
   Therefore, Fran's glove is not green.

5. Some cars are red.
   Amy owns a car.
   Therefore, Amy's car is red.

6. All 6th graders are students.
   David is not a 6th grader.
   Therefore, David is not a student.

7. Bob is at the park or at the library.
   He is not at the park.
   Therefore, he is at the library.

8. Marybeth is at school or at the movies.
   She is not at school.
   Therefore, she is not at the movies.

9. The flowers are either red or yellow.
   Steve buys a flower.
   Therefore, the flower is red.

10. Samantha is at the park or at the pool.
    She is not at the pool.
    Therefore, she is not at the park.

Problem Solving: Extensions

LOGIC PUZZLES

Murdock Soames is a detective. He is called in to solve a crime.

A jeweled hatpin has been stolen from Countess Monica. Four suspects are in the room with Mr. Soames. He knows that the three innocent people will tell the truth and that the guilty person will lie. Soames asks, "Who stole the hatpin?"

> Jim: "Tara did it."
> Kate: "Jim took it."
> Tara: "Jim lied when he said I did it."
> Pablo: "I didn't take it."

Soames quickly identified the guilty person. Who was it?

To solve this puzzle, try some "If. . ., then. . ." thinking. If Jim is telling the truth, then Tara is lying. But then Kate is also lying. (Remember: Only one statement is false.)

Try some more "If. . ., then. . ." thinking.
Use the clues to solve each problem.

1. There are three boxes. One contains only red marbles. One contains only white marbles. One contains red marbles and white marbles. The boxes are labeled "RED," "WHITE," and "MIXED." But each label is incorrect. How could you take one marble from one box and be able to identify all three boxes?

2. Karen traveled to the lands of Prairieville and Contrary many times. One day she woke up from a nap and said, "I don't remember if I am in Prairieville or in Contrary." Then she remembered that the people in Prairieville always tell the truth and that the people in Contrary always say the opposite of what they mean. Karen asked a person, "Please go to that man and ask him whether he lives in Prairieville or in Contrary." The person went, returned, and said, "The man says he lives in Prairieville." Then Karen knew where she was. Was Karen in Prairieville or in Contrary?

Problem Solving: Extensions

VISUALIZING

Here are two views of the same cube.
The letter *A* is opposite the letter *D*.

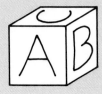 

Which letter is opposite *C*?

You can solve this problem by
imagining the figure at the right so
that *D* is opposite *A*. Visualize the
positions of *E* and *F*. Check by cutting
out and folding a pattern of the cube.

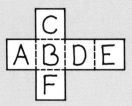

Solve each problem.

Visualize this pattern folded to
form a cube.

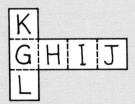

1. Which letter would be opposite *H*?

2. Which letter would be opposite *I*?

3. *P* is opposite *Q* on this cube. Two
   views of the cube are shown.
   Which letter is opposite *R*?

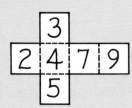

4. Which two patterns would form identical cubes?

   a.
   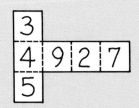

   b.

   c.

   d.
   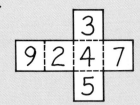

Problem Solving: Extensions

MAKING INFERENCES

A set of blocks has spheres, cubes, rectangular prisms, and triangular pyramids. Blocks of the same shape weigh the same amount.

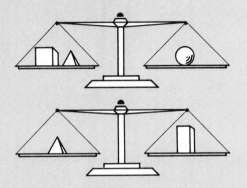 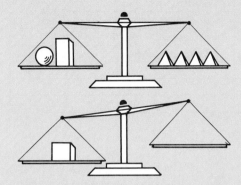

The first three scales balance. What block or set of blocks will balance the cube on the fourth scale?

One way to solve this problem is to start with the scale that has one block on each side.

Think: If like weights are removed from both sides of the scale, the scale will still balance.

If blocks balance the scale, one block can be substituted for the other.

Solve each problem.

1. What is equal to ✦ if the following are true?

    ✦
    ✖✖✖=▢
    ✖✖=△
    ✖✦=◯◯

2. There are three coins that look exactly alike. But one is counterfeit and weighs slightly less than the other two coins. How could you weigh the coins once on a balance scale and be able to tell which is the counterfeit coin?

3. There are nine coins that look exactly alike. One is counterfeit and is lighter in weight. How could you use two weighings of the balance scale to find the counterfeit coin?

Problem Solving: Extensions

ESTIMATING BY SAMPLING

FISH AND WILDLIFE SERVICE	
Job: *estimate number of fish in Bass Lake*	
Date	Procedure
6/21	Placed 200 marked fish in lake.
7/19	Took sample of 100 fish.
	8 were marked.

About how many fish are there in Bass Lake?

One way to solve this problem is to find the ratio of marked fish to all fish in the sample. Then write an equal ratio of marked fish to all fish in the lake.

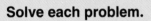

$$\frac{\text{marked fish in sample}}{\text{all fish in sample}} = \frac{\text{marked fish in lake}}{\text{all fish in lake}}$$

Solve each problem.

1. 300 marked fish were placed in Pike Lake. Later a sample of 100 fish was taken from the lake. 15 of the sample fish were marked. About how many fish are there in Pike Lake?

An African game preserve is roughly rectangular in shape. Observers took a survey of the elephant population. They flew over the shaded sample regions to make a count.

200 m 200 m 200 m 200 m 200 m

30 km

60 km

2. How many square kilometers of the game preserve are shaded?

3. What is the ratio of the shaded area to the total area?

4. The count in the shaded area was 20 elephants. About how many elephants are there in the entire preserve?

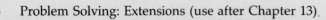

Problem Solving: Extensions

USING REFERENCES

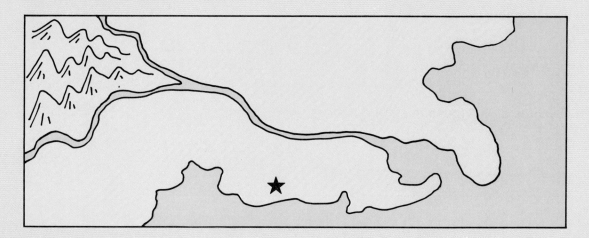

Suppose your state were divided equally among its residents. How much of the area would each person get? (Suggestion: Use a calculator.)

To solve this problem, what two facts do you need? What references could be used to find this information?

Use a calculator. Find the area per resident for each of the following.

1. the largest state in the United States

2. the smallest state in the United States

3. the state with the largest population

4. the state with the smallest population

5. Which of the 50 states has the greatest area per resident?

6. Which state has the least area per resident?

Solve each problem.

7. Which state has an area about $\frac{1}{4}$ that of Massachusetts?

8. Which New England state has an area about $\frac{1}{8}$ that of Kentucky?

More Practice

SET 1 (pp. 2–3)

Write each number.

1. 19 thousand 36
2. 96 thousand 218
3. seven hundred fifty thousand, four hundred thirty-six

What does the digit 4 mean in each number?

4. 364,912   5. 3,746   6. 426,331   7. 299,416   8. 745,823

SET 2 (pp. 4–5)

Write >, <, or =.

1. 637 ▧ 367   2. 4,915 ▧ 4,519   3. 800,701 ▧ 800,701

Write in order from least to greatest.

4. 437   4,370   4,037   4,703   5. 97,012   79,120   97,120   97,210

SET 3 (pp. 6–7)

Round to the nearest thousand.

1. 4,767   2. 12,790   3. 132,100   4. 56,500   5. 813,342

Round to the nearest ten-thousand.

6. 34,300   7. 45,000   8. 18,046   9. 321,247   10. 924,700

SET 4 (pp. 8–11)

What does the digit 7 mean in each number?

1. 276,400,321   2. 47,001,399   3. 712,345,906,200   4. 67,414,359

Write each number.

5. 94 million 26 thousand 19
6. 32 million 127 thousand 216
7. 25 billion 92 million 600
8. 614 billion 9 thousand 23

SET 5 (pp. 14–19)

Add.

1.
$$\begin{array}{r} 39 \\ +86 \\ \hline \end{array}$$

2.
$$\begin{array}{r} \$4.59 \\ +\ 9.87 \\ \hline \end{array}$$

3.
$$\begin{array}{r} 65 \\ 230 \\ +486 \\ \hline \end{array}$$

4.
$$\begin{array}{r} 17,216 \\ +\ 9,378 \\ \hline \end{array}$$

5.
$$\begin{array}{r} 634,215 \\ +246,599 \\ \hline \end{array}$$

6. $(7 + 4) + 9$

7. $\$26.54 + \$4.25$

8. $35,018 + 217,594 + 27,933$

Solve each problem.

9. Mr. Earl spent $46.50 on lumber and $18.79 on paint. How much did he spend in all?

10. A factory made 465 brown shutters, 614 red shutters, and 2,500 black shutters. How many were made in all?

SET 6 (pp. 20–25)

Subtract.

1.
$$\begin{array}{r} 74 \\ -29 \\ \hline \end{array}$$

2.
$$\begin{array}{r} \$3.84 \\ -\ 1.59 \\ \hline \end{array}$$

3.
$$\begin{array}{r} 600 \\ -468 \\ \hline \end{array}$$

4.
$$\begin{array}{r} 914 \\ -356 \\ \hline \end{array}$$

5.
$$\begin{array}{r} \$70.00 \\ -\ 26.59 \\ \hline \end{array}$$

6. $709 - 82$

7. $362 - 176$

8. $\$95.00 - \$36.45$

Use the bar graph on page 22 to solve each problem.

9. Which grade had the fewest number of students?

10. How many more students were in 6th grade than in 5th grade?

SET 7 (pp. 26–31)

Subtract. Estimate to check.

1.
$$\begin{array}{r} 4,325 \\ -1,879 \\ \hline \end{array}$$

2.
$$\begin{array}{r} 3,814 \\ -\ 965 \\ \hline \end{array}$$

3.
$$\begin{array}{r} 49,014 \\ -\ 9,478 \\ \hline \end{array}$$

4.
$$\begin{array}{r} 507,061 \\ -266,907 \\ \hline \end{array}$$

5.
$$\begin{array}{r} 789,216 \\ -\ 69,758 \\ \hline \end{array}$$

Solve each problem.

6. The Burke family drove 655 km to a hotel. The next day they drove 214 km to a museum. About how many kilometers did they drive in all?

7. In June, 4,465 people visited the museum. In July, 8,725 people visited the museum. Admission is $6.50. How many people visited the museum in June and July?

SET 8 (pp. 40–45)

Multiply.

1. $\begin{array}{r} 9 \\ \times 4 \\ \hline \end{array}$
2. $\begin{array}{r} 67 \\ \times 5 \\ \hline \end{array}$
3. $\begin{array}{r} 217 \\ \times 8 \\ \hline \end{array}$
4. $\begin{array}{r} \$5.35 \\ \times 3 \\ \hline \end{array}$
5. $\begin{array}{r} 6,420 \\ \times 9 \\ \hline \end{array}$

6. $8 \times 4,259$ 7. $6 \times 9,083$ 8. $4 \times 8,763$ 9. $7 \times 6,089$

Solve each problem.

10. Annette buys 4 boxes of pencils. There are 18 pencils in each box. How many pencils are there altogether?

11. José bought 3 books. Each book cost $8.95. He gave the clerk $40. How much change did José receive?

SET 9 (pp. 46–53)

Multiply.

1. $\begin{array}{r} 36 \\ \times 50 \\ \hline \end{array}$
2. $\begin{array}{r} 54 \\ \times 23 \\ \hline \end{array}$
3. $\begin{array}{r} \$9.25 \\ \times 64 \\ \hline \end{array}$
4. $\begin{array}{r} 27 \\ \times 300 \\ \hline \end{array}$
5. $\begin{array}{r} 7,207 \\ \times 4,000 \\ \hline \end{array}$

6. 40×70 7. 76×92 8. 100×379 9. $\$84 \times 5,000$

10. $56 \times 8,095$ 11. $49 \times 3,276$ 12. $38 \times 5,601$ 13. $\$73 \times 9,644$

SET 10 (pp. 54–61)

Multiply. Estimate to check.

1. $\begin{array}{r} 318 \\ \times 264 \\ \hline \end{array}$
2. $\begin{array}{r} \$7.75 \\ \times 310 \\ \hline \end{array}$
3. $\begin{array}{r} 4,216 \\ \times 525 \\ \hline \end{array}$
4. $\begin{array}{r} 6,045 \\ \times 2,173 \\ \hline \end{array}$
5. $\begin{array}{r} \$59.35 \\ \times 7,178 \\ \hline \end{array}$

Multiply to find each product.

6. 2^3 7. 4^6 8. 10^5 9. 8^4 10. 19^2

Solve each problem.

11. A publisher charges $9.95 for a 1-year subscription to a magazine. It receives 4,875 orders. About how much money should the publisher receive?

12. Jane works 4 hours in the morning. She works 2 hours in the afternoon. She works 20 days per month. How many hours does Jane work each month?

SET 11 (pp. 70–77)

Divide.

1. $5 \overline{)30}$ **2.** $9 \overline{)31}$ **3.** $4 \overline{)139}$ **4.** $6 \overline{)24,196}$ **5.** $9 \overline{)\$45.36}$ **6.** $3 \overline{)18,059}$

7. $179 \div 2$ **8.** $\$68.95 \div 7$ **9.** $36,215 \div 8$

10. $25,018 \div 4$ **11.** $19,756 \div 8$ **12.** $87,095 \div 6$

Solve each problem.

13. A store received a shipment of 9 coats, each the same price. The total cost was $402.75. How much did each coat cost?

14. The following number of sweaters were sold on each of 5 days: 8, 6, 14, 9, 3. What was the average number of sweaters sold each day?

SET 12 (pp. 78–83)

Divide.

1. $60 \overline{)2,500}$ **2.** $80 \overline{)6,415}$ **3.** $19 \overline{)2,033}$ **4.** $53 \overline{)21,528}$ **5.** $88 \overline{)\$528.00}$

6. $49 \overline{)52,175}$ **7.** $22 \overline{)406}$ **8.** $68 \overline{)3,880}$ **9.** $31 \overline{)122}$ **10.** $62 \overline{)12,152}$

11. $286 \div 47$ **12.** $17,208 \div 30$ **13.** $\$28.00 \div 35$

14. $24,850 \div 20$ **15.** $\$33.75 \div 45$ **16.** $68,158 \div 36$

SET 13 (pp. 86–93)

Estimate each quotient. Then divide.

1. $200 \overline{)82,645}$ **2.** $500 \overline{)4,567}$ **3.** $489 \overline{)2,518}$ **4.** $726 \overline{)492,273}$

5. $61,346 \div 189$ **6.** $510,095 \div 478$

Solve each problem. If information is missing, tell what you need to know.

7. Bruce receives $3.50 per hour to do gardening. He worked at the Herman residence on Friday. How much did he charge Mrs. Herman?

8. Bruce needs 216 tomato stakes for his customers. Each package contains 12 stakes. How many packages must Bruce buy?

SET 14 (pp. 102–105)

Write as a decimal.

1. 6 and 9 tenths
2. 518 thousandths
3. 75 hundredths
4. 14 and 256 ten-thousandths
5. three hundred twenty and seven hundredths

Write an equivalent decimal.

6. 0.6   7. 0.30   8. 8.2   9. 3.70   10. 0.1   11. 84.90

What does the digit 8 mean in each number?

12. 28.67   13. 536.782   14. 28,615.9   15. 34.98   16. 9.2468

SET 15 (pp. 106–109)

Write >, <, or =.

1. 6.4 ▇ 6.47
2. 1.04 ▇ 0.96
3. 75.02 ▇ 75.0023
4. 9.004 ▇ 9.40
5. 2.648 ▇ 2.648
6. 18.92 ▇ 18.092

Round to the nearest tenth.

7. 2.63   8. 0.867   9. 1.45   10. 0.354   11. 26.82

SET 16 (pp. 112–119)

Estimate each answer. Then add or subtract.

1.	2.	3.	4.	5.
8.6 +17.4	6.45 −2.89	$62.75 − 11.92	150.46 +482.25	91.8 +37.93

6. 3.8 + 41 + 9.16
7. 18.991 − 1.086
8. 20.9 + 1.78 + 15.756
9. 403.8 − 9.8623
10. $7.02 + $28.92
11. 500.95 − 128.6

Solve each problem.

12. Kay has a balance of $617.47 in her checking account. She writes a check for $98.59. What is the new balance?

13. Mr. Jeffrey has a balance of $85.02 in his checking account. He deposits $708.85. What is his new balance?

SET 17 (pp. 128–131)

Multiply.

1.	**2.**	**3.**	**4.**	**5.**
3.2	36.1	42.5	$15.04	0.06
×6.8	× 5	×0.34	× 8.5	×0.07

6. 0.04 × 9.3   **7.** 0.02 × 2   **8.** 0.031 × 0.03

SET 18 (pp. 134–139)

Divide.

1. $7\overline{)6.3}$ **2.** $8\overline{)198.08}$ **3.** $34\overline{)0.9214}$ **4.** $9\overline{)47.07}$

Divide. Round to the nearest tenth.

5. 1.285 ÷ 5   **6.** 26.86 ÷ 79   **7.** 39.28 ÷ 4

Solve each problem.

8. How many 3-meter sections can Betty cut from a piece of tubing 8.4 meters long?

9. Which is a better buy, 8 ounces of nuts for $1.28 or 12 ounces of nuts for $1.80?

SET 19 (pp. 140–145)

Multiply or divide.

1. 10 × 0.8   **2.** 18.6 ÷ 10   **3.** 1,000 × 9.45
4. 8,245 ÷ 100   **5.** 100 × 6.97   **6.** 23.6 ÷ 1,000

Divide. Round each quotient to the nearest tenth.

7. 2.45 ÷ 0.11   **8.** 47.7 ÷ 0.09   **9.** 6.741 ÷ 0.21

SET 20 (pp. 146–149)

Estimate each answer.

1. 24.8 × 2.8   **2.** 0.619 × 4.23   **3.** $4.89 × 39
4. 23.65 ÷ 4.3   **5.** $22.12 ÷ 4   **6.** 781.5 ÷ 0.43

Solve each problem. Use a sales tax of $.06 on the dollar.

7. Mr. Andrew spends $34.95 at the hardware store. What is the total cost of his purchase?

8. Mrs. Johns buys a brush for $3.09 and a wrench for $9.50. What is the total cost of her purchase?

SET 21   (pp. 158–161)

What time is it?

1. 3 hours 18 minutes after 11:56 A.M.

2. 2 hours 48 minutes before 6:14 P.M.

Copy and complete.

3. 64 hours = ▧ days ▧ hours

5. 3 minutes 25 seconds = ▧ seconds

4. 6 weeks 2 days = ▧ days

6. 80 days = ▧ weeks ▧ days

SET 22   (pp. 162–169)

Choose the sensible measurement.

1. A car is about ▧ long.

a. 6 cm   **b.** 60 m   **c.** 6 m

2. A bottle holds about ▧ of milk.

a. 1 L   **b.** 1 mL   **c.** 10 mL

3. An apple weighs about ▧.

a. 300 kg   **b.** 300 g   **c.** 3 kg

Copy and complete.

4. 8 cm = ▧ mm

5. 245 cm = ▧ m

6. 4.8 km = ▧ m

7. 50 mL = ▧ L

8. 0.7 kg = ▧ g

9. 2.4 L = ▧ mL

Solve each problem.

10. A 3-L pitcher is full of water. Joan pours out 750 mL. How much water is left in the pitcher?

11. A can weighs 250 g. There are 24 cans in a carton. What is the total weight of the cans in kilograms?

SET 23   (pp. 172–181)

Choose the sensible measurement.

1. Your foot is about ▧ long.

a. 8 in.   **b.** 8 ft   **c.** 8 yd

2. A rug is about ▧ long.

a. 12 mi   **b.** 12 ft   **c.** 12 in.

3. A container holds about ▧ of milk.

a. 2 oz   **b.** 20 gal   **c.** 2 qt

Copy and complete.

4. 4 c = ▧ fl oz

5. 3 tons = ▧ lb

6. 2 mi = ▧ ft

7. 8 yd = ▧ in.

8. 72 in. = ▧ ft

9. 51 oz = ▧ lb ▧ oz

Solve each problem.

10. A doll weighs 4 lb 8 oz. The case weighs 1 lb 10 oz. What is the total weight of the doll and the case?

11. Use the graph on page 181. How much snow had fallen in Granger at 5 P.M.?

SET 24 (pp. 191–195)

Is the first number divisible by the second? Write *yes* or *no*.

1. 32, 4 **2.** 53, 6 **3.** 80, 7 **4.** 196, 10 **5.** 510, 6

Find the least common multiple. Do not use 0.

6. 2, 7 **7.** 3, 15 **8.** 18, 9 **9.** 7, 9 **10.** 6, 4

Find the greatest common factor of each pair of numbers.

11. 12, 16 **12.** 6, 9 **13.** 15, 50 **14.** 6, 8 **15.** 2, 11

SET 25 (pp. 196–197, 200–201)

Write *prime* or *composite*.

1. 8 **2.** 7 **3.** 18 **4.** 50 **5.** 73

Show each number as a product of primes.

6. 4 **7.** 12 **8.** 25 **9.** 36 **10.** 52

Use the graph on page 201 to solve each problem.

11. How many more women than men worked for the company in 1970?

12. In which years was the total number of employees under 15,000?

SET 26 (pp. 210–215)

Copy and complete.

1. $\dfrac{1}{2} = \dfrac{\blacksquare}{8}$ **2.** $\dfrac{2}{3} = \dfrac{\blacksquare}{12}$ **3.** $\dfrac{8}{24} = \dfrac{1}{\blacksquare}$ **4.** $\dfrac{40}{60} = \dfrac{\blacksquare}{3}$

Write each fraction in lowest terms.

5. $\dfrac{8}{40}$ **6.** $\dfrac{4}{18}$ **7.** $\dfrac{9}{36}$ **8.** $\dfrac{50}{100}$ **9.** $\dfrac{24}{30}$ **10.** $\dfrac{80}{100}$

Write each fraction as a whole number or as a mixed number in lowest terms.

11. $\dfrac{5}{2}$ **12.** $\dfrac{18}{3}$ **13.** $\dfrac{23}{4}$ **14.** $\dfrac{37}{8}$ **15.** $\dfrac{50}{2}$ **16.** $\dfrac{83}{10}$

SET 27 (pp. 216–223)

Add or subtract. Simplify if possible.

1. $\dfrac{1}{4} + \dfrac{2}{4}$
2. $\dfrac{4}{9} - \dfrac{1}{9}$
3. $\dfrac{7}{10} + \dfrac{1}{2}$
4. $\dfrac{7}{8} - \dfrac{2}{3}$

5. $\dfrac{9}{10} - \dfrac{1}{2}$
6. $\dfrac{5}{7} + \dfrac{2}{3}$
7. $\dfrac{5}{7} + \dfrac{5}{7}$
8. $\dfrac{5}{6} - \dfrac{1}{3}$

Write >, <, or =.

9. $\dfrac{1}{2} \blacksquare \dfrac{2}{3}$
10. $\dfrac{5}{7} \blacksquare \dfrac{2}{9}$
11. $\dfrac{4}{5} \blacksquare \dfrac{2}{3}$
12. $2\dfrac{1}{2} \blacksquare 2\dfrac{5}{8}$

SET 28 (pp. 226–233)

Add or subtract. Simplify if possible.

1. $\begin{array}{r} 5\frac{7}{10} \\ -3\frac{3}{10} \\ \hline \end{array}$
2. $\begin{array}{r} 8\frac{1}{2} \\ +2\frac{2}{5} \\ \hline \end{array}$
3. $\begin{array}{r} 9\frac{1}{3} \\ +6\frac{2}{3} \\ \hline \end{array}$
4. $\begin{array}{r} 7 \\ -4\frac{3}{4} \\ \hline \end{array}$
5. $\begin{array}{r} 11\frac{1}{3} \\ -5\frac{4}{5} \\ \hline \end{array}$

Solve each problem.

6. April bought $2\dfrac{1}{4}$ yards of blue ribbon and $3\dfrac{2}{3}$ yards of red ribbon. How much ribbon did she buy in all?

7. Frank worked $5\dfrac{1}{2}$ hours on Saturday and $3\dfrac{3}{4}$ hours on Sunday. Write a question. Then answer it.

SET 29 (pp. 242–251)

Write each mixed number as a fraction.

1. $2\dfrac{2}{3}$
2. $5\dfrac{5}{6}$
3. $4\dfrac{1}{4}$
4. $1\dfrac{5}{9}$
5. $7\dfrac{1}{2}$
6. $3\dfrac{7}{10}$

Multiply or divide. Simplify if possible.

7. $\dfrac{1}{2} \times \dfrac{4}{5}$
8. $\dfrac{4}{7} \times \dfrac{3}{4}$
9. $\dfrac{2}{3} \div 9$
10. $4\dfrac{1}{2} \times \dfrac{2}{9}$

11. $2\dfrac{1}{4} \div 3\dfrac{3}{8}$
12. $\dfrac{7}{9} \times \dfrac{18}{21}$
13. $\dfrac{1}{5} \div 2$
14. $\dfrac{1}{8} \div \dfrac{3}{4}$

SET 30 (pp. 254–259)

Write each decimal as a fraction or as a mixed number.

1. 0.7   **2.** 6.5   **3.** 5.45   **4.** 3.8   **5.** 0.64   **6.** 9.73

Write each fraction as a decimal. Use a bar to show repeating digits.

7. $\frac{3}{10}$ **8.** $\frac{5}{12}$ **9.** $\frac{4}{25}$ **10.** $\frac{2}{3}$ **11.** $2\frac{3}{4}$ **12.** $\frac{2}{8}$

Solve each problem.

13. Richard had $3\frac{1}{4}$ ft of wire. He cut off 0.5 foot to use on a kite. How much wire was left?

14. Richard worked on the kite for $2\frac{3}{4}$ hours. He earns $4.20 per hour. How much money did he earn?

SET 31 (pp. 268–273)

Write each ratio.

1. circles to squares   **2.** triangles to circles   **3.** circles to all shapes

Are the ratios equal? Write *yes* or *no*.

4. $\frac{1}{2}$ and $\frac{50}{100}$ **5.** $\frac{35}{60}$ and $\frac{2}{3}$ **6.** $\frac{30}{18}$ and $\frac{5}{4}$ **7.** $\frac{16}{20}$ and $\frac{4}{5}$

Solve for *n*.

8. $\frac{4}{10} = \frac{6}{n}$ **9.** $\frac{n}{16} = \frac{15}{20}$ **10.** $\frac{16}{18} = \frac{24}{n}$ **11.** $\frac{15}{10} = \frac{n}{8}$

SET 32 (pp. 274–277, 280–283)

Write each fraction or decimal as a percent.

1. $\frac{46}{100}$ **2.** $\frac{17}{20}$ **3.** $\frac{5}{8}$ **4.** 0.72   **5.** 0.11   **6.** 0.03

Write each percent as a decimal.

7. 82%   **8.** 45%   **9.** 9%   **10.** 1%   **11.** 99%   **12.** 6%

Solve each problem.

13. Joe's shadow was 0.8 mm long. He is 2 m tall. At the same time, the shadow of a flagpole was 2.4 m long. How high is the flagpole?

14. On a map, 1 cm stands for 20 km. What is the actual distance between two towns that are 3.4 cm apart on the map?

SET 33 (pp. 284–287)

Solve.

1. 20% of $40　　　　　**2.** 5% of $100　　　　　**3.** 75% of $160

4. 2% of $30　　　　　**5.** 98% of $65　　　　　**6.** 45% of $500

Solve each problem.

7. Mr. Gold borrowed $3,000 for 2 years at an interest rate of 15% per year. He agreed to repay the entire loan at the end of 2 years. What will the interest be on his loan?

8. Lilia has $1,800 in her savings account. The bank pays interest at a rate of 7% per year. How much interest will Lilia's money earn in 3 months?

SET 34 (pp. 296–301)

Use this figure to answer exercises 1–8.

1. Name five points.

2. Name four lines.

3. Name two line segments.

4. Name two intersecting lines.

5. Name two parallel lines.

6. Name two perpendicular lines.

7. Name three rays.

8. Name one right angle.

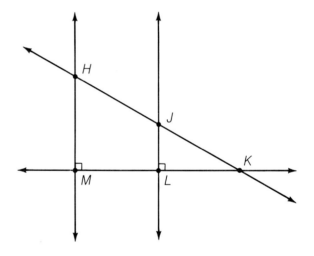

SET 35 (pp. 302–309)

Name each polygon. Give the special name for each triangle and each quadrilateral.

1. 　　**2.** 　　**3.** 　　**4.**

5. 　　**6.** 　　**7.** 　　**8.**

9. Which figures in exercises 1–8 are congruent?

SET 36 (pp. 310–319)

Use the circle to answer exercises 1–4.

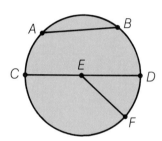

1. Name three radii.

2. Name a chord.

3. Name a diameter.

4. Find the length of the diameter.

Is the red line a line of symmetry? Write *yes* or *no*.

5.   **6.**   **7.**   **8.**

9. Which figures in exercises 5–8 are similar?

SET 37 (pp. 318–321)

Name the shape of each object.

1. 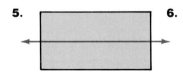   **2.** 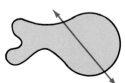   **3.** 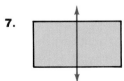   **4.**

Name the point for each ordered pair.

5. (3, 2)   **6.** (1, 0)   **7.** (4, 5)

Name the ordered pair for each point.

8. B   **9.** C   **10.** E

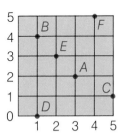

SET 38 (pp. 332–335, 344–347)

Use this figure to answer exercises 1–4.

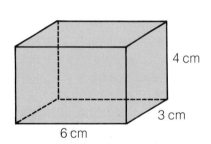

1. Find the perimeter of the front face.

2. Find the area of the top face.

3. Find the surface area of the figure.

4. Find the volume of the figure.

SET 39 (pp. 338–343, 350–351)

Find the circumference and the area of each circle. Use 3.14 for π.

1.
2 m

2.
7 m

3.
4 ft

Solve each problem.

4. A triangle has a base of 8 cm and a height of 4 cm. What is the area of the triangle?

5. Use the graph on page 351. If the price of juice was $.70 per serving, how much money would be collected on the 5 days shown?

SET 40 (pp. 360–367)

Find the range, the mean, the median, and the mode for each set of numbers.

1. 55, 56, 62, 55

2. 22, 17, 26, 19, 20, 22

Solve each problem.

3. Doris saw 10 red cars, 6 blue cars, and 8 black cars. Which color car had the least frequency? The greatest frequency?

4. A forest is in the shape of a rectangle 8 km by 12 km. Two sample areas, each 2 km by 2 km, were chosen for a count of oak trees. In one sample area, 20 trees were counted. In the other, 18 trees were counted. Estimate the number of oak trees in the forest.

SET 41 (pp. 368–371, 374–375)

Solve each problem.

1. A spinner has 9 sections. The sections are numbered from 1 through 9. What is the probability of spinning an odd number?

2. There is a 25% chance of snow. Is it more likely to snow or not to snow?

3. You have a nickel, a dime, and a quarter. How many possible combinations of heads and tails are there?

4. You toss 4 coins. What is the probability of tossing at least 3 heads?

SET 42 (pp. 384–387)

Write the opposite of each integer.

1. $^+3$ **2.** $^-1$ **3.** $^+9$ **4.** 0 **5.** $^-100$ **6.** $^+321$

Write $>$ or $<$.

7. $^-2 \blacksquare 0$ **8.** $^+8 \blacksquare ^-5$ **9.** $0 \blacksquare ^-7$ **10.** $^-6 \blacksquare ^+6$

11. $^+16 \blacksquare ^-7$ **12.** $^-9 \blacksquare ^+10$ **13.** $0 \blacksquare ^-12$ **14.** $^+37 \blacksquare ^-61$

Write in order from least to greatest.

15. $^+5 \quad 0 \quad ^-3$ **16.** $^+5 \quad ^+10 \quad ^-8$ **17.** $^-7 \quad ^+4 \quad 0 \quad ^+7$

18. $^+10 \quad ^-7 \quad ^+3 \quad ^-4$ **19.** $^-8 \quad ^-9 \quad ^+3 \quad ^+7$ **20.** $^-9 \quad 0 \quad ^+2 \quad ^-5$

SET 43 (pp. 388–389, 392–395)

Add.

1. $^+3 + ^-1$ **2.** $^+2 + ^-2$ **3.** $^-7 + ^-3$ **4.** $^+6 + ^-8$

5. $^-3 + ^-8$ **6.** $^-4 + ^-4$ **7.** $^-5 + ^+9$ **8.** $^+9 + ^+4$

Subtract.

9. $^+6 - ^-1$ **10.** $^-5 - ^+5$ **11.** $^-7 - ^-3$ **12.** $^+3 - ^-8$

13. $^+8 - ^-8$ **14.** $^-3 - ^-4$ **15.** $^+2 - ^+1$ **16.** $0 - ^+6$

Solve each problem.

17. Amy spun $^+3$ points in the first round of a game. She spun $^-2$ points in the second round. What was her score after the two rounds?

18. Use the table on page 395. How much more did JFM gain on Tuesday than Delray?

SET 44 (pp. 396–397)

Name the ordered pair for each point.

1. A **2.** B **3.** C

4. D **5.** E **6.** F

Name the point for each ordered pair.

7. $(^-4, ^-3)$ **8.** $(^+2, ^-1)$ **9.** $(0, 0)$

10. $(^-5, ^+1)$ **11.** $(^+4, 0)$ **12.** $(0, ^+3)$

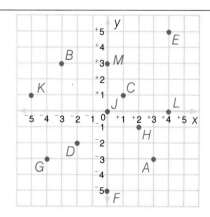

Glossary

addition   An operation that gives the total number, or amount in all.

$$\begin{array}{r} 27 \\ +32 \\ \hline 59 \end{array} \leftarrow \text{addends}$$
$$59 \leftarrow sum$$

$$27 + 32 = 59$$
addends   sum

angle   An angle is formed when two rays have the same endpoint.

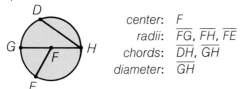

45°

A *degree* (°) is a unit used for measuring angles. A *right angle* has a measure of 90°. An *acute angle* has a measure less than 90°. An *obtuse angle* has a measure greater than 90°.

area   The number of square units needed to cover a region. *Square millimeters*, *square centimeters*, *square meters*, and *square kilometers* are units used to measure area in the metric system. *Square inches*, *square feet*, and *square yards* are units used to measure area in the customary system.

capacity   Capacity is the amount of a substance that a container can hold.

circle   A simple closed figure. All of the points are an equal distance from the center.

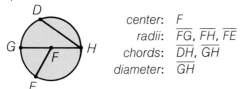

center: *F*
radii: $\overline{FG}$, $\overline{FH}$, $\overline{FE}$
chords: $\overline{DH}$, $\overline{GH}$
diameter: $\overline{GH}$

circumference   The distance around a circle. The formula for the circumference of a circle is $C = \pi \times d$.

common factor   *See* greatest common factor.

common multiple   *See* least common denominator.

composite number   A whole number with more than two different factors.

cone   A space figure with a circular base and a curved lateral surface that extends to a single vertex.

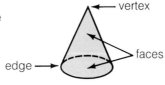

vertex

faces

edge

congruent   Figures that have the same size and shape are congruent. Two angles or two line segments are congruent if they have the same measurement. Two polygons are congruent if they coincide by sliding, turning, or flipping.

cross products   If two ratios are equal, their cross products are equal.

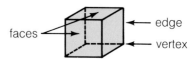

$\frac{2}{6} \qquad \frac{3}{9}$

$2 \times 9 \qquad 6 \times 3$
$18 \ = \ 18$

The cross products are equal.

cube   A space figure with 6 square faces, 12 edges, and 8 vertices.

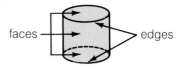

faces

edge

vertex

customary system   A system of measurement used primarily in the United States. The *inch*, the *foot*, the *yard*, and the *mile* are units used to measure length. The *fluid ounce*, the *cup*, the *pint*, the *quart*, and the *gallon* are units used to measure capacity. The *ounce*, the *pound*, and the *ton* are units used to measure weight.

cylinder   A space figure with 2 congruent flat faces, 1 curved face, 2 curved edges, and no vertices.

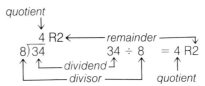

faces

edges

data   Information, usually given in numerical form.

decagon   A polygon with 10 sides and 10 angles.

decimal   A whole number, fraction, or mixed number that is expressed using a decimal point.

division   An operation that gives the quotient of two numbers or amounts.

quotient
$\downarrow$
$4 \text{ R}2 \leftarrow$ remainder
$8)\overline{34}$
dividend
divisor

$34 \div 8 \ = 4 \text{ R}2$

quotient

equivalent decimals   Decimals that name the same number. 0.9 and 0.90 are equivalent decimals.

equivalent fractions   Fractions that name the same number. $\frac{1}{2}$, $\frac{2}{4}$, and $\frac{3}{6}$ are equivalent fractions.

estimate   To find an approximate answer mentally by rounding the numbers before solving.

even number   A number that has 2 as a factor.

expanded form   A form in which a whole number is written to show the value of each digit.

$$2{,}589 = 2{,}000 + 500 + 80 + 9$$

exponent   An exponent tells how many times a number is used as a factor.

$$4^3 = 4 \times 4 \times 4 = 64$$

expression   A sentence that names a number. These are some expressions for the number 5: $3 + 2$; $25 \div 5$; $9 - 4$

fraction   A number such as $\frac{5}{6}$. A fraction may name part of a region or part of a set.

$$\frac{5}{6} \quad \begin{array}{l} \leftarrow \textit{numerator} \\ \leftarrow \textit{denominator} \end{array}$$

The numerator and the denominator are the *terms* of a fraction.

greater than (>)   A way to compare numbers.

$$46 > 43 \qquad 2.7 > 2.1 \qquad \frac{4}{5} > \frac{2}{5}$$

greatest common factor   The largest number that is a common factor of two or more numbers.

1, 2, 4, and 8 are factors of 16 and 24.
They are common factors of 16 and 24.
The greatest common factor of 16 and 24 is 8.

hexagon   A polygon with 6 sides and 6 angles.

integers   The set of numbers . . . $^-3$, $^-2$, $^-1$, 0, $^+1$, $^+2$, $^+3$, ... This is the set consisting of all whole numbers (positive integers and zero) and their opposites (negative integers and zero). Zero is neither positive nor negative.

interest   A percent of a loan that must be repaid to a bank, along with the amount of the loan.

intersect   Lines that meet at a common point intersect.

least common denominator   The *least common multiple* of the denominators of two or more fractions. The least common multiple of 6 and 8 is 24, so 24 is the least common denominator of $\frac{5}{6}$ and $\frac{3}{8}$.

least common multiple   *See* least common denominator.

less than (<)   A way to compare numbers.

$$52 < 57 \qquad 1.4 < 1.9 \qquad \frac{3}{8} < \frac{6}{8}$$

line   A line is a set of points that continues without end in opposite directions.

line AB ($\overleftrightarrow{AB}$) or line BA ($\overleftrightarrow{BA}$)

line of symmetry   A line that divides a figure into two parts that match.

line segment   A line segment is part of a line. The *endpoints* show where a line segment begins and ends.

line segment AB ($\overline{AB}$) or line segment BA ($\overline{BA}$)

lowest terms   A fraction is in lowest terms when the numerator and the denominator have no common factor greater than 1.

mass   Mass is the amount of matter contained in an object.

mean   Mean is another name for average. It is a single number used to represent a set of numbers.

metric system   A system of measurement used throughout the world. The *millimeter*, the *centimeter*, the *decimeter*, the *meter*, and the *kilometer* are units used to measure length. The *liter* and the *milliliter* are units used to measure capacity. The *milligram*, the *gram*, and the *kilogram* are units used to measure mass.

mixed number   A number such as $1\frac{3}{4}$ that has a whole number part (1) and a fraction part $\left(\frac{3}{4}\right)$.

mode   The value that occurs most often in a set of numbers.

numbers: 90, 100, 90, 90, 80, 100
mode: 90

multiple: A product is a multiple of each of its factors. 15 is a multiple of 3 and 5.

multiplication   An operation that gives the product of two numbers or amounts.

$$\begin{array}{r} 6 \\ \times 8 \\ \hline 48 \end{array} \begin{array}{l} \leftarrow \\ \leftarrow \end{array} \textit{factors} \qquad 8 \times 6 = 48$$

$$\leftarrow \textit{product} \qquad \textit{factors} \quad \textit{product}$$

octagon   A polygon with 8 sides and 8 angles.

odd number   A number that is not divisible by 2.

ordered pair   A pair of numbers that names a point on a graph. (1, 5) is an ordered pair. The 1 tells how many units to the right of 0. The 5 tells how many units up.

parallel   Two lines in a plane that do not meet are parallel.

parallelogram A quadrilateral whose opposite sides are parallel and congruent. Opposite angles of a parallelogram are also congruent.

pentagon A polygon with 5 sides and 5 angles.

percent (%) A ratio that compares a number to 100. 2% means 2 hundredths.

$$2\% = \frac{2}{100} = 0.02$$

perimeter The distance around a figure. To find the perimeter, add the lengths of the sides.
The formula for the perimeter of a rectangle is:
Perimeter = (2 × length) + (2 × width)

perpendicular Two lines that intersect to form right angles are perpendicular.

pi (π) The ratio of the circumference of a circle to its diameter. To the nearest ten-thousandth, π is 3.1416.

plane A flat surface that goes on and on in all directions.

point A point is a position in space.

polygon A closed figure with sides that are line segments. The line segments meet at a *vertex* to form an angle. A *diagonal* of a polygon is a line segment that connects vertices that are not next to each other.

prime number A whole number with exactly two different factors, itself and 1.

prism A space figure with bases that are congruent polygons in parallel planes. The remaining faces are rectangular. A prism is named for the shape of its bases.

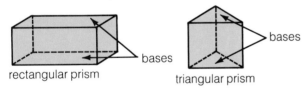

rectangular prism   triangular prism

probability The chance that a certain event will occur.

proportion A statement that two ratios are equal.

pyramid A space figure with a base that is a polygon. The remaining faces are triangular and meet at a point. A pyramid is named for the shape of its base.

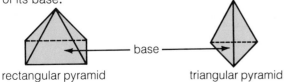

rectangular pyramid   triangular pyramid

quadrilateral A polygon with 4 sides and 4 angles.

range The difference between the greatest number and the least number of given information.

ratio A way to compare two numbers.

ray A part of a line. It has one endpoint and extends without end in one direction.

A ————————— B ——→ ray AB ($\overrightarrow{AB}$)

reciprocal If the product of two numbers is 1, the numbers are reciprocals of each other.

The reciprocal of $\frac{3}{4}$ is $\frac{4}{3}$. $\frac{3}{4} \times \frac{4}{3} = \frac{12}{12} = 1$

rectangle A parallelogram with 4 right angles.

repeating decimal A decimal in which a digit or a set of digits repeats over and over again.
$$0.212121 \ldots = 0.\overline{21}$$

rhombus A parallelogram with all sides congruent.

sample You can draw conclusions about a large set of data by using a sample, or part of the set.

scale drawing A figure drawn using equal ratios between the distances on the drawing and the actual distances. A map is a scale drawing of a region.

similar figures Figures that have the same shape, but not necessarily the same size.

simplify To write a fraction in lowest terms.

space figure A three-dimensional object.

sphere A space figure that has the shape of a ball.

square A rectangle with 4 congruent sides.

square root One of two equal factors of a number. The square root of 16 is 4.

subtraction An operation that gives the difference between two numbers or amounts.

$$\begin{array}{r} 17 \\ -\ 9 \\ \hline 8 \end{array} \leftarrow \text{difference}$$ $17 - 9 = 8$

surface area The sum of the areas of all the faces of a space figure.

time The *second*, the *minute*, the *hour*, the *day*, the *week*, the *month*, and the *year* are units used to measure time.

trapezoid   A quadrilateral with a pair of parallel sides.

triangle   A polygon with 3 sides and 3 angles. An *equilateral triangle* has 3 congruent sides. An *isosceles triangle* has at least 2 congruent sides. A *scalene triangle* has no congruent sides. In an *acute triangle*, every angle is less than 90°. A *right triangle* has 1 right angle. An *obtuse triangle* has 1 angle greater than 90°.

unit price   The price per item or per unit of weight, volume, or capacity.

volume   The number of cubic units needed to fill a space figure. *Cubic millimeters*, *cubic centimeters*, and *cubic meters* are units used to measure volume in the metric system. *Cubic inches*, *cubic feet*, and *cubic yards* are units used to measure volume in the customary system.

whole numbers   The set of numbers 0, 1, 2, 3, 4, 5, 6, 7, 8, ...

Computer Terms

*   A symbol that means multiplied by.

BACK (BK)   A Logo command to move the turtle a certain number of steps backward.

BASIC (Beginner's All-Purpose Symbolic Instruction Code)   A computer language.

CLEARSCREEN (CS)   A Logo command that erases all graphics displays from the monitor.

:   A BASIC function that combines more than one statement in a single program line.

command (BASIC)   An instruction to a computer that tells it to prepare to or start to do work for you.

command (Logo)   A single instruction to the computer.

CONTROL-C   A computer command that instructs the computer to interrupt any program that is in progress.

display   Any text or graphics that appear on the screen.

DOT   A Logo command that uses ordered pairs to instruct the turtle to plot a point at a specified position on the screen.

END   The last statement in a BASIC program or Logo procedure.

ERASE   A Logo command that removes a procedure from the computer's memory.

flowchart   A diagram that shows the step-by-step procedures of a program.

FOR...NEXT   A pair of BASIC statements used to create a loop in a program.

FORWARD (FD)   A Logo command to move the turtle a certain number of steps forward.

GOSUB   A BASIC statement that instructs the program to execute the subroutine beginning on a stated line number.

GOTO   A BASIC statement that instructs the program to go directly to a stated line number.

graphics   Pictures and designs generated by the computer.

hardware   The equipment that you can use in computing: computer, disk drive, printer, monitor, etc.

HOME (BASIC)   A command that moves the cursor to the top left corner of the monitor.

HOME (Logo)   A command that places the turtle in the middle of the screen.

IF...THEN   A BASIC statement. IF sets up a comparison of two data items. THEN specifies an action to be taken should the comparison be true.

IFFALSE   A Logo command that tells the computer to look at the most recent test and to take a given action if the test is false.

IFTRUE   A Logo command that tells the computer to look at the most recent test and to take a given action if the test is true.

INPUT   A BASIC statement that requests information from the user and then assigns that information to a specified variable.

INT   A BASIC function that removes any decimal part of a number: INT(123.454) would equal 123.

LEFT (LT)   A Logo command to turn the turtle a certain number of degrees to the left.

LET   A BASIC statement that tells what piece of data a variable will stand for.

Logo   A computer language generally used to tell a turtle how to draw shapes on the screen.

loop   Part of a computer program that repeats.

MAKE   A Logo command that tells what piece of data a variable will stand for.

NEW   A BASIC command used to clear the computer's memory of any stored program.

PENDOWN (PD)   A Logo command that restores the turtle's drawing capability after a PENUP.

PENUP (PU)   A Logo command that allows the turtle to move without drawing a line.

PRINT   A computer command to display the data that follow it.

procedure   A set of Logo instructions stored in the computer that enable it to carry out a specific task.

program   A set of BASIC instructions stored in the computer that enable it to carry out a specific task.

RANDOM   A Logo command that generates a random integer greater than or equal to 0 but 1 less than the given number.

REM   A BASIC statement that enables a programmer to insert remarks or comments in a program. It does not affect the operation of the program.

REPEAT   A Logo command that causes a procedure to happen a specified number of times.

RETURN   The last instruction in a BASIC subroutine. It instructs the computer to go back to the line following the instruction that called for the subroutine.

RIGHT (RT)   A Logo command to turn the turtle a certain number of degrees to the right.

RND(1)   A BASIC statement that returns a random number between .00000000 and .999999999. It is used in conjunction with the INT statement to generate a random number greater than or equal to 0 but 1 less than the given factor; e.g., PRINT INT(4 ∗ RND(1)).

ROUND   A Logo command.

RUN   A BASIC command to start a program.

SAVE   A computer command to store a program on a disk or a cassette for later use.

;   A BASIC function that enables the user to combine strings, variables, and string variables in a single PRINT statement.

SENTENCE   A Logo command that combines lists and variables to form sentences.

SETPOS   A Logo command that uses ordered pairs to send the turtle to a specified position on the screen.

/   A symbol that means divided by.

software   Computer programs and procedures.

[ ]   Used in Logo to delineate the beginning and end of a list.

statement   A BASIC instruction that gets a computer to do a specific piece of work for you.

STOP   A Logo command that halts the procedure that is running and returns control to the user.

string   A group of characters or words to be used in a program as a single data item. Strings must be enclosed in quote marks; e.g., "YOUR NAME".

string variable   A variable ending with a $ symbol that stands for a string; e.g., LET A$ = "YOUR NAME". String variables can never be used for math.

subroutine   A part of a BASIC program designed to perform a specific task. Subroutines may be called from any point within a program. They return control to the main program after execution.

SYNTAX ERROR   A message generated by the computer when a BASIC command is used incorrectly or is not entered properly.

TEST READLIST   A user is asked for a response. Then this Logo command compares the user's response to a predetermined answer and sets up a true-or-false condition for the IFTRUE and IFFALSE commands to detect.

user   The person operating the computer.

variable   A name that is assigned by the user to a number or data item. BASIC variables must be a letter or begin with a letter. Logo variables begin with a colon. Variables are used for math.

INDEX

(**Boldface** indicates the page on which the term is defined.)

PHOTO CREDITS